Microsoft

W9-BFC-667

Microsoft®

Internet & Networking Dictionary

DISCARD

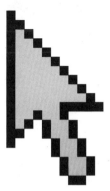

PUBLISHED BY
Microsoft Press
A Division of Microsoft Corporation
One Microsoft Way
Redmond, Washington 98052-6399

Library of Congress Cataloging-in-Publication Data
Microsoft Internet & Networking Dictionary / Microsoft Press.

     p. cm.
   ISBN 0-7356-1813-5
   1. Computer networks--Dictionaries. 2. Internet--Dictionaries. I. Microsoft Press.

   TK5105.5 .M5474 2002
   004.67'8--dc21   2002075312

Printed and bound in the United States of America.

1 2 3 4 5 6 7 8 9   QWE   7 6 5 4 3 2

Distributed in Canada by H.B. Fenn and Company Ltd.

A CIP catalogue record for this book is available from the British Library.

Microsoft Press books are available through booksellers and distributors worldwide. For further information about international editions, contact your local Microsoft Corporation office or contact Microsoft Press International directly at fax (425) 936-7329. Visit our Web site at www.microsoft.com/mspress. Send comments to *mspinput@microsoft.com*.

Acquisitions Editor: Alex Blanton
Project Editor: Sandra Haynes

Body Part No. X08-92505

Dictionary of Computer Terms. 1

Introduction

The *Microsoft Internet & Networking Dictionary* is designed to provide easy reference to the Internet and networking terms you're likely to encounter most often. This dictionary also emphasizes terminology that you're likely to encounter in documentation, online help, computer manuals, marketing and sales materials, the popular media, and the computer trade press. In some cases, related terms or specialized or highly technical language is included to help you better understand a technology, service, or product.

Order of Presentation

Entries are alphabetized by letter. Spaces are ignored, as are characters such as hyphens, slashes, and periods; for example, *V.Fast Class* falls between *V.everything* and *VFAT*. Numbers and symbols are located at the beginning of the book and are listed in ascending ASCII order. If an entry begins with a letter or letters but contains a number, it is listed alphabetically, according to the initial letter(s), and then according to ASCII order. Thus, *V.120* precedes *V.32terbo*.

Entries

Entries are of two types: main entries, which contain full definitions, and synonymous cross-references, which contain *See* references to the appropriate main entries. Synonymous cross-references are generally secondary or less common ways of referring to a main entry. The definition at the main entry can be substituted as a definition for the synonymous cross-reference.

Format

Information in each entry is presented in a consistent format: entry name in boldface, spelling variants (if any), part of speech, definition, table reference (if any), acronym (if any), alternative names (if any), and cross-references (if any).

Main Entries

Entries that are acronyms or abbreviations for one or more words or concatenations of two or more words have those words spelled out at the beginning of the definition. The letters in these words or phrases that make up the acronym, abbreviation, or concatenation are in boldface.

When a main entry is spelled exactly the same as another main entry, the two entries are differentiated by the use of a superscript numeral after each term. These entries are called homographs, and they are generally different parts of speech. For example: **e-mail**[1] (*noun*); **e-mail**[2] (*verb*).

Spelling Variants

When a main entry has one or more variations in the way it is spelled, each spelling variant follows the main entry after the word *or*.

Parts of Speech

Entries are broken down into four parts of speech, in addition to prefixes, abbreviated as follows: *n.* noun; *vb.* verb; *adj.* adjective; *adv.* adverb.

Definitions

Each of the more than 3,000 entries included in this dictionary is written in clear, standard English. Many go beyond a simple definition to provide additional detail and to put the term in context for a typical computer user. When an entry has more than one sense or definition, the definitions are presented in a numbered list, to make it easier to distinguish the particular, sometimes subtle, variations in meaning.

Table References

Some entries have affiliated tables that aid in defining the entry. In most cases, tables appear on the same page as the entries to which they apply. In some instances, however, page layout requirements have forced them to a subsequent page. Entries with tables usually have the reference (see the table) at the end of the definition.

Acronyms

Some terminology in the computer field, particularly computer standards and Internet slang, can be shortened to form acronyms. Sometimes the acronym is the more common way to refer to the concept or object; in these cases, the acronym is the main entry. In other cases, the acronym is not as commonly used as the words or phrase for which it stands. In these cases, the words or phrase constitute the main entry. The acronym is given after the definition (*Acronym:*).

Alternative Names

Some items or concepts in the computer field can be referred to by more than one name. Generally, though, one way is preferred. The preferred terminology is the main entry. Alternative names are listed after any acronyms; otherwise they are listed after the definition (*Also called:*).

Cross-References

Cross-references are of three types: *See*, *See also*, and *Compare*. A *See* reference is used in an entry that is a synonymous cross-reference and simply points to another entry that contains the information sought. A *See also* reference points to one or more entries that contain additional or supplemental information about a topic and follows and acronyms or alternative names after the definition. A *Compare* reference points to an entry or entries that offer contrast and follows any *See also* references; otherwise it follows any acronyms or alternative names after the definition.

Future Printings

Every effort has been made to ensure the accuracy and completeness of this book. If you find an error, think that an entry does not contain enough information, or seek an entry that does not appear in this book, please let us know. Address your letter to: Dictionary Editor, Microsoft Press, One Microsoft Way, Redmond, WA 98052-6390. Or send e-mail to mspcd@microsoft.com.

Numbers and Symbols

$0.02 *n. See* my two cents.

& *n.* The default character used to designate a character entity (special character) in an HTML or SGML document. *See also* HTML, SGML.

/ *n.* A character used to separate parts of a directory path in UNIX and FTP or parts of an Internet address (URL) in Web browsers.

// *n.* Notation used with a colon to separate the URL protocol (such as http or ftp) from the URL host machine name, as in http://www.yahoo.com. *See also* URL.

: *n.* Colon, a symbol used after the protocol name (such as http or ftp) in a URL. *See also* URL.

<> *n.* **1.** Angle brackets, a pair of symbols used to enclose a keyword, comprising a tag in an HTML, SGML, or XML document. *See also* HTML, SGML, XML. **2.** In an Internet Relay Chat (IRC) or multiuser dungeon (MUD), a set of symbols used to designate some action or reaction, as in <chuckle>. *See also* emotag, IRC, MUD. **3.** A pair of symbols used to enclose a return address in an e-mail header.

> *n.* **1.** Right angle bracket, a symbol used in some operating systems, such as MS-DOS and UNIX, to direct the output resulting from some command into a file. **2.** A symbol commonly used in e-mail messages to designate text included from another message.

@ *n.* The separator between account names and domain names in Internet e-mail addresses. When spoken, @ is read as "at." Therefore, user@host.com would be read as "user at host dot com."

100Base-FX *n.* An Ethernet standard for baseband LANs (local area networks) using fiber optic cable carrying 100 Mbps (megabits per second). *Also called:* Fast Ethernet. *See also* Ethernet (definition 1).

100Base-VG *n.* An Ethernet standard for baseband LANs (local area networks) using voice-grade twisted-pair cable carrying 100 Mbps (megabits per second). Unlike other Ethernet networks, 100Base-VG relies on an access method called demand priority, in which nodes send requests to hubs, which in turn give permission to transmit based on the priority levels included with the requests. *Also called:* 100Base-VG-AnyLAN. *See also* Ethernet (definition 1).

100Base-VG-AnyLAN *n. See* 100Base-VG.

100Base-X *n.* Descriptor used for any of three forms of 100 Mbps Ethernet networks: 100Base-T4, 100Base-TX, or 100Base-FX. *Also called:* Fast Ethernet. *See also* 100Base-T, 100Base-FX, Ethernet (definition 1).

 # 10Base2 *n.* The Ethernet and IEEE 802.3 standard for baseband LANs (local area networks) using a thin coaxial cable (3/16 inch) up to 200 meters long and carrying 10 Mbps (megabits per second) in a bus topology. A network node is connected to the cable by a BNC connector on the adapter card. *Also called:* Cheapernet, thin Ethernet ThinNet ThinWire. *See also* BNC connector, bus network, coaxial cable, Ethernet (definition 1), IEEE 802.x.

10Base5 *n.* The Ethernet and IEEE 802.3 standard for baseband LANs (local area networks) using a thick coaxial cable (3/8 inch) up to 500 meters long and carrying 10 Mbps (megabits per second) in a bus topology. A network node is equipped with a transceiver that plugs into a 15-pin AUI connector on the adapter card and taps into the cable. This form of Ethernet is generally used for network backbones. *Also called:* thick Ethernet, ThickNet, ThickWire. *See also* coaxial cable, Ethernet (definition 1), IEEE 802.x.

10Base-F *n.* The Ethernet standard for baseband LANs (local area networks) using fiber-optic cable carrying 10 Mbps (megabits per second) in a star topology. All nodes are connected to a repeater or to a central concentrator. A node is equipped with a fiber-optic transceiver that plugs into an AUI connector on the adapter card and attaches to the cable with an ST or SMA fiber-optic connector. The 10Base-F standard comprises 10Base-FB for a backbone, 10Base-FL for the link between the central concentrator and a station, and 10Base-FP for a star network. *See also* Ethernet (definition 1), fiber optics, star network.

10Base-FB *n.* *See* 10Base-F.

10Base-FL *n.* *See* 10Base-F.

10Base-FP *n.* *See* 10Base-F.

10Base-T *n.* The Ethernet standard for baseband LANs (local area networks) using twisted-pair cable carrying 10 Mbps (megabits per second) in a star topology. All nodes are connected to a central hub known as a multiport repeater. *See also* Ethernet (definition 1), star network, twisted-pair cable.

/16 network *n.* IP address class B. This class has 16,382 networks available and more than sixty-five thousand hosts available. *See also* host[1], IP address classes, network.

/24 network *n.* IP address class A. This class has more than two million networks available and 254 hosts available. *See also* host[1], IP address classes, network.

33.6 *n.* A modem with a maximum data transfer rate of 33.3 Kbps (kilobits per second).

400 *n.* HTTP status code—Bad Request. A Hypertext Transfer Protocol message from an HTTP server indicating that a client request cannot be completed because the syntax of the request is incorrect. *See also* HTTP server (definition 1), HTTP status codes.

401 *n.* HTTP status code—Unauthorized. A Hypertext Transfer Protocol message from an HTTP server indicating that a client request cannot be completed because the

#

transaction requires an Authorization header, which was not supplied. *See also* HTTP server (definition 1), HTTP status codes.

402 *n.* HTTP status code—Payment Required. A Hypertext Transfer Protocol message from an HTTP server indicating that a client request cannot be completed because the transaction requires a payment, and no ChargeTo header was supplied. *See also* HTTP server (definition 1), HTTP status codes.

403 *n.* HTTP status code—Forbidden. A Hypertext Transfer Protocol message from an HTTP server indicating that a client request cannot be completed because access is restricted. *See also* HTTP server (definition 1), HTTP status codes.

404 *n.* HTTP status code—Not Found. A Hypertext Transfer Protocol message from an HTTP server indicating that a client request cannot be completed because the server is unable to find an address that matches the URL requested. *See also* HTTP server (definition 1), HTTP status codes, URL.

56K[1] *adj.* Having 56 kilobits per second (Kbps) available for traffic on a communications circuit. One voice channel can carry up to 64 Kbps (called a T0 carrier); 8 Kbps are used for signaling, leaving 56 Kbps available for traffic. *See also* T-carrier.

56K[2] *n. See* 56-Kbps modem.

56-Kbps modem *n.* An asymmetric modem that operates over POTS (Plain Old Telephone Service) to deliver data downstream at 56 Kbps, with upstream speeds of 28.8 and 33.6 Kbps. Earlier, slower modems invoke a two-conversion transmission process: digital data from a computer is converted into analog form for transmission over the telephone wire and is then reconverted to digital data by the receiving modem. In contrast, 56-Kbps modems achieve faster speeds by converting analog data to digital data only once, typically at the telephone company's switching office near the beginning of the transmission's journey. Designed to improve download times for Internet users, 56-Kbps modems rely on a public phone network that allows for a single conversion and on the availability of a digital connection, such as ISDN or T1, at the ISP (Internet service provider) location that provides the actual connection to the Internet. *See also* cdigital data transmission, modem.

802.x standards *n. See* IEEE 802.x.

802.11 standards *n. See* IEEE 802.11.

8-N-1 *n.* Short for **8** bits, **N**o parity, **1** stop bit. Typical default settings for serial communications, such as modem transmissions.

/8 network *n.* IP address class C. This class has 126 networks available and more than sixteen million hosts available. *See also* host[1], IP address classes, network.

9600 *n.* A modem with a maximum data transfer rate of 9600 bps (bits per second).

A

A

Abeline *n.* A high-performance network developed by Qwest Communications, Nortel, and Cisco Systems to provide a backbone network for the Internet2 project. Abeline interconnects the gigaPoPs created by the Internet2 project and its member institutions, enabling connected institutions to develop advanced network services and applications. *See also* gigaPoP, Internet2.

A-Bone *n.* The Asian-Pacific Internet backbone that connects users in East and South Asian countries and Australia at T1 speeds or better, without the need to send data through North American facilities. The A-Bone was launched by Asia Internet Holding Co., Ltd. in 1996. By 1998, a total of 13 countries were connected to the A-Bone's hub in Japan. A-Bone also includes links to both Europe and the United States. *See also* backbone.

absolute link *n.* A hyperlink to the exact location of a file on a file server, the World Wide Web, or a company intranet. Absolute links use an exact path; if you move the file containing the hyperlink or a hyperlink destination, the link breaks.

absolute URL *n.* The full Internet address of a page or other World Wide Web resource. The absolute URL includes a protocol, such as "http," network location, and optional path and file name—for example, http://example.microsoft.com/.

access control *n.* The mechanisms for limiting access to certain items of information or to certain controls based on users' identities and their membership in various predefined groups. Access control is typically used by system administrators for controlling user access to network resources, such as servers, directories, and files. *See also* access privileges, system administrator.

access control list *n.* A list associated with a file or a resource that contains information about which users or groups have permission to access a resource or modify the file. *Acronym:* ACL.

access permission *n. See* permission.

access point *n.* In a wireless LAN (local area network), a transceiver that connects the LAN to a wired network. *See also* wireless LAN.

access privileges *n.* The type of operations permitted a given user for a certain system resource on a network or a file server. A variety of operations, such as the ability to access a server, view the contents of a directory, open or transfer files, and create, modify, or delete files or directories, can be allowed or disallowed by the system administrator. Assigning access privileges to users helps the system administrator to maintain security on the system, as well as the privacy of confidential information, and to allocate system resources, such as disk space. *Also called:* access rights. *See also* file protection, file server, permission, system administrator.

access provider *n. See* ISP.

account *n.* The record-keeping mechanism used by networks and multiuser operating systems for keeping track of authorized users. Network accounts are created by network administrators and are used both to validate users and to administer policies—for example, permissions—related to each user.

account lockout *n.* A security feature in Windows XP that locks a user account if a number of failed logon attempts occur within a specified amount of time, based on security policy lockout settings. Locked accounts cannot log on.

A

account name *n.* The part of an e-mail address that identifies a user or an account on an e-mail system. An e-mail address on the Internet typically consists of an account name, followed by the @ (at) symbol, a host name, and a domain name. *See also* account, domain name, e-mail address.

account policy *n.* On local area networks and multi-user operating systems, a set of rules governing whether a new user is allowed access to the system and whether an existing user's rights are expanded to include additional system resources. An account policy also generally states the rules with which the user must comply while using the system in order to maintain access privileges.

ACK *n.* Short for **ack**nowledgment. A message sent by the receiving unit to the sending station or computer indicating either that the unit is ready to receive transmission or that a transmission was received without error. *Compare* NAK.

ACL *n.* *See* access control list.

ACPI *n.* Acronym for **A**dvanced **C**onfiguration and **P**ower **I**nterface. An open specification developed jointly by Microsoft, Intel, and Toshiba for managing power consumption on mobile, desktop, and server computers. Unlike earlier, BIOS-based management solutions, ACPI provides a means of integrating power management through all parts of a PC, including applications, hardware, and the operating system (OS). ACPI enables an OS to control a computer's power state in response to input from the user, from an application, or from a device driver. For example, an ACPI-enabled OS could turn a CD-ROM drive, a printer, or even a television on or off as needed. ACPI is part of the industry-wide OnNow initiative that allows system manufacturers to deliver computers that start at the touch of a keyboard. *See also* plug and play.

activation *n.* In Sun Microsystem's J2EE network platform, the process of transferring Enterprise JavaBean (EJB) from secondary storage to memory. *See also* EJB, J2EE. *Compare* passivation.

Active Channel *n.* A Web site described by a Channel Definition Format (CDF) file. Developers can use Active Channels to automatically download content to a user on a subscription basis, to send content to users on a regular schedule, to deliver personalized content to individual users, and to provide content to a Windows screen saver. Active Channels were introduced in Microsoft Internet Explorer 4 and can be used to deliver information through either the Internet or an intranet. *See also* pull, webcasting.

active content *n*. Material on a Web page that changes on the screen with time or in response to user action. Active content is implemented through ActiveX controls. *See also* ActiveX control.

Active Desktop *n*. The feature introduced with Microsoft's Internet Explorer 4 that enables end users to display active—that is, updateable, customizable—HTML content on the Windows desktop. Active content includes such items as channels, Web pages, ActiveX controls, and Java applets. *See also* Active Channel, ActiveX, HTML, Internet Explorer, Java.

Active Directory *n*. A Microsoft technology, part of the Active Platform, that is designed to enable applications to find, use, and manage directory resources (for example, user names, network printers, and permissions) in a distributed computing environment. Distributed environments are usually heterogeneous collections of networks that often run proprietary directory services from different providers. To simplify directory-related activities associated with locating and administering network users and resources, Active Directory presents applications with a single set of interfaces that eliminates the need to deal with differences between and among these proprietary services. Active Directory is a component of the Windows Open Services Architecture (WOSA). *See also* directory service, WOSA.

Active Directory Services Interface *n*. An administrative tool known as a Microsoft Management Console (MMC) snap-in that allows administrators to manage objects in the domain. *Acronym:* ADSI.

active hub *n*. **1.** The central computer that regenerates and retransmits all signals in an active star network. *See also* active star. **2.** A type of hub used on ARCnet networks that both regenerates (boosts) signals and passes them along. *Compare* intelligent hub, passive hub.

Active Platform *n*. A Microsoft development platform that offers a standardized approach to incorporating Internet and distributed computing technologies in client/server applications. Microsoft Windows 9x, Microsoft Windows NT, and Microsoft Internet Explorer 4.*x* (and later) provide the basis for the Active Platform. On the client side, users are given a consistent interface that enables them to easily access both local and remote information. On the server side, developers can take advantage of the tools and technologies that span the client and the server. Active Platform supports development of the modular object-oriented programs known as component software and allows creation of cross-platform applications that can run on multiple chips and operating systems. Active Platform includes support for HTML and the creation of small programs in several languages through client-side scripting. *See also* Active Desktop, Active Server, ActiveX.

Active Server *n*. The server-based component of Microsoft's Active Platform. Comprised of a set of technologies that includes DCOM (distributed component object model), Active Server Pages, Microsoft Transaction Server, and message queues, Active Server provides support for developing component-based, scalable, high-performance Web applications on Microsoft Windows NT servers. Active Server is designed to allow developers to concentrate on creating Internet and intranet software in a variety of languages without having to focus on the intricacy of the network itself. *See also* Active Desktop, Active Platform, Active Server Pages, ActiveX.

Active Server Pages *n.* A Web-oriented technology developed by Microsoft that is designed to enable server-side (as opposed to client-side) scripting. Active Server Pages are text files that can contain not only text and HTML tags as in standard Web documents, but also commands written in a scripting language (such as VBScript or JavaScript) that can be carried out on the server. This server-side work enables a Web author to add interactivity to a document or to customize the viewing or delivery of information to the client without worrying about the platform the client is running. All Active Server Pages are saved with an .asp extension and can be accessed like standard URLs through a Web browser, such as Microsoft Internet Explorer or Netscape Navigator. When an Active Server Page is requested by a browser, the server carries out any script commands embedded in the page, generates an HTML document, and sends the document back to the browser for display on the requesting (client) computer. Active Server Pages can also be enhanced and extended with ActiveX components. *Acronym:* ASP. *See also* Active Server, ActiveX.

active star *n.* A form of the star network topology in which the central computer actively regenerates and retransmits all signals. *See also* star network.

ActiveX *n.* A set of technologies that enables software components to interact with one another in a networked environment, regardless of the language in which the components were created. ActiveX, which was developed by Microsoft in the mid 1990s and is currently administered by the Open Group, is built on Microsoft's Component Object Model (COM). Currently, ActiveX is used primarily to develop interactive content for the World Wide Web, although it can be used in desktop applications and other programs. ActiveX controls can be embedded in Web pages to produce animation and other multimedia effects, interactive objects, and sophisticated applications. *See also* ActiveX control, COM. *Compare* applet, plug-in (definition 2).

ActiveX control *n.* A reusable software component based on Microsoft's ActiveX technology that is used to add interactivity and more functionality, such as animation or a popup menu, to a Web page, applications, and software development tools. An ActiveX control can be written in any of a number of languages, including Java, C++, and Visual Basic. *See also* ActiveX. *Compare* helper program.

adapter or **adaptor** *n.* A printed circuit board that enables a personal computer to use a peripheral device, such as a CD-ROM drive, modem, or joystick, for which it does not already have the necessary connections, ports, or circuit boards. Commonly, a single adapter card can have more than one adapter on it. *Also called:* interface card. *See also* network adapter, port.

7

A

adapter card or **adaptor card** *n. See* adapter.

adaptive answering *n.* The ability of a modem to detect whether an incoming call is a fax or a data transmission and respond accordingly. *See also* modem.

adaptive load balancing *n. See* load balancing.

adaptive routing *n. See* dynamic routing.

A-D converter *n. See* analog-to-digital converter.

address *n.* **1.** A name or token specifying a particular computer or site on the Internet or other network. **2.** A code used to specify an e-mail destination.

address classes *n.* Predefined groupings of Internet addresses with each class defining networks of a certain size. The range of numbers that can be assigned for the first octet in the IP address is based on the address class. Class A networks (values 1 to 126) are the largest, with more than 16 million hosts per network. Class B networks (128 to 191) have up to 65,534 hosts per network, and Class C networks (192 to 223) can have up to 254 hosts per network.

addressing *n.* The process of assigning or referring to an address. In programming, the address is typically a value specifying a memory location.

address mapping table *n.* A table used by routers or DNS (Domain Name System) servers to obtain the corresponding IP (Internet Protocol) address of a text name of a computer resource, such as the name of a host computer on the Internet. *Acronym:* AMT. *See also* DNS server, IP address, router.

address mask *n.* A number that, when compared by the computer with a network address number, will block out all but the necessary information. For example, in a network that uses XXX.XXX.XXX.YYY and where all computers within the network use the same first address numbers, the mask will block out XXX.XXX.XXX and use only the significant numbers in the address, YYY. *See also* address (definition 2).

address munging *n.* The practice of modifying an e-mail address in posts to newsgroups or other Internet forums to foil computer programs that gather e-mail addresses. The host name in an e-mail address is altered to create a fictitious address in such a way that a human can still easily determine the correct address. For example, a person with an e-mail address of Jane@myispoffersusersfreeemail.com could modify, or "mung," her address to read Jane@remove-this-to-reply-myispoffersusersfreeemail.com. Address munging is generally used to prevent delivery of unsolicited junk e-mail or spam. *Also called:* munging. *See also* address (definition 2), host name, spam.

address resolution *n.* The identification of a computer's IP (Internet Protocol) address by finding the corresponding match in an address mapping table. *See also* address mapping table.

Address Resolution Protocol *n. See* ARP.

ad-hoc network *n.* A temporary network formed by communicating stations or computers in a wireless LAN. *See also* wireless LAN.

ADN *n. See* Advanced Digital Network.

ADO.NET *n.* The suite of data access technologies included in the .NET Framework class libraries that provide access to relational data and XML. ADO.NET consists of classes that make up the DataSet (such as tables, rows, columns, relations, and so on), .NET Framework data providers, and custom type definitions (such as SqlTypes for SQL Server).

ADSL *n.* Acronym for **a**symmetric **d**igital **s**ubscriber **l**ine. Technology and equipment allowing high-speed digital communication, including video signals, across an ordinary twisted-pair copper phone line, with speeds up to 8 Mbps (megabits per second) downstream (to the customer) and up to 640 Kbps (kilobits per second) upstream. ADSL access to the Internet is offered by some regional telephone companies, offering users faster connection times than those available through connections made over standard phone lines. *Also called:* asymmetric digital subscriber loop. *Compare* SDSL.

Advanced Digital Network *n.* A dedicated line service capable of transmitting data, video, and other digital signals with exceptional reliability, offered as a premier service by communications companies. Usually Advanced Digital Network refers to speeds at or above 56 kilobits per second (Kbps).

Advanced Encryption Standard *n. See* AES.

Advanced Research Projects Agency Network *n. See* ARPANET.

Advanced Streaming Format *n.* An open file format specification for streaming multimedia files containing text, graphics, sound, video, and animation. Advanced Streaming Format (ASF) does not define the format for any media streams within the file. Rather, it defines a standardized, extensible file "container" that is not dependent on a particular operating system or communication protocol, or on a particular method (such as HTML or MPEG-4) used to compose the data stream in the file. An ASF file consists of three objects: a Header object containing information about the file itself, a Data object containing the media streams, and an optional Index object that can help support random access to data within the file. The ASF specification has been submitted to the ISO (International Organization for Standardization) for consideration. *Acronym:* ASF. *See also* streaming.

.aero *n.* One of seven new top-level domain names approved in 2000 by the Internet Corporation for Assigned Names and Numbers (ICANN). .aero is meant for use with air-transport industry-related Web sites. The seven new domain names became available for use in the spring of 2001.

AES *n.* Acronym for **A**dvanced **E**ncryption **S**tandard. A cryptographic algorithm specified by the National Institute of Standards and Technology (NIST) to protect sensitive information. AES is specified in three key sizes: 128, 192, and 256 bits. AES replaces the 56-bit key Data Encryption Standard (DES), which was adopted in 1976. *See also* DES.

affinity *n.* For Network Load Balancing, the method used to associate client requests to cluster hosts. When no affinity is specified, all network requests are load balanced across the cluster without respect to their source. Affinity is implemented by directing all client requests from the same IP address to the same cluster host. *See also* IP address.

AFIPS *n.* Acronym for American Federation of Information Processing Societies. An organization formed in 1961 for the advancement of computing and information-related concerns. The U.S. representative of the International Federation of Information Processing, AFIPS was replaced by the Federation on Computing in the United States (FOCUS) in 1990.

AFP *n.* Acronym for AppleTalk Filing Protocol. A remote filing system protocol that provides a standard means for a workstation on an AppleTalk network to access and manipulate files on an AFP-implemented server. *Also called:* AppleShare File Server.

agent *n.* **1.** A program that performs a background task for a user and reports to the user when the task is done or some expected event has taken place. **2.** A program that searches through archives or other repositories of information on a topic specified by the user. Agents of this sort are used most often on the Internet and are generally dedicated to searching a single type of information repository, such as postings on Usenet groups. Spiders are a type of agent used on the Internet. *Also called:* intelligent agent. *See also* spider. **3.** In client/server applications, a process that mediates between the client and the server. **4.** In Simple Network Management Protocol (SNMP), a program that monitors network traffic. *See also* SNMP.

aggregated links *n.* *See* link aggregation.

aggregation of links *n.* *See* link aggregation.

AH *n.* Authentication Header. A form of IP packet authentication included in the IPSec security standard. AH attaches a header to the packet with authentication information but does not encrypt the packet data, which allows its use in cases where encryption is not allowed. *See also* IPSec.

AIM *n.* Acronym for America Online Instant Messenger. A popular instant-messaging service provided for free by America Online. With the AIM service, instant messages can be sent over an Internet connection using the AIM software or directly from a Web browser using AIM Express. *See also* America Online, instant messaging. *Compare* ICQ, .NET Messenger Service, Yahoo! Messenger.

AirPort *n.* A wireless connectivity option introduced by Apple in 1999. AirPort provides wireless network and Internet communications to all AirPort card–equipped Macintosh computers within 150 feet of an AirPort base station. AirPort was developed around the IEEE 802.11 Direct Sequence Spectrum (DSSS) industry standard and is interoperable with other 802.11-based equipment.

AirSnort *n.* A hacking tool used to gather and decrypt passwords in data sent over wireless networks. AirSnort monitors wireless transmissions and collects packets of data. When it has collected enough data, AirSnort is able to compute the encryption key used in the transmission. AirSnort takes advantage of security flaws in the Wired Equivalent Protocol (WEP) standard. *See also* password sniffing.

A

ALB *n. See* load balancing.

alias *n.* A name used to direct e-mail messages to a person or group of people on a network.

ALOHA *n. See* ALOHAnet.

ALOHAnet *n.* The first wireless packet-switched network and the first large network to be connected to the ARPANET. ALOHAnet was built in 1970 at the University of Hawaii by Norm Abramson and was funded by Larry Roberts. ALOHAnet enabled computers at seven campuses on four different islands to communicate bidirectionally with the central computer on Oahu using a network of radio transmitters. The ALOHA protocol was the basis for Ethernet. *See also* ARPANET, Ethernet, network.

AltaVista *n.* A World Wide Web search site and portal hosted by Digital Equipment Corporation. *See also* portal.

alt. newsgroups *n.* Internet newsgroups that are part of the alt. ("alternative") hierarchy and have the prefix alt. Unlike the seven Usenet newsgroup hierarchies (comp., misc., news., rec., sci., soc., talk.) that require formal votes among users in the hierarchy before official newsgroups can be established, anybody can create an alt. newsgroup. Therefore, newsgroups devoted to discussions of obscure or bizarre topics are generally part of the alt. hierarchy.

always on *n.* An Internet connection that is maintained continuously, whether or not the computer user is online. Always-on connections provide convenience to users who don't need to dial in or log on to access the Internet, but also provide more opportunities for hackers to attempt to access the system or use the computer to spread malicious programs.

American Registry for Internet Numbers *n. See* ARIN.

America Online *n.* An online information service, based in Vienna, Virginia, that provides e-mail, news, educational and entertainment services, and Internet access. America Online is one of the largest American ISPs (Internet service providers). In 2000 America Online merged with media giant Time Warner Inc. to become AOL Time Warner Inc. Intended for mass-market delivery of branded content and communication services, the merged companies form a communication and media conglomerate with the Internet's largest user base and a wide range of entertainment, publishing, and cable properties. *Acronym:* AOL.

A

America Online Instant Messenger *n. See* AIM.

analog *adj.* Pertaining to or being a device or signal that is continuously varying in strength or quantity, such as voltage or audio, rather than based on discrete units, such as the binary digits 1 and 0. A lighting dimmer switch is an analog device because it is not based on absolute settings. *Compare* digital (definition 2).

analog-to-digital converter *n.* A device that converts a continuously varying (analog) signal, such as sound or voltage, from a monitoring instrument to binary code for use by a computer. *Acronym:* ADC. *Also called:* A-D converter. *See also* modem. *Compare* digital-to-analog converter.

anchor *n.* A tag in an HTML document that defines a section of text, an icon, or other element as a link to another element in the document or to another document or file. *See also* hyperlink.

annoybot *n.* A bot on an Internet Relay Chat (IRC) channel or a multiuser dungeon (MUD) that interacts with the user in an obnoxious manner. *See also* bot, IRC, MUD.

anonymity *n.* The ability to send an e-mail message or an article to a newsgroup without one's identity becoming known. Ordinarily, the e-mail address of the sender appears automatically in a message's header, which is created by the client software. To achieve anonymity, a message must be sent through an anonymous remailer— which, however, maintains a record of the sender's identity to enable replies. *See also* anonymous remailer.

anonymous *n.* On the Internet, the standard login name used to obtain access to a public FTP file archive. *See also* anonymous FTP.

anonymous FTP *n.* The ability to access a remote computer system on which one does not have an account, via the Internet's File Transfer Protocol (FTP). Users have restricted access rights with anonymous FTP and usually can only copy files to or from a public directory, often named /pub, on the remote system. Users can also typically use FTP commands, such as listing files and directories. When using anonymous FTP, the user accesses the remote computer system with an FTP program and generally uses *anonymous* or *ftp* as a logon name. The password is usually the user's e-mail address, although a user can often skip giving a password or give a false e-mail address. In other cases, the password can be the word *anonymous*. Many FTP sites do not permit anonymous FTP access in order to maintain security. Those that do permit anonymous FTP sometimes restrict users to only downloading files for the same reason. *See also* FTP[1] (definition 1), logon, /pub.

anonymous post *n.* A message in a newsgroup or mailing list that cannot be traced to its originator. Generally this is accomplished by using an anonymous server for newsgroup posts or an anonymous remailer for e-mail. *See also* anonymous remailer.

anonymous remailer *n.* An e-mail server that receives incoming messages, replaces the headers that identify the original sources of the messages, and sends the messages to their ultimate destinations. The purpose of an anonymous remailer is to hide the identities of the senders of the e-mail messages.

anonymous server *n.* **1.** The software used by an anonymous remailer. *See also* anonymous remailer. **2.** Software that provides anonymous FTP service. *See also* anonymous FTP.

ANSI *n.* **1.** Acronym for American National Standards Institute. A voluntary, non-profit organization of business and industry groups formed in 1918 for the development and adoption of trade and communication standards in the United States. ANSI is the American representative of ISO (the International Organization for Standardization). Among its many concerns, ANSI has developed recommendations for the use of programming languages including FORTRAN, C, and COBOL, and various networking technologies. *See also* SCSI. **2.** The Microsoft Windows ANSI character set. This set is includes ISO 8859/x plus additional characters. This set was originally based on an ANSI draft standard. The MS-DOS operating system uses the ANSI character set if ANSI.SYS is installed.

anti-replay *n.* An IP packet–level security feature that prevents packets that have been intercepted and changed from being inserted into the data stream. Anti-replay creates a security association between a source and destination computer, with each agreeing on a numbering sequence for transmitted packets. The anti-replay mechanism detects packets tagged with numbers that fall outside the accepted sequence, discards them, sends an error message, and logs the event. The anti-replay protocol is included as part of the IPSec standard. *See also* IPSec.

antivirus program *n.* A computer program that scans a computer's memory and mass storage to identify, isolate, and eliminate viruses, and that examines incoming files for viruses as the computer receives them.

anti-worm *n.* *See* automatic patching, do-gooder virus.

anycasting *n.* Communication between a single sender and the nearest receiver in a group. In IPv6, anycasting enables one host to initiate the updating of routing tables for a group of hosts. *See also* IPv6. *Compare* multicasting, unicast.

AOL *n.* *See* America Online.

AOL Instant Messenger *n.* *See* AIM.

AOL NetFind *n.* Resident Web-finding tool of America Online (AOL) information service. Searches by keyword and concept. Using Intelligent Concept Extraction (ICE) and Excite technology, this tool finds relationships between words and ideas; for example, between "elderly people" and "senior citizen." *See also* Excite, Intelligent Concept Extraction.

Apache *n.* A free open-source HTTP (Web) server introduced in 1995 by the Apache Group as an extension to, and improvement of, the National Center for Supercomputing Applications' earlier HTTPd (version 1.3). Apache is popular on

UNIX-based systems, including Linux, and also runs on Windows NT and other operating systems, such as BeOS. Because the server was based on existing code with a series of patches, it became known as "A Patchy server," which led to the official name Apache. *See also* HTTPd.

A

Apache Group *n.* A non-profit organization of volunteers from around the world that operates and contributes to the Apache HTTP Server Project.

Apache HTTP Server Project *n.* A collaborative effort by the members of the Apache Group to design, develop, and maintain the Apache HTTP (Web) server. *See also* Apache, Apache Group.

Apache project *n. See* Apache HTTP Server Project.

APNIC *n.* Acronym for **A**sian-**P**acific **N**etwork **I**nformation **C**enter, a nonprofit, voluntary membership organization covering the Asia/Pacific Rim region. APNIC, like its European counterpart RIPE and its American counterpart ARIN, devotes itself to matters related to the Internet, among them such tasks as registering new members, allocating IP addresses, and maintaining database information. *See also* ARIN, RIPE.

APPC *n.* Acronym for **A**dvanced **P**rogram-to-**P**rogram **C**ommunication. A specification developed as part of IBM's SNA (Systems Network Architecture) model and designed to enable applications programs running on different computers to communicate and exchange data directly. APPC extends SNA to include minicomputers and PCs.

Apple Filing Protocol *n. See* AFP.

applet *n.* A program that can be downloaded over the Internet and executed on the recipient's machine. Applets are often written in the Java programming language and run within browser software, and they are typically used to customize or add interactive elements to a Web page.

AppleShare *n.* A file server software developed by Apple Computer, Inc., that works with the Mac OS and allows one Macintosh computer to share files with another on the same network. *See also* file server, Mac OS.

AppleTalk *n.* An inexpensive local area network developed by Apple Computer, Inc., for Macintosh computers that can be used by Apple and non-Apple computers to communicate and share resources such as printers and file servers. Non-Apple computers must be equipped with AppleTalk hardware and suitable software. The network uses a layered set of protocols similar to the ISO/OSI reference model and transfers information in the form of packets called frames. AppleTalk supports connections to other AppleTalk networks through devices known as bridges, and it supports connections to dissimilar networks through devices called gateways. *See also* bridge, frame (definition 2), gateway.

AppleTalk Phase 2 *n.* The extended AppleTalk Internet model designed by Apple Computer, Inc., that supports multiple zones within a network and extended addressing capacity.

AppleWorks *n.* A suite of productivity applications, formerly known as Claris-Works, distributed by Apple Computer, Inc., and shipped on the iMac computer. AppleWorks/ClarisWorks is an integrated product that includes support for word processing, spreadsheets, databases, drawing, painting, charting, and the Internet.

A

appliance server *n.* **1.** An inexpensive computing device used for specific tasks including Internet connectivity or file-and-print services. The server is usually easy to use but does not possess the capabilities or software of a typical server for general office use. **2.** *See* server appliance.

application programming interface *n.* A set of routines used by an application program to direct the performance of procedures by the computer's operating system. *Acronym:* API. *Also called:* application program interface.

application server *n.* **1.** A server program on a computer in a distributed network that handles the business logic between users and backend business applications or databases. Application servers also can provide transaction management, failover, and load balancing. An application server is often viewed as part of a three-tier application consisting of a front-end GUI server such as an HTTP server (first tier), an application server (middle tier), and a backend database and transaction server (third tier). *Also called:* appserver. *Compare* HTTP server (definition 1). **2.** Any machine on which an application-server program is running. *Also called:* appserver.

application service provider *n.* A third-party company or organization that hosts applications or services for individuals or business customers. The customer connects to a data center maintained by the application service provider (ASP) through Internet or private lines to access applications that would otherwise need to be housed on the customer's local servers or individual PCs. This arrangement allows the customer to free up disk space that would otherwise be taken by applications, as well as to access the most recent software updates. ASPs deliver solutions ranging from high-end applications to services for small and medium-sized businesses. *Acronym:* ASP.

appserver *n.* *See* application server.

arbitration *n.* A set of rules for resolving competing demands for a machine resource by multiple users or processes. *See also* contention.

Archie *n.* An Internet utility for finding files in public archives obtainable by anonymous FTP. The master Archie server at McGill University in Montreal downloads FTP indexes from participating FTP servers, merges them into a master list, and sends updated copies of the master list to other Archie servers each day. Archie is a shortened form of *archive. See also* anonymous FTP, FTP[1] (definition 1). *Compare* Jughead, Veronica.

Archie client *n.* *See* Archie.

Archie server *n.* On the Internet, a server that contains Archie indexes to the names and addresses of files in public FTP archives. *See also* Archie, FTP[1] (definition 1), server (definition 2).

architecture *n.* **1.** The physical construction or design of a computer system and its components. *See also* cache, closed architecture, network architecture. **2.** The data-handling capacity of a microprocessor. **3.** The design of application software incorporating protocols and the means for expansion and interfacing with other programs.

A

ARCnet *n.* Short for **A**ttached **R**esource **C**omputer **Net**work. A form of token bus network architecture for PC-based LANs developed by Datapoint Corporation. ARCnet relies on a bus or star topology and can support up to 255 nodes. Different versions run at speeds of 1.5 Mbps, 20 Mbps (ARCnet Plus), and 100 Mbps.

ARCnet Plus *n. See* ARCnet.

ARIN *n.* Acronym for **A**merican **R**egistry for **I**nternet **N**umbers. A nonprofit organization formed to register and administer Internet Protocol (IP) addresses in North and South America. The American Registry for Internet Numbers separates the allocation of IP addresses from the administration of top-level Internet domains, such as .com and .edu. Both of these tasks were previously managed by Network Solutions, Inc., as part of the InterNIC consortium. Its international counterparts are RIPE, in Europe, and APNIC, in Asia and the Pacific Rim. *See also* APNIC, InterNIC, IP address, RIPE.

ARP *n.* Acronym for **A**ddress **R**esolution **P**rotocol. A TCP/IP protocol for determining the hardware address (or physical address) of a node on a local area network connected to the Internet, when only the IP address (or logical address) is known. An ARP request is sent to the network, and the node that has the IP address responds with its hardware address. Although ARP technically refers only to finding the hardware address, and RARP (for Reverse ARP) refers to the reverse procedure, ARP is commonly used for both senses. *See also* IP address, TCP/IP.

ARPANET *n.* A large wide area network created in the 1960s by the U.S. Department of Defense Advanced Research Projects Agency (ARPA, renamed DARPA in the 1970s) for the free exchange of information between universities and research organizations, although the military also used this network for communications. In the 1980s MILNET, a separate network, was spun off from ARPANET for use by the military. ARPANET was the network from which the Internet evolved. *See also* ALOHAnet, Internet, MILNET.

ARP request *n.* Short for **A**ddress **R**esolution **P**rotocol **request**. An ARP packet containing the Internet address of a host computer. The receiving computer responds with or passes along the corresponding Ethernet address. *See also* ARP, Ethernet, IP address, packet.

article *n.* A message that appears in an Internet newsgroup. *Also called:* post. *See also* newsgroup.

AS *n. See* autonomous system.

ASCII *n.* Acronym for **A**merican **S**tandard **C**ode for **I**nformation **I**nterchange. A coding scheme using 7 or 8 bits that assigns numeric values to up to 256 characters, including letters, numerals, punctuation marks, control characters, and other symbols. ASCII was developed in 1968 to standardize data transmission among disparate hardware and software systems and is built into most minicomputers and all PCs. ASCII is divided into two sets: 128 characters (standard ASCII) and an additional 128 (extended ASCII). *Compare* EBCDIC.

A

Asian-Pacific Network Information Center *n. See* APNIC.

.asp *n.* A file extension that identifies a Web page as an Active Server Page.

ASP *n.* **1.** *See* Active Server Pages. **2.** *See* application service provider.

ASP.NET *n.* A set of technologies in the Microsoft .NET Framework for building Web applications and XML Web services. ASP.NET pages execute on the server and generate markup (such as HTML, WML, or XML) that is sent to a desktop or mobile browser. ASP.NET pages use a compiled, event-driven programming model that improves performance and enables the separation of application logic and user interface. ASP.NET pages and XML Web services files created using ASP.NET contain server-side (rather than client-side) logic written in Visual Basic .NET, C# .NET, or any .NET-compatible language. Web applications and XML Web services take advantage of the features of the common language runtime, such as type safety, inheritance, language interoperability, versioning, and integrated security.

ASP.NET server control *n.* A server-side component that encapsulates user-interface and related functionality. An ASP.NET server control derives directly or indirectly from the System.Web.UI.Control class. The superset of ASP.NET server controls includes Web server controls, HTML server controls, and mobile controls. The page syntax for an ASP.NET server control includes a runat="server" attribute on the control's tag. *See also* Web server control, HTML server control, validation server controls.

ASP.NET Web application *n.* An application that processes HTTP requests (Web requests) and executes on top of the ASP.NET runtime. An ASP.NET application can include ASP.NET pages, XML Web services, HTTP handlers, and HTTP modules.

asymmetric digital subscriber line *n. See* ADSL.

asymmetric digital subscriber loop *n. See* ADSL.

asymmetric modem *n.* A modem that transmits data to the telephone network and receives data from the network at different speeds. Most commonly, an asymmetric modem will have a maximum download speed substantially higher than its upload speed. *See also* modem.

asynchronous *adj.* Pertaining to, being, or characteristic of something that is not dependent on timing. For example, asynchronous communications can start and stop at any time instead of having to match the timing governed by a clock.

asynchronous communications *n.* Computer-to-computer communications in which the sending and receiving computers do not rely on timing as a means of determining where transmissions begin and end. *Compare* synchronous communications.

Asynchronous Protocol Specification *n.* The X.445 standard. *See also* X series.

Asynchronous Transfer Mode *n. See* ATM (definition 1).

ATM *n.* **1.** Acronym for **A**synchronous **T**ransfer **M**ode. A network technology capable of transmitting data, voice, audio, video, and frame relay traffic in real time. Data, including frame relay data, is broken into packets containing 53 bytes each, which are switched between any two nodes in the system at rates ranging from 1.5 Mbps to 622 Mbps (over fiber optic cable). The basic unit of ATM transmission is known as a cell, a packet consisting of 5 bytes routing information and a 48-byte payload (data). These cells are transmitted to their destination, where they are reassembled into the original traffic. During transmission, cells from different users may be intermixed asynchronously to maximize utilization of network resources. ATM is defined in the broadband ISDN protocol at the levels corresponding to levels 1 and 2 of the ISO/OSI reference model. It is currently used in LANs (local area networks) involving workstations and personal computers, but it is expected to be adopted by the telephone companies, which will be able to charge customers for the data they transmit rather than for their connect time. *See also* broadband, ISDN, ISO/OSI reference model. **2.** Acronym for **a**utomated **t**eller **m**achine. A special-purpose terminal that bank customers can use to make deposits, obtain cash, and perform other transactions.

ATM Adaptation Layer *n.* The ATM layer that mediates between higher-level and lower-level services, converting different types of data (such as audio, video, and data frames) to the 48-byte payloads required by ATM. *Acronym:* AAL. *See also* ATM (definition 1).

ATM Forum *n.* Forum created in 1991 and including more than 750 companies related to communications and computing, as well as government agencies and research groups. The forum aims to promote Asynchronous Transfer Mode for data communication. *See also* ATM (definition 1).

at sign *n. See* @.

Attached Resource Computer Network *n. See* ARCnet.

attenuation *n.* The weakening of a transmitted signal, such as the distortion of a digital signal or the reduction in amplitude of an electrical signal, as it travels farther from its source. Attenuation is usually measured in decibels and is sometimes desirable, as when signal strength is reduced electronically, for example, by a radio volume control, to prevent overloading.

attribute *n.* **1.** In a database record, the name or structure of a field. For example, the files LASTNAME, FIRSTNAME, and PHONE would be attributes of each record in a PHONELIST database. The size of a field or the type of information it contains would also be attributes of a database record. **2.** In screen displays, an element of additional information stored with each character in the video buffer of a video adapter running in character mode. Such attributes control the background and foreground colors of the character, underlining, and blinking. **3.** In markup languages such as SGML and HTML, a name-value pair within a tagged element that modifies certain features of that element. *See also* HTML, SGML.

authentication *n.* In a multiuser or network operating system, the process by which the system validates a user's logon information. A user's name and password are compared against an authorized list, and if the system detects a match, access is granted to the extent specified in the permission list for that user. *See also* logon, password, permission, user account, user name.

authentication center *n.* Secure database used to identify and prevent wireless phone fraud. Authentication centers verify whether a wireless phone is registered with a wireless carrier's network.

Authentication Header *n. See* AH.

Authenticode *n.* A security feature of Microsoft Internet Explorer. Authenticode allows vendors of downloadable executable code (plug-ins or ActiveX controls, for example) to attach digital certificates to their products to assure end users that the code is from the original developer and has not been altered. Authenticode lets end users decide for themselves whether to accept or reject software components posted on the Internet before downloading begins. *See also* ActiveX control, Internet Explorer, security.

author¹ *vb.* **1.** To create a product for implementation via computer technology. **2.** To write a computer program. **3.** To assemble multimedia components, such as graphics, text, audio, and animation, in a publication or product, for delivery on a CD-ROM or DVD or on line, to be viewed on a computer. **4.** To create Web pages. Traditionally, to author meant to write a literary work or journalistic piece; in the cyberworld, to write is "to provide content"; thus, to author in the traditional sense is to be a "content provider."

author² *n. See* Web author.

authoring software *n.* A type of computer program used for creating Web pages and other hypertext and multimedia applications. Authoring software provides a way to define relationships between different types of objects, including text, graphics, and sound, and to present them in a desired order. This type of program is sometimes known as authorware, although the latter name is generally associated with a specific product from Macromedia. *Also called:* authoring tool.

authority *n.* A DNS server responsible for resolving names and IP addresses of sites and resources on the Internet at a particular level of authority: top-level domain, second-level domain, or subdomain.

authorization *n.* In reference to computing, especially remote computers on a network, the right granted an individual to use the system and the data stored on it. Authorization is typically set up by a system administrator and verified by the computer based on some form of user identification, such as a code number or password. *Also called:* access privileges, permission. *See also* network, system administrator.

authorization code *n. See* password.

AutoIP *n.* Short for **auto**matic **I**nternet **P**rotocol addressing. A technique used by a device to obtain a valid IP address without a DHCP server or other IP-configuration authority. With AutoIP, a device randomly chooses an IP address from a set of reserved addresses and queries the local network to determine whether another client already is using that address. The device repeats the steps of picking and verifying until an unused address is found. AutoIP, based on an Internet Engineering Task Force (IETF) Internet Draft, is used in Universal Plug and Play (UPnP) networking. *See also* UPnP networking.

automatic IP addressing *n. See* AutoIP.

automatic patching *n.* A process in which vulnerabilities caused by a destructive computer virus infection are tracked down and corrected by a do-gooder virus or other anti-virus program. Automatic patching may be initiated by the user, or may be done by a virus entering a back door left by a malicious virus, without the consent of the user. *See also* anti-worm, do-gooder virus.

Automatic Private IP Addressing *n.* A feature of Windows XP TCP/IP that automatically configures a unique IP address from the range 169.254.0.1 through 169.254.255.254 and a subnet mask of 255.255.0.0 when the TCP/IP protocol is config-ured for dynamic addressing and Dynamic Host Configuration Protocol (DHCP) is not available. *Acronym:* APIPA. *See also* DHCP server, DHCP, IP address, TCP/IP.

autonomous system *n.* A group of routers or networks controlled by a single administrative authority using a common Interior Gateway Protocol (IGP) for routing packets. Each autonomous system is assigned a globally unique number called an autonomous-system number (ASN). *Acronym:* AS. *Also called:* routing domain. *See also* IGP.

availability *n.* **1.** In processing, the accessibility of a computer system or resource, such as a printer, in terms of usage or of the percentage of the total amount of time the device is needed. **2.** A measure of the fault tolerance of a computer and its programs. A highly available computer runs 24 hours a day, 7 days a week. *See also* fault tolerance.

available time *n. See* uptime.

avatar *n.* In virtual-reality environments such as certain types of Internet chat rooms, a graphical representation of a user. An avatar typically is a generic picture or animation of a human of either gender, a photograph or caricature of the user, a pic-ture or animation of an animal, or an object chosen by the user to depict his or her vir-tual-reality "identity." *See* superuser.

B

b[1] *adj.* Short for **b**inary.

b[2] *n.* **1.** Short for **b**it. **2.** Short for **b**aud.

B1FF *n.* Slang for a new online user who is prone to making mistakes in e-mail, newsgroup articles, or chats that show his or her inexperience. Examples of typical mistakes made by B1FFs include sentences ending with multiple exclamation points (!!!!) and messages typed in ALL CAPS. Although it's spelled B-1(one)-F-F, the term is pronounced "bif."

B

B2B *n.* Short for **b**usiness-**to**-**b**usiness. The electronic exchange of products and services between businesses without the direct involvement of consumers. B2B's effects on business include streamlining purchasing, accounting, and other administrative functions; lowering transaction costs; and simplifying the sale of excess inventory. Related businesses have collaborated on the creation of Internet-based supply-chain networks.

B2C *n.* Short for **b**usiness-**to**-**c**onsumer. The direct electronic exchange of products and services between businesses and consumers. B2C's effects on business include improving the efficiency in delivering goods and services to consumers.

backbone *n.* **1.** A network of communication transmission that carries major traffic between smaller networks. The backbones of the Internet, including communications carriers such as Sprint and MCI, can span thousands of miles using microwave relays and dedicated lines. **2.** The smaller networks (compared with the entire Internet) that perform the bulk of the packet switching of Internet communication. Today these smaller networks still consist of the networks that were originally developed to make up the Internet—the computer networks of the educational and research institutions of the United States—especially NSFnet, the computer network of the National Science Foundation in Oak Ridge, Tennessee. *See also* NSFnet, packet switching. **3.** The wires that carry major communications traffic within a network. In a local area network, a backbone may be a bus. *Also called:* collapsed backbone.

backbone cabal *n.* On the Internet, a term for the group of network administrators responsible for naming the hierarchy of Usenet newsgroups and devising the procedures for creating new newsgroups. The backbone cabal no longer exists.

back door *n.* A means of gaining access to a program or system by bypassing its security controls. Programmers often build back doors into systems under development so that they can fix bugs. If the back door becomes known to anyone other than the programmer, or if it is not removed before the software is released, it becomes a security risk. *Also called:* trapdoor.

back end *n.* **1.** In a client/server application, the part of the program that runs on the server. *See also* client/server architecture. *Compare* front end. **2.** In networking, a server computer or the processing that takes place on it.

background noise *n.* The noise inherent in a line or circuit, independent of the presence of a signal. *See also* noise.

BackOffice *n.* A suite of software developed by Microsoft that provides certain network services. Designed to work with Windows NT and Windows 2000, BackOffice includes such services as e-mail (Exchange), intranet capabilities (Site Server), network management (Systems Management Server), and high-end database development (SQL Server), among others.

Back Orifice *n.* A hostile application tool used by hackers to gain control of a remote computer. Back Orifice consists of client and server applications. The client application is used to control a computer running the server application. A target computer is taken over after an executable file, typically delivered by an e-mail attachment or a removable disk, is opened. Back Orifice then copies itself to the Windows System directory and transfers control to the machine running the client application. Back Orifice first appeared in the summer of 1998 and was quickly contained through updated security software. Its name is a play on words for the Microsoft BackOffice suite of servers.

bacterium *n.* A type of computer virus that repeatedly replicates itself, eventually taking over the entire system. *See also* virus.

bandpass filter *n.* An electronic circuit that passes signals that are within a certain frequency range (band) but blocks or attenuates signals above or below the band. *See also* attenuation.

bandwidth *n.* **1.** The difference between the highest and lowest frequencies that an analog communications system can pass as measured in Hertz (Hz) or cycles per second. For example, a telephone accommodates a bandwidth of 3000 Hz: the difference between the lowest (300 Hz) and highest (3300 Hz) frequencies it can carry. **2.** The data transfer capacity, or speed of transmission, of a digital communications system as measured in bits per second (bps).

bandwidth allocation *n. See* bandwidth reservation.

bandwidth brokerage *n. See* bandwidth trading.

bandwidth exchange *n. See* bandwidth trading.

bandwidth management *n.* The analysis and control of traffic on WAN (wide area network) and Internet links to prioritize bandwidth and improve quality of service (QoS). *See also* quality of service (definition 2), traffic shaping.

bandwidth on demand *n.* In telecommunications, the capability of increasing throughput, in increments, as required by the channel to be serviced. *See also* bandwidth, channel (definition 2), throughput.

bandwidth reservation *n.* Process of assigning in advance a percentage of bandwidth to each user or application served by a network. Bandwidth reservation optimizes the use of available traffic by prioritizing time-critical packets. *Also called:* bandwidth allocation, custom queuing. *See also* bandwidth management, traffic shaping.

bandwidth shaping *n. See* traffic shaping.

bandwidth test *n.* A benchmark test that determines the speed of a network connection. Bandwidth tests estimate the downstream and upstream speeds by sending a series of packets over the network and measuring how many packets are received in a given amount of time. *Also called:* throughput test. *See also* throughput.

bandwidth trading *n.* The exchange of excess bandwidth capacity. Although considered a possible commodity market, bandwidth trading currently lacks standardized contracts and instantaneous provisioning needed to simplify the trading process. *Also called:* bandwidth brokerage, bandwidth exchange.

bang *n.* The pronunciation for an exclamation point, particularly when the exclamation point is used in a file name or in a path on UNIX systems. *See also* bang path.

bang path *n.* Slang for an older form of e-mail address used in UUCP (UNIX-to-UNIX copy). A bang address supplies the path that the message needs to take to reach its destination, including the name of each host through which the message is to be passed. Exclamation points called "bangs" separate the elements of the e-mail address, such as the user account and host names. The address name!location, where "name" is the user account and "location" is the host name, would be spoken as "name bang location."

baseband *adj.* Of or relating to communications systems in which the medium of transmission (such as a wire or fiber-optic cable) carries a single message at a time in digital form. Baseband communication is found in local area networks such as Ethernet and Token Ring. *See also* Ethernet, Token Ring network. *Compare* broadband.

baseband network *n.* A type of local area network in which messages travel in digital form on a single transmission channel between machines connected by coaxial cable or twisted-pair wiring. Machines on a baseband network transmit only when the channel is not busy, although a technique called *time-division multiplexing* can enable channel sharing. Each message travels as a packet that contains information about the source and destination machines as well as message data. Baseband networks operate over short distances at speeds ranging from about 50 kilobits per second (50 Kbps) to 16 megabits per second (16 Mbps). Receiving, verifying, and converting a message, however, add considerably to the actual time, reducing throughput. The maximum recommended distance for such a network is about 2 miles, or considerably less if the network is heavily used. *See also* coaxial cable, multiplexer, packet (definition 2), throughput, twisted-pair cable. *Compare* broadband network.

Basic Rate Interface *n. See* BRI.

Basic Service Set *n.* The communicating stations, or nodes, on a wireless LAN. *See also* wireless LAN.

batch job *n.* A program or set of commands that runs without user interaction. *See also* batch processing.

batch processing *n.* The practice of storing transactions for a period of time before they are posted to a master file, typically in a separate operation undertaken at night. *Compare* transaction processing.

B

baud *n.* One signal change per second, a measure of data transmission speed. Named after the French engineer and telegrapher Jean-Maurice-Emile Baudot and originally used to measure the transmission speed of telegraph equipment, the term now most commonly refers to the data transmission speed of a modem. *See also* baud rate.

baud rate *n.* The speed at which a modem can transmit data. The baud rate is the number of events, or signal changes, that occur in one second—not the number of bits per second (bps) transmitted. In high-speed digital communications, one event can actually encode more than one bit, and modems are more accurately described in terms of bits per second than baud rate. For example, a so-called 9600-baud modem actually operates at 2400 baud but transmits 9600 bits per second by encoding 4 bits per event (2400 x 4 = 9600) and thus is a 9600-bps modem. *Compare* bit rate, transfer rate.

B

BBS *n.* **1.** Acronym for **b**ulletin **b**oard **s**ystem. A computer system equipped with one or more modems or other means of network access that serves as an information and message-passing center for remote users. Often BBSs are focused on special interests, such as science fiction, movies, Windows software, or Macintosh systems, and can have free or fee-based access, or a combination. Users dial into a BBS with their modems and post messages to other BBS users in special areas devoted to a particular topic, in a manner reminiscent of the posting of notes on a cork bulletin board. Many BBSs also allow users to chat online with other users, send e-mail, download and upload files that include freeware and shareware software, and access the Internet. Many software and hardware companies run proprietary BBSs for customers that include sales information, technical support, and software upgrades and patches. **2.** Acronym for **b**e **b**ack **s**oon. A shorthand expression often seen in Internet discussion groups by a participant leaving the group who wishes to bid a temporary farewell to the rest of the group.

bcc *n.* Acronym for **b**lind **c**ourtesy **c**opy. A feature of e-mail programs that allows a user to send a copy of an e-mail message to a recipient without notifying other recipients that this was done. Generally, the recipient's address is entered into a field called "bcc:" in the mail header. *Also called:* blind carbon copy. *See also* e-mail[1] (definition 1), header. *Compare* cc.

B channel *n.* Short for **bearer channel**. One of the 64-Kbps communications channels that carry data on an ISDN circuit. A BRI (Basic Rate Interface) ISDN line has two B channels and one D (data) channel. A PRI (Primary Rate Interface) ISDN line has 23 B channels (in North America) or 30 B channels (in Europe) and one D channel. *See also* BRI, D channel, ISDN.

beacon *n.* On an FDDI network, a special frame generated and passed along when a node detects a problem. *See also* frame (definition 2).

beam *vb.* To transfer information from one device to another through an infrared wireless connection. The term typically refers to data sharing using handheld devices such as Palm organizers, Pocket PCs, mobile phones, and pagers.

bearer channel *n.* *See* B channel.

Bell communications standards *n.* A series of data transmission standards originated by AT&T during the late 1970s and early 1980s that, through wide acceptance in North America, became de facto standards for modems. Bell 103, now mostly obsolete, governed transmission at 300 bits per second (bps) with full-duplex, asynchronous communications over dial-up telephone lines using frequency-shift keying (FSK). Bell 212A governed modem operations at 1200 bps with full-duplex, asynchronous communications over dial-up telephone lines using phase-shift keying (PSK). An international set of transmission standards, known as the CCITT recommendations, has become generally accepted as the primary source of standardization, especially for communications at speeds greater than 1200 bps. *See also* CCITT V series.

B

Bell-compatible modem *n.* A modem that operates according to the Bell communications standards. *See also* Bell communications standards.

Bellman-Ford distance-vector routing algorithm *n.* An algorithm that helps to determine the shortest route between two nodes on a network. The Routing Information Protocol (RIP) is based on the Bellman-Ford distance-vector routing algorithm. *See also* RIP.

benign virus *n.* A program that exhibits properties of a virus, such as self-replication, but does not otherwise do harm to the computer systems that it infects.

Berkeley Internet Name Domain *n. See* BIND.

Berkeley Sockets API *n. See* sockets API.

biff¹ *n.* **1.** A BSD utility that issues a signal when new mail has arrived. Biff was named after a University of California graduate student's dog who had a habit of barking at the mailman at the time the utility was developed. **2.** *See* B1FF.

biff² *vb.* To provide notification of new (incoming) e-mail.

binary *n.* In an FTP client program, the command that instructs the FTP server to send or receive files as binary data. *See also* FTP client, FTP server. *Compare* ASCII.

binary file transfer *n.* Transfer of a file containing arbitrary bytes or words, as opposed to a text file containing only printable characters (for example, ASCII characters with codes 10, 13, and 32–126). On modern operating systems a text file is simply a binary file that happens to contain only printable characters, but some older systems distinguish the two file types, requiring programs to handle them differently. *Acronym:* BFT.

binary format *n.* Any format that structures data in 8-bit form. Binary format is generally used to represent object code (program instructions translated into a machine-readable form) or data in a transmission stream.

binary synchronous protocol *n. See* BISYNC.

BIND *n.* Acronym for **B**erkeley **I**nternet **N**ame **D**omain. A domain name server originally written for the BSD version of UNIX developed at the Berkeley campus of the University of California but now available for most versions of UNIX. As a domain name server, BIND translates between human-readable domain names and Internet-friendly, numeric IP addresses. It is widely used on Internet servers. *See also* DNS, DNS server, IP address.

binding *n.* The process by which protocols are associated with one another and the network adapter to provide a complete set of protocols needed for handling data from the application layer to the physical layer. *See also* ISO/OSI reference model.

BinHex *n.* Short for **bin**ary to **hex**adecimal. A format for converting binary data files into ASCII text so they can be transmitted via e-mail to another computer or in a newsgroup post. This method can be used when standard ASCII characters are needed for transmission, as they are on the Internet. BinHex is used most frequently by Mac users. *See also* MIME.

BioAPI *n.* An open system specification for use in biometric security and authentication technologies. BioAPI supports a wide range of biometric technology, from handheld devices to large-scale networks, and applications include fingerprint identification, facial recognition, speaker verification, dynamic signatures, and hand geometry. BioAPI was developed for the BioAPI Consortium, a group of organizations with ties to biometrics. BioAPI incorporates compatibility with existing biometric standards such as HA-API, which allows applications to operate BioAPI-compliant technologies without modification.

bionics *n.* The study of living organisms, their characteristics, and the ways they function, with a view toward creating hardware that can simulate or duplicate the activities of a biological system. *See also* cybernetics.

bipartite virus *n.* *See* multipartite virus.

BISDN *n.* *See* broadband ISDN.

BISYNC *n.* Short for **bi**nary **sync**hronous communications protocol. A communications standard developed by IBM. BISYNC transmissions are encoded in either ASCII or EBCDIC. Messages can be of any length and are sent in units called frames, optionally preceded by a message header. BISYNC uses synchronous transmission, in which message elements are separated by a specific time interval, so each frame is preceded and followed by special characters that enable the sending and receiving machines to synchronize their clocks. STX and ETX are control characters that mark the beginning and end of the message text; BCC is a set of characters used to verify the accuracy of transmission. *Also called:* BSC.

bit *n.* Short for **bi**nary digi**t**. The smallest unit of information handled by a computer. One bit expresses a 1 or a 0 in a binary numeral, or a true or false logical condition, and is represented physically by an element such as a high or low voltage at one point in a circuit or a small spot on a disk magnetized one way or the other. A single bit conveys little information a human would consider meaningful. A group of 8 bits, however, makes up a byte, which can be used to represent many types of information, such as a letter of the alphabet, a decimal digit, or other character. *See also* ASCII, binary.

bitmap *n.* A data structure in memory that represents information in the form of a collection of individual bits. A bit map is used to represent a bit image. Another use of a bit map in some systems is the representation of the blocks of storage on a disk, indicating whether each block is free (0) or in use (1).

BITNET *n.* Acronym for **B**ecause **I**t's **T**ime **Net**work. A WAN (wide area network) founded in 1981 and operated by the Corporation for Research and Educational Networking (CREN) in Washington, D.C. Now defunct, BITNET provided e-mail and file transfer services between mainframe computers at educational and research institutions in North America, Europe, and Japan. BITNET used the IBM Network Job Entry (NJE) protocol rather than TCP/IP, but it could exchange e-mail with the Internet. The listserv software for maintaining mailing lists was originated on BITNET.

B

bit. newsgroups *n.* A hicrarchy of Internet newsgroups that mirror the content of some BITNET mailing lists. *See also* BITNET.

bit-oriented protocol *n.* A communications protocol in which data is transmitted as a steady stream of bits rather than as a string of characters. Because the bits transmitted have no inherent meaning in terms of a particular character set (such as ASCII), a bit-oriented protocol uses special sequences of bits rather than reserved characters for control purposes. The HDLC (high-level data link control) defined by ISO is a bit-oriented protocol. *Compare* byte-oriented protocol.

bit rate *n.* **1.** The speed at which binary digits are transmitted. *See also* transfer rate. **2.** The streaming speed of digital content on a network. Bit rate is usually measured in kilobits per second (Kbps).

bit stream *n.* **1.** A series of binary digits representing a flow of information transferred through a given medium. **2.** In synchronous communications, a continuous flow of data in which characters in the stream are separated from one another by the receiving station rather than by markers, such as start and stop bits, inserted into the data.

bit stuffing *n.* The practice of inserting extra bits into a stream of transmitted data. Bit stuffing is used to ensure that a special sequence of bits appears only at desired locations. For example, in the HDLC, SDLC, and X.25 communications protocols, six 1 bits in a row can appear only at the beginning and end of a frame (block) of data, so bit stuffing is used to insert a 0 bit into the rest of the stream whenever five 1 bits appear in a row. The inserted 0 bits are removed by the receiving station to return the data to its original form. *See also* HDLC, SDLC, X.25.

bit transfer rate *n. See* transfer rate.

BIX *n.* Acronym for **BYTE I**nformation **Ex**change. An online service originated by *BYTE* magazine, now owned and operated by Delphi Internet Services Corporation. BIX offers e-mail, software downloads, and hardware and software conferences.

.biz *n.* One of seven new top-level domain names approved in 2000 by the Internet Corporation for Assigned Names and Numbers (ICANN), .biz is meant for use in business-related Web sites.

biz. news groups *n.* Usenet newsgroups that are part of the biz. hierarchy and have the prefix of biz. These newsgroups are devoted to discussions related to business. Unlike most other newsgroup hierarchies, biz. newsgroups permit users to post advertisement and other marketing material. *See also* newsgroup, traditional newsgroup hierarchy.

BizTalk Server *n.* An application developed by Microsoft Corporation to streamline business processes within a large company's internal network and between business partners over the Internet. BizTalk Server enables the integration of business applications written in different computer languages and running on various operating systems.

BlackBerry *n.* A wireless handheld device that allows mobile users to send and receive e-mail, as well as view appointment calendars and contact lists. The BlackBerry features a display screen and a built-in keyboard operated by pressing the keys with the thumbs. BlackBerry's ease of use and its ability to send and receive messages silently have made it a popular device for wireless text messaging in a business environment.

black hat *n.* A hacker who operates with malicious or criminal intent. A black hat will break into a system to alter or damage data or to commit theft. *Compare* white hat.

black hole *n.* A mysterious "place" on a computer network where messages, such as e-mail and news items, disappear without a trace. The usage is derived from stellar black holes, which have such strong gravitational fields that even light cannot escape them. The term is sometimes also used to refer to projects that consume vast amounts of time with no apparent product.

blind carbon copy *n. See* bcc.

blind courtesy copy *n. See* bcc.

blog^1 *n. See* Weblog.

blog^2 *vb.* To create or maintain a Weblog.

blogger *n.* One who creates or maintains a Weblog.

Bluetooth *n.* Technology protocol developed to wirelessly connect electronic devices such as wireless phones, personal digital assistants (PDAs), and computers. Devices equipped with Bluetooth chips can exchange information within about a 30-foot range via radio waves in the 2.45 gigahertz (GHz) spectrum. Bluetooth was developed by the Bluetooth Special Interest Group, a consortium of telecommunications, computing, consumer electronics, and related industry groups.

Bluetooth Special Interest Group *n.* A group of companies from the telecommunications, computing, and networking industries that promotes the development and deployment of Bluetooth technology. *See also* Bluetooth.

Bluetooth wireless technology *n.* A specification for radio links between mobile PCs, mobile phones, and other portable devices. These radio links are small-form factor, low cost, and short range.

.bmp *n.* The file extension that identifies raster graphics stored in bitmap file format. *See also* bitmap.

BNC *n.* Acronym for **b**ayonet-**N**eill-**C**oncelman. Named for Paul Neill of Bell Labs and Carl Concelman (affiliation unknown), who developed two earlier types of coaxial connectors known as the N connector and C connector, BNC is a type of connector used to join segments of coaxial cable. When one connector is inserted into another and rotated 90 degrees, they lock. BNC connectors are often used with closed-circuit television. The letters BNC are sometimes also considered an acronym for British Naval Connector. *Also called:* BNC connector. *See also* coaxial cable.

B

BNC connector *n. See* BNC.

body *n.* **1.** In e-mail and Internet newsgroups, the content of a message. The body of a message follows the header, which contains information about the sender, origin, and destination of the message. *See also* header. **2.** In HTML, SGML, and XML, a section of a document that contains the content of the document, along with tags describing characteristics of the content—for example, format. **3.** A segment of a data packet containing the actual data.

BOF *n.* Acronym for **b**irds **o**f a **f**eather. Meetings of special interest groups at trade shows, conferences, and conventions. BOF sessions provide an opportunity for people working on the same technology at different companies or research institutions to meet and exchange their experiences.

bomb *n.* A program planted surreptitiously, with intent to damage or destroy a system in some way—for example, to erase a hard disk or cause it to be unreadable to the operating system. *See also* Trojan horse, virus, worm.

bonding *n.* **1.** Acronym for **B**andwidth **O**n **D**emand **In**teroperability **G**roup. **2.** The process of combining two or more ISDN B (bearer) channels to form a single channel with a bandwidth greater than the standard B channel bandwidth of 64 Kbps. Bonding two B channels, for example, provides a bandwidth of 128 Kbps, which is four times faster than a 28.8 Kbps modem. Such high-speed channels are ideal for video conferencing, imaging, and transferring large-scale data. *See also* B channel, BRI, ISDN.

bonding *vb. See* link aggregation.

bookmark *n.* **1.** A marker inserted at a specific point in a document to which the user may wish to return for later reference. **2.** In Netscape Navigator, a link to a Web page or other URL that a user has stored in a local file in order to return to it later. *See also* Favorites folder, hotlist, URL.

bookmark file *n.* **1.** A Netscape Navigator file containing the addresses of preferred Web sites. It is synonymous with the Favorites folder in Internet Explorer and the hotlist in Mosaic. *See also* Favorites folder, hotlist, Internet Explorer, Mosaic. **2.** A rendering of such a file in HTML format, generally posted on a Web page for the benefit of other people. *See also* HTML.

boost *vb.* To strengthen a network signal before it is transmitted further.

BOOTP *n. See* Bootstrap Protocol.

Bootstrap Protocol *n.* A protocol used primarily on TCP/IP networks to configure diskless workstations. RFCs 951 and 1542 define this protocol. DHCP is a later boot configuration protocol that uses this protocol. The Microsoft DGCP service provided limited support for BOOTP service. *Acronym:* BOOTP. *Also called:* Boot Protocol. *See also* DHCP, RFC, TCP/IP.

B

Border Gateway Protocol *n.* A protocol used by NSFnet that is based on the External Gateway Protocol. *Acronym:* BGP. *See also* External Gateway Protocol, NSFnet.

bot *n.* **1.** Short for ro**bot**. A displayed representation of a person or other entity whose actions are based on programming. **2.** A program that performs some task on a network, especially a task that is repetitive or time consuming. **3.** On the Internet, a program that performs a repetitive or time-consuming task, such as searching Web sites and newsgroups for information and indexing them in a database or other record-keeping system (called *spiders*); automatically posting one or more articles to multiple newsgroups (often used in spamming and called *spambots*); or keeping IRC channels open. *Also called:* Internet robot. *See also* IRC, newsgroup, spam, spambot, spider.

bozo *n.* A slang term used frequently on the Internet, particularly in newsgroups, for a foolish or eccentric person.

bozo filter *n.* On the Internet, slang for a feature in some e-mail clients and newsgroup readers or a separate utility that allows the user to block, or filter out, incoming e-mail messages or newsgroup articles from specified individuals. Generally these individuals are ones that the user does not want to hear from, such as bozos. *Also called:* kill file. *See also* bozo.

bps *n.* Short for **b**its **p**er **s**econd. The measure of transmission speed used in relation to networks and communication lines. Although bps represents the basic unit of measure, networks and communications devices, such as modems, are so fast that speeds are usually given in multiples of bps—Kbps (kilobits, or thousands of bits, per second), Mbps (megabits, or millions of bits, per second), and Gbps (gigabits, or billions of bits, per second). Speed in bps is not the same as the baud rate for a modem. *See also* baud rate.

braindamaged *adj.* Performing in an erratic or destructive manner. A braindamaged application or utility program is characterized by some or all of the following traits: a mysterious and unintuitive user interface, failure to respond predictably to commands, failure to release unused memory, failure to close open files, and use of "reserved" elements of the operating system that can result in a fatal error in a program or the operating system. Braindamaged programs are also often responsible for causing problems across local area networks.

brain dump *n.* A large, unorganized mass of information, presented in response to a query via e-mail or a newsgroup article, that is difficult to digest or interpret.

branch *n.* Any connection between two items such as blocks in a flowchart or nodes in a network.

BRB *n.* Acronym for (I'll) **b**e **r**ight **b**ack. An expression used commonly on live chat services on the Internet and online information services by participants signaling their temporary departure from the group. *See also* chat[1] (definition 1).

BRI *n.* Acronym for **B**asic **R**ate **I**nterface. An ISDN subscriber service that uses two B (64 Kbps) channels and one D (64 Kbps) channel to transmit voice, video, and data signals. *See also* ISDN.

bridge *n.* **1.** A device that connects networks using the same communications protocols so that information can be passed from one to the other. *Compare* gateway. **2.** A device that connects two LANs (local area networks), whether or not they use the same protocols, and allows information to flow between them. The bridge operates at the ISO/OSI data-link layer. *Also called:* layer switch. *See also* data-link layer. *Compare* router.

bridge page *n. See* doorway page.

bridge router *n.* A device that supports the functions of both a bridge and router. A bridge router links two segments of a local or wide area network, passing packets of data between the segments as necessary, and uses Level 2 addresses for routing. *Also called:* Brouter. *See also* bridge (definition 2), router.

Briefcase *n.* A system folder in Windows 9x used for synchronizing files between two computers, usually between desktop and laptop computers. The Briefcase can be transferred to another computer via disk, cable, or network. When files are transferred back to the original computer, the Briefcase updates all files to the most recent version.

British Naval Connector *n. See* BNC.

broadband *adj.* Of or relating to communications systems in which the medium of transmission (such as a wire or fiber-optic cable) carries multiple messages at a time, each message modulated on its own carrier frequency by means of modems. Broadband communication is found in wide area networks. *Compare* baseband.

broadband ISDN *n.* Next-generation ISDN based on ATM (Asynchronous Transfer Mode) technology. Broadband ISDN divides information into two categories: interactive services, which are controlled by the user, and distributed (or distribution) services that can be broadcast to the user. *Acronym:* BISDN. *See also* ATM (definition 1), ISDN.

broadband modem *n.* A modem for use on a broadband network. Broadband technology allows several networks to coexist on a single cable. Traffic from one network does not interfere with traffic from another, since the conversations happen on different frequencies, rather like the commercial radio system. *See also* broadband network.

broadband network *n.* A local area network on which transmissions travel as radio-frequency signals over separate inbound and outbound channels. Stations on a

B

broadband network are connected by coaxial or fiber-optic cable, which can carry data, voice, and video simultaneously over multiple transmission channels that are distinguished by frequency. A broadband network is capable of high-speed operation (20 megabits or more), but it is more expensive than a baseband network and can be difficult to install. Such a network is based on the same technology used by cable television (CATV). *Also called:* wideband transmission. *Compare* baseband network.

broadcast storm *n.* A network broadcast that causes multiple hosts to respond simultaneously, overloading the network. A broadcast storm may occur when old TCP/IP routers are mixed with routers that support a new protocol. *See also* communications protocol, router, TCP/IP.

Brouter *n. See* bridge router.

browse *vb.* To scan a database, a list of files, or the Internet, either for a particular item or for anything that seems to be of interest. Generally, browsing implies observing, rather than changing, information. In unauthorized computer hacking, browsing is a (presumably) nondestructive means of finding out about an unknown computer after illegally gaining entry.

browser *n. See* Web browser.

browser box *n. See* WebTV.

browser CLUT *n.* A color look-up table consisting of the 216 colors deemed safe when viewed with most Web browsers on most computer operating systems. *See also* CLUT, websafe palette.

BSD/OS *n.* A version of the UNIX operating system based on BSD UNIX and sold by Berkeley Software Design, Inc. *See also* BSD UNIX.

BSD UNIX *n.* Acronym for **B**erkeley **S**oftware **D**istribution **UNIX**. A UNIX version developed at the University of California at Berkeley, providing additional capabilities such as networking, extra peripheral support, and use of extended filenames. BSD UNIX was instrumental in gaining widespread acceptance of UNIX and in getting academic institutions connected to the Internet. BSD UNIX is now being developed by Berkeley Software Design, Inc. *Also called:* Berkeley UNIX. *See also* BSD/OS, UNIX.

BSS *n. See* Basic Service Set.

bucket brigade attack *n. See* man-in-the-middle attack.

bulletin board system *n. See* BBS.

Business Software Alliance *n.* International organization of computer software companies that promotes the interests of the software industry. This alliance focuses on educating the public on the importance of software, advancing free and open world trade, and supporting legislation opposing software piracy and Internet theft. The Business Software Alliance has offices in the United States, Europe, and Asia, with members in more than 60 nations around the world. *Acronym:* BSA.

business-to-business *n. See* B2B.

business-to-consumer *n. See* B2C.

bus *n.* A set of hardware lines (conductors) used for data transfer among the components of a computer system. A bus is essentially a shared highway that connects different parts of the system—including the processor, disk-drive controller, memory, and input/output ports—and enables them to transfer information. The bus consists of specialized groups of lines that carry different types of information. One group of lines carries data; another carries memory addresses (locations) where data items are to be found; yet another carries control signals. Buses are characterized by the number of bits they can transfer at a single time, equivalent to the number of wires within the bus. A computer with a 32-bit address bus and a 16-bit data bus, for example, can transfer 16 bits of data at a time from any of 2^{32} memory locations. Most PCs contain one or more expansion slots into which additional boards can be plugged to connect them to the bus.

B

bus network *n.* A topology (configuration) for a LAN in which all nodes are connected to a main communications line (bus). On a bus network, each node monitors activity on the line. Messages are detected by all nodes but are accepted only by the node(s) to which they are addressed. A malfunctioning node ceases to communicate but does not disrupt operation (as it might on a ring network, in which messages are passed from one node to the next). To avoid collisions that occur when two or more nodes try to use the line at the same time, bus networks commonly rely on collision detection or token passing to regulate traffic. *Also called:* bus topology, linear bus. *See also* contention, CSMA/CD, token bus network, token passing. *Compare* ring network, star network.

bus topology *n. See* bus network.

button bomb *n.* A button on Web pages with the image of a bomb.

BYTE Information Exchange *n. See* BIX.

byte-oriented protocol *n.* A communications protocol in which data is transmitted as a string of characters in a particular character set, such as ASCII, rather than as a stream of bits as in a bit-oriented protocol. To express control information, a byte-oriented protocol relies on control characters, most of which are defined by the coding scheme used. The asynchronous communications protocols commonly used with modems and IBM's BISYNC protocol are byte-oriented protocols. *Compare* bit-oriented protocol.

C

C2 *n.* A security class of the U.S. Department of Defense Trusted Computer System Evaluation Criteria (DOD 4200.28.STD). C2 is the lowest level of security in the U.S. National Computer Security Center's hierarchy of criteria for trusted computer systems, requiring user logon with password and a mechanism for auditing. The C2 level is outlined in the Orange Book. *See also* Orange Book (definition 1).

CA *n. See* certificate authority.

cable modem *n.* A modem that sends and receives data through a coaxial cable television network instead of telephone lines, as with a conventional modem. Cable modems, which have speeds of 500 kilobits per second (Kbps), can generally transmit data faster than current conventional modems. However, cable modems do not operate at the same rate upstream (when sending information) and downstream (when receiving information). Upstream rates vary from about 2 Mbps to 10 Mbps, downstream rates from about 10 Mbps to 36 Mbps. *See also* coaxial cable, modem.

cache *n.* A special memory subsystem in which frequently used data values are duplicated for quick access. A memory cache stores the contents of frequently accessed RAM locations and the addresses where these data items are stored. When the processor references an address in memory, the cache checks to see whether it holds that address. If it does hold the address, the data is returned to the processor; if it does not, a regular memory access occurs. A cache is useful when RAM accesses are slow compared with the microprocessor speed because cache memory is always faster than main RAM memory.

cache farm *n.* A group of servers that save copies of Web pages to caches to fulfill successive requests without calling the pages up repeatedly from the Web server. In essence, the servers are dedicated to caching. By saving Web pages where they can be accessed without increasing traffic on the Web site, the cache farm allows higher-performance Web access for the end user and a reduction in network congestion and volume. *See also* cache.

cache poisoning *n.* Deliberate corruption of Internet Domain Name System (DNS) information through alteration of data that equates host names with their IP addresses. Misleading information of this type, when cached (saved) by one DNS server and later passed to another, exposes DNS servers to attacks in which data sent from one host to another can be accessed or corrupted. Cache poisoning has been used to redirect network requests from a legitimate server to an alternate Web site. *See also* DNS.

CAL *n.* Acronym for **C**ommon **A**pplication **L**anguage. An object-oriented communications language for controlling home-networking products. CAL, originally part of the CEBus (Consumer Electronic Bus) standard for home automation, can be implemented with various communication protocols, home-networking standards, and home electronic products. *See also* CEBus, home automation.

call *vb.* To establish a connection through a telecommunications network.

callback or **callback security** *n.* A security feature used to authenticate users calling in to a network. During callback, the network validates the caller's username and password, hangs up, and then returns the call, usually to a preauthorized number. This security measure usually prevents unauthorized access to an account even if an individual's logon ID and password have been stolen. *See also* authentication, remote access server.

callback modem *n.* A modem that, instead of answering an incoming call, requires the caller to enter a touch-tone code and hang up so that the modem can return the call. When the modem receives the caller's code, it checks the code against a stored set of phone numbers. If the code matches an authorized number, the modem dials the number and then opens a connection for the original caller. Callback modems are used when communications lines must be available to outside users but data must be protected from unauthorized intruders.

CALS *n.* Acronym for Computer-Aided Acquisition and Logistics Support. A U.S. Department of Defense standard for electronic exchange of data with commercial suppliers.

cancelbot *n.* Short for **cancel ro**bot. A program that identifies articles in newsgroups based on a set of criteria and cancels the distribution of those articles. Although the criteria for cancellation is set by the owner of the cancelbot, most cancelbots exist to identify and eliminate spam messages posted to dozens or hundreds of newsgroups. *See also* spam.

cancel message *n.* A message sent to Usenet news servers indicating that a certain article is to be canceled, or deleted, from the server. *See also* article, news server, Usenet.

Carnivore *n.* Digital wiretap technology developed by the U.S. Federal Bureau of Investigation. Carnivore's purpose is to track and capture e-mail and other Internet-based communications sent from and received by a suspect. Carnivore copies all of an ISP's network traffic into a collection system where a filter sifts through all communications, disregarding all data but that related to the suspect.

cascade *n.* **1.** Additional elements displayed by a menu item or list box from which the user can choose in order to interact with other screen elements. **2.** In newsgroup articles, the accumulation of quotation marks (often angle brackets) added by newsgroup readers each time an article is replied to. Most newsgroup readers will copy the original article in the body of the reply; after several replies, the original material will have several quotation marks. *See also* article, newsgroup, newsreader.

cascaded star topology *n.* A star network in which nodes connect to hubs and hubs connect to other hubs in a hierarchical (cascaded) parent/child relationship. This topology is characteristic of 100Base-VG networks.

Cascading Style Sheet mechanism *n. See* cascading style sheets.

cascading style sheets *n.* A Hypertext Markup Language (HTML) specification developed by The World Wide Web Consortium (W3C) that allows authors of HTML

35

documents and users to attach style sheets to HTML documents. The style sheets include typographical information on how the page should appear, such as the font of the text in the page. This specification also directs the way in which the style sheets of the HTML document and the user's style will blend. Cascading style sheets have been proposed for the HTML 3.2 standard. *Acronym:* CSS. *Also called:* Cascading Style Sheet mechanism, CSS1. *See also* HTML, style sheet (definition 2).

Category 3 cable *n.* Network cable that supports frequencies up to 16 MHz and transmission speeds up to 10 Mbps (standard Ethernet). Category 3 cable has four unshielded twisted pairs (UTPs) of copper wire and RJ-45 connectors, and is used in voice and 10Base-T applications. *Also called:* Cat 3 cable.

Category 4 cable *n.* Network cable that supports frequencies up to 20 MHz and transmission speeds up to 16 Mbps. Category 4 cable has four unshielded twisted pairs (UTPs) of copper wire and RJ-45 connectors. Less popular than Category 3 and Category 5 cables, it is used primarily for token ring networks. *Also called:* Cat 4 cable.

Category 5 cable *n.* Network cable that supports frequencies up to 100 MHz and transmission speeds up to 100 Mbps (using two pairs) or 1000 Mbps (using four pairs and called gigabit over copper). Category 5 cable has four unshielded twisted pairs (UTPs) of copper wire and RJ-45 connectors, and is used for 10/100/1000 Base-T, ATM, and token ring networks. *Also called:* Cat 5 cable.

Category 5e cable *n.* Network cable that supports frequencies up to 100 MHz and transmission speeds up to 1000 Mbps (half-duplex mode) or 2000 Mbps (full-duplex mode). Category 5e cable has four unshielded twisted pairs (UTPs) of copper wire, RJ-45 connectors, and enhanced shielding to prevent signal degradation. Category 5e cable can be used for 10/100/1000 Base-T, ATM, and token ring networks. *Also called:* Cat 5e cable. *See also* duplex[2] (definition 1), half-duplex[1].

CATV *n.* Acronym for community antenna television or cable television. A television broadcasting system that uses coaxial or fiber-optic cable to distribute a broadband signal containing many separate television program channels. CATV systems are also increasingly being used to carry digital data—for example, Internet connections—to and from subscribers.

CatXML *n.* Acronym for Catalogue XML. An open standard for using XML in catalogue information exchanges over the Internet. CatXML uses a flexible XML schema with multiple profiles that can be adapted to meet the needs of individual businesses. CatXML supports existing information structures and provides distributed query information grid models and dynamic output formats.

cavity virus *n.* A type of virus that overwrites and hides within a section of the file it has infected. A cavity virus overwrites only a part of the host file filled with a constant, allowing the file to continue to function.

cc *n.* Acronym for courtesy copy. A directive to an e-mail program to send a complete copy of a given piece of mail to another individual. The use of cc mail addressing, as opposed to directly addressing the mail to a person, generally implies that the recipient is not required to take any action; the message is for informational purposes only. In a cc directive, the fact that this recipient received the mail is printed in the mail header and is thus known to all other recipients. *Also called:* carbon copy. *See also* e-mail[1] (definition 1), header. *Compare* bcc.

CCITT *n.* Acronym for Comité Consultatif International Télégraphique et Téléphonique, now called the International Telecommunication Union-Telecommunication Standardization Sector (ITU-TSS, often abbreviated as ITU-T). CCITT was the organization that performed the standardization functions for the International Telecommunication Union (ITU). Following a reorganization of the ITU in 1992, CCITT ceased to exist as a separate body, although several standards are still known by the CCITT prefix. *See also* ITU.

CCITT Groups 1–4 *n.* A set of four standards recommended by the Comité Consultatif International Télégraphique et Téléphonique (International Telegraph and Telephone Consultative Committee) for the encoding and transmission of images over fax machines. Groups 1 and 2 relate to analog devices and are generally out of use. Groups 3 and 4, which deal with digital devices, are outlined below. Group 3 is a widespread standard that supports standard images of 203 horizontal dots per inch (dpi) by 98 vertical dpi and fine images of 203 horizontal dpi by 198 vertical dpi; supports two methods of data compression, one (based on the Huffman code) reducing an image to 10 to 20 percent of the original, the second (READ, for relative element address designate) compressing images to 6 to 12 percent of the original; and provides for password protection and for polling so that a receiving machine can request transmission as appropriate. Group 4, a newer standard, supports images of up to 400 dpi; supports data compression based on a beginning row of white pixels (dots), with each succeeding line encoded as a series of changes from the line before, compressing images to 3 to 10 percent of the original; does not include error-correction information in the transmission; and requires an Integrated Services Digital Network (ISDN) phone line rather than a dial-up line.

CCITT V series *n.* *See* V series.

CCITT X series *n.* *See* X series.

cc:Mail *n.* An e-mail program originally introduced by cc:mail, Inc., and currently produced by the Lotus Development Corporation. Lotus cc:Mail runs on multiple networking platforms and the Internet and is closely integrated with Lotus Notes collaborative software.

CDMA *n.* *See* Code Division Multiple Access.

CDN *n.* Acronym for content delivery network. A service that caches the pages of a Web site on geographically dispersed servers to enable faster delivery of Web pages. When a page is requested at a URL that is content delivery–enabled, the content delivery network routes the user's request to a cache server close to the user. *See also* content delivery.

CeBIT *n.* One of the world's leading tradeshows for the information technology, telecommunications, and office automation industries. Held annually in Hannover, Germany, CeBIT attracts hundreds of thousands of visitors and exhibitors from more than 60 countries.

CEBus *n.* Short for **C**onsumer **E**lectronic **Bus**. CEBus is an open architecture set of specification documents that define protocols for how to make products communicate through power line wires, low voltage twisted pairs, coax, infrared, RF, and fiber optics. Anyone, anywhere can get a copy of the plans and develop products that work with the CEBus standard.

C

cell *n.* **1.** The intersection of a row and a column in a spreadsheet. Each row and column in a spreadsheet is unique, so each cell can be uniquely identified—for example, cell B17, at the intersection of column B and row 17. Each cell is displayed as a rectangular space that can hold text, a value, or a formula. **2.** An addressable (named or numbered) storage unit for information. A binary cell, for example, is a storage unit that can hold 1 bit of information—that is, it can be either on or off. **3.** A fixed-length packet, the basic transmission unit on high-speed networks, such as ATM. *See also* ATM. **4.** Coverage area for wireless phones served by a single base station (cell tower), usually surrounded by six other cells. As a wireless phone moves across the boundary between cells, the conversation is handed from one cell to the next. Cells may be less than a half mile or more than 15 miles in radius, depending on the volume of wireless calls or the presence of large buildings or terrain that might interfere with signals.

Cellular Telecommunications and Internet Association *n.* Association based in Washington, D.C. that represents the wireless telecommunications industry and its equipment manufacturers. *Acronym:* CTIA.

censorship *n.* The action of preventing material that a party considers objectionable from circulating within a system of communication over which that party has some power. The Internet as a whole is not censored, but some parts of it come under varying degrees of control. A news server, for example, often is set to exclude any or all of the alt. newsgroups, such as alt.sex.* or alt.music.white-power, which are unmoderated and tend to be controversial. A moderated newsgroup or mailing list might be considered to be "censored" because the moderator will usually delete highly controversial and obscene content or content that is on a different topic from that followed by the newsgroup. Online services have identifiable owners, who often take some share of responsibility for what reaches their users' computer screens. In some countries, censorship of certain political or cultural Web sites is a matter of national policy.

censorware *n.* Software that imposes restrictions on what Internet sites, newsgroups, or files may be accessed by the user.

centralized network *n.* A network in which nodes connect to and use resources on a single central computer, typically a mainframe.

central office *n.* In communications, the switching center where interconnections between customers' communications lines are made.

CERN *n.* Acronym for **C**onseil **E**uropéen pour la **R**echerche **N**ucléaire (the European Laboratory for Particle Physics). CERN, a physics research center located in Geneva, Switzerland, is where the original development of the World Wide Web took place by Tim Berners-Lee in 1989 as a method to facilitate communication among members of the scientific community. *See also* NCSA (definition 1).

CERN server *n.* One of the first Hypertext Transfer Protocol (HTTP) servers, developed at CERN by Tim Berners-Lee. The CERN server is still in wide use and is free of charge. *See also* CERN, HTTP server (definition 1).

CERT *n.* Acronym for **C**omputer **E**mergency **R**esponse **T**eam. An organization that provides a round-the-clock security consultation service for Internet users and provides advisories whenever new virus programs and other computer security threats are discovered.

certificate *n.* A certificate is sent when a message is digitally signed. The certificate proves the sender's identity and supplies the recipient with a public key with which to decrypt the sender's encrypted messages. *Also called:* digital certificate.

certificate authority *n.* An issuer of digital certificates, the cyberspace equivalent of identity cards. A certificate authority may be an external issuing company (such as VeriSign) or an internal company authority that has installed its own server (such as the Microsoft Certificate Server) for issuing and verifying certificates. A certificate authority is responsible for providing and assigning the unique strings of numbers that make up the "keys" used in digital certificates for authentication and to encrypt and decrypt sensitive or confidential incoming and outgoing online information. *Acronym:* CA. *See also* digital certificate, encryption.

certification *n.* **1.** The act of awarding a document to demonstrate a computer professional's competence in a particular field. Some hardware and software suppliers, such as Microsoft and Novell, offer certification in the use of their products; other organizations, such as the Institute for Certification of Computer Professionals (ICCP) and the Computing Technology Industry Association (CompTIA), offer more general certification. **2.** The act of awarding a document to demonstrate that a hardware or software product meets some specification, such as being able to work with a certain other hardware or software product. **3.** The issuance of a notice that a user or site is trusted for the purpose of security and computer authentication. Often certification is used with Web sites.

certification authority *n.* An organization that assigns encryption keys. *See also* certificate authority.

CGI *n.* Acronym for **C**ommon **G**ateway **I**nterface. The specification that defines communications between information servers (such as HTTP servers) and resources on the server's host computer, such as databases and other programs. For example, when a user submits a form through a Web browser, the HTTP server executes a program (often called a CGI script) and passes the user's input information to that program via CGI. The program then returns information to the server via CGI. Use of CGI can make a Web page much more dynamic and add interactivity for the user. *See also* CGI script, HTTP server (definition 1).

cgi-bin *n.* Short for Common Gateway Interface-**bin**aries. A file directory that holds external applications to be executed by HTTP servers via CGI. *See also* CGI.

CGI program *n. See* CGI script.

CGI script *n.* Short for Common Gateway Interface **script**. An external application that is executed by an HTTP server machine in response to a request by a client, such as a Web browser. Generally, the CGI script is invoked when the user clicks on some element in a Web page, such as a link or an image. Communication between the CGI script and the server is carried out via the CGI specification. CGI scripts can be written in many programming languages, including C, C++, and Visual Basic. However, the most commonly used language for CGI scripts is Perl because it is a small but robust language and it is common on UNIX, which is the platform on which the majority of Web sites run. CGI scripts don't necessarily need to be scripts; they can also be batch programs or compiled programs. CGI scripts are used to provide interactivity on a Web page, including such features as providing a form that users can fill out, image maps that contain links to other Web pages or resources, and links that users can click on to send e-mail to a specified address. ActiveX controls and Java applets can provide much the same functionality as CGI scripts, through different means. *See also* CGI, cgi-bin, image map. *Compare* ActiveX control, Java applet.

Challenge Handshake Authentication Protocol *n.* An authentication scheme used by PPP servers to validate the identity of the originator of a connection, upon connection or any time later. *Acronym:* CHAP. *See also* authentication, PPP.

change file *n.* A file that records transactional changes occurring in a database, providing a basis for updating a master file and establishing an audit trail. *Also called:* transaction log.

channel *n.* **1.** A path or link through which information passes between two devices. A channel can be either internal or external to a microcomputer. **2.** In communications, a medium for transferring information. Depending on its type, a communications channel can carry information (data, sound, and/or video) in either analog or digital form. A communications channel can be a physical link, such as the cable connecting two stations in a network, or it can consist of some electromagnetic transmission on one or more frequencies within a bandwidth in the electromagnetic spectrum, as in radio and television, or in optical, microwave, or voice-grade communication. *Also called:* circuit, line. *See also* analog, bandwidth, digital.

channel access *n.* **1.** A method used in networked systems to gain access to the data communication channel that links two or more computers. Common methods of channel access are contention, polling, and the token ring network. *See also* channel, contention, token ring network. **2.** In wireless technology, an access method such as CDMA (Code Division Multiple Access). *See also* Code Division Multiple Access.

channel adapter *n.* A device that enables hardware using two different types of communications channels to communicate.

channel aggregator *n. See* content aggregator.

channel capacity *n.* The speed at which a communications channel can transfer information, measured in bits per second (bps) or in baud.

Channel Definition Format *n.* A file format based on XML that describes a channel—a collection of Web pages—on a server. The Channel Definition Format is used with the Active Channel feature in Microsoft Internet Explorer to deliver selected, often personalized, information to individuals on a subscription basis. *See also* Active Channel, webcasting.

channel hop *vb.* To switch repeatedly from one IRC channel to another. *See also* IRC.

channel op *n.* Short for **channel op**erator. A user on an IRC channel who has the privilege of expelling undesirable participants. *See also* IRC.

channel operator *n. See* channel op.

Channel Service Unit *n. See* DDS.

CHAP *n. See* Challenge Handshake Authentication Protocol.

character entity *n.* In HTML and SGML, the notation for a special character. A character entity begins with an & (ampersand), followed by either a string of letters or of numbers, and ends with a semicolon. The special characters represented by character entities include acute and grave accents, the tilde, and Greek letters, among others. *Also called:* named entity.

character-oriented protocol *n. See* byte-oriented protocol.

character set *n.* A grouping of alphabetic, numeric, and other characters that have some relationship in common. For example, the standard ASCII character set includes letters, numbers, symbols, and control codes that make up the ASCII coding scheme.

chat[1] *n.* **1.** Real-time conversation via computer. When a participant types a line of text and then presses the Enter key, that participant's words appear on the screens of the other participants, who can then respond in kind. Most online services support chat; on the Internet, IRC is the usual system. *See also* IRC. **2.** An Internet utility program that supports chat. IRC has largely superseded it.

chat[2] *vb.* To carry on a real-time conversation with other users by computer. *See also* IRC.

chat room *n.* The informal term for a data communication channel that links computers and permits users to "converse" by sending text messages to one another in real time. Similar to the channels provided by IRC (Internet Relay Chat), chat rooms are available through online services and some electronic bulletin board systems

(BBSs). Chat rooms are often devoted to a particular subject or are conducted on a certain schedule. *See also* BBS, chat, IRC.

Cheapernet *n. See* 10Base2.

Cheese worm *n.* An Internet worm that patches security holes created by the Lion worm. The Cheese worm searches out and infects Linux-based systems that were previously compromised by the Lion worm, repairing vulnerabilities and closing a back door left by the earlier infection. It then uses the healed computer to scan for other vulnerable computers connected to the Internet and sends itself to them.

Chernobyl packet *n.* A form of network attack in which a data packet sent by a hacker activates every available option for the protocol in use on the receiving system. The Chernobyl packet will cause a packet storm that will eventually overload and crash the network. *Also called:* kamikaze packet.

Chernobyl virus *n. See* CIH virus.

Children's Online Privacy Protection Act *n. See* COPPA.

CIFS *n. See* Common Internet File System.

CIH virus *n.* A highly destructive virus that first appeared in early 1998. When activated, the CIH virus code will attempt to overwrite the flash BIOS of infected machines, rendering the computer unbootable. The CIH virus is also known as the Chernobyl virus because in its original form it was set to activate on the anniversary of the Chernobyl nuclear accident. Although the CIH virus lacks stealth or sophisticated replication capabilities and is easily detected by current virus security programs, it continues to appear regularly. *Also called:* Chernobyl virus. *See also* virus.

CIP *n.* **1.** Short for **C**ommerce **I**nterchange **P**ipeline. A Microsoft technology that provides for secure routing of business data between applications over a public network such as the Internet. CIP is independent of data format and supports encryption and digital signatures, as well as various transport protocols including SMTP, HTTP, DCOM, and EDI value-added networks. Typically, data such as invoices and purchase orders travel over a network through a transmit pipeline and are read from the network by a receive pipeline that decodes and prepares the data for the receiving application. **2.** Short for **C**ommon **I**ndexing **P**rotocol. A protocol defined by the Internet Engineering Task Force (IETF) for enabling servers to share indexing information. CIP was developed to provide servers with a standard means of sharing information about the contents of their databases. With such sharing, a server unable to resolve a particular query would be able to route the query to other servers that might contain the desired information—for example, to find the e-mail address of a particular user on the Web.

circuit switching *n.* A method of opening communications lines, as through the telephone system, by creating a physical link between the initiating and receiving parties. In circuit switching, the connection is made at a switching center, which physically connects the two parties and maintains an open line between them for as long as needed. Circuit switching is typically used on the dial-up telephone network, and it is also used on a smaller scale in privately maintained communications networks. Unlike other methods of transmission, such as packet switching, it requires the link to be established before any communication can take place. *Compare* message switching, packet switching.

CIS *n.* Acronym for CompuServe Information Service *See* CompuServe.

CIX *n. See* Commercial Internet Exchange.

ClariNet *n.* A commercial service that distributes news articles from United Press International (UPI) and other news agencies in newsgroups that are part of the clari. hierarchy. Unlike most other newsgroups, access to the clari. newsgroups is restricted to Internet service providers who pay a subscription fee to ClariNet.

C

clari. newsgroups *n.* Internet newsgroups maintained by ClariNet Communications, Inc. ClariNet newsgroups contain news articles obtained from the Reuters and United Press International wire services, SportsTicker, Commerce Business Daily, and other sources. Unlike most other newsgroups, ClariNet groups are only accessible through Internet service providers who purchase the service. *See also* ClariNet, ISP, newsgroup.

Class A IP address *n.* A unicast IP address that ranges from 1.0.0.1 through 126.255.255.254. The first octet indicates the network, and the last three octets indicate the host on the network. *See also* Class B IP address, Class C IP address, IP address classes.

Class A network *n.* An Internet network that can define a maximum of 16,777,215 hosts. Class A networks use the first byte of an IP address to designate the network, with the first (high-order) bit set to 0. The host is designated by the last 3 bytes. Class A addressing currently allows for a maximum of 128 networks. Class A networks are best suited for sites with few networks but numerous hosts and are usually designated for use by large government or educational institutions. *See also* host, IP address.

Class B IP address *n.* A unicast IP address that ranges from 128.0.0.1 through 191.255.255.254. The first two octets indicate the network, and the last two octets indicate the host on the network. *See also* Class A IP address, Class C IP address, IP address classes.

Class C IP address *n.* A unicast IP address that ranges from 192.0.0.1 to 223.255.255.254. The first three octets indicate the network, and the last octet indicates the host on the network. *See also* Class A IP address, Class B IP address, IP address classes.

classful IP addressing *n.* An IP addressing scheme where IP addresses are organized into classes: Class A, Class B, and Class C. *See also* IP address classes.

classless interdomain routing *n.* An address scheme that uses aggregation strategies to minimize the size of top-level Internet routing tables. Routes are grouped with the objective of minimizing the quantity of information carried by core routers. The main requirement for this scheme is the use of routing protocols that support it, such as Border Gateway Protocol (BGP) version 4 and RIP version 2. *Acronym:* CIDR. *See also* Border Gateway Protocol, communications protocol, RIP, router, supernetting.

CLEC *n.* Acronym for Competitive Local Exchange Carrier. A company that sells access to the public switched telephone network, or other last mile network connections, in competition with a traditional telephone company. *See also* ILEC, last mile.

clickstream *n.* The path a user takes while browsing a Web site. Each distinct selection made on a Web page adds one click to the stream. The further down the clickstream the user goes without finding the sought item, the more likely he or she is to depart to another Web site. Analysis of usage patterns helps Web site designers create user-friendly site structures, links, and search facilities. *See also* Web site.

clickthrough *n.* The number of times that visitors to a Web site click on an advertising banner within a specified period of time. Clickthrough is one of the elements that Web site producers use to decide how much to charge advertisers. *See also* clickthrough rate.

clickthrough rate *n.* The proportion of visitors to a Web site who click on a banner advertisement there, expressed as a percentage of total visitors to the Web site. *Also called:* click rate. *See also* clickthrough.

client *n.* On a local area network or the Internet, a computer that accesses shared network resources provided by another computer (called a *server*). *See also* client/server architecture, server.

client error *n.* A problem reported by the Hypertext Transfer Protocol (HTTP) client module as the result of difficulty in interpreting a command or the inability to connect properly to a remote host.

client/server architecture *n.* An arrangement used on LANs (local area networks) that makes use of distributed intelligence to treat both the server and the individual workstations as intelligent, programmable devices, thus exploiting the full computing power of each. This is done by splitting the processing of an application between two distinct components: a "front-end" client and a "back-end" server. The client component is a complete, stand-alone personal computer (not a "dumb" terminal), and it offers the user its full range of power and features for running applications. The server component can be a personal computer, a minicomputer, or a mainframe that provides the traditional strengths offered by minicomputers and mainframes in a time-sharing environment: data management, information sharing between clients, and sophisticated network administration and security features. The client and server machines work together to accomplish the processing of the application being used. Not only does this increase the processing power available over older architectures but it also uses that power more efficiently. The client portion of the application is typically optimized for user interaction, whereas the server portion provides the centralized, multiuser functionality. *See also* distributed intelligence. *Compare* peer-to-peer network.

client/server network *n. See* client/server architecture.

closed architecture *n.* **1.** Any computer design whose specifications are not freely available. Such proprietary specifications make it difficult or impossible for third-party vendors to create ancillary devices that work correctly with a closed-architecture machine; usually only its original maker can build peripherals and add-ons for such a machine. **2.** A computer system that provides no expansion slots for adding new types of circuit boards within the system unit. The original Apple Macintosh was an example of a closed architecture.

cluster *n.* A group of independent network servers that operate—and appear to clients—as if they were a single unit. A cluster network is designed to improve network capacity by, among other things, enabling the servers within a cluster to shift work in order to balance the load. By enabling one server to take over for another, a cluster network also enhances stability and minimizes or eliminates downtime caused by application or system failure. *See also* client/server architecture.

cluster analysis *n.* A technique used in data mining and knowledge discovery to group observations by identifying and extracting like or similar group conditions. Cluster analysis aims to describe the structure of a complex data set. *See also* data mining.

cluster controller *n.* An intermediary device that is situated between a computer and a group (cluster) of subsidiary devices, such as terminals on a network, and is used to control the cluster.

clustering *n.* The grouping of multiple servers in a way that allows them to appear to be a single unit to client computers on a network. Clustering is a means of increasing network capacity, providing live backup in case one of the servers fails, and improving data security. *See also* cluster, server.

cluster network *n. See* cluster.

cluster virus *n.* A type of virus that infects once but gives the appearance of infecting every application launched. A cluster virus modifies the file system so that it is loaded before any application that the user attempts to open. Because the virus is also run when running any program, it appears that every program on the disk is infected.

CLUT *n.* Acronym for Color Look Up Table. In digital graphics applications, a specific set of colors used in the creation of graphics. When a graphic is created or edited, the user may specify a CLUT that corresponds with the needs of print, Web, or other destination media. In Web design, a specific CLUT of browser-safe colors is used to be certain graphics and designs will display consistently across different platforms and with different browsers. *See also* browser CLUT, websafe palette.

C

coaxial cable *n.* A round, flexible, two-conductor cable consisting of—from the center outwards—a copper wire, a layer of protective insulation, a braided metal mesh sleeve, and an outer shield, or jacket of PVC or fire-resistant material. The shield prevents signals transmitted on the center wire from affecting nearby components and prevents external interference from affecting the signal carried on the center wire. Coaxial cable is widely used in networks. It is the same type of wiring as that used for cable television. *Compare* fiberoptic cable, twisted-pair wiring.

cobweb site *n.* A Web site that is far out of date. *See also* Web site.

code *n.* A system of symbols used to convert information from one form to another. A code for converting information in order to conceal it is often called a *cipher*.

Code Division Multiple Access *n.* A form of multiplexing in which the transmitter encodes the signal, using a pseudo-random sequence that the receiver also knows and can use to decode the received signal. Each different random sequence corresponds to a different communication channel. Motorola uses Code Division Multiple Access for digital cellular phones. *Acronym:* CDMA. *Also called:* spread spectrum. *See also* multiplexer, transmitter.

Code Red worm *n.* A fast-spreading and pernicious Internet worm first discovered in mid-2001. The Code Red worm propagates quickly, and any machine that was infected once is potentially vulnerable to re-infection. The Code Red worm is time sensitive, spreading in propagation mode from the 1st to the 19th of each month, attacking in flood mode from the 20th to the 27th, and finally hiding in hibernation mode until the 1st of the next month when the cycle begins again. The worm maintains a list of all computers previously infected, and all these computers will be attacked each month by every newly infected machine. This makes total eradication of the worm difficult because a single machine remaining infected from earlier propagation/attack cycles can potentially re-infect every machine on the list, and each computer might be subject to multiple attacks. At least three versions of the Code Red worm are known to exist. The Code Red worm was named for a caffeinated soft drink by the security team that first tracked the worm.

code signing *n.* The process of adding a digital signature to additions and updates made to source code and applications published on the Internet. Code signing is intended to provide a level of security and trust to Internet software distribution. *See also* digital signature.

Coffee Pot Control Protocol *n. See* HTCPCP.

collaborative filtering *n.* A means of deriving information from the experiences and opinions of a number of people. The term was coined by Doug Terry at Xerox PARC, who first used the technique by allowing users to annotate documents as they read them and to choose which documents to read next based not only on their content but also on what others wrote about them. A common use of collaborative filtering is the creation of lists of World Wide Web pages of interest to particular people;

by documenting the experiences of several people, a list of interesting Web sites can be "filtered." Collaborative filtering is also used as a marketing research tool; by keeping a database of opinions and ratings regarding several products, researchers can predict which new products the people contributing to the database will like.

collapsed backbone *n. See* backbone (definition 3).

Color Look Up Table *n. See* CLUT.

color space *n.* A means of describing color in digital environments. RGB is the most common color space on the Web, and with other color, the most common color space viewed on computer displays, while CMYK is the main color space for desktop publishing and other digital print media.

.com *n.* **1.** In the Internet's Domain Name System, the top-level domain that identifies addresses operated by commercial organizations. The domain name .com appears as a suffix at the end of the address. *See also* DNS (definition 1), domain (definition 3). *Compare* .edu, .gov, .mil, .net, .org. **2.** In MS-DOS, the file extension that identifies a command file. *See also* COM (definition 3).

COM *n.* **1.** A name reserved by the MS-DOS operating system for serial communications ports. For example, if a modem is connected to one serial port and a serial printer to another, the devices are identified as COM1 and COM2 by the operating system. **2.** Acronym for **C**omponent **O**bject **M**odel. A specification developed by Microsoft for building software components that can be assembled into programs or add functionality to existing programs running on Microsoft Windows platforms. COM components can be written in a variety of languages, although most are written in C++, and can be unplugged from a program at runtime without having to recompile the program. COM is the foundation of the OLE (object linking and embedding), ActiveX, and DirectX specifications. *See also* ActiveX, component (definition 2), OLE. **3.** The extension reserved by MS-DOS for a type of executable binary (program) file limited to a single 64-kilobyte (KB) segment. COM files are often used for utility programs and short routines. They are not supported in OS/2.

COMDEX *n.* Any of a series of annual computer trade shows operated by Softbank COMDEX, Inc. One of these shows takes place in Las Vegas each November and is the largest computer trade show in the United States.

Commerce Interchange Pipeline *n. See* CIP.

commerce server *n.* An HTTP server designed for conducting online business transactions. Data is transferred between the server and Web browser in an encrypted form to keep information such as credit card numbers reasonably secure. Commerce servers are typically used by online stores and companies that are set up for mail order business. The wares or services offered by the store or company are described and displayed in photographs on the store or company Web site and users can order directly from the site using their Web browser. A number of companies market commerce servers, including Netscape, Microsoft, and Quarterdeck. *See also* HTTP server (definition 1), SSL, Web browser.

Commercial Internet Exchange *n.* A nonprofit trade organization of public Internet service providers. In addition to the usual representational and social activities, the organization also operates an Internet backbone router that is accessible to its members. *Acronym:* CIX. *See also* backbone (definition 1), ISP, router.

Common Indexing Protocol *n. See* CIP.

Common Internet File System *n.* A standard proposed by Microsoft that would compete directly with Sun Microsystems' Web Network File System. A system of file sharing of Internet or intranet files. *Acronym:* CIFS.

common language runtime *n.* The engine at the core of managed code execution. The runtime supplies managed code with services such as cross-language integration, code access security, object lifetime management, and debugging and profiling support.

communications *n.* The vast discipline encompassing the methods, mechanisms, and media involved in information transfer. In computer-related areas, communications involves data transfer from one computer to another through a communications medium, such as a telephone, microwave relay, satellite link, or physical cable. Two primary methods of computer communications exist: temporary connection of two computers through a switched network, such as the public telephone system, and permanent or semipermanent linking of multiple workstations or computers in a network. The line between the two is indistinct, however, because microcomputers equipped with modems are often used to access both privately owned and public-access network computers. *See also* CCITT, channel (definition 2), communications protocol, IEEE, ISDN, ISO/OSI reference model, LAN, modem, network, synchronous transmission. *Compare* telecommunications.

Communications Act of 1934 *n. See* FCC.

Communication Satellite Corporation *n.* Corporation created by the U.S. government to provide international satellite services for telecommunications. *Acronym:* COMSAT.

communications channel *n. See* channel (definition 2).

communications controller *n.* A device used as an intermediary in transferring communications to and from the host computer to which it is connected. By relieving the host computer of the actual tasks of sending, receiving, deciphering, and checking transmissions for errors, a communications controller helps to make efficient use of the host computer's processing time—time that might be better used for noncommunications tasks. A communications controller can be either a programmable machine in its own right or a nonprogrammable device designed to follow certain communications protocols. *See also* front-end processor (definition 2).

communications parameter *n.* Any of several settings required in order to enable computers to communicate. In asynchronous communications, for example, modem speed, number of data bits and stop bits, and type of parity are parameters that must be set correctly to establish communication between two modems.

communications port *n. See* COM.

communications protocol *n.* A set of rules or standards designed to enable computers to connect with one another and to exchange information with as little error as possible. The protocol generally accepted for standardizing overall computer communications is a seven-layer set of hardware and software guidelines known as the OSI (Open Systems Interconnection) model. A somewhat different standard, widely used before the OSI model was developed, is IBM's SNA (Systems Network Architecture). The word *protocol* is often used, sometimes confusingly, in reference to a multitude of standards affecting different aspects of communication, such as file transfer (for example, XMODEM and ZMODEM), handshaking (for example, XON/XOFF), and network transmissions (for example, CSMA/CD). *See also* ISO/OSI reference model, SNA.

communications satellite *n.* A satellite stationed in geosynchronous orbit that acts as a microwave relay station, receiving signals sent from a ground-based station (earth station), amplifying them, and retransmitting them on a different frequency to another ground-based station. Initially used for telephone and television signals, communications satellites can also be used for high-speed transmission of computer data. Two factors affecting the use of satellites with computers, however, are propagation delay (the time lag caused by the distance traveled by the signal) and security concerns. *See also* downlink, uplink.

communications server *n.* A gateway that translates packets on a local area network (LAN) into asynchronous signals, such as those used on telephone lines or in RS-232-C serial communications, and allows all nodes on the LAN access to its modems or RS-232-C connections. *See also* gateway, RS-232-C standard.

communications slot *n.* On many models of the Apple Macintosh, a dedicated expansion slot for network interface cards. *Acronym:* CS.

communications software *n.* The software that controls the modem in response to user commands. Generally such software includes terminal emulation as well as file transfer facilities. *See also* modem, terminal emulation.

Communications Terminal Protocol *n.* A terminal protocol that enables a user at a remote location to access a computer as if the remote computer were directly connected (hardwired) to the computer. *Acronym:* CTERM.

COMNET Conference & Expo *n.* Conference and exposition for the communications networking industry. The conference features educational sessions and exhibitions on technical and business issues affecting communications networks.

comp. newsgroups *n.* Usenet newsgroups that are part of the comp. hierarchy and have the prefix comp. These newsgroups are devoted to discussions of computer hardware, software, and other aspects of computer science. Comp. newsgroups are one of the seven original Usenet newsgroup hierarchies. The other six are misc., news., rec., sci., soc., and talk. *See also* newsgroup, traditional newsgroup hierarchy, Usenet.

component *n.* **1.** A discrete part of a larger system or structure. **2.** An individual modular software routine that has been compiled and dynamically linked, and is ready to use with other components or programs. *See also* link (definition 1). **3.** In Sun Microsystem's J2EE network platform, an application-level software unit supported by a container. Components are configurable at deployment time. The J2EE platform defines four types of components: enterprise java beans, Web components, applets, and application clients. *See also* applet, container (definition 3), Enterprise JavaBeans, J2EE.

Component Object Model *n.* *See* COM (definition 2).

Compressed SLIP *n.* Short for **Compressed Serial Line Internet Protocol**. A version of SLIP using compressed Internet address information, thereby making the protocol faster than SLIP. *Acronym:* CSLIP. *See also* SLIP.

CompuServe *n.* An online information service that is a subsidiary of America Online. CompuServe provides information and communications capabilities, including Internet access. It is primarily known for its technical support forums for commercial hardware and software products and for being one of the first large commercial online services. CompuServe also operates various private network services.

computer game *n.* A class of computer program in which one or more users interacts with the computer as a form of entertainment. Computer games run the gamut from simple alphabet games for toddlers to chess, treasure hunts, war games, and simulations of world events. The games are controlled from a keyboard or with a joystick or other device and are supplied on disks, on CD-ROMs, as game cartridges, on the Internet, or as arcade devices.

computer network *n.* *See* network.

computer users' group *n.* *See* user group.

computer virus *n.* *See* virus.

congestion *n.* The condition of a network when the current load approaches or exceeds the available resources and bandwidth designed to handle that load at a particular location in the network. Packet loss and delays are associated with congestion.

connection *n.* A physical link via wire, radio, fiberoptic cable, or other medium between two or more communications devices.

connection-based session *n.* A communications session that requires a connection to be established between hosts prior to an exchange of data.

connectionless *adj.* In communications, of, pertaining to, or characteristic of a method of data transmission that does not require a direct connection between two nodes on one or more networks. Connectionless communication is achieved by passing, or routing, data packets, each of which contains a source and destination address, through the nodes until the destination is reached. *See also* node (definition 2), packet (definition 2). *Compare* connection-oriented.

connectionless session *n.* A communications session that does not require a connection to be established between hosts prior to an exchange of data.

connection-oriented *adj.* In communications, of, pertaining to, or characteristic of a method of data transmission that requires a direct connection between two nodes on one or more networks. *Compare* connectionless.

connectivity *n.* **1.** The nature of the connection between a user's computer and another computer, such as a server or a host computer on the Internet or a network. This may describe the quality of the circuit or telephone line, the degree of freedom from noise, or the bandwidth of the communications devices. **2.** The ability of hardware devices or software packages to transmit data between other devices or packages. **3.** The ability of hardware devices, software packages, or a computer itself to work with network devices or with other hardware devices, software packages, or a computer over a network connection.

connectoid *n.* In Windows 9x and Windows NT, an icon representing a dial-up networking connection that will also execute a script for logging onto the network dialed.

console game *n.* A special-purpose computer system designed specifically for the home user to play video games. A game console typically includes a CPU, one or more game controllers, audio output, and a video output that connects to a television set. Individual games and memory cards are supplied on plug-in cartridges or compact discs. Many recent versions are 128-bit systems and also include a modem for online gaming over the Internet. Well-known console games include Microsoft Xbox, Sony PlayStation 2, Nintendo GameCube, and Sega Dreamcast. *Also called:* game console. *See also* computer game, Dreamcast, GameCube, PlayStation, Xbox.

container *n.* **1.** In OLE terminology, a file containing linked or embedded objects. *See also* OLE. **2.** In SGML, an element that has content as opposed to one consisting solely of the tag name and attributes. *See also* element, SGML, tag. **3.** In Sun Microsystem's J2EE network platform, an entity that provides life cycle management, security, deployment, and runtime services to components such as beans, Web components, applets, and application clients. Each type of container created (for example, EJB, Web, JSP, servlet, applet, and application client) also provides component-specific services. *See also* applet, component (definition 3), Enterprise JavaBean, JSP, servlet.

container object *n.* An object that can logically contain other objects. For example, a folder is a container object. *See also* object.

content *n.* **1.** The data that appears between the starting and ending tags of an element in an SGML, XML, or HTML document. The content of an element may consist of plain text or other elements. *See also* element, HTML, SGML, tag (definition 3). **2.** The message body of a newsgroup article or e-mail message. **3.** The "meat" of a document, as opposed to its format or appearance.

content aggregator *n.* **1.** Broadly, an organization or business that groups Internet-based information by topic or area of interest—for example, sports scores, business news, or online shopping—to provide users with a means of accessing that content from a single location. **2.** In terms of push technology and multicasting, a service business that mediates between subscribers ("customers") and content providers by gathering and organizing information for broadcast over the Internet. Content aggregators supply subscribers with client software through which content providers broadcast (push) information via "channels" that allow users both to choose the kind of information they receive and to decide when they want it updated. *Also called:* channel aggregator. *See also* push[1], webcasting. *Compare* content provider.

content caching *n.* *See* content delivery.

content delivery *n.* The process of caching the pages of a Web site on geographically dispersed servers to enable faster delivery of Web pages. When a page is requested at a URL that is content-delivery enabled, the content-delivery network routes the user's request to a cache server closer to the user. Content delivery frequently is used for high-traffic Web sites or for specific high-traffic events. *Also called:* content distribution, content caching.

content distribution *n.* *See* content delivery.

contention *n.* On a network, competition among nodes for the opportunity to use a communications line or network resource. In one sense, contention applies to a situation in which two or more devices attempt to transmit at the same time, thus causing a collision on the line. In a somewhat different sense, contention also applies to a free-for-all method of controlling access to a communications line, in which the right to transmit is awarded to the station that wins control of the line. *See also* CSMA/CD. *Compare* token passing.

Content Management Server *n.* Automated software application developed by Microsoft Corporation to assist nontechnical users in creating, tracking, and publishing content for Web sites. A workflow system delineates the tasks each user can perform, assigns content to individuals or groups, and allows users to monitor the status of content with which they are associated.

content provider *n.* **1.** Broadly, an individual, group, or business that provides information for viewing or distribution on the Internet or on private or semiprivate intranets or extranets. Content in this sense includes not only information but also video, audio, software, listings of Web sites, and product-specific materials such as online catalogs. **2.** A service business that makes Internet information resources available to users. Content providers include online services such as America Online and CompuServe, Internet service providers (ISPs), and an increasing number of media companies representing television, long-distance telephone, and publishing industries. *See also* ISP, online information service. *Compare* content aggregator.

Content Scrambling System *n. See* CSS.

cookie *n.* **1.** A block of data that a server returns to a client in response to a request from the client. **2.** On the World Wide Web, a block of data that a Web server stores on a client system. When a user returns to the same Web site, the browser sends a copy of the cookie back to the server. Cookies are used to identify users, to instruct the server to send a customized version of the requested Web page, to submit account information for the user, and for other administrative purposes. **3.** Originally an allusion to fortune cookie, a UNIX program that outputs a different message, or "fortune," each time it is used. On some systems, the cookie program is run during user logon.

cookie filtering tool *n.* A utility that prevents a cookie on a Web browser from relaying information about the user requesting access to a Web site. *See also* cookie (definition 2).

cookies policy *n.* A statement that describes a Web site's policy regarding cookies. The policy usually defines a cookie, explains the types of cookies used by the Web site, and describes how the Web site uses the information stored in the cookies.

.coop *n.* One of seven new top-level domain names approved in 2000 by the Internet Corporation for AssignedNames and Numbers (ICANN), .coop is meant for use with the Web sites of nonprofit cooperatives. The seven new domain names became available for use in the spring of 2001.

COPPA *n.* Acronym for Children's Online Privacy Protection Act. A U.S. federal law enacted in April 2000 and designed to protect the online privacy of children under the age of 13. COPPA requires Web sites that collect personal information from children under 13 to receive permission from parents or guardians first, and to monitor and supervise children's experiences with interactive Web elements such as chat rooms and e-mail.

copyright *n.* A method of protecting the rights of an originator of a creative work, such as a text, a piece of music, a painting, or a computer program, through law. In many countries the originator of a work has copyright in the work as soon as it is fixed in a tangible medium (such as a piece of paper or a disk file); that rule applies in the United States for works created after 1977. Registration of a copyright, or the use of a copyright symbol, is not needed to create the copyright but does strengthen the originator's legal powers. Unauthorized copying and distribution of copyrighted material can lead to severe penalties, whether done for profit or not. Copyrights affect the computer community in three ways: the copyright protection of software, the copyright status of material (such as song lyrics) distributed over a network such as the Internet, and the copyright status of original material distributed over a network (such as a newsgroup post). The latter two involve electronic media that are arguably not tangible, and legislation protecting the information disseminated through electronic media is still evolving. *See also* fair use, General Public License.

CORBA *n.* Acronym for **C**ommon **O**bject **R**equest **B**roker **A**rchitecture. A specification developed by the Object Management Group in 1992 in which pieces of programs (objects) communicate with other objects in other programs, even if the two programs are written in different programming languages and are running on different platforms. A program makes its request for objects through an *object request broker*, or *ORB*, and thus does not need to know the structure of the program from which the object comes. CORBA is designed to work in object-oriented environments. *See also* IIOP, object (definition 2).

courtesy copy *n. See* cc.

CPCP *n. See* HTCPCP.

CPRM *n.* Acronym for **C**ontent **P**rotection for **R**ecordable **M**edia. Technology developed to control the use of copyrighted digital music and video material by blocking the transfer of protected files to portable media such as zip disks and smart cards. CPRM would be added to storage devices and provide data scrambling and identification codes to block the copying of copyrighted files.

cracker *n.* A person who overcomes the security measures of a computer system and gains unauthorized access. The goal of some crackers is to obtain information illegally from a computer system or use computer resources. However, the goal of the majority is only to break into the system. *See also* hacker (definition 2).

crawl *vb.* To compile and organize entries for a search engine by reading Web pages and related information. Crawling is typically performed by programs called "spiders."

crawler *n. See* spider, Web browser.

cross-post *vb.* To copy a message or news article from one newsgroup, conference topic, e-mail system, or other communications channel to another—for example, from a Usenet newsgroup to a CompuServe forum or from e-mail to a newsgroup.

cross-site scripting *n.* A security vulnerability of dynamic Web pages generated from a database in response to user input. With cross-site scripting, a malicious user introduces unwanted executable script or code into another user's Web session. Once running, this script could allow others to monitor the user's Web session, change what is displayed on the screen, or shut down the Web browser. Web sites that allow visitors to add comments or make other additions or changes to the pages are the most vulnerable to this flaw. Cross-site scripting is not restricted to the products of a particular vendor or a particular operating system. *See also* script.

crypto *n. See* cryptography.

cryptoanalysis *n.* The decoding of electronically encrypted information for the purpose of understanding encryption techniques. *See also* cryptography, encryption.

CryptoAPI *n.* An application programming interface (API) that is provided as part of Microsoft Windows. CryptoAPI provides a set of functions that allows applications to encrypt or digitally sign data in a flexible manner while providing protection for the user's sensitive private key data. Actual cryptographic operations are performed by independent modules known as cryptographic service providers (CSPs). *See also* cryptographic service provider, private key.

cryptographic service provider *n.* An independent module that performs cryptographic operations, such as creating and destroying keys. A cryptographic service provider consists of, at a minimum, a DLL and a signature file. *Acronym:* CSP.

cryptography *n.* The use of codes to convert data so that only a specific recipient will be able to read it using a key. The persistent problem of cryptography is that the key must be transmitted to the intended recipient and may be intercepted. Public key cryptography is a recent significant advance. *Also called:* crypto. *See also* code, encryption, PGP, private key, public key.

CSLIP *n.* *See* Compressed SLIP.

CSMA/CA *n.* Acronym for **C**arrier **S**ense **M**ultiple **A**ccess with **C**ollision **A**voidance, a protocol for controlling network access similar to CSMA/CD, in that nodes (stations) listen to the network and transmit only when it is free. But in CSMA/CA, nodes avoid data collisions by signaling their intention with a brief Request to Send (RTS) signal and then waiting for acknowledgment before actually transmitting.

CSMA/CD *n.* Acronym for **C**arrier **S**ense **M**ultiple **A**ccess with **C**ollision **D**etection. A network protocol for handling situations in which two or more nodes (stations) transmit at the same time, thus causing a collision. With CSMA/CD, each node on the network monitors the line and transmits when it senses that the line is not busy. If a collision occurs because another node is using the same opportunity to transmit, both nodes stop transmitting. To avoid another collision, both then wait for differing random amounts of time before attempting to transmit again. *Compare* token passing.

CSO *n.* Acronym for **C**omputing **S**ervices **O**ffice. An Internet directory service that matches users' own names with e-mail addresses, generally at colleges and universities. The CSO service, which can be reached through Gopher, was originally developed at the Computing Services Office at the University of Illinois.

CSO name server *n.* A facility that provides e-mail directory information through the CSO system. *See also* CSO.

CSS *n.* **1.** *See* cascading style sheets. **2.** Acronym for **C**ontent **S**crambling **S**ystem. An encryption feature added to DVDs distributed with approval of the MPAA. CSS looks for a matching region code on the DVD and the playback device. If the codes do not match (such as for a DVD purchased in Japan and a DVD player purchased in the United States), CSS will not allow the DVD to play. CSS also will not allow a DVD to be played on playback equipment not approved by the MPAA. *See also* deCSS, region code.

CSS1 *n. See* cascading style sheets.

CSU *n. See* DDS.

CTERM *n. See* Communications Terminal Protocol.

CT Expo *n.* Acronym for Computer Telephony Expo. Annual exposition on data and communications issues involving the computer, telecommunications, and Internet industries. Held in Los Angeles, California, CT Expo features exhibits by hundreds of companies displaying their latest products and services, as well as conferences on a range of subjects affecting computer telephony.

CTI *n.* Acronym for computer-telephony integration. The practice of using a computer to control one or more telephone and communications functions.

CTIA *n. See* Cellular Telecommunications and Internet Association.

CTIA Wireless *n.* Annual conference of the wireless data, mobile Internet, and handheld computing industries. Sponsored by the Cellular Telecommunications and Internet Association, CTIA Wireless showcases products and technical developments in the field of wireless communications and data.

CTO *n.* Acronym for Chief Technology Officer. A corporate executive in charge of managing a company's information technology (IT) architecture and other technological assets. The CTO's responsibilities may include oversight of IT centers, networks and intranet, applications, databases, Web presence, and other technological resources.

CTS *n.* Acronym for Clear To Send. In serial communications, a signal sent, as from a modem to its computer, to indicate that transmission can proceed. CTS is a hardware signal sent over line 5 in RS-232-C connections. *Compare* RTS.

CUL8R *n.* A fanciful shorthand notation meaning "See you later," sometimes seen in Internet discussion groups as a farewell by a participant temporarily leaving the group.

CUSeeMe *n.* A video conferencing program developed at Cornell University. It was the first program to give Windows and Mac OS users the ability to engage in real-time video conferencing over the Internet, but it requires a lot of bandwidth (at least 128 Kbps speed) to function properly.

custom control *n.* A control authored by a user or a third-party software vendor that does not belong to the .NET Framework class library. This is a generic term that includes user controls. A custom server control is used in Web Forms (ASP.NET pages). A custom client control is used in Windows Forms applications.

custom queuing *n.* A form of queuing on Cisco routers where the wide area network (WAN) link is divided into micropipes based on a percentage of the total bandwidth available on the pipe. *See also* bandwidth reservation.

CVS *n.* Acronym for Concurrent Versions System. An open-source network-transparent version control system which allows multiple developers to view and edit code simultaneously. Popular because the client-server function allows operation over the Internet. CVS maintains a single copy of the source code with a record of who initiated changes and when the changes were made. CVS was developed for the UNIX operating system and is commonly used by programmers working with Linux, Mac OS X, and other UNIX-based environments.

cXML *n.* Acronym for commerce **XML**. A set of document definitions for Extensible Markup Language (XML) developed for use in business-to-business e-commerce. cXML defines standards for product listings, allows for electronic requests and responses between procurement applications and suppliers, and provides for secure financial transactions via the Internet.

C

cyber- *prefix* A prefix attached to "everyday" words in order to give them a computer-based or online meaning, as in cyberlaw (the practice of law either in relation to or through the use of the Internet) and cyberspace (the virtual online world). The prefix is derived from the word *cybernetics*, which refers to the study of mechanisms used to control and regulate complex systems, either human or machine.

cyberart *n.* The artwork of artists who use computers to create or distribute their efforts.

cybercafe or **cyber café** *n.* **1.** A coffee shop or restaurant that offers access to PCs or other terminals that are connected to the Internet, usually for a per-hour or per-minute fee. Users are encouraged to buy beverages or food to drink or eat while accessing the Internet. **2.** A virtual café on the Internet, generally used for social purposes. Users interact with each other by means of a chat program or by posting messages to one another through a bulletin board system, such as in a newsgroup or on a Web site.

cybercash *n. See* e-money.

cyberchat *n. See* IRC.

cybercop *n.* A person who investigates criminal acts committed on line, especially fraud and harassment.

cyberculture *n.* The behavior, beliefs, customs, and etiquette that characterize groups of individuals who communicate or socialize over computer networks, such as the Internet. The cyberculture of one group can be vastly different from the cyberculture of another.

Cyberdog *n.* Apple's Internet suite for Web browsing and e-mail, based on OpenDoc for easy integration with other applications. *See also* OpenDoc.

cyberlawyer *n.* **1.** An attorney whose practice involves the law related to computers and online communication, including elements of communications law, intellectual property rights, privacy and security issues, and other specialties. **2.** An attorney who advertises or distributes information over the Internet and the World Wide Web.

cyberlife *n.* In the gaming world, a technology that mimics biological DNA. *See also* digital DNA.

cybernaut *n.* One who spends copious time on line, exploring the Internet. *Also called:* Internaut. *See also* cyberspace.

cybernetics *n.* The study of control systems, such as the nervous system, in living organisms and the development of equivalent systems in electronic and mechanical devices. Cybernetics compares similarities and differences between living and non-living systems (whether those systems comprise individuals, groups, or societies) and is based on theories of communication and control that can be applied to either living or nonliving systems or both. *See also* bionics.

cyberpunk *n.* **1.** A genre of near-future science fiction in which conflict and action take place in virtual-reality environments maintained on global computer networks in a worldwide culture of dystopian alienation. The prototypical cyberpunk novel is William Gibson's *Neuromancer* (1982). **2.** A category of popular culture that resembles the ethos of cyberpunk fiction. **3.** A person or fictional character who resembles the heroes of cyberpunk fiction.

cybersex *n.* Communication via electronic means, such as e-mail, chat, or newsgroups, for the purpose of sexual stimulation or gratification. *See also* chat[1] (definition 1), newsgroup.

cyberspace *n.* **1.** The advanced shared virtual-reality network imagined by William Gibson in his novel *Neuromancer* (1982). **2.** The universe of environments, such as the Internet, in which persons interact by means of connected computers. A defining characteristic of cyberspace is that communication is independent of physical distance.

cyberspeak *n.* Terminology and language (often jargon, slang, and acronyms) relating to the Internet (computer-connected) environment, that is, cyberspace. *See also* cyberspace.

cybersquatter *n.* A person who registers company names and other trademarks as Internet domain names in order to force the named companies or owners of the trademarks to buy them at an inflated price.

cyberwidow *n.* The spouse of a person who spends inordinate amounts of time on the Internet.

cybrarian *n.* Software used at some libraries that allows one to query a database through the use of an interactive search engine.

D

DAC *n. See* digital-to-analog converter.

daemon *n.* A program associated with UNIX systems that performs a housekeeping or maintenance utility function without being called by the user. A daemon sits in the background and is activated only when needed, for example, to correct an error from which another program cannot recover.

daisy chain[1] *n.* A set of devices connected in series. In order to eliminate conflicting requests to use the channel (bus) to which all the devices are connected, each device is given a different priority. SCSI (**S**mall **C**omputer **S**ystem **I**nterface) and the newer USB (**U**niversal **S**erial **B**us) both support daisy-chained devices. *See also* SCSI, USB.

daisy chain[2] *vb.* To connect a series of devices, one to another, like daisies in a chain of flowers.

DAP *n. See* Directory Access Protocol.

DARPA *n. See* Defense Advanced Research Projects Agency.

DARPANET *n.* Short for **D**efense **A**dvanced **R**esearch **P**rojects **A**gency **Net**work. *See* ARPANET.

data bank *n.* Any substantial collection of data.

database *n.* A file composed of records, each containing fields together with a set of operations for searching, sorting, recombining, and other functions. *Acronym:* DB.

database administrator *n.* One who manages a database. The administrator determines the content, internal structure, and access strategy for a database, defines security and integrity, and monitors performance. *Acronym:* DBA. *Also called:* database manager.

database machine *n.* **1.** A peripheral that executes database tasks, thereby relieving the main computer from performing them. **2.** A database server that performs only database tasks.

database management system *n.* A software interface between the database and the user. A database management system handles user requests for database actions and allows for control of security and data integrity requirements. *Acronym:* DBMS. *Also called:* database manager.

database manager *n. See* database administrator, database management system.

database publishing *n.* The use of desktop publishing or Internet technology to produce reports containing information obtained from a database.

database server *n.* A network node, or station, dedicated to storing and providing access to a shared database. *Also called:* database machine.

database structure *n.* A general description of the format of records in a database, including the number of fields, specifications regarding the type of data that can be entered in each field, and the field names used.

datacom *n.* Short for **data com**munications. *See* communications.

data communications *n.* *See* communications.

data conferencing *n.* Simultaneous data communication among geographically separated participants in a meeting. Data conferencing involves whiteboards and other software that enable a single set of files at one location to be accessed and modified by all participants. *See also* desktop conferencing, whiteboard. *Compare* video conferencing.

data-driven attack *n.* A form of attack in which malicious code is hidden in a program or other innocuous data. When the data is executed, the virus or other destructive code is activated. A data-driven attack is typically used to bypass a firewall or other security measures.

data encryption *n.* *See* encryption.

data encryption key *n.* A sequence of secret information, such as a string of decimal numbers or binary digits, that is used to encrypt and decrypt data. *Acronym:* DEK. *See also* decryption, encryption, key (definition 3).

data encryption standard *n.* *See* DES.

datagram *n.* One packet, or unit, of information, along with relevant delivery information such as the destination address, that is sent through a packet-switching network. *See also* packet switching.

data link *n.* A connection between any two devices capable of sending and receiving information, such as a computer and a printer or a main computer and a terminal. Sometimes the term is extended to include equipment, such as a modem, that enables transmission and receiving. Such devices follow protocols that govern data transmission. *See also* communications protocol, data-link layer, DCE, DTE.

Data Link Connection Identifier *n.* A virtual circuit on frame relay networks that permanently identifies the path to a particular destination. *See also* frame relay, virtual circuit.

data-link layer *n.* The second of seven layers in the ISO/OSI reference model for standardizing computer-to-computer communications. The data-link layer is one layer above the physical layer. Its concern is packaging and addressing data and managing the flow of transmissions. It is the lowest of the three layers (data-link, network, and transport) involved in actually moving data between devices. *See also* ISO/OSI reference model.

data migration *n.* **1.** The process of moving data from one repository or source, such as a database, to another, usually via automated scripts or programs. Often data migration involves transferring data from one type of computer system to another. **2.** In supercomputing applications, the process of storing large amounts of data off line while making them appear to be on line as disk-resident files.

data mining *n.* The process of identifying commercially useful patterns, problems, or relationships in a database, a Web server, or other computer repository through the use of advanced statistical tools. Some Web sites use data mining to monitor the efficiency of site navigation and to determine changes in the Web site's design based on how consumers are using the site.

data model *n.* A collection of related object types, operators, and integrity rules that form the abstract entity supported by a database management system (DBMS). Thus, one speaks of a relational DBMS, a network DBMS, and so on, depending on the type of data model a DBMS supports. In general, a DBMS supports only one data model as a practical rather than a theoretical restriction.

data network *n.* A network designed for transferring data encoded as digital signals, as opposed to a voice network, which transmits analog signals.

Data Over Cable Service Interface Specification *n.* *See* DOCSIS.

data-overrun error *n.* An error that occurs when more data is being acquired than can be processed. *See also* bps.

data packet *n.* *See* packet.

data path *n.* The route that a signal follows as it travels through a computer network.

data rate *n.* The speed at which a circuit or communications line can transfer information, usually measured in bits per second (bps).

Data Service Unit *n.* *See* DDS.

data set *n.* **1.** A collection of related information made up of separate elements that can be treated as a unit in data handling. **2.** In communications, a modem. *See also* modem.

Data Set Ready *n.* *See* DSR.

data sharing *n.* The use of a single file by more than one person or computer. Data sharing can be done by physically transferring a file from one computer to another, or, more commonly, by networking and computer-to-computer communications.

data signal *n.* The information transmitted over a line or circuit. It consists of binary digits and can include actual information or messages and other elements such as control characters or error-checking codes.

data sink *n.* **1.** Any recording medium where data can be stored until needed. **2.** In communications, the portion of a Data Terminal Equipment (DTE) device that receives transmitted data.

data source *n.* **1.** The originator of computer data, frequently an analog or digital data collection device. **2.** In communications, the portion of a Data Terminal Equipment (DTE) device that sends data.

data stream *n.* An undifferentiated, byte-by-byte flow of data.

data switch *n.* A device in a computer system that routes incoming data to various locations.

Data Terminal Equipment *n. See* DTE.

Data Terminal Ready *n. See* DTR.

data traffic *n.* The exchange of electronic messages—control and data—across a network. Traffic capacity is measured in bandwidth; traffic speed is measured in bits per unit of time.

data transfer *n.* The movement of information from one location to another, either within a computer (as from a disk drive to memory), between a computer and an external device (as between a file server and a computer on a network), or between separate computers.

data warehouse[1] *n.* A database, frequently very large, that can access all of a company's information. While the warehouse can be distributed over several computers and may contain several databases and information from numerous sources in a variety of formats, it should be accessible through a server. Thus, access to the warehouse is transparent to the user, who can use simple commands to retrieve and analyze all the information. The data warehouse also contains data about how the warehouse is organized, where the information can be found, and any connections between data. Frequently used for decision support within an organization, the data warehouse also allows the organization to organize its data, coordinate updates, and see relationships between information gathered from different parts of the organization. *See also* database, server (definition 1), transparent (definition 1).

data warehouse[2] *vb.* To acquire, collect, manage, and disseminate information gathered from various sources into a single location; or to implement an informational database used to store sharable data. Data warehousing is a four-step process: gathering data; managing the data in a centralized location; providing access to the data along with tools for interpreting, analyzing, and reporting on the data; and producing reports on the data to be used for decision making.

date and time stamp *n. See* time stamp.

date stamp *n. See* time stamp.

DAV connector *n. See* digital audio/video connector.

DBA *n. See* database administrator.

DB connector *n.* Any of various connectors that facilitate parallel input and output. The initials DB (for data bus) are followed by a number that indicates the number of lines (wires) within the connector. For example, a DB-9 connector has nine pins and supports up to nine lines, each of which can connect to a pin on the connector.

DBMS *n. See* database management system.

DBS *n. See* direct broadcast satellite.

dbXML *n.* Acronym for **d**atabase **XML**. A native XML database server designed to manage large collections of XML documents. dbXML may be embedded in custom applications or run as a stand-alone database.

DCA *n.* Acronym for **D**ocument **C**ontent **A**rchitecture. A formatting guideline used in IBM's Systems Network Architecture (SNA) that enables the exchange of text-only documents between differing types of computers. DCA provides for two types of document formatting: Revisable-Form-Text DCA (RFTDCA), which allows for modification of formatting, and Final-Form-Text DCA (FFTDCA), which cannot be modified. *See also* DIA, SNA.

DCD *n.* **1.** Acronym for **D**ata **C**arrier **D**etected. A signal in serial communications that is sent from a modem to its computer to indicate that the modem is ready for transmitting. *Also called:* RLSD. *See also* RS-232-C standard. **2.** Acronym for **D**ocument **C**ontent Description. A specification governing the rules for defining the structure and content of XML documents. The specification was created by IBM and Microsoft in 1998 and was submitted to the World Wide Web Consortium for approval. *See also* XML.

D

DCE *n.* Acronym for **D**ata **C**ommunications **E**quipment. The term used in RS-232 and X.25 specifications for a device, such as a modem, that provides another device (known as the Data Terminal Equipment or DTE) with access to a communications line. A DCE is an intermediary device that often transforms input from a DTE before sending it to a recipient. *See also* RS-232-C standard, X series. *Compare* DTE.

D channel *n.* Short for **d**ata **channel**. In the ISDN communications architecture, the channel dedicated to carrying control signals, such as packet-switching information; and user-related data, such as phone numbers. The basic ISDN connection, called the Basic Rate Interface (BRI), is composed of two B (bearer) channels, which carry as much as 64 Kbps of actual data each, and one D channel, which transmits at either 16 Kbps or 64 Kbps. The faster Primary Rate Interface (PRI) is composed of one 64-Kbps D channel and either 23 or 30 B channels operating at 64 Kbps. *See also* B channel, BRI, ISDN.

DCOM *n.* Acronym for **D**istributed **C**omponent **O**bject **M**odel. The version of Microsoft's Component Object Model (COM) specification that stipulates how components communicate over Windows-based networks. It permits the distribution of different components for a single application across two or more networked computers, running an application distributed across a network so that the distribution of components is not apparent to the user, and remotely displaying an application. *Also called:* Distributed COM. *See also* COM (definition 2), component (definition 2).

DDE *n.* Acronym for **D**ynamic **D**ata **E**xchange. An interprocess communication method featured in Microsoft Windows and OS/2. DDE allows two or more programs that are running simultaneously to exchange data and commands. In Windows 3.1, DDE was largely supplanted by OLE, which is an extension of DDE. In Windows 95 and Windows NT, OLE and ActiveX are more commonly used. *See also* ActiveX, OLE.

DDoS *n.* Acronym for **d**istributed **d**enial of **s**ervice attack. A form of denial of service attack (DoS) originating from several computers that seeks to disrupt Web access by overwhelming a target with connection requests that cannot be completed. A DDoS attack involves cracking into a number of computers and planting programs that lie dormant until sent a signal to attack. At that point the computers send a steady stream of data packets to the targeted Web site, overwhelming the ability of·the Web server to respond. Because the attack is coming from many computers, security features that might otherwise recognize the attack and stop accepting data packets from a single source are unable to shut down connections to all the attackers. *See also* DoS, packet, zombie.

DDS *n.* Acronym for **d**igital **d**ata **s**ervice, a dedicated communications line that provides transmission at speeds up to 56 Kbps. DDS lines use a device known as a CSU/DSU rather than a modem for connecting two networks. The CSU, or Channel Service Unit, connects the network to the transmission line; the DSU, or Data Service Unit, converts data for transmission by the CSU and controls data flow.

dead-letter box *n.* In e-mail or message systems, a file to which undeliverable messages are sent.

declarative markup language *n.* In text processing, a system of text-formatting codes that indicates only that a unit of text is a certain part of a document. Document formatting is then done by another program, called a parser. SGML and HTML are examples of declarative markup languages. *Acronym:* DML. *Also called:* data manipulation language. *See also* HTML, SGML.

DECnet *n.* A hardware, software, and protocol stack designed by Digital Equipment Corporation for its Digital Network Architecture (DNA).

decryption *n.* The process of restoring encrypted data to its original form. *See also* data encryption key. *Compare* encryption.

deCSS *n.* Decrypt CSS. A utility capable of cracking the CSS encryption system used on DVD discs. By decrypting the CSS code, DVD movies and other copyrighted material can be used with any DVD playback device without regard to license or region coding. The origin of deCSS can be traced to a number of individuals interested in creating a DVD player for the Linux OS. The term deCSS is sometimes used generically for any software capable of defeating CSS technology. *See also* CSS, region code.

dedicated server *n.* A computer—usually quite powerful—that is used solely as a network server. *See also* server. *Compare* nondedicated server.

Defense Advanced Research Projects Agency *n.* The U.S. government agency that provided the original support for the development of the interconnected networks that later grew into the Internet. *Acronym:* DARPA. *See also* ARPANET.

deferral time *n.* The length of time that nodes on a CSMA/CD network wait before trying to retransmit after a collision. *See also* CSMA/CD.

DEK *n. See* data encryption key.

demand priority *n.* A network access method in which hubs control network access; a feature of 100Base-VG Ethernet networks. With demand priority, nodes send requests to hubs and the hubs give permission to transmit based on priority levels assigned to the requests by the nodes. *See also* 100Base-VG.

demodulation *n.* In communications, the means by which a modem converts data from modulated carrier frequencies (waves that have been modified in such a way that variations in amplitude and frequency represent meaningful information) over a telephone line. Data is converted to the digital form needed by a computer to which the modem is attached, with as little distortion as possible. *Compare* modulation (definition 1).

demon dialer *n. See* war dialer.

denial of service attack *n. See* DoS.

denizen *n.* A participant in a Usenet newsgroup.

DES *n.* Acronym for **D**ata **E**ncryption **S**tandard. A specification for encryption of computer data developed by IBM and adopted by the U.S. government as a standard in 1976. DES uses a 56-bit key. *See also* encryption, key (definition 3).

D

desktop conferencing *n.* The use of computers for simultaneous communication among geographically separated participants in a meeting. This communication may include input to and display from application programs as well as audio and video communication. *See also* data conferencing, teleconferencing, video conferencing.

DHCP *n.* Acronym for **D**ynamic **H**ost **C**onfiguration **P**rotocol. A TCP/IP protocol that enables a network connected to the Internet to assign a temporary IP address to a host automatically when the host connects to the network. *See also* IP address, TCP/IP. *Compare* dynamic SLIP.

DHTML *n. See* dynamic HTML.

DIA *n.* Acronym for **D**ocument **I**nterchange **A**rchitecture. A document exchange guideline used in IBM's Systems Network Architecture (SNA). DIA specifies methods of organizing and addressing documents for transmission between computers of different sizes and models. DIA is supported by IBM's Advanced Program-to-Program Communication (APPC) and by Logical Unit (LU) 6.2, which establish the capabilities and types of interactions possible in an SNA environment. *See also* DCA, SNA.

dialog *n.* **1.** In computing, the exchange of human input and machine responses that forms a "conversation" between an interactive computer and the person using it. **2.** The exchange of signals by computers communicating on a network.

dial-up access *n.* Connection to a data communications network through a public switched telecommunication network.

dial-up networking *n.* Connection to a remote network through use of a modem. Dial-up networking is typically used in reference to telecommuting, although the term is equally applicable to connecting to the Internet.

DIB *n.* Acronym for **D**irectory **I**nformation **B**ase. A directory of user and resource names in an X.500 system. The DIB is maintained by a Directory Server Agent (DSA). *Also called:* white pages.

dictionary attack *n.* Originally a method of guessing a user's password or PIN by trying every word in the dictionary until successful. Currently used to identify any attack that tries known words or alphanumeric character strings to break a simple password.

Diffie-Hellman *n.* Diffie-Hellman key agreement protocol. A public-key cryptography method that allows two hosts to create and share a secret key. Diffie-Hellman is used for key management by virtual private networks (VPNs) operating on the IPSec standard. *See also* IPSec.

digerati *n.* Cyberspace populace that can be roughly compared to *literati*. Digerati are people renowned as or claiming to be knowledgeable about topics and issues related to the digital revolution; more specifically, they are people "in the know" about the Internet and online activities.

digest *n.* **1.** An article in a moderated newsgroup that summarizes multiple posts submitted to the moderator. *See also* moderator, newsgroup. **2.** A message in a mailing list that is sent to subscribers in place of the multiple individual posts that the digest contains. If the mailing list is moderated, the digest may be edited. *See also* moderated.

digicash *n. See* e-money.

digital *adj.* **1.** A reference to something based on digits (numbers) or their representation. **2.** In computing, analogous in use, though not in meaning, to *binary* because the computers familiar to most people process information coded as different combinations of the binary digits (bits) 0 and 1. *Compare* analog.

digital audio/video connector *n.* An interface on some high-end video cards or TV tuner cards that allows the simultaneous transmission of digital audio and video signals. *Also called:* DAV connector.

digital broadcast satellite *n. See* direct broadcast satellite.

digital cash *n. See* e-money.

digital certificate *n.* **1.** An assurance that software downloaded from the Internet comes from a reputable source. A digital certificate provides information about the software—such as the identity of the author and the date on which the software was registered with a certificate authority (CA), as well as a measure of tamper-resistance. **2.** A user identity card or "driver's license" for cyberspace. Issued by a certificate authority (CA), a digital certificate is an electronic credential that authenticates a user on the Internet and intranets. Digital certificates ensure the legitimate online transfer of confidential information, money, or other sensitive materials by means of public encryption technology. A digital certificate holder has two keys (strings of numbers): a private key held only by the user, for "signing" outgoing messages and decrypting incoming messages; and a public key, for use by anyone, for encrypting data to send to a specific user. *See also* certificate authority, encryption, private key, public key.

digital communications *n.* Exchange of communications in which all information is transmitted in binary-encoded (digital) form.

digital data service *n. See* DDS.

digital data transmission *n.* The transfer of information encoded as a series of bits rather than as a fluctuating (analog) signal in a communications channel.

digital fingerprinting *n. See* digital watermark.

digital home *n. See* smart home.

digital DNA *n.* **1.** Broadly, a reference to the bits that comprise digital information. **2.** In the gaming world, a technology called "Cyberlife" that mimics biological DNA in the creation and development of trainable creatures known as Norns. Like real DNA, digital DNA is passed from parent to offspring and determines the artificial creature's characteristics and adaptability.

D

digital modem *n.* **1.** A communications device that acts as the intermediary between a digital device such as a computer or terminal and a digital communications channel, such as a high-speed network line, an ISDN circuit, or a cable TV system. Although a digital modem supports standard (analog) modem protocols, it is not a "typical" modem in the sense of being a device whose primary function is to modulate (convert digital to analog) before transmission and demodulate (convert analog to digital) after transmission. It uses advanced digital modulation techniques for changing data frames into a format suitable for transmission over a digital line. *See also* terminal adapter. *Compare* modem. **2.** A 56 Kbps modem. Such a modem is not purely digital but does eliminate the traditional digital-to-analog conversion for downstream transmissions—that is, transmissions moving from the Internet to the end user. A 56 Kbps modem is also digital in that it requires a digital connection, such as T1, between the telephone company and the user's Internet Service Provider (ISP) in order to achieve its highest speed. *See also* 56-Kbps modem. **3.** A term used to distinguish all-digital communications devices, such as ISDN and cable "modems" from the more traditional analog-to-digital, phone-based modems.

Digital Network Architecture *n.* A multilayered architecture and set of protocol specifications for networks. Designed by the Digital Equipment Corporation, Digital Network Architecture is implemented in the set of products known by the name *DECnet. Acronym:* DNA. *See also* DECnet.

Digital Rights Management *n. See* DRM.

digital satellite system *n.* A high-powered satellite system with the capability to deliver high-quality transmissions of hundreds of channels directly to television receivers. A DSS broadcast begins as a digital signal sent from a service provider's station to a satellite. From there, it is directed to a satellite dish (typically 18 inches) at the user's premises. The dish next transmits the signal to a converter box, which changes it to an analog signal before sending it to the television set. *Acronym:* DSS.

Digital Services *n. See* DS.

digital signature *n.* A security mechanism used on the Internet that relies on two keys, one public and one private, that are used to encrypt messages before transmission and to decrypt them on receipt.

Digital Signature Algorithm *n.* The U.S. government standard for digital signatures, as specified by the National Institute of Standards and Technology, in FIPS 186, Digital Signature Standard. DSA is based on signature encryption based on a public and a private key. *Acronym:* DSA. *See also* digital signature.

Digital Signature Standard *n.* A public key cryptographic standard issued in 1994 by the United States National Institute of Standards and Technology (NIST) to authenticate electronic documents. The DSS uses a Digital Signature Algorithm (DSA) to generate and verify digital signatures based on a public key, which is not secret, and a private key, which is known or held only by the person generating the signature. A digital signature serves to authenticate both the identity of the signer and the integrity of the transmitted information. *Acronym:* DSS. *See also* public key encryption.

Digital Simultaneous Voice and Data *n.* A modem technology by Multi-Tech Systems, Inc., that allows a single telephone line to be used for conversation together with data transfer. This is accomplished by switching to packet-mode communications when the need for voice transfer is detected; digitized voice packets are then transferred along with data and command packets. *Acronym:* DSVD.

digital subscriber line or **Digital Subscriber Line** *n. See* DSL.

Digital Subscriber Line Access Multiplexer or **Digital Subscriber Line Multiplexer** *n. See* DSLAM.

digital-to-analog converter *n.* A device that translates digital data to an analog signal. A digital-to-analog converter takes a succession of discrete digital values as input and creates an analog signal whose amplitude corresponds, moment by moment, to each digital value. *Acronym:* DAC. *Compare* analog-to-digital converter.

digital TV or **digital television** *n.* The transmission of television signals using digital rather than the conventional analog signals. A digital TV standard for the United States was approved by the FCC in 1996. Digital TV provides a better television experience and new information services. Digital signals produce higher quality pictures and CD-quality sound, compared to the analog signals used with today's television. Digital TV can support interactive television, electronic program guides, and a variety of digital services, such as Internet channel broadcasting and data services. *Acronym:* DTV. *Compare* HDTV.

digital video *n.* Video images and sound stored in a digital format. *Acronym:* DV.

digital watermark *n.* A unique identifier embedded in a file to deter piracy and prove file ownership and quality. Digital watermarking is often used with graphics and audio files to identify the owner's rights to these works. *See also* fingerprint[2].

digiterati *n. See* digerati.

DIN connector *n.* A multipin connector conforming to the specification of the German national standards organization (Deutsch Industrie Norm). DIN connectors are used to link various components in personal computers.

direct broadcast satellite *n.* A digital telecommunications service that delivers television programming via the Digital Satellite System (DSS). Direct broadcast satellite technology uses a geostationary orbit satellite (GEO) to receive digitized signals sent by ground-based uplink centers; the satellite then beams the signal across a wide swath on Earth. Subscribers within that swath use small (18-inch) satellite dishes to bring the signal into a set-top box decoder for playback. Although primarily used for television broadcasts, the technology is seen as having potential to also deliver high-quality, digital communications and multimedia content in the future. *Acronym:* DBS. *Also called:* digital broadcast satellite. *See also* digital satellite system, geostationary orbit satellite, webcasting.

direct cable connection *n.* A link between the I/O ports of two computers that uses a single cable rather than a modem or other active interface device. In most cases, a direct cable connection requires a null modem cable.

direct-connect modem *n.* A modem that uses standard telephone wire and connectors and that plugs directly into a telephone jack, eliminating the need for an intermediary telephone.

directory *n.* **1.** A catalog for file names and other directories stored on a disk. A directory is a way of organizing and grouping the files so that the user is not overwhelmed by a long list of them. The uppermost directory is called the *root directory*; the directories within a directory are called *subdirectories*. Depending on how an operating system supports directories, file names in a directory can be viewed and ordered in various ways—for example, alphabetically, by date, by size, or as icons in a graphical user interface. What the user views as a directory is supported in the operating system by tables of data, stored on the disk, that indicate characteristics and the location of each file. In the Macintosh and Windows 9x operating systems, directories are called *folders*. **2.** On a network, an index of names and pertinent information related to authorized users and network resources.

Directory Access Protocol *n.* The protocol that governs communications between X.500 clients and servers. *See also* CCITT X series.

Directory Client Agent *n. See* DUA.

Directory Information Base *n. See* DIB (definition 2).

directory replication *n.* The copying of a master set of directories from a server (called an *export server*) to specified servers or workstations (called *import computers*) in the same or other domains. Replication simplifies the task of maintaining identical sets of directories and files on multiple computers because only a single master copy of the data must be maintained. *See also* directory, server.

Directory Server Agent *n. See* DSA.

directory service *n.* A service on a network that returns mail addresses of other users or enables a user to locate hosts and services.

Directory System Agent *n. See* DSA.

dirty *adj.* Of, pertaining to, or characteristic of a communications line that is hampered by excessive noise, degrading the quality of the signal. *See also* noise (definition 2).

discretionary access control list *n.* The part of an object's security descriptor that grants or denies specific users and groups permission to access the object. Only the owner of an object can change permissions granted or denied in a discretionary access control list (DACL); thus, access to the object is at the owner's discretion. *Acronym:* DACL. *See also* distribution group.

discussion group *n.* Any of a variety of online forums in which people communicate about subjects of common interest. Forums for discussion groups include electronic mailing lists, Internet newsgroups, and IRC channels.

diskless workstation *n.* A station on a computer network that is not equipped with a disk drive and that uses files stored in a file server. *See also* file server.

disk server *n.* A node on a local area network that acts as a remote disk drive shared by network users. Unlike a file server, which performs the more sophisticated tasks of managing network requests for files, a disk server functions as a storage medium on which users can read and write files. A disk server can be divided into sections (volumes), each of which appears to be a separate disk. *Compare* file server.

Distributed COM *n. See* DCOM.

Distributed Component Object Model *n. See* DCOM.

distributed database *n.* A database implemented on a network. The component partitions are distributed over various nodes (stations) of the network. Depending on the specific update and retrieval traffic, distributing the database can significantly enhance overall performance.

distributed database management system *n.* A database management system capable of managing a distributed database. *Acronym:* DDBMS. *See also* distributed database.

distributed denial of service attack *n. See* DDoS.

distributed file system *n.* A file management system in which files may be located on multiple computers connected over a local or wide area network. *Acronym:* DFS.

distributed intelligence *n.* A system in which processing ability (intelligence) is distributed among multiple computers and other devices, each of which can work independently to some degree but can also communicate with the other devices to function as part of the larger system. *See also* distributed processing.

distributed network *n.* A network in which processing, storage, and other functions are handled by separate units (nodes) rather than by a single main computer.

distributed processing *n.* A form of information processing in which work is performed by separate computers linked through a communications network. Distributed processing is usually categorized as either plain distributed processing or true distributed processing. Plain distributed processing shares the workload among computers that can communicate with one another. True distributed processing has separate computers perform different tasks in such a way that their combined work can contribute to a larger goal. The latter type of processing requires a highly structured environment that allows hardware and software to communicate, share resources, and exchange information freely.

distributed services *n. See* BISDN.

distributed system *n.* A noncentralized network consisting of numerous computers that can communicate with one another and that appear to users as parts of a single, large, accessible "storehouse" of shared hardware, software, and data.

Distributed System Object Model *n.* IBM's System Object Model (SOM) in a shared environment, where binary class libraries can be shared between applications on networked computers or between applications on a given system. The Distributed System Object Model complements existing object-oriented languages by allowing SOM class libraries to be shared among applications written in different languages. *Acronym:* DSOM. *See also* SOM (definition 1).

distributed transaction processing *n.* Transaction processing that is shared by one or more computers communicating over a network. *Acronym:* DTP. *See also* distributed processing, transaction processing.

distributed workplace *n.* An environment other than the traditional office or factory, in which work is carried out on a regular basis. The flexibility afforded by the combination of communications and computing technologies enables many workers to conduct business anywhere the appropriate computer and data communications infrastructure has been set up. *See also* SOHO, telecommute.

distribution group *n.* A group that is used solely for e-mail distribution and that is not security-enabled. Distribution groups cannot be listed in discretionary access control lists (DACLs) used to define permissions on resources and objects. Distribution groups can be used only with e-mail applications (such as Microsoft Exchange) to send e-mail messages to collections of users. If you do not need a group for security purposes, create a distribution group instead of a security group. *See also* discretionary access control list.

distribution list *n.* A list of recipients on an e-mail mailing list. This can be in the form of either a mailing list program, such as LISTSERV, or an alias in an e-mail program for all recipients of an e-mail message. *See also* alias, LISTSERV, mailing list.

D

distribution services *n. See* BISDN.

distro¹ *n.* **1.** A distribution of software (usually a version of Linux), digital music, or an online magazine or e-zine. *See also* e-zine, Linux. **2.** A company or individual that sells items, typically software, music CDs, or books, via the Web.

distro² *vb.* To distribute or sell software releases, digital music, or text items via the Web.

DLC *n.* Acronym for **D**ata **L**ink **C**ontrol. An error-correction protocol in the Systems Network Architecture (SNA) responsible for transmission of data between two nodes over a physical link. Supported by Microsoft Windows NT and Windows 2000, DLC is designed to provide access to IBM mainframe computers and to Hewlett-Packard printers connected to the network. *See also* HDLC, SNA.

DLCI *n. See* Data Link Connection Identifier.

DML *n. See* declarative markup language.

DNA *n. See* digital DNA, Digital Network Architecture, distributed network, Windows DNA.

DNS *n.* **1.** Acronym for **D**omain **N**ame **S**ystem. The hierarchical system by which hosts on the Internet have both domain name addresses (such as bluestem.prairienet.org) and IP addresses (such as 192.17.3.4). The domain name address is used by human users and is automatically translated into the numerical IP address, which is used by the packet-routing software. DNS names consist of a top-level domain (such as .com, .org, and .net), a second-level domain (the site name of a business, an organization, or an individual), and possibly one or more subdomains (servers within a second-level domain). *See also* domain name address, IP address. **2.** Acronym for **D**omain **N**ame **S**ervice. The Internet utility that implements the Domain Name System. DNS servers, also called name servers, maintain databases containing the addresses and are accessed transparently to the user. *See also* DNS server.

DNS name server *n. See* DNS server.

DNS server *n.* Short for **D**omain **N**ame **S**ystem **server**, a computer that can answer Domain Name System (DNS) queries. The DNS server keeps a database of host computers and their corresponding IP addresses. Presented with the name apex.com, for example, the DNS server would return the IP address of the hypothetical company Apex. *Also called:* name server. *See also* DNS (definition 2), IP address.

DNS zone transfer *n. See* zone transfer.

DOCSIS *n.* Acronym for **D**ata **O**ver **C**able **S**ervice **I**nterface **S**pecification. The International Telecommunications Union standard (ITU Recommendation J.112) that specifies functions and internal and external interfaces for high-speed, bidirectional transfer of digital data between cable television networks and subscribers. DOCSIS-compliant equipment ensures interoperability between cable modems and the cable television infrastructure, regardless of manufacturer or provider. Initially developed by a group of cable television providers, including Time Warner and TCI, DOCSIS was designed to support data, video, and rapid Internet access. Data rates are 27 Mbps to 36 Mbps downstream (from the cable network) and 320 Kbps to 10 Mbps upstream (to the cable network). *See also* cable modem.

Document Content Architecture *n. See* DCA.

Document Content Description *n. See* DCD (definition 2).

Document Interchange Architecture *n. See* DIA.

document management *n.* The full spectrum of electronic document creation and distribution within an organization.

document management system *n.* A server-based network facility designed for the storage and handling of an organization's documents. A document management system, or DMS, is built around a central library known as a repository and typically supports controlled access, version tracking, cataloging, search capabilities, and the ability to check documents in and out electronically. The open interface specification known as ODMA (Open Document Management API) enables desktop applications that support ODMA to interface with a DMS so that users can access and manage documents from within their client applications. *Acronym:* DMS. *Also called:* EDMS, electronic document management system.

Document Object Model *n.* A World Wide Web Consortium specification that describes the structure of dynamic HTML and XML documents in a way that allows them to be manipulated through a Web browser. In the Document Object Model, or DOM, a document is presented as a logical structure rather than as a collection of tagged words. In essence, DOM is a means of defining a document as a treelike hierarchy of nodes in which the document is an object containing other objects, such as images and forms. Through DOM, programs and scripts can access these objects in order to change aspects such as their appearance or behavior. DOM is a vehicle for adding depth and interactivity to what would otherwise be a static Web page. *Acronym:* DOM.

document source *n.* The plain-text HTML form of a World Wide Web document, with all tags and other markup displayed as such rather than being formatted. *Also called:* source, source document. *See also* HTML.

Document Style Semantics and Specification Language *n.* An ISO standard derived from SGML that addresses the semantics of high-quality composition in a manner independent of particular formatting systems or processes. Like CSS and XSL, it can be used to format XML documents. *Acronym:* DSSSL. *See also* ISO, SGML.

document type definition *n. See* DTD.

DoD *n. See* U.S. Department of Defense.

do-gooder virus *n.* A virus or worm that has been released with the intention of correcting problems caused by other, more malicious viruses. The do-gooder virus typically looks for computers that have been compromised and then infects the system and fixes back doors and other vulnerabilities left behind by the malicious program. The do-gooder virus may then use the repaired computer as a platform to infect other computers. *See also* anti-worm, automatic patching.

DOM *n. See* Document Object Model.

domain *n.* **1.** In database design and management, the set of valid values for a given attribute. For example, the domain for the attribute AREA-CODE might be the list of all valid three-digit numeric telephone area codes in the United States. *See also* attribute (definition 1). **2.** For Windows NT Advanced Server, a collection of computers that share a common domain database and security policy. Each domain has a unique name. **3.** In the Internet and other networks, the highest subdivision of a domain name in a network address, which identifies the type of entity owning the address (for example, .com for commercial users or .edu for educational institutions) or the geographical location of the address (for example, .fr for France or .sg for Singapore). The domain is the last part of the address (for example, www.acm.org). *See also* domain name.

domain controller *n.* In Windows NT, the master server that holds the directory services database that identifies all network users and resources.

domain name *n.* An address of a network connection that identifies the owner of that address in a hierarchical format: *server.organization.type.* For example, www.whitehouse.gov identifies the Web server at the White House, which is part of the U.S. government.

domain name address *n.* The address of a device connected to the Internet or any other TCP/IP network, in the hierarchical system that uses words to identify servers, organizations, and types, such as www.logos.net. *See also* TCP/IP.

Domain Name Server *n. See* DNS server.

Domain Name Service *n. See* DNS (definition 2).

Domain Name System *n. See* DNS (definition 1).

Domain Naming System *n. See* DNS (definition 1).

domain slamming *n.* The practice of transferring ownership of domain names from one customer to another without the permission of the first customer.

Domino *n. See* Lotus Domino.

doorway page *n.* A Web page that functions as a doorway into a Web site. Usually a doorway page contains keywords, which Internet search engines seek when they scan the Internet. Placing the correct keywords on a doorway page can increase the number of viewers visiting a site.

DoS *n.* Acronym for denial of service attack. A computerized assault, usually planned, that seeks to disrupt Web access. A denial of service attack can occur in a number of forms. The most common form of attack is to overwhelm an Internet server with connection requests that cannot be completed. This causes the server to become so busy attempting to respond to the attack that it ignores legitimate requests for connections. One example of this type of attack, known as a SYN flood, inundates the server's entry ports with false connection messages. Another, known as the Ping of Death, sends a ping command with an oversized IP packet that causes the server to freeze, crash, or restart. Other forms of denial of service attacks include the destruction or alteration of a server's configuration data, such as router information; unauthorized access to physical components of a system; and the sending of large or invalid data that causes a system to crash or freeze. *See also* packet, Ping of Death, SYN flood.

dot *n.* **1.** In the UNIX, MS-DOS, OS/2, and other operating systems, the character that separates a file name from an extension as in TEXT.DOC (pronounced "text-dot-doc"). **2.** In computer graphics and printing, a small spot combined with others in a matrix of rows and columns to form a character or a graphic element in a drawing or design. The dots forming an image on the screen are called pixels. The resolution of a display or printing device is often expressed in dots per inch (dpi). Dots are not the same as spots, which are groups of dots used in the halftoning process. **3.** In an Internet address, the character that separates the different parts of the domain name, such as the entity name from the domain. *See also* domain (definition 3), domain name.

D

dot address *n.* An IP address in dotted quad form. *See also* IP address.

dot-bomb *n.* An Internet-based company or organization that has failed or downsized significantly. *See also* dot-commed.

dot-com *n.* A company doing business primarily or entirely on the Internet. The term is derived from the top-level domain, .com, at the end of the Web addresses of commercial Web sites.

dot-commed *adj.* Losing a job because of the downsizing or failure of an Internet-based company or organization. *See also* dot-bomb.

double posting *n.* In newsgroup discussions, the practice of replying to one's own posts. Because it may be seen as the digital equivalent to talking to one's self, double posting is considered an undesirable practice.

down *adj.* Not functioning, in reference to computers, printers, communications lines on networks, and other such hardware.

downlink *n.* The transmission of data from a communications satellite to an earth station.

download *vb.* In communications, to transfer a copy of a file from a remote computer to the requesting computer by means of a modem or network.

downsample *n.* To decrease the number of audio samples or pixels, by applying an operation such as averaging. Popular internet music formats, such as MP3, use downsampling to reduce file size.

downsizing *n.* In computing, the practice of moving from larger computer systems, such as mainframes and minicomputers, to smaller systems in an organization, generally to save costs and to update to newer software. The smaller systems are usually client/server systems composed of a combination of PCs, workstations, and some legacy system such as a mainframe, connected in one or more local area networks or wide area networks. *See also* client/server architecture.

downstream¹ *n.* The direction in which information, such as a news feed for a newsgroup or data from an http (Web) server, is passed from one server to the next. *See also* newsfeed, newsgroup, server.

downstream² *adv.* **1.** The location of a client computer in relation to a server. **2.** The direction in which data moves from the server to the client.

downstream³ *adj.* Refers to data that moves *from* a remote network *to* an individual computer. In some Internet-related communications technologies, data flows more quickly downstream than upstream; cable modems, for example, can transfer data as fast as 30 Mbps downstream but support much slower rates, from 128 Kbps to around 2 Mbps, upstream. *Compare* upstream.

downtime *n.* The amount or percentage of time a computer system or associated hardware remains nonfunctional. Although downtime can occur because hardware fails unexpectedly, it can also be a scheduled event, as when a network is shut down to allow time for maintenance.

Dreamcast *n.* A console game system designed by the Sega corporation. It features a Hitachi 128-bit graphics engine with an on-board SH-4 RISC processor (operating frequency of 200 MHz 360 MIPS/1.4 GFLOPS) and a customized OS using Windows CE as its base (supporting DirectX). Game developers for the Dreamcast platform use an environment supported by Microsoft Visual Studio and refined Visual C++. *See also* computer game, console game. *Compare* GameCube, PlayStation, Xbox.

dribbleware *n.* Updates, patches, and new drivers for a software product that are released one at a time, as they become available, rather than being issued together in a new version of the product. A company using the dribbleware technique might distribute new and replacement files on diskette or CD-ROM, or make them available for download through the Internet or a private network.

drill down *vb.* To start at a top-level menu, directory, or Web page and pass through several intermediate menus, directories, or linked pages, until the file, page, menu command, or other item being sought is reached. Drilling down is common practice in searching for files or information on the Internet, where high-level Gopher menus and World Wide Web pages are frequently very general and become more specific at each lower level. *See also* Gopher, Web page.

DRM *n.* Acronym for **D**igital **R**ights **M**anagement. A group of technologies developed to protect intellectual property from online piracy by controlling who can view protected content and in what form. A DRM package may allow the purchaser to view protected content, but prevent printing or forwarding. Content may also be set to expire after a set amount of time or if distributed to multiple users. DRM technology is meant to protect multiple forms of digital and analog content, and includes encryption, digital watermarking, and content tracking software.

DS *n.* Acronym for **D**igital **S**ervices or **D**igital **S**ignal, a category used in referencing the speed, number of channels, and transmission characteristics of T1, T2, T3, and T4 communications lines. The basic DS unit, or level, is known as DS-0, which corresponds to the 64 Kbps speed of a single T1 channel. Higher levels are made up of multiple DS-0 levels. DS-1 represents a single T1 line that transmits at 1.544 Mbps. For higher rates, T1 lines are multiplexed to create DS-2 (a T2 line consisting of four T1 channels that transmits at 6.312 Mbps), DS-3 (a T3 line consisting of 28 T1 channels that transmits at 44.736 Mbps), and DS-4 (a T4 line consisting of 168 T1 channels that transmits at 274.176 Mbps).

DSA *n.* **1.** Acronym for **D**irectory **S**ystem **A**gent or **D**irectory **S**erver **A**gent. An X.500 server program that looks up the address of a user on the network when requested by a DUA (Directory User Agent). *See also* agent (definition 3), CCITT X series, DUA. **2.** *See* Digital Signature Algorithm.

DSL *n.* Acronym for **D**igital **S**ubscriber **L**ine, a recently developed (late 1990s) digital communications technology that can provide high-speed transmissions over standard copper telephone wiring. DSL is often referred to as xDSL, where the *x* stands for one or two characters that define variations of the basic DSL technology. Currently, ADSL (Asymmetric DSL) is the form most likely to be provided, but even it is, as yet, available only to limited groups of subscribers. *See also* ADSL, DSL Lite, HDSL, RADSL, SDSL, VDSL.

DSLAM *n.* Acronym for **D**igital **S**ubscriber **L**ine **A**ccess **M**ultiplexer. A device in a telephone company central office that splits DSL subscriber lines and connects them to Internet network hosts and to the public telephone network. The use of a DSLAM makes it possible to provide both voice and data service through a single pair of copper wires.

DSL Lite *n.* Short for **D**igital **S**ubscriber **L**ine **L**ite. A variation of ADSL currently under development that simplifies installation but transmits more slowly, at 1.544 Mbps. *See also* ADSL, DSL.

DSO *n.* Acronym for **D**ynamic **S**hared **O**bject. An Apache HTTP server module that supports all UNIX-based platforms. DSO uses a dynamically linked shared library of resources that are loaded and executed only at run time when necessary. DSO is most commonly used with Linux and is included in most Linux distributions.

DSOM *n.* *See* Distributed System Object Model.

DSR *n.* Acronym for **D**ata **S**et **R**eady. A signal used in serial communications sent, for example, by a modem to the computer to which it is attached, to indicate that it is ready to operate. DSR is a hardware signal sent over line 6 in RS-232-C connections. *See also* RS-232-C standard. *Compare* CTS.

DSSSL *n. See* Document Style Semantics and Specification Language.

DSVD *n. See* Digital Simultaneous Voice and Data.

DTD *n.* Acronym for **d**ocument **t**ype **d**efinition. A separate document that contains formal definitions of all of the data elements in a particular type of HTML, SGML, or XML document, such as a report or a book. By consulting the DTD for a document, a program called a parser can work with the markup codes that the document contains. *See also* HTML, SGML.

DTE *n.* Acronym for **D**ata **T**erminal **E**quipment. In the RS-232-C and X.25 specifications, a device, such as a PC, that has the ability to transmit information in digital form over a cable or a communications line to a mediating device (known as the DCE). *See also* RS-232-C standard. *Compare* DCE.

DTR *n.* Acronym for **D**ata **T**erminal **R**eady. A signal used in serial communications sent, for example, by a computer to its modem to indicate that the computer is ready to accept an incoming transmission. *See also* RS-232-C standard.

DUA *n.* Acronym for **D**irectory **U**ser **A**gent. An X.500 client program that sends a request to a DSA for the address of a user on the network. *Also called:* DCA, Directory Client Agent. *See also* agent (definition 3), DSA.

dual attachment station *n.* An FDDI node with two connections to the network—either through a node and a concentrator or through two concentrators. *Compare* single attachment station.

dual-band phone *n.* Wireless phone that broadcasts and receives signals on both 800-MHz (digital cellular) and 1900-MHz (personal communications service, or PCS) networks.

dual homing *n.* A form of fault tolerance used with critical network devices on FDDI networks, in which such devices are attached to both the primary and secondary (backup) rings through two concentrators to provide the maximum possible security in case the primary ring fails.

dual-mode phone *n.* Wireless phone that broadcasts and receives signals on both analog and digital networks. Dual-mode phones allow wireless phone users with digital service to send and receive calls on analog networks in areas where wireless carriers do not provide digital service.

dual-ring topology *n.* A token-passing ring topology implemented in FDDI networks that consists of two rings in which information travels in opposite directions. One ring, the primary ring, carries information; the second ring is used for backup. *See also* FDDI.

DUN *n. See* dial-up networking.

duplex[1] *adj.* Capable of carrying information in both directions over a communications channel. A system is full-duplex if it can carry information in both directions at once; it is half-duplex if it can carry information in only one direction at a time.

duplex[2] *n.* Simultaneous communications, in both directions, between the sender and receiver. *Also called:* duplex transmission, full-duplex transmission. *See also* half-duplex[2].

duplex channel *n.* A communications link that allows for duplex (two-way) transmission.

DV *n. See* digital video.

Dynamic Host Configuration Protocol *n. See* DHCP.

dynamic HTML *n.* A technology designed to add richness, interactivity, and graphical interest to Web pages by providing those pages with the ability to change and update themselves dynamically—that is, in response to user actions, without the need for repeated downloads from a server. This is done by enabling the interaction of HTML, cascading style sheets (CSS), and JavaScript. Examples of dynamic HTML actions include moving graphics on the page and displaying information, such as menus or tables, in response to mouse movements or clicks. Interoperability is governed by the World Wide Web Consortium (W3C) Document Object Model (DOM) specification, a platform- and language-neutral interface to ensure that programs and scripts can dynamically access and update the content, structure, and style of documents. *Acronym:* DHTML.

dynamic page *n.* An HTML document that contains animated GIFs, Java applets, or ActiveX controls. *See also* ActiveX control, GIF, HTML, Java applet.

dynamic routing *n.* Routing that adjusts automatically to the current conditions of a network. Dynamic routing typically uses one of several dynamic-routing protocols such as Routing Information Protocol (RIP) and Border Gateway Protocol (BGP). *Compare* static routing.

dynamic SLIP *n.* Short for **dynamic S**erial **L**ine **I**nternet **P**rotocol. Internet access under SLIP in which the user's IP address is not permanent but is reassigned from a pool each time the user connects. The number of IP addresses an Internet service provider needs to offer is reduced to the number of connections that can be in use at once, rather than the total number of subscribers. *See also* IP address, ISP, SLIP. *Compare* DHCP.

dynamic Web page *n.* A Web page that has fixed form but variable content, allowing it to be tailored to a customer's search criteria.

E

e- *prefix* Short for **e**lectronic. A prefix indicating that a word refers to the computer-based version of some traditionally nonelectronic term, as e-mail, e-commerce, and e-money.

EAI *n.* Acronym for **E**nterprise **A**pplication **I**ntegration. The process of coordinating the operation of the various programs, databases, and existing technologies of a business or enterprise so that they function as an efficient, business-wide system.

EBCDIC *n.* Acronym for **E**xtended **B**inary **C**oded **D**ecimal **I**nterchange **C**ode. An IBM code that uses 8 bits to represent 256 possible characters, including text, numbers, punctuation marks, and transmission control characters. It is used primarily in IBM mainframes and minicomputers. *Compare* ASCII.

eavesdropper *n. See* lurker.

e-bomb *n.* Short for **e**-mail **bomb**. A technique used by some hackers in which a target is put on a large number of mailing lists so that network traffic and storage are tied up by e-mail sent by other mailing list subscribers to the lists' recipients.

e-book *n.* Format allowing books and other large texts to be downloaded from a Web site and viewed digitally. Typically, reading an e-book requires using a small computer appliance that is about the size of a paperback book and consists of a display screen and basic controls. Users can bookmark, highlight, or annotate text, but rights management features may prevent users from e-mailing, printing, or otherwise sharing e-book contents. *Also called:* electronic book.

e-cash *n. See* e-money.

echo *n.* In communications, a signal transmitted back to the sender that is distinct from the original signal. Network connections can be tested by sending an echo back to the main computer.

echo cancellation *n.* A technique for eliminating unwanted incoming transmissions in a modem that are echoes of the modem's own transmission. The modem sends a modified, reversed version of its transmission on its receiving path, thus erasing echoes while leaving incoming data intact. Echo cancellation is standard in V.32 modems.

echo check *n.* In communications, a method for verifying the accuracy of transmitted data by retransmitting it to the sender, which compares the echoed signal with the original.

echo loop attack *n.* A form of denial of service (DoS) attack in which a connection is established between User Datagram Protocol (UDP) services on two or more host machines that bounce an increasing volume of packets back and forth. The echo loop attack ties up the host machines and causes network congestion.

echoplex *n.* In communications, a technique for error detection. The receiving station retransmits data back to the sender's screen, where it can be displayed visually to check for accuracy.

echo suppressor *n.* In communications, a method for preventing echoes in telephone lines. Echo suppressors inhibit signals from the listener to the speaker, creating a one-way channel. For modems that send and receive on the same frequency, the echo suppressor must be disabled to allow two-way transmission. This disabling produces the high-pitched tone heard in modem-to-modem connections.

ECML *n.* *See* Electronic Commerce Modeling Language.

e-commerce *n.* Short for **electronic commerce**. Commercial activity that takes place by means of computers connected through a network. Electronic commerce can occur between a user and a vendor through the Internet, an online information service, or a bulletin board system (BBS), or between vendor and customer computers through electronic data interchange (EDI). *Also called:* e-tail. *See also* EDI.

e-credit *n.* *See* electronic credit.

e-currency *n.* *See* e-money.

E

EDGE *n.* Acronym for **E**nhanced **D**ata Rates for **G**lobal **E**volution or **E**nhanced **D**ata Rates for **GSM** and TDMA **E**volution. A third-generation enhancement to the Global System for Mobile Communications (GSM) wireless service, which allows data, multimedia services, and applications to be delivered on broadband at rates up to 384 Kbps.

EDI *n.* Acronym for **E**lectronic **D**ata **I**nterchange. A standard for exchanging bundles of data between two companies via telephone lines or the Internet. EDI transmits much larger bundles of data than can be transmitted via e-mail. For EDI to be effective, users must agree on certain standards for formatting and exchanging information, such as the X.400 protocol. *See also* CCITT X series, standard (definition 1).

EDMS *n.* Acronym for **e**lectronic **d**ocument **m**anagement **s**ystem. *See* document management system.

.edu *n.* In the Internet's Domain Name System, the top-level domain that identifies addresses operated by four-year, degreed educational institutions. The domain name .edu appears as a suffix at the end of the address. In the United States, schools that offer kindergarten through high school classes use the top-level domain of .k12.us or just .us. *See also* DNS (definition 1), domain (definition 3). *Compare* .com, .gov, .mil, .net, .org.

edutainment *n.* Multimedia content in software, on CD-ROM, or on a Web site that purports to educate the user as well as entertain.

EFF *n.* *See* Electronic Frontier Foundation.

e-form *n.* Short for **electronic form**. An online document that contains blank spaces for a user to fill in with requested information and that can be submitted through a network to the organization requesting the information. On the Web, e-forms are often coded in CGI script and secured via encryption. *See also* CGI (definition 1).

ego-surfing *n.* The practice of using a Web search engine to search for one's own name on the Internet.

e-home *n. See* smart home.

EIA *n.* Acronym for Electronic Industries Association. An association based in Washington, D.C., with members from various electronics manufacturers. It sets standards for electronic components. RS-232-C, for example, is the EIA standard for connecting serial components. *See also* RS-232-C standard.

EJB *n. See* Enterprise JavaBeans.

electronic bulletin board *n. See* BBS (definition 1).

electronic cash *n. See* e-money.

electronic commerce *n. See* e-commerce.

E

Electronic Commerce Modeling Language *n.* A computer language developed by leading e-commerce companies as a standard for inputting e-wallet information into the payment fields of Web sites. This allows for one-click transfer of e-wallet information at compatible Web sites. *Acronym:* ECML.

electronic credit *n.* A form of electronic commerce involving credit card transactions carried out over the Internet. *Also called:* e-credit. *See also* e-commerce.

electronic data interchange *n. See* EDI.

electronic form *n. See* e-form.

Electronic Frontier Foundation *n.* A public advocacy organization dedicated to the defense of civil liberties for computer users. The organization was founded in 1990 by Mitchell Kapor and John Perry Barlow as a response to U.S. Secret Service raids on hackers. *Acronym:* EFF.

electronic funds transfer *n.* The transfer of money via automated teller machine, telephone lines, or Internet connection. Examples of electronic fund transfers include using a credit card to make purchases from an e-commerce site, or using an automated teller machine or automated telephone banking system to move funds between bank accounts. *Acronym:* EFT.

Electronic Industries Association *n. See* EIA.

electronic journal *n. See* journal.

electronic mail *n. See* e-mail[1].

electronic mail services *n.* Services that allow users, administrators, or daemons to send, receive, and process e-mail. *See also* daemon.

electronic office *n.* A term used especially in the late 1970s to mid-1980s to refer to a hypothetical paperless work environment to be brought about by the use of computers and communications devices.

Electronic Privacy Information Center *n. See* EPIC.

electronic publishing *n.* A general term for distributing information via electronic media, such as communications networks or CD-ROM.

Electronics Industries Association *n. See* EIA.

electronic storefront *n.* A business that displays its merchandise on the Internet and has provisions for contact or online sales.

electronic text *n. See* e-text.

element *n.* In markup languages such as HTML and SGML, the combination of a set of tags, any content contained between the tags, and any attributes the tags may have. Elements can be nested, one within the other. *See also* attribute (definition 3), HTML, markup language, SGML.

elm *n.* Short for electronic mail. A program for reading and composing e-mail on UNIX systems. The elm program has a full-screen editor, making it easier to use than the original mail program, but elm has largely been superseded by pine. *See also* e-mail[1]. *Compare* Eudora, pine.

e-mail[1] or **email** or **E-mail** *n.* **1.** Short for electronic mail. The exchange of text messages and computer files over a communications network, such as a local area network or the Internet, usually between computers or terminals. **2.** An electronic text message.

e-mail[2] or **email** or **E-mail** *vb.* To send an e-mail message.

e-mail address *n.* A string that identifies a user so that the user can receive Internet e-mail. An e-mail address typically consists of a name that identifies the user to the mail server, followed by an at sign (@) and the host name and domain name of the mail server. For example, if Anne E. Oldhacker has an account on the machine called baz at Foo Enterprises, she might have an e-mail address aeo@baz.foo.com, which would be pronounced "A E O at baz dot foo dot com."

e-mail filter *n.* A feature in e-mail-reading software that automatically sorts incoming mail into different folders or mailboxes based on information contained in the message. For example, all incoming mail from a user's Uncle Joe might be placed in a folder labeled "Uncle Joe." Filters may also be used either to block or accept e-mail from designated sources.

e-mail management system *n.* An automated e-mail response system used by an Internet-based business to sort incoming e-mail messages into predetermined categories and either reply to the sender with an appropriate response or direct the e-mail to a customer service representative. *Acronym:* EMS.

E

embedded hyperlink *n.* A link to a resource that is embedded within text or is associated with an image or an image map. *See also* hyperlink, image map.

e-money or **emoney** *n.* Short for electronic **money**. A generic name for the exchange of money through the Internet. *Also called:* cybercash, digicash, digital cash, e-cash, e-currency.

emotag *n.* In an e-mail message or newsgroup article, a letter, word, or phrase that is encased in angle brackets and that, like an emoticon, indicates the attitude the writer takes toward what he or she has written. Often emotags have opening and closing tags, similar to HTML tags, that enclose a phrase or one or more sentences. For example: <joke>You didn't think there would really be a joke here, did you?</joke>. Some emotags consist of a single tag, such as <grin>. *See also* emoticon, HTML.

emoticon *n.* A string of text characters that, when viewed sideways, form a face expressing a particular emotion. An emoticon is often used in an e-mail message or newsgroup post as a comment on the text that precedes it. Common emoticons include :-) or :) (meaning "I'm smiling at the joke here"), ;-) ("I'm winking and grinning at the joke here"), :-(("I'm sad about this"), :-7 ("I'm speaking with tongue in cheek"), :D or :-D (big smile; "I'm overjoyed"), and :-O (either a yawn of boredom or a mouth open in amazement). *Compare* emotag.

encoder *n.* **1.** In general, any hardware or software that encodes information—that is, converts the information to a particular form or format. For example, the Windows Media Encoder converts audio and video to a form that can be streamed to clients over a network. **2.** In reference to MP3 digital audio in particular, technology that converts a WAV audio file into an MP3 file. An MP3 encoder compresses a sound file to a much smaller size, about one-twelfth as large as the original, without a perceptible drop in quality. *Also called:* MP3 encoder. *See also* MP3, WAV. *Compare* rip, ripper.

encryption *n.* The process of encoding data to prevent unauthorized access, especially during transmission. Encryption is usually based on one or more keys, or codes, that are essential for decoding, or returning the data to readable form. The U.S. National Bureau of Standards created a complex encryption standard, Data Encryption Standard (DES), which is based on a 56-bit variable that provides for more than 70 quadrillion unique keys to encrypt documents. *See also* DES.

encryption key *n.* A sequence of data that is used to encrypt other data and that, consequently, must be used for the data's decryption. *See also* decryption, encryption.

End-User License Agreement *n.* A legal agreement between a software manufacturer and the software's purchaser with regard to terms of distribution, resale, and restricted use. *Acronym:* EULA.

enhanced Category 5 cable *n.* *See* Category 5e cable.

Enhanced Data Rates for Global Evolution *n.* *See* EDGE.

Enhanced Data Rates for GSM and TDMA Evolution *n.* *See* EDGE.

Enterprise JavaBeans *n.* An application programming interface (API) designed to extend the JavaBean component model to cross-platform, server-side applications that can run on the various systems usually present in an enterprise environment. Enterprise JavaBeans are defined in the Enterprise JavaBean specification released by Sun Microsystems, Inc. The goal of the API is to provide developers with a means of applying Java technology to the creation of reusable server components for business applications, such as transaction processing. *Acronym:* EJB. *See also* Java, JavaBean.

enterprise computing *n.* In a large enterprise such as a corporation, the use of computers in a network or series of interconnected networks that generally encompass a variety of different platforms, operating systems, protocols, and network architectures. *Also called:* enterprise networking.

enterprise network *n.* In a large enterprise such as a corporation, the network (or interconnected networks) of computer systems owned by the enterprise, which fills the enterprise's various computing needs. This network can span diverse geographical locations and usually encompasses a range of platforms, operating systems, protocols, and network architectures.

enterprise networking *n. See* enterprise computing.

EPIC *n.* Short for Electronic Privacy Information Center. A public-interest research center based in Washington, D.C., dedicated to directing public attention toward civil liberties and online privacy related to electronic communication, cryptography, and related technologies.

error checking *n.* A method for detecting discrepancies between transmitted and received data during file transfer.

error message *n.* A message from the system or program indicating that an error requiring resolution has occurred.

ESP IEEE standard *n.* Short for Encapsulating Security Payload **IEEE standard**. A standard for providing integrity and confidentiality to IP (Internet Protocol) datagrams. In some circumstances, it can also provide authentication to IP datagrams. *See also* authentication, IEEE, IP.

ESRB *n.* Acronym for Entertainment Software Rating Board. An independent, self-regulatory body providing ratings to the public and support to companies in the interactive software entertainment industry. The ESRB provides ratings for computer games and other interactive products such as Web sites, online games, and interactive chat.

e-tail *n. See* e-commerce.

e-text *n.* Short for electronic **text**. A book or other text-based work that is available on line in an electronic media format. An e-text can be read online or downloaded to a user's computer for offline reading. *See also* e-zine.

Ethernet *n.* **1.** The IEEE 802.3 standard for contention networks. Ethernet uses a bus or star topology and relies on the form of access known as Carrier Sense Multiple

E

Access with Collision Detection (CSMA/CD) to regulate communication line traffic. Network nodes are linked by coaxial cable, by fiberoptic cable, or by twisted-pair wiring. Data is transmitted in variable-length frames containing delivery and control information and up to 1500 bytes of data. The Ethernet standard provides for baseband transmission at 10 megabits (10 million bits) per second and is available in various forms, including those known as Thin Ethernet, Thick Ethernet, 10Base2, 10Base5, 10Base-F, and 10Base-T. The IEEE standard dubbed 802.3z, or Gigabit Ethernet, operates at 10 times 100 Mbps speed. *See also* ALOHAnet, baseband, bus network, coaxial cable, contention, CSMA/CD, Gigabit Ethernet, twisted-pair cable. **2.** A widely used local area network system developed by Xerox in 1976, from which the IEEE 802.3 standard was developed.

Ethernet/802.3 *n.* The IEEE standard for 10- or 100-Mbps transmissions over an Ethernet network. Ethernet/802.3 defines both hardware and data packet construction specifications. *See also* Ethernet.

Eudora *n.* An e-mail client program originally developed as freeware for Macintosh computers by Steve Dorner at the University of Illinois, now maintained in both freeware and commercial versions for both Macintosh and Windows by Qualcomm, Inc.

EULA *n. See* End-User License Agreement.

event handler *n.* **1.** A method within a program that is called automatically whenever a particular event occurs. **2.** A core function in JavaScript that handles client-side events. It is the mechanism that causes a script to react to an event. For example, common JavaScript event handlers coded in Web pages include onClick, onMouseOver, and onLoad. When the user initiates the action, such as a mouse over, the event handler executes, or carries out, the desired outcome. **3.** In Java applets, rather than having a specific starting point, the applet has a main loop where it waits for an event or series of events (keystroke, mouse click, and so on). Upon occurrence of the event, the event handler carries out the instructions specified. *See also* applet, client, JavaScript.

event log *n.* A file that contains information and error messages for all activities on the computer.

event logging *n.* The process of recording an audit entry in the audit trail whenever certain events occur, such as starting and stopping, or users logging on and off and accessing resources. *See also* service.

e-wallet *n.* A program used in e-commerce that stores a customer's shipping and billing information to facilitate Web-based financial transactions. An e-wallet allows customers to instantly enter encrypted shipping and billing information when placing an order, rather than manually typing the information into a form on a Web page.

Excite *n.* A World Wide Web search engine developed by Excite, Inc. After conducting a search, Excite provides both a summary of each matching Web site it has located and a link to more information of the same type.

Explorer *n. See* Internet Explorer, Windows Explorer.

ExploreZip *n.* A destructive virus that attacks computers running Windows, where it first appears as an e-mail attachment named zipped_files.exe. ExploreZip affects local drives, mapped drives, and accessible network machines and destroys both document and source-code files by opening and immediately closing them, leaving a zero-byte file. Described as both a Trojan horse (because it requires the victim to open the attachment) and a worm (because it can propagate itself in certain instances), ExploreZip spreads by mailing itself to the return address of every unread e-mail in the inbox of the computer's e-mail program, as well as by searching for—and copying itself to—the Windows directory on mapped drives and networked machines. *See also* Trojan horse, virus, worm.

Extensible Forms Description Language or **eXtensible Forms Description Language** *n. See* XFDL.

Extensible Hypertext Markup Language *n. See* XHTML.

Extensible Markup Language or **eXtensible Markup Language** *n. See* XML.

extensible style language *n. See* XSL.

eXtensible Stylesheet Language *n. See* XSL.

eXtensible Stylesheet Language Formatting Objects *n. See* XSL-FO.

Extensible Stylesheets Language-Transformations *n. See* XSLT.

exterior gateway protocol *n.* A protocol used by routers (gateways) on separate, independent networks for distributing routing information between and among themselves—for example, between hosts on the Internet. *Acronym:* EGP. *Also called:* external gateway protocol. *Compare* Interior Gateway Protocol.

External Gateway Protocol *n.* A protocol for distributing information regarding availability to the routers and gateways that interconnect networks. *Acronym:* EGP. *See also* gateway, router.

external gateway protocol *n. See* exterior gateway protocol.

external modem *n.* A stand-alone modem that is connected via cable to a computer's serial port. *See also* internal modem.

extranet *n.* An extension of a corporate intranet using World Wide Web technology to facilitate communication with the corporation's suppliers and customers. An extranet allows customers and suppliers to gain limited access to a company's intranet in order to enhance the speed and efficiency of their business relationship. *See also* intranet.

eyeballs *n.* The individuals or the number of individuals who view a Web site or its advertising.

e-zine or **ezine** *n.* Short for electronic magazine. A digital publication available on the Internet, a bulletin board system (BBS), or other online service, often free of charge.

F

F2F *adv.* Short for **f**ace-**to**-**f**ace. In person, rather than over the Internet. The term is used in e-mail.

face time *n.* Time spent dealing face-to-face with another person, rather than communicating electronically.

failback *n.* In a cluster network system (one with two or more interconnected servers), the process of restoring resources and services to their primary server after they have been temporarily relocated to a backup system while repairs were implemented on the original host. *See also* cluster, failover.

failover *vb.* In a cluster network system (one with two or more interconnected servers), to relocate an overloaded or failed resource, such as a server, a disk drive, or a network, to its redundant, or backup, component. For example, when one server in a two-server system stops processing because of a power outage or other malfunction, the system automatically fails over to the second server, with little or no disruption to the users. *See also* cluster, failback.

fair queuing *n.* A technique used to improve quality of service that gives each session flow passing through a network device a fair share of network resources. With fair queuing, no prioritization occurs. *Acronym:* FQ. *See also* quality of service, queuing. *Compare* weighted fair queuing.

fair use *n.* A legal doctrine describing the boundaries of legitimate use of copyrighted software or other published material.

fanzine *n.* A magazine, distributed on line or by mail, that is produced by and devoted to fans of a particular group, person, or activity. *See also* e-zine.

FAQ *n.* Acronym for **f**requently **a**sked **q**uestions. A document listing common questions and answers on a particular subject. FAQs are often posted on Internet newsgroups where new participants tend to ask the same questions that regular readers have answered many times.

FARNET *n. See* Federation of American Research Networks.

Fast Ethernet *n. See* 100Base-X.

fast packet *n.* A standard for high-speed network technology that utilizes fast switching of fixed-length cells or packets for real-time transmission of data. *Also called:* Asynchronous Transfer Mode, ATM. *See also* packet (definition 2), packet switching.

fast packet switching *adj.* Of, describing, or pertaining to high-speed packet-switching networks that perform little or no error checking. The term is often, however, restricted to high-speed networking technologies, such as ATM, that transmit fixed-length cells rather than including those, such as frame relay, that transmit variable-length packets.

Fast SCSI *n.* A form of the SCSI-2 interface that can transfer data 8 bits at a time at up to 10 megabytes per second. The Fast SCSI connector has 50 pins. *Also called:* Fast SCSI-2. *See also* SCSI, SCSI-2. *Compare* Fast/Wide SCSI, Wide SCSI.

Fast/Wide SCSI *n.* A form of the SCSI-2 interface that can transfer data 16 bits at a time at up to 20 megabytes per second. The Fast/Wide SCSI connector has 68 pins. *Also called:* Fast/Wide SCSI-2. *See also* SCSI, SCSI-2. *Compare* Fast SCSI, Wide SCSI.

fat client *n.* In a client/server architecture, a client machine that performs most or all of the processing, with little or none performed by the server. The client handles presentation and functions, and the server manages data and access to it. *See also* client (definition 3), client/server architecture, server (definition 2), thin server. *Compare* fat server, thin client.

FAT file system *n.* The system used by MS-DOS to organize and manage files. The FAT (file allocation table) is a data structure that MS-DOS creates on the disk when the disk is formatted. When MS-DOS stores a file on a formatted disk, the operating system places information about the stored file in the FAT so that MS-DOS can retrieve the file later when requested. The FAT is the only file system MS-DOS can use; OS/2, Windows NT, and Windows 9x operating systems can use the FAT file system in addition to their own file systems (HPFS, NTFS, and VFAT, respectively). *See also* HPFS, NTFS, VFAT, Windows.

fat server *n.* In a client/server architecture, a server machine that performs most of the processing, with little or none performed by the client. Applications logic and data reside on the server, and presentation services are handled by the client. *See also* client (definition 3), client/server architecture, server (definition 2), thin client. *Compare* fat client, thin server.

F

fault resilience *n. See* high availability.

fault tolerance *n.* The ability of a computer or an operating system to respond to a catastrophic event or fault, such as a power outage or a hardware failure, in a way that ensures that no data is lost and any work in progress is not corrupted. This can be accomplished with a battery-backed power supply, backup hardware, provisions in the operating system, or any combination of these. In a fault-tolerant network, the system has the ability either to continue the system's operation without loss of data or to shut the system down and restart it, recovering all processing that was in progress when the fault occurred.

Favorites folder *n.* In Microsoft Internet Explorer, a collection of shortcuts to Web sites that a user has selected for future reference. Other Web browsers refer to this collection by other names, such as bookmarks or hotlists. *See also* bookmark file (definition 1), Internet Explorer, URL. *Compare* bookmark (definition 2), hotlist.

fax modem *n.* A modem that sends (and possibly receives) data encoded in a fax format (typically CCITT fax format), which a fax machine or another modem decodes and converts to an image. The image must already have been encoded on the host computer. Text and graphic documents can be converted into fax format by special software usually provided with the modem; paper documents must first be scanned in. Fax modems may be internal or external and may combine fax and conventional modem capabilities. *See also* modem.

fax server *n.* A computer on a network capable of sending and receiving fax transmissions to and from other computers on the network. *See also* server (definition 1).

FCC *n.* Acronym for Federal Communications Commission. The U.S. agency created by the Communications Act of 1934, which regulates interstate and international wire, radio, and other broadcast transmissions, including telephone, telegraph, and telecommunications.

FDDI *n.* Acronym for Fiber Distributed Data Interface. A standard developed by the American National Standards Institute (ANSI) for high-speed fiber-optic LANs (local area networks). FDDI provides specifications for transmission rates of 100 megabits (100 million bits) per second on networks based on the token ring standard. *See also* token ring network.

FDDI II *n.* Acronym for Fiber Distributed Data Interface. An extension of the FDDI standard, FDDI II contains additional specifications for the real-time transmission of analog data in digitized form for high-speed fiber-optic LANs (local area networks). *See also* FDDI.

FDHP *n.* Acronym for Full Duplex Handshaking Protocol. A protocol used by duplex modems to determine the source type of the transmission and match it. *See also* duplex[1], handshake.

Federal Communications Commission *n. See* FCC.

Federal Information Processing Standards *n.* A system of standards, guidelines, and technical methods for information processing within the U.S. federal government. *Acronym:* FIPS.

Federal Internet Exchange *n. See* FIX.

federated database *n.* A database to which scientists contribute their findings and knowledge regarding a particular field or problem. A federated database is designed for scientific collaboration on problems of such scope that they are difficult or impossible for an individual to solve. *See also* database.

Federation of American Research Networks *n.* A nonprofit association of internetworking technology companies in the United States that serves as a national advocate for internetworking, with a primary focus on the education, research, and related communities. *Acronym:* FARNET. *See also* internetwork.

Federation on Computing in the United States *n.* The U.S. representative of the International Federation of Information Processing (IFIP). *Acronym:* FOCUS. *See also* IFIP.

feed *n. See* newsfeed.

fiberoptic cable or **fiber-optic cable** *n.* A form of cable used in networks that transmits signals optically, rather than electrically as do coaxial and twisted-pair cable. The light-conducting heart of a fiberoptic cable is a fine glass or plastic fiber called the core. This core is surrounded by a refractive layer called the cladding that effectively traps the light and keeps it bouncing along the central fiber. Outside both the core and the cladding is a final layer of plastic or plastic-like material called the coat, or jacket. Fiberoptic cable can transmit clean signals at speeds as high as 2 Gbps. Because it transmits light, not electricity, it is also immune to eavesdropping.

fiber to the curb *n. See* FTTC.

fiber to the home *n. See* FTTH.

Fidonet *n.* **1.** A protocol for sending e-mail, newsgroup postings, and files over telephone lines. The protocol originated on the Fido BBS, initiated in 1984 by Tom Jennings, and maintaining low costs has been a factor in its subsequent development. Fidonet can exchange e-mail with the Internet. **2.** The network of BBSs, private companies, NGOs (nongovernment organizations), and individuals that use the Fidonet protocol.

file protection *n.* A process or device by which the existence and integrity of a file are maintained. Methods of file protection range from allowing read-only access and assigning passwords to covering the write-protect notch on a disk and locking away floppy disks holding sensitive files.

file server *n.* A file-storage device on a local area network that is accessible to all users on the network. Unlike a disk server, which appears to the user as a remote disk drive, a file server is a sophisticated device that not only stores files but manages them and maintains order as network users request files and make changes to them. To deal with the tasks of handling multiple—sometimes simultaneous—requests for files, a file server contains a processor and controlling software as well as a disk drive for storage. On local area networks, a file server is often a computer with a large hard disk that is dedicated only to the task of managing shared files. *Compare* disk server.

File Server for Macintosh *n.* An AppleTalk network integration service that allows Macintosh clients and personal computers clients to share files. *Also called:* MacFile.

File Transfer Protocol *n. See* FTP[1] (definition 1).

film at 11 *n.* A phrase sometimes seen in newsgroups. An allusion to a brief newsbreak on TV that refers to a top news story that will be covered in full on the 11 o'clock news, it is used sarcastically to ridicule a previous article's lack of timeliness or newsworthiness. *See also* newsgroup.

filter *n.* **1.** A program or set of features within a program that reads its standard or designated input, transforms the input in some desired way, and then writes the output to its standard or designated output destination. A database filter, for example, might flag information of a certain age. **2.** In communications and electronics, hardware or software that selectively passes certain elements of a signal and eliminates or minimizes others. A filter on a communications network, for example, must be designed to transmit a certain frequency but attenuate (dampen) frequencies above it (a lowpass filter), those below it (a highpass filter), or those above and below it (a bandpass filter). **3.** A pattern or mask through which data is passed to weed out specified items. For instance, a filter used in e-mail or in retrieving newsgroup messages can allow users to filter out messages from other users. *See also* e-mail filter.

finger¹ *n.* An Internet utility, originally limited to UNIX but now available on many other platforms, that enables a user to obtain information on other users who may be at other sites (if those sites permit access by finger). Given an e-mail address, finger returns the user's full name, an indication of whether or not the user is currently logged on, and any other information the user has chosen to supply as a profile. Given a first or last name, finger returns the logon names of users whose first or last names match.

finger² *vb.* To obtain information on a user by means of the finger program.

fingerprint¹ *vb.* To scan a computer system to discover what operating system (OS) the computer is running. By detecting a computer's OS through fingerprinting, a hacker is better able to specify attacks on system vulnerabilities and therefore better able to plan an attack on that system. A hacker may use several different fingerprinting schemes separately and in tandem to pinpoint the OS of a target computer.

fingerprint² *n.* Information embedded or attached to a file or image to uniquely identify it. *Compare* digital watermark.

FIPS *n. See* Federal Information Processing Standards.

FIPS 140-1 *n.* Acronym for **F**ederal **I**nformation **P**rocessing **S**tandard 140-1. A U.S. Government standard, issued by the National Institute of Standards and Technology (NIST), entitled Security Requirements for Cryptographic Modules. FIPS 140-1 defines four levels of security requirements related to cryptographic hardware and software modules within computer and telecommunications systems used for sensitive but unclassified data. The four security levels range from basic module design through increasingly stringent levels of physical security. The standard covers such security-related features as hardware and software security, cryptographic algorithms, and management of encryption keys. FIPS 140-1products can be validated for federal use in both the United States and Canada after independent testing under the Cryptographic Module Validation (CMV) Program, developed and jointly adopted by NIST and the Canadian Communication Security Establishment. *See also* cryptography.

firewall *n.* A security system intended to protect an organization's network against external threats, such as hackers, coming from another network, such as the Internet. Usually a combination of hardware and software, a firewall prevents computers in the organization's network from communicating directly with computers external to the network and vice versa. Instead, all communication is routed through a proxy server outside of the organization's network, and the proxy server decides whether it is safe to let a particular message or file pass through to the organization's network. *See also* proxy server.

firewall sandwich *n.* The use of load-balancing appliances on both sides of Internet-worked firewalls to distribute both inbound and outbound traffic among the firewalls. The firewall sandwich architecture helps to prevent firewalls from degrading network performance and creating a single point of network failure. *See also* firewall, load balancing.

FireWire *n.* A high-speed serial bus from Apple that implements the IEEE 1394 standard. *See also* IEEE 1394.

FIR port *n.* Short for **f**ast **i**nfrared **port**. A wireless I/O port, most common on a portable computer, that exchanges data with an external device using infrared light. *See also* infrared.

FIRST *n.* Acronym for **F**orum of **I**ncident **R**esponse and Security **T**eams. An organization within the Internet Society (ISOC) that coordinates with CERT in order to encourage information sharing and a unified response to security threats. *See also* CERT, Internet Society.

first in, first out *n.* A method of processing a queue, in which items are removed in the same order in which they were added—the first in is the first out. Such an order is typical of a list of documents waiting to be printed. *Acronym:* FIFO. *See also* queue. *Compare* last in, first out.

fishbowl *n.* A secure area within a computer system in which intruders can be contained and monitored. A fishbowl is typically set up by a security administrator to impersonate important applications or information so that the system administrator can learn more about hackers who have broken into the network without the hacker learning more about or damaging the system. *See also* honeypot.

five-nines availability *n.* The availability of a system 99.999 percent of the time. *See also* high availability.

FIX *n.* Acronym for **F**ederal **I**nternet **E**xchange. A connection point between the U.S. government's various internets and the Internet. There are two Federal Internet Exchanges: FIX West, in Mountain View, California; and FIX East, in College Park, Maryland. Together, they link the backbones of MILNET, ESnet (the TCP/IP network of the Department of Energy), and NSInet (NASA Sciences Internet) with NSFnet. *See also* backbone (definition 1), MILNET, NSFnet, TCP/IP.

flame[1] *n.* An abusive or personally insulting e-mail message or newsgroup posting.

flame[2] *vb.* **1.** To send an abusive or personally insulting e-mail message or newsgroup posting. **2.** To criticize personally by means of e-mail messages or newsgroup postings.

flame bait *n.* A posting to a mailing list, newsgroup, or other online conference that is likely to provoke flames, often because it expresses a controversial opinion on a highly emotional topic. *See also* flame[1], flame war. *Compare* troll.

flamefest *n.* A series of inflammatory messages or articles in a newsgroup or other online conference.

flamer *n.* A person who sends or posts abusive messages via e-mail, in newsgroups and other online forums, and in online chats. *See also* chat[1] (definition 1), newsgroup.

flame war *n.* A discussion in a mailing list, newsgroup, or other online conference that has turned into a protracted exchange of flames. *See also* flame[1].

F

flooding *n.* The networking technique of forwarding a frame onto all ports of a switch except the port on which it arrived. Flooding can be used for robust data distribution and route establishment. *Also called:* flood routing.

flow analysis *n.* A method of tracing the movement of different types of information through a computer system, especially with regard to security and the controls applied to ensure the integrity of the information.

FOCUS *n. See* Federation on Computing in the United States.

follow-up *n.* A post to a newsgroup that replies to an article. The follow-up has the same subject line as the original article, with the prefix "Re:" attached. An article and all of its follow-ups, in the order they were received, constitute a thread, which a user can read together using a newsreader.

Fortezza *n.* A cryptographic technology developed by the United States National Security Agency (NSA) for enabling secure communication of sensitive information. Fortezza is based on encryption, authentication, and other technologies built into a personalized card known as the Fortezza Crypto Card that can be inserted into a PCMCIA slot on a computer. This card works with Fortezza-enabled hardware and software to secure applications such as e-mail, Web browsing, e-commerce, and file encryption. An RS-232 token can also be used with legacy systems that do not have card-reading capability. The technology is supported by a number of commercial vendors.

F

fortune cookie *n.* A proverb, prediction, joke, or other phrase chosen at random from a collection of such items and output to the screen by a program. Fortune cookies are sometimes displayed at logon and logoff times by UNIX systems.

forum *n.* A medium provided by an online service or BBS for users to carry on written discussions of a particular topic by posting messages and replying to them. On the Internet, the most widespread forums are the newsgroups in Usenet.

Forum of Incident Response and Security Teams *n. See* FIRST.

forward *vb.* In e-mail, to send a received message, either modified or in its entirety, to a new recipient.

four-nines availability *n.* The availability of a system 99.99 percent of the time. *See* high availability.

FQ *n. See* fair queuing.

fractional T1 *n.* A shared connection to a T1 line, in which only a fraction of the 24 T1 voice or data channels are used. *Acronym:* FT1. *See also* T1.

fraggle attack *n. See* smurf attack.

frame *n.* **1.** In asynchronous serial communications, a unit of transmission that is sometimes measured in elapsed time and begins with the start bit that precedes a character and ends with the last stop bit that follows the character. **2.** In synchronous communications, a package of information transmitted as a single unit. Every frame follows the same basic organization and contains control information, such as synchronizing characters, station address, and an error-checking value, as well as a variable amount of data. For example, a frame used in the widely accepted HDLC and related SDLC protocols begins and ends with a unique flag (01111110). *See also* HDLC, SDLC. **3.** A single screen-sized image that can be displayed in sequence with other, slightly different, images to create animated drawings. **4.** The storage required to hold one screen-sized image of text, graphics, or both. **5.** A rectangular space containing, and defining the proportions of, a graphic. **6.** A rectangular section of the page displayed by a Web browser that is a separate HTML document from the rest of the page. Web pages can have multiple frames, each of which is a separate document. Associated with each frame are the same capabilities as for an unframed Web page, including scrolling and linking to another frame or Web site; these capabilities can be used independently of other frames on the page. Frames, which were introduced in Netscape Navigator 2.0, are often used as a table of contents for one or more HTML documents on a Web site. Most current Web browsers support frames, although older ones do not. *See also* HTML document, Web browser.

frame relay *n.* A packet-switching protocol for use on WANs (wide area networks). Frame relay transmits variable-length packets at up to 2 Mbps over predetermined, set paths known as PVCs (permanent virtual circuits). It is a variant of X.25 but dispenses with some of X.25's error detection for the sake of speed. *See also* ATM (definition 1), X.25.

frame relay access device *n. See* frame relay assembler/disassembler.

frame relay assembler/disassembler *n.* A combination channel service unit/ digital service unit (CSU/DSU) and router that connects an internal network to a frame relay connection. The device converts data (which may be in the form of IP packets or conform to some other network protocol) into packets for transmission over the frame relay network and converts such packets back to the original data. Since this type of connection is direct—without a firewall—other network protection is necessary. *Acronym:* FRAD. *See also* firewall, frame relay, IP.

frame source *n.* In the HTML frames environment, a contents document that will look for the source document to display within a frame drawn by the local browser. *See also* HTML.

frames page *n.* A Web page that divides a Web browser window into different scrollable areas that can independently display several Web pages. One window can remain unchanged, while the other windows change based on hyperlinks that the user selects.

FreeBSD *n.* A freely distributed version of BSD UNIX (Berkeley Software Distribution UNIX) for IBM and IBM-compatible PCs. *See also* BSD UNIX.

freenet or **free-net** *n.* A community-based computer BBS and Internet service provider, usually operated by volunteers and providing free access to subscribers in the community or access for a very small fee. Many freenets are operated by public libraries or universities. *See also* ISP.

free software *n.* Software, complete with source code, that is distributed freely to users who are in turn free to use, modify, and distribute it, provided that all alterations

F

are clearly marked and that the name and copyright notice of the original author are not deleted or modified in any way. Unlike freeware, which a user might or might not have permission to modify, free software is protected by a license agreement. Free software is a concept pioneered by the Free Software Foundation in Cambridge, Massachusetts. *Compare* freeware, open source, public-domain software, shareware.

Free Software Foundation *n.* An advocacy organization founded by Richard Stallman, dedicated to eliminating restrictions on people's right to use, copy, modify, and redistribute computer programs for noncommercial purposes. The Free Software Foundation is the maintainer of GNU software, which is UNIX-like software that can be freely distributed. *See also* GNU.

freeware *n.* A computer program given away free of charge and often made available on the Internet or through user groups. An independent program developer might offer a product as freeware either for personal satisfaction or to assess its reception among interested users. Freeware developers often retain all rights to their software, and users are not necessarily free to copy or distribute it further. *Compare* free software, public-domain software, shareware.

frequently asked questions *n. See* FAQ.

fringeware *n.* Freeware whose reliability and value are questionable. *See also* freeware.

front end *n.* **1.** In a client/server application, the part of the program that runs on the client. *See also* client/server architecture. *Compare* back end (definition 1). **2.** In networking, a client computer or the processing that takes place on it. *Compare* back end (definition 2).

front-end processor *n.* **1.** Generally, a computer or processing unit that produces and manipulates data before another processor receives it. **2.** In communications, a computer that is located between communications lines and a main (host) computer and is used to relieve the host of housekeeping chores related to communications; sometimes considered synonymous with communications controller. A front-end processor is dedicated entirely to handling transmitted information, including error detection and control; receipt, transmission, and possibly encoding of messages; and management of the lines running to and from other devices. *See also* communications controller.

FTAM *n.* Acronym for **F**ile-**T**ransfer **A**ccess and **M**anagement. A communications standard for transferring files between different makes and models of computer.

FTP¹ *n.* **1.** Acronym for **F**ile **T**ransfer **P**rotocol, a fast, application-level protocol widely used for copying files to and from remote computer systems on a network using TCP/IP, such as the Internet. This protocol also allows users to use FTP commands to work with files, such as listing files and directories on the remote system. *See also* TCP/IP. **2.** A common logon ID for anonymous FTP.

FTP² *vb.* To download files from or upload files to remote computer systems, via the Internet's File Transfer Protocol. The user needs an FTP client to transfer files to and from the remote system, which must have an FTP server. Generally, the user also needs to establish an account on the remote system to FTP files, although many FTP sites permit the use of anonymous FTP. *See also* FTP client, FTP server.

FTP client or **ftp client** *n.* A program that enables the user to upload and download files to and from an FTP site over a network, such as the Internet, using the File Transfer Protocol. *See also* FTP[1] (definition 1). *Compare* FTP server.

FTP commands *n.* Commands that are part of the File Transfer Protocol. *See also* FTP[1] (definition 1).

FTP program or **ftp program** *n. See* FTP client.

FTP server *n.* A file server that uses the File Transfer Protocol to permit users to upload or download files through the Internet or any other TCP/IP network. *See also* file server, FTP[1] (definition 1), TCP/IP. *Compare* FTP client.

FTP site *n.* The collection of files and programs residing on an FTP server. *See also* FTP[1] (definition 1), FTP server.

FTTC *n.* Acronym for fiber to the curb. The installation and use of fiber-optic cable from the central office (CO) to within a thousand feet of a user's home or office. With FTTC, coaxial cable or another medium carries the signals from the curb into the home or office. FTTC is a replacement for Plain Old Telephone Service (POTS) that enables the distribution of telephony, cable TV, Internet access, multimedia, and other communications over one line. *Compare* FTTH.

FTTH *n.* Acronym for fiber to the home. The installation and use of fiber-optic cable from the central office (CO) directly into a user's home or office. FTTH is a replacement for Plain Old Telephone Service (POTS) that enables the distribution of telephony, cable TV, Internet access, multimedia, and other communications over one line. *Compare* FTTC.

fulfillment *n.* The process of delivering goods and services ordered by a consumer. Fulfillment involves establishing a reliable procedure for tracking orders and delivering products.

fulfillment service provider *n.* A company that provides fulfillment services for an e-commerce Web site by tracking, packing, and shipping goods ordered via the e-commerce site. A fulfillment service provider allows an e-business to save time, costs, and labor by outsourcing order processing.

FWIW *adv.* Acronym for for what it's worth. An expression used in e-mail and newsgroups.

FYI *n.* **1.** Acronym for for your information. An expression used in e-mail and newsgroups to introduce information that is thought to be useful to the reader. **2.** An electronic document distributed through InterNIC like a request for comments (RFC), but intended to explain an Internet standard or feature for users rather than to define it for developers, as the RFC does. *See also* InterNIC. *Compare* RFC.

F

G

Game Boy *n.* Nintendo Corporation's popular battery-powered, portable handheld gaming system first introduced in 1990 and updated frequently. Games are supplied on cartridges. The latest Game Boy, Game Boy Advance, features a 32-bit ARM CPU with embedded memory and a 2.9-inch TFT reflective screen with 240x160 resolution. *See also* computer game.

GameCube *n.* Nintendo Corporation's console gaming system. It features a developer-friendly format and introduces 1T-RAM technology, which reduces delays to the main memory and the graphics LSI mixed memory. The microprocessor is a custom IBM Power PC "Gekko" featuring a secondary cache (Level One: Instruction 32 KB, Data 32 KB (8-way); Level Two: 256 KB (2-way)). Games are supplied on a GameCube game disc. *See also* computer game, console game. *Compare* Dreamcast, PlayStation, Xbox.

gamer *n.* Refers to a person who plays games, sometimes role-playing games or trading card games; often a person who plays computer, console, arcade, or online games as a primary hobby or avocation.

gated *adj.* Transmitted through a gateway to a subsequent network or service. For example, a mailing list on BITNET may be gated to a newsgroup on the Internet.

gateway *n.* A device that connects networks using different communications protocols so that information can be passed from one to the other. A gateway both transfers information and converts it to a form compatible with the protocols used by the receiving network. *Compare* bridge.

gateway page *n. See* doorway page.

gatored *vb.* To have been the victim of a hijackware program that seized control of an Internet shopping or surfing experience and caused the victim's browser to display ads and Web sites chosen by the program. Users may be gatored when they have unknowingly installed a program or plug-in with a hidden marketing agenda, which intrudes on the user's Web shopping to display ads or Web sites promoting competing products. The term gatored comes from the name of a plug-in that was one of the first hijackware products to be used by Web marketers. *See also* hijackware.

Gecko *n.* A cross-platform Web browsing engine introduced by Netscape in 1998, distributed and developed as open-source software through Mozilla.org. Designed to be small, fast, and modular, the Gecko engine supports Internet standards including HTML, cascading style sheets (CSS), XML, and the Document Object Model (DOM). Gecko is the layout engine in Netscape's Communicator software.

GENA *n.* Acronym for General Event Notification Architecture. An extension to HTTP defined by an Internet Engineering Task Force (IETF) Internet-Draft and used to communicate events over the Internet between HTTP resources. Universal Plug and Play (UPnP) services use GENA to send XML event messages to control points.

General Event Notification Architecture *n. See* GENA.

General Inter-ORB Protocol *n. See* IIOP.

General Packet Radio Service *n. See* GPRS.

General Public License *n.* The agreement under which software, such as the GNU (GNU's Not UNIX) utilities, is distributed by the Free Software Foundation. Anyone who has a copy of such a program may redistribute it to another party and may charge for distribution and support services, but may not restrict the other party from doing the same. A user may modify the program, but if the modified version is distributed, it must be clearly identified as such and is also covered under the General Public License. A distributor must also either provide source code or indicate where source code can be obtained. *Acronym:* GPL. *Also called:* copyleft. *See also* free software, Free Software Foundation, GNU.

Genie *n.* An online information service originally developed by General Electric (GE) Information Services as GEnie (**G**eneral **E**lectric **n**etwork for **i**nformation **e**xchange); currently owned and provided by IDT Corporation as Genie (lowercase *e*). Genie provides business information, forums, home shopping, and news and can exchange e-mail with the Internet.

GEO *n. See* geostationary orbit satellite.

GEOS *n.* An operating system developed by Geoworks Corporation, used in some handheld devices. GEOS is designed to provide broad functionality in resource-constrained environments that have limited storage or memory capability, such as enhanced phones, some Internet access devices, and PDAs and other handheld computers.

geostationary orbit satellite *n.* A communications satellite that rotates with the earth and thus appears to remain fixed, or stationary, over a particular location. This travels in orbit 22,282 miles above the equator, where its period of rotation matches the earth's rotation. The service area, or *footprint,* of the satellite is approximately one-third of the earth's surface, so global satellite coverage can be achieved with three satellites in orbit. In a voice communication system, a round-trip to and from this satellite takes approximately 250 milliseconds. Satellite-based data communications are necessary for delivering high bandwidth options to rural areas. *Acronym:* GEO.

GGA *n.* Acronym for **G**ood **G**ame **A**ll. GGA is often used in online and chat games at the conclusion of play. *See also* role-playing game.

ghost *n.* An abandoned or no-longer-maintained Web site that remains accessible to visitors.

.gif *n.* The file extension that identifies GIF bit map images. *See also* GIF.

GIF *n.* **1.** Acronym for **G**raphics **I**nterchange **F**ormat. A graphics file format developed by CompuServe and used for transmitting raster images on the Internet. An image may contain up to 256 colors, including a transparent color. The size of the file depends on the number of colors actually used. The LZW compression method is used to reduce the file size still further. **2.** A graphic stored as a file in the GIF format.

G

GIF animation *n.* A file containing a series of graphics that are displayed in rapid sequence in a Web browser to appear as though they are a moving picture.

Gigabit Ethernet *n.* The IEEE standard dubbed 802.3z, which includes support for transmission rates of 1 Gbps (gigabit per second)—1000 Mbps (megabits per second)—over an Ethernet network. The usual Ethernet standard (802.3) supports only up to 100 Mbps. *Compare* Ethernet/802.3.

gigabit over copper *n.* *See* Category 5 cable.

gigabits per second *n.* A measurement of data transfer speed, as on a network, in multiples of 1,073,741,824 (2^{30}) bits. *Acronym:* Gbps.

gigaPoP *n.* Short for **giga**bit **P**oint **o**f **P**resence. A point of access for Internet2 (and possibly other high-speed networks) that supports data transfer speeds of at least 1 Gbps. Approximately 30 gigaPoPs are located at various points across the United States.

GIMP *n.* Acronym for **G**NU **I**mage **M**anipulation **P**rogram. A free and expandable graphics program for image creation and photo manipulation. GIMP is available for various UNIX-related platforms, including Linux and Mac OS X.

GIOP *n.* Short for **G**eneral **I**nter-**ORB** **P**rotocol. *See* IIOP.

globally unique identifier *n.* In the Component Object Model (COM), a 16-byte code that identifies an interface to an object across all computers and networks. Such an identifier is unique because it contains a time stamp and a code based on the network address hardwired on the host computer's LAN interface card. These identifiers are generated by a utility program. *Acronym:* GUID.

Global System for Mobile Communications *n.* *See* GSM.

global universal identification *n.* An identification scheme in which only one name is associated with a particular object; this name is accepted across platforms and applications. *Acronym:* GUID. *See also* globally unique identifier.

GNU *n.* Acronym for **G**NU's **N**ot **U**NIX. A collection of software based on the UNIX operating system maintained by the Free Software Foundation. GNU is distributed under the GNU General Public License, which requires that anyone who distributes GNU or a program based on GNU may charge only for distribution and support and must allow the user to modify and redistribute the code on the same terms. *See also* Free Software Foundation, General Public License. *Compare* Linux.

GNU Image Manipulation Program *n.* *See* GIMP.

Gnutella *n.* A file-sharing protocol that forms the basis of a number of peer-to-peer networking products. Gnutella forms a loose decentralized network with each user able to see and access all shared files of other Gnutella users. Unlike Napster, Gnutella does not require a central server, and any file type can be exchanged. Gnutella was originally developed by researchers at America Online's Nullsoft group but the original implemen-

G

tation of the protocol was never publicly released. An open-source Gnutella preview appeared that resulted in a number of variations becoming available. *See also* Napster.

Godwin's Law *n.* As originally proposed by Internet activist Michael Godwin, the theory that as an online discussion grows longer, a comparison involving Nazis or Hitler will inevitably be made. When a participant in an online discussion resorts to invoking such a comparison, other participants might cite Godwin's Law to indicate both that the person has lost the argument and that the discussion has continued too long.

Good Times virus *n.* A purported e-mail virus alluded to in a warning that has been propagated widely across the Internet, as well as by fax and standard mail. The letter claims that reading an e-mail message with the subject "Good Times" will cause damage to the user's system. In fact, it is currently impossible to harm a system by reading an e-mail message, although it is possible to include a virus in a file that is attached to an e-mail message. Some consider the chain letter itself to be the "virus" that wastes Internet bandwidth and the reader's time. Information on such hoaxes and on real viruses can be obtained from CERT (http://www.cert.org/). *See also* urban legend, virus.

Gopher or **gopher** *n.* An Internet utility for finding textual information and presenting it to the user in the form of hierarchical menus, from which the user selects submenus or files that can be downloaded and displayed. One Gopher client may access all available Gopher servers, so the user accesses a common "Gopherspace." The name of the program is a three-way pun: it is designed to go for desired information; it tunnels through the Internet and digs the information up; and it was developed at the University of Minnesota, whose athletic teams are named the Golden Gophers. Gopher is being subsumed by the World Wide Web.

Gopher server *n.* The software that provides menus and files to a Gopher user. *See also* Gopher.

Gopher site *n.* A computer on the Internet on which a Gopher server runs. *See also* Gopher, Gopher server.

Gopherspace *n.* The total set of information on the Internet that is accessible as menus and documents through Gopher. *See also* Gopher.

GOSIP *n.* Acronym for **G**overnment **O**pen **S**ystems **I**nterconnection **P**rofile. A U.S. government requirement that all of its new network purchases comply with the ISO/OSI standards. GOSIP went into effect on August 15, 1990, but was never fully implemented and was replaced by POSIT.

.gov *n.* In the Internet's Domain Name System, the top-level domain that identifies addresses operated by government agencies. The domain name .gov appears as a suffix at the end of the address. In the United States, only nonmilitary federal government agencies may use the .gov domain. State governments in the United States use the top-level domain of .state.us, with .us preceded by the two-letter abbreviation for the state, or just .us; other regional governments in the United States are registered under the .us domain. *See also* DNS (definition 1), domain (definition 3). *Compare* .com, .edu, .mil, .net, .org.

Government Open Systems Interconnection Profile *n. See* GOSIP.

GPRS *n.* Acronym for **G**eneral **P**acket **R**adio **S**ervice. A third-generation enhancement to the Global System for Mobile Communications (GSM), which supports non-voice applications such as Web browsing and other servicing requiring transfer of data packets without limits in message size. Systems using the service can be immediately connected when needed and therefore seem to the users to be always on. *See also* GSM, TDMA.

grade *n.* In communications, the range of frequencies available for transmission on a single channel. For example, voice-grade telephone frequencies range from about 300 hertz (Hz) through 3400 Hz.

grade of service *n.* The probability that a user of a shared communications network, such as a public telephone system, will receive an "all channels busy" signal. The grade of service is used as a measure of the traffic-handling ability of the network and is usually applied to a specific period, such as the peak traffic hour. A grade of service of 0.002, for example, assumes that a user has a 99.8 percent chance that a call made during the specified period will reach its intended destination.

Graphics Interchange Format *n. See* GIF.

Great Plains *n.* Microsoft Corporation's suite of business solution applications for finance, accounting, and management. Microsoft acquired the Great Plains applications in December 2000, when it purchased Great Plains Software, which had originally developed the suite of business accounting and management solutions. Great Plains Business Solutions include applications for accounting and finance, customer relations management, e-commerce, human resources, manufacturing, project accounting, and supply-chain management.

Great Renaming *n.* The changeover to the current system of Usenet hierarchies throughout the Internet. Before the Great Renaming, which took place in 1985, non-local newsgroup names had the form net.*; for example, a group that carried source code, formerly named net.sources, was renamed comp.sources.misc. *See also* local newsgroups, newsgroup, traditional newsgroup hierarchy, Usenet.

Green Book *n.* A specifications book written by the Sony and Philips Corporations, covering the CD-I (compact disc-interactive) technology. *See also* CD-I. *Compare* Orange Book (definition 2), Red Book (definition 2).

group *n.* A collection of elements that can be treated as a whole. In various multiuser operating systems, a group is a set of user accounts, sometimes called *members*; privileges can be specified for the group, and each member will then have those privileges. *See also* user account.

groupware *n.* Software intended to enable a group of users on a network to collaborate on a particular project. Groupware may provide services for communication (such as e-mail), collaborative document development, scheduling, and tracking. Documents may include text, images, or other forms of information.

GSL *n.* Acronym for **G**rammar **S**pecification **L**anguage. A grammar description format used by VoiceXML applications and other speech recognition systems. GSL was developed by Nuance and supports a number of XML-based speech editing and voice-browsing applications.

GSM *n.* Acronym for **G**lobal **S**ystem for **M**obile Communications. A digital cellular phone technology first deployed in 1992. In 2000, GSM was the predominant phone technology in Europe, and was used by 250 million subscribers worldwide. GSM phones offer a removable smart card containing subscriber account information. This card can be transferred from phone to phone quickly and easily, allowing the user to access his account from any phone in the system. Various enhancements to the GSM system allow increased Web browsing and data transfer options. *See also* GPRS, TDMA.

guest *n.* A common name for a login account that can be accessed without a password. Bulletin board systems (BBSs) and service providers often maintain such an account so that prospective subscribers can sample the services offered.

guest account *n.* An account used to log onto a system or domain where the user does not have access. Generally, resources and access are severely limited. On Windows NT technology, this account is built in to all domains. *See also* domain.

GUID *n. See* globally unique identifier, global universal identification.

gunzip *n.* A GNU utility for decompressing files compressed with gzip. *See also* GNU. *Compare* gzip.

gzip *n.* A GNU utility for compressing files. *See also* GNU. *Compare* gunzip.

G

H

H.320 *n.* An International Telecommunications Union (ITU) standard that enables interoperability among video-conferencing equipment from different manufacturers over circuit-switched services such as ISDN, thus making desktop video conferencing viable. H.320 establishes the common formats necessary to make audio and video inputs and outputs compatible and defines a protocol that makes it possible for a multimedia terminal to use audio/visual communications links and synchronization. *See also* International Telecommunications Union, ISDN, video conferencing.

H.323 *n.* An International Telecommunications Union (ITU) interoperability protocol enabling cross-communication of multimedia products and applications over packet-based networks. Under H.323, multimedia products offered by one vendor can work with those of another, regardless of hardware compatibility. For example, a PC can share audio and video streams over either an intranet or the Internet. Applications are thus network-, platform-, and application-independent. *See also* International Telecommunications Union, packet switching.

H.324 *n.* An International Telecommunications Union (ITU) standard for simultaneously transmitting video, data, and voice over POTS (Plain Old Telephone Service) modem connections.

hack *vb.* **1.** To apply creative ingenuity to a programming problem or project. **2.** To alter the behavior of an application or an operating system by modifying its code rather than by running the program and selecting options.

hacker *n.* **1.** A computerphile; a person who is totally engrossed in computer technology and computer programming or who likes to examine the code of operating systems and other programs to see how they work. **2.** A person, more commonly considered a cracker, who uses computer expertise for illicit ends, such as by gaining access to computer systems without permission and tampering with programs and data. *Also called:* cracker. *See also* hacktivist.

hacktivist *n.* An individual who furthers political or social agendas through hacking activity. Hacktivists may break into computer systems to disrupt traffic or cause confusion, and may alter Web pages or e-mail to display content sympathetic to a specific cause. *See also* hacker.

HAGO *n.* Acronym for **h**ave **a g**ood **o**ne. An expression used to conclude e-mail messages or in signing off from IRC.

HailStorm *n. See* .NET My Services.

half-duplex[1] *adj.* Of or pertaining to two-way communication that takes place in only one direction at a time. For example, transmission between half-duplex modems occurs when one modem waits to transmit until the other has finished sending. *Compare* duplex[1].

half-duplex[2] *n.* Two-way electronic communication that takes place in only one direction at a time. *Also called:* half-duplex transmission. *Compare* duplex[2], simplex.

half router *n.* A device that connects a local area network (LAN) to a communications line (such as one to the Internet) using a modem and that controls the routing of data to individual stations on the LAN.

Handheld Device Markup Language *n. See* HDML.

Handheld Device Transport Protocol *n. See* HDTP.

handle *n.* **1.** In online communication, such as chats and bulletin boards, the name a person uses to identify himself or herself. A handle is comparable to an alias or a nickname and is like those used with CB radio. **2.** A unique alphanumeric identifier of up to 10 characters assigned by InterNIC to the domain names, contacts, and network records in its domain name database. The NIC handle is used as a shorthand means of finding records and ensuring accuracy in the database. *Also called:* NIC handle.

handshake *n.* A series of signals acknowledging that communication or the transfer of information can take place between computers or other devices. A hardware handshake is an exchange of signals over specific wires (other than the data wires) in which each device indicates its readiness to send or receive data. A software handshake consists of signals transmitted over the same wires used to transfer data, as in modem-to-modem communications over telephone lines.

hardware handshake *n. See* handshake.

hardwired *adj.* **1.** Built into a system using hardware such as logic circuits, rather than accomplished through programming. **2.** Physically connected to a system or a network, as by means of a network connector board and cable.

hash *n.* In many FTP client programs, a command that instructs the FTP client to display a pound sign (#) each time it sends or receives a block of data. *See also* FTP client.

HDCP *n.* Acronym for **H**igh-bandwidth **D**igital **C**ontent **P**rotection. An encryption and authentication specification created by Intel for Digital Video Interface (DVI) devices such as digital cameras, high-definition televisions, and video disk players. HDCP is designed to protect transmissions between DVI devices from being copied.

HDLC *n.* Acronym for **H**igh-level **D**ata **L**ink **C**ontrol. A protocol for information transfer adopted by the ISO. HDLC is a bit-oriented, synchronous protocol that applies to the data-link (message-packaging) layer (layer 2 of the ISO/OSI reference model) for computer-to-microcomputer communications. Messages are transmitted in units called frames, which can contain differing amounts of data but which must be organized in a particular way. *See also* frame (definition 1), ISO/OSI reference model.

HDML *n.* Acronym for **H**andheld **D**evice **M**arkup **L**anguage. A simple, first-generation markup language used to define hypertext-like content and applications for wireless

H

and other handheld devices with small displays. This language is used primarily to create Web sites viewed via wireless phones and personal digital assistants (PDAs). HDML provides content consisting mainly of text with limited graphics. *See also* WML.

HDSL *n.* Acronym for **H**igh-**b**it-rate **D**igital **S**ubscriber **L**ine. A form of DSL, HDSL is a protocol for digital transmission of data over standard copper telecommunications lines (as opposed to fiber-optic lines) at rates of 1.544 Mbps in both directions. *Also called:* High-data-rate Digital Subscriber Line. *See also* DSL.

HDTP *n.* Acronym for **H**andheld **D**evice **T**ransport **P**rotocol. Protocol that enables a handheld device, such as a wireless phone or personal digital assistant (PDA), to access the Internet. HDTP regulates the input and output of data interpreted by the device's microbrowser. *See also* WAP.

HDTV *n.* Acronym for **H**igh-**D**efinition **Tele**Vision. A new television display standard that doubles the existing screen resolution and increases the screen aspect ratio from 4:3 to 16:9. This aspect ratio creates a television screen that is shaped like a movie screen.

HDTV-over-IP *n.* An Internet-based delivery option for High Definition Television (HDTV). HDTV-over-IP provides options for new and expanded services to ISPs, cable companies, telecommunications carriers, and business intranets, with its most extensive use in education. Universities use high-speed networks such as Internet2 to provide the intensive bandwidth demanded by HDTV-over-IP. Because HDTV-over-IP offers extreme image fidelity and sharpness, it is seen as ideal for delivery of distance education courses requiring precise visuals for which conventional video cannot provide sufficient resolution. *Also called:* iHDTV.

head *n.* In HTML, a section of coding that precedes the body of a document and is used to describe the document itself (title, author, and so on) rather than the elements within the document.

H

header *n.* An information structure that precedes and identifies the information that follows, such as a block of bytes in communications, a file on a disk, a set of records in a database, or an executable program.

helper application *n.* An application intended to be launched by a Web browser when the browser downloads a file that it is not able to process itself. Examples of helper applications are sound and movie players. Helper applications generally must be obtained and installed by users; they usually are not included in the browser itself. Many current Web browsers no longer require helper applications for common multimedia file formats. *Also called:* helper program. *Compare* ActiveX control, plug-in (definition 2).

helper program *n.* *See* helper application.

HHOK *n.* Acronym for **h**a, **h**a, **o**nly **k**idding. An indication of humor or facetiousness often used in e-mail and online communications.

hierarchical computer network *n.* **1.** A network in which one host computer controls a number of smaller computers, which may in turn act as hosts to a group of

PC workstations. **2.** A network in which control functions are organized according to a hierarchy and in which data processing tasks may be distributed.

high availability *n.* The ability of a system or device to be usable when it is needed. When expressed as a percentage, high availability is the actual service time divided by the required service time. Although high availability does not guarantee that a system will have no downtime, a network often is considered highly available if it achieves 99.999 percent network uptime. *Also called:* RAS (reliability/availability/serviceability), fault resilience. *See also* five-nines availability, four-nines availability, three-nines availability, two-nines availability. *Compare* fault tolerance.

High-bit-rate Digital Subscriber Line *n. See* HDSL.

High-data-rate Digital Subscriber Line *n. See* HDSL.

High-Definition Television *n. See* HDTV.

High-Performance File System *n. See* HPFS.

High-Performance Serial Bus *n. See* IEEE 1394.

hijackware *n.* Software that appears to be a useful plug-in or utility, but which will take over a user's Internet surfing or shopping activity by creating pop-up advertisements for competing products or redirecting the user to competitor's Web sites. Typically users will download and install a hijackware product believing it to be free browser enhancement software. Businesses pay the makers of hijackware products to push their shopping sites and product advertising onto Internet users, sometimes to the point of denying the user access to competing Web sites. *See also* gatored.

history *n.* A list of the user's actions within a program, such as commands entered in an operating system shell, menus passed through using Gopher, or links followed using a Web browser.

H

hit *n.* **1.** A successful retrieval of data from a cache rather than from the slower hard disk or RAM. *See also* cache. **2.** A successful retrieval of a record matching a query in a database. **3.** Retrieval of a file from a Web site. Each separate file accessed on a Web page, including HTML documents and graphics, counts as a hit. **4.** In computer war and other games, when a character is successfully fired on, attacked, or otherwise taken out.

holy war *n.* An argument in a mailing list, newsgroup, or other forum over some emotional and controversial topic, such as abortion or Northern Ireland. Introducing a holy war that is off the purported topic of the forum is considered a violation of netiquette.

home automation *n.* The process of programmatically controlling appliances, lighting, heating and cooling systems, and other devices in a home network. *See also* home network (definition 1).

homebrew *n.* Hardware or software developed by an individual at home or by a company for its own use rather than as a commercial product, such as hardware developed by electronics hobbyists when microcomputers first appeared in the 1970s.

home controller *n.* A software or hardware interface used to control the systems in a home network for home automation.

home network *n.* **1.** A communications network in a home or building used for home automation. Home networks can use wiring (existing or new) or wireless connections. *See also* home automation, home controller. **2.** Two or more computers in a home that are interconnected to form a local area network (LAN).

home page *n.* **1.** A document intended to serve as a starting point in a hypertext system, especially the World Wide Web. A home page is called a *start page* in Microsoft Internet Explorer. **2.** An entry page for a set of Web pages and other files in a Web site. **3.** A personal Web page, usually for an individual.

Home Phoneline Networking Alliance *n. See* HomePNA.

HomePNA *n.* Short for **H**ome **P**honeline **N**etworking **A**lliance. An association of more than 100 companies working toward the adoption of a unified technology for setting up home networks over existing telephone wiring. Phoneline networking allows multiple PCs, printers, and peripheral devices to be connected for such purposes as multiplayer gaming, sharing printers and other peripherals, and rapid downloads over the Internet. The alliance was founded by a number of companies including IBM, Intel, AT&T, and Lucent Technologies.

Home Radio Frequency *n. See* HomeRF.

HomeRF *n.* Acronym for **H**ome **R**adio **F**requency. A wireless home-networking specification that uses the 2.4-GHz frequency band to communicate between computers, peripherals, cordless phones, and other devices. HomeRF is supported by Siemens, Compaq, Motorola, National Semiconductor, Proxim, and other companies.

homogeneous network *n.* A network on which all the hosts are similar and only one protocol is used.

Honeynet Project *n.* A nonprofit security research group created to collect and analyze data on hacking tools and methods by maintaining a decoy network of computers that is potentially attractive to hackers. The Honeynet Project sets up entire networks of computers in different combinations of operating systems and security to realistically simulate those used in businesses and organizations. Hackers are lured to the network where all inbound and outbound data is captured and contained to help researchers learn about hacker tactics and motives.

honeypot *n.* A security program designed to lure and distract a network attacker with decoy data. The honeypot appears to be a system that the intruder would like to crack but which, in reality, is safely separated from the actual network. This allows network administrators to observe attackers and study their activities without the intruders knowing they are being monitored. Honeypot programs get their name from the "like a bear to honey" metaphor.

honker *n.* A slang term for a hacker, the term originated in China. The Honker Union of China is an active group of Chinese hackers with nationalistic or hacktivist aims. The Honker Union of China has claimed patriotic motivation for defacing Japanese and U.S. Web sites, hacking U.S. networks, and releasing the Lion worm and other malicious programs. *See also* hacktivist, Lion worm.

hop *n.* In data communications, one segment of the path between routers on a geographically dispersed network. A hop is comparable to one "leg" of a journey that includes intervening stops between the starting point and the destination. The distance between each of those stops (routers) would be a communications hop.

host[1] *n.* **1.** The main computer in a mainframe or minicomputer environment—that is, the computer to which terminals are connected. **2.** In PC-based networks, a computer that provides access to other computers. **3.** On the Internet or other large networks, a server computer that has access to other computers on the network. A host computer provides services, such as news, mail, or data, to computers that connect to it.

host[2] *vb.* To provide services to client computers that connect from remote locations—for example, to offer Internet access or to be the source for a news or mail service.

hosting *n.* The practice of providing computer and communication facilities to businesses or individuals, especially for use in creating Web and electronic commerce sites. A hosting service can provide high-speed access to the Internet, redundant power and data storage, and 24-hour maintenance at lower cost than implementing the same services independently. *See also* host[2], virtual hosting.

Host Integration Server *n.* A software application from Microsoft Corporation to allow businesses to integrate existing application, data, and network assets with new business applications and technologies. Host Integration Server preserves a company's existing legacy infrastructure and investments, while providing out-of-the-box development tools that enable integration with client/server and Web networks.

host name *n.* The name of a specific server on a specific network within the Internet, leftmost in the complete host specification. For example, www.microsoft.com indicates the server called "www" within the network at Microsoft Corporation.

host not responding *n.* An error message issued by an Internet client indicating that the computer to which a request has been sent is refusing the connection or is otherwise unavailable to respond to the request.

host unreachable *n.* An error condition that occurs when the particular computer to which the user wishes to connect over a TCP/IP network cannot be accessed on its LAN because it is either down or disconnected from the network. The error message the user sees may or may not be phrased in this manner. *See also* TCP/IP.

HotBot *n.* An Internet search engine developed by Inktomi Corporation and Hot-Wired, Inc. Using Slurp, a Web robot, this tool maintains a database of documents that can be matched to key words entered by the user, in a fashion similar to other

H

search engines. HotBot incorporates many workstations in parallel to search and index Web pages. *See also* spider.

HotJava *n.* A Web browser developed by Sun Microsystems, Inc., that is optimized to run Java applications and applets embedded in Web pages. *See also* applet, Java, Java applet.

hot link *n.* A connection between two programs that instructs the second program to make changes to data when changes occur in the first program. For example, a word processor or desktop publishing program could update a document based on information obtained from a database through a hot link. *See* hyperlink.

hotlist *n.* A list of frequently accessed items, such as Web pages in a Web browser, from which the user can select one. The hotlist of Web pages is called the bookmark list in Netscape Navigator and Lynx and is called the Favorites folder in Microsoft Internet Explorer.

Hotmail *n.* A Web-based e-mail service launched in 1996 and owned and operated by Microsoft since December 1997. Hotmail provides free e-mail accounts and can be used by anyone with Internet access and Web browsing software.

hot-potato routing *n.* A packet routing scheme that relies on keeping data moving, even if it may temporarily move away from its final destination. *Also called:* deflection routing.

HotWired *n.* A Web site affiliated with *Wired* magazine that contains news, gossip, and other information about the culture of the Internet.

hover button *n.* Text or an image on a Web page, usually in the form of a button, that changes appearance when a cursor passes over it. The hover button may change color, blink, display a pop-up with additional information, or produce other similar effects. Hover buttons are usually implemented through ActiveX objects and scripting, although hover behavior can also be set through HTML attributes.

HPFS *n.* Acronym for **H**igh **P**erformance **F**ile **S**ystem. A file system available with OS/2 versions 1.2 and later. *See also* NTFS.

HTCPCP *n.* Acronym for **H**yper **T**ext **C**offee **P**ot **C**ontrol **P**rotocol. A protocol defined in jest as an April Fools' Day spoof of open Internet standards. HTCPCP/1.0 was proposed in RFC 2324 on April 1, 1998 by Larry Masinter of Xerox PARC. In this RFC, Masinter described a protocol for controlling, monitoring, and diagnosing coffee pots.

.htm *n.* The MS-DOS/Windows 3.*x* file extension that identifies Hypertext Markup Language (HTML) files, most commonly used as Web pages. Because MS-DOS and Windows 3.*x* cannot recognize file extensions longer than three letters, the .html extension is truncated to three letters in those environments. *See also* HTML.

.html *n.* The file extension that identifies Hypertext Markup Language (HTML) files, most commonly used as Web pages. *See also* HTML.

HTML *n.* Acronym for **H**ypertext **M**arkup **L**anguage. The markup language used for documents on the World Wide Web. A tag-based notation language used to format documents that can then be interpreted and rendered by an Internet browser. HTML is an application of SGML (Standard Generalized Markup Language) that uses tags to mark elements, such as text and graphics, in a document to indicate how Web browsers should display these elements to the user and should respond to user actions such as activation of a link by means of a key press or mouse click. HTML 2, defined by the Internet Engineering Task Force (IETF), included features of HTML common to all Web browsers as of 1994 and was the first version of HTML widely used on the World Wide Web. HTML+ was proposed for extending HTML 2 in 1994, but it was never implemented. HTML 3, which also was never standardized or fully implemented by a major browser developer, introduced tables. HTML 3.2 incorporated features widely implemented as of early 1996, including tables, applets, and the ability to flow text around images. HTML 4, the latest specification, supports style sheets and scripting languages and includes internationalization and accessibility features. Future HTML development will be carried out by the World Wide Web Consortium (W3C). Most Web browsers, notably Netscape Navigator and Internet Explorer, recognize HTML tags beyond those included in the present standard. *See also* .htm, .html, SGML, tag (definition 3), Web browser.

HTML attribute *n.* A value within an HTML tag that assigns additional properties to the object being defined. Some HTML editing software assigns some attributes automatically when you create an object such as a paragraph or table.

HTML code fragment *n.* HTML code that you add to a Web page to create features such as a script, a counter, or a scrolling marquee. Often used in the context of webrings to add a link and standard graphics or automation to an individual page to indicate membership.

HTML document *n.* A hypertext document that has been coded with HTML. *See* Web page.

HTML editor *n.* A software program used to create and modify HTML documents (Web pages). Most HTML editors include a method for inserting HTML tags without actually having to type out each tag. A number of HTML editors will also automatically reformat a document with HTML tags, based on formatting codes used by the word processing program in which the document was created. *See also* tag (definition 3), Web page.

HTML extensions *n.* A feature or setting that is an extension to the formal HTML specification. Extensions may not be supported by all Web browsers, but they may be used widely by Web authors. An example of an extension is marquee scrolling text.

HTML page *n. See* Web page.

HTML server control *n.* An ASP.NET server control that belongs to the System.Web.UI.HtmlControls namespace. An HTML server control maps directly to an HTML element and is declared on an ASP.NET page as an HTML element marked by a runat=server attribute. In contrast to Web server controls, HTML server controls do not have an <asp:ControlName> tag prefix. *See also* Web server control.

HTML tag *n. See* tag (definition 3).

HTML validation service *n.* A service used to confirm that a Web page uses valid HTML according to the latest standard and/or that its hyperlinks are valid. An HTML validation service can catch small syntactical errors in HTML coding as well as deviations from the HTML standards. *See also* HTML.

HTTP *n.* Acronym for **H**yper**t**ext **T**ransfer **P**rotocol. The protocol used to carry requests from a browser to a Web server and to transport pages from Web servers back to the requesting browser. Although HTTP is almost universally used on the Web, it is not an especially secure protocol.

HTTPd *n.* Acronym for **H**yper**t**ext **T**ransfer **P**rotocol **D**aemon. A small, fast HTTP server that was available free from NCSA. HTTPd was the predecessor for Apache. *Also called:* HTTP Daemon. *See also* Apache, HTTP server, NCSA (definition 1).

HTTP Daemon *n. See* HTTPd.

HTTP Next Generation *n. See* HTTP-NG.

HTTP-NG *n.* Acronym for **H**yper**t**ext **T**ransfer **P**rotocol **N**ext **G**eneration. A standard under development by the World Wide Web Consortium (W3C) for improving performance and enabling the addition of features such as security. Whereas the current version of HTTP establishes a connection each time a request is made, HTTP-NG will set up one connection (which consists of separate channels for control information and data) for an entire session between a particular client and a particular server.

HTTPS *n.* **1.** Acronym for **H**yper**t**ext **T**ransfer **P**rotocol **S**ecure. A variation of HTTP that provides for encryption and transmission through a secure port. HTTPS was devised by Netscape and allows HTTP to run over a security mechanism known as SSL (Secure Sockets Layer). *See also* HTTP, SSL. **2.** Web server software for Windows NT. Developed by the European Microsoft Windows NT Academic Centre (EMWAC) at the University of Edinburgh, Scotland, it offers such features as WAIS search capability. *See also* HTTP server, WAIS.

HTTP server *n.* **1.** Server software that uses HTTP to serve up HTML documents and any associated files and scripts when requested by a client, such as a Web browser. The connection between client and server is usually broken after the requested document or file has been served. HTTP servers are used on Web and Intranet sites. *Also called:* Web server. *See also* HTML, HTTP, server (definition 2). *Compare* application server. **2.** Any machine on which an HTTP server program is running.

HTTP status codes *n.* Three-digit codes sent by an HTTP server that indicate the results of a request for data. Codes beginning with 1 respond to requests that the client may not have finished sending; with 2, successful requests; with 3, further action that the client must take; with 4, requests that failed because of client error; and with 5, requests that failed because of server error. *See also* 400, 401, 402, 403, 404, HTTP.

HTTP streaming *n.* The process of downloading streaming digital media using an HTTP server (a standard Internet server) rather than a server designed specifically to transmit streaming media. HTTP streaming downloads the media file onto a computer, which plays the downloaded file as it becomes available. *See also* real-time streaming.

hub *n.* In a network, a device joining communication lines at a central location, providing a common connection to all devices on the network. The term is an analogy to the hub of a wheel. *See also* active hub, switching hub.

hybrid network *n.* A network constructed of different topologies, such as ring and star. *See also* bus network, ring network, star network, Token Ring network, topology.

Hybris virus *n.* A slow-spreading but persistent self-updating Internet worm first detected in late 2000. The Hybris virus is activated whenever an infected computer is connected to the Internet. It attaches itself to all outgoing e-mail messages, maintains a list of all e-mail addresses in the headers of incoming e-mail messages, and sends copies of itself to all e-mail addresses on the list. Hybris is difficult to eradicate because it updates itself regularly, accessing and downloading updates and plug-ins from anonymous postings to the alt.comp.virus newsgroup. Hybris incorporates downloaded extensions into its code, and it e-mails its modified form to additional potential victims. Hybris often includes a spiral plug-in which produces a spinning disk on top of any active windows on a user's screen.

hyperlink *n.* A connection between an element in a hypertext document, such as a word, a phrase, a symbol, or an image, and a different element in the document, another document, a file, or a script. The user activates the link by clicking on the linked element, which is usually underlined or in a color different from the rest of the document to indicate that the element is linked. Hyperlinks are indicated in a hypertext document through tags in markup languages such as SGML and HTML. These tags are generally not visible to the user. *Also called:* hot link, hypertext link, link. *See also* anchor, HTML, hypermedia, hypertext, URL.

H

hypermedia *n.* The combination of text, video, graphic images, sound, hyperlinks, and other elements in the form typical of Web documents. Essentially, hypermedia is the modern extension of hypertext, the hyperlinked, text-based documents of the original Internet. Hypermedia attempts to offer a working and learning environment that parallels human thinking—that is, one in which the user can make associations between topics, rather than move sequentially from one to the next, as in an alphabetic list. For example, a hypermedia presentation on navigation might include links to astronomy, bird migration, geography, satellites, and radar. *See also* hypertext.

hypertext *n.* Text linked together in a complex, nonsequential web of associations in which the user can browse through related topics. For example, in an article with the word *iron*, traveling among the links to *iron* might lead the user to the periodic table of the elements or a map of the migration of metallurgy in Iron Age Europe. The term *hypertext* was coined in 1965 to describe documents presented by a computer that express the nonlinear structure of ideas as opposed to the linear format of books, film, and speech. The term *hypermedia*, more recently introduced, is nearly synonymous but emphasizes the nontextual element, such as animation, recorded sound, and video. *See also* hypermedia.

Hyper Text Coffee Pot Control Protocol *n. See* HTCPCP.

hypertext link *n. See* hyperlink.

Hypertext Markup Language *n. See* HTML.

Hypertext Transfer Protocol *n. See* HTTP.

Hypertext Transfer Protocol Daemon *n. See* HTTPd.

Hypertext Transfer Protocol Next Generation *n. See* HTTP-NG.

HyperWave *n.* A World Wide Web server that specializes in database manipulation and multimedia.

HYTELNET *n.* A menu-driven index of Internet resources that are accessible via telnet, including library catalogs, databases and bibliographies, bulletin boards, and network information services. HYTELNET can operate through a client program on a computer connected to the Internet, or through the World Wide Web.

HyTime *n.* Acronym for **Hypermedia/Time**-based Structuring Language. A markup language standard that describes links within and between documents and hypermedia objects. The standard defines structures and some semantic features, enabling description of traversal and presentation information of objects.

H

I

IAB *n. See* Internet Architecture Board.

IANA *n.* Acronym for **I**nternet **A**ssigned **N**umbers **A**uthority. The organization historically responsible for assigning IP (Internet Protocol) addresses and overseeing technical parameters, such as protocol numbers and port numbers, related to the Internet protocol suite. Under the direction of the late Dr. Jon Postel, IANA operated as an arm of the Internet Architecture Board (IAB) of the Internet Society (ISOC) under contract with the U.S. government. However, given the international nature of the Internet, IANA's functions, along with the domain name administration handled by U.S.-based Network Solutions, Inc. (NSI), were privatized in 1998 and turned over to a new, nonprofit organization known as ICANN (Internet Corporation for Assigned Names and Numbers). *See also* ICANN, NSI.

IC *adj.* Acronym for **I**n **C**haracter. Used to refer to events going on within a role-playing game, such as MUD, as opposed to events in real life. It is also used in the context of online chat, e-mail, and newsgroup postings. *See also* MUD, role-playing game.

ICANN *n.* Acronym for **I**nternet **C**orporation for **A**ssigned **N**ames and **N**umbers. The private, nonprofit corporation to which the U.S. government in 1998 delegated authority for administering IP (Internet Protocol) addresses, domain names, root servers, and Internet-related technical matters, such as management of protocol parameters (port numbers, protocol numbers, and so on). The successor to IANA (IP address administration) and NSI (domain name registration), ICANN was created to internationalize and privatize Internet management and administration. *See also* IANA, NSI.

ICE *n.* **1.** Acronym for **I**nformation and **C**ontent **E**xchange. A protocol based on XML (Extensible Markup Language) designed to automate the distribution of syndicated content over the World Wide Web. Based on the concept of content syndicators (distributors) and subscribers (receivers), ICE defines the responsibilities of the parties involved, as well as the format and means of exchanging content so that data can easily be transferred and reused. The protocol has been submitted to the World Wide Web Consortium by Adobe Systems, Inc., CNET, Microsoft, Sun Microsystems, and Vignette Corporation. It is intended to help in both publishing and inter-business exchanges of content. **2.** Acronym for **I**ntrusion **C**ountermeasure **E**lectronics. A fictional type of security software, popularized by science fiction novelist William Gibson, that responds to intruders by attempting to kill them. The origin of the term is attributed to a USENET subscriber, Tom Maddox. **3.** *See* Intelligent Concept Extraction.

ICMP *n.* Acronym for **I**nternet **C**ontrol **M**essage **P**rotocol. A network-layer (ISO/OSI level 3) Internet protocol that provides error correction and other information relevant to IP packet processing. For example, it can let the IP software on one machine inform another machine about an unreachable destination. *See also* communications protocol, IP, ISO/OSI reference model, packet (definition 1).

ICP *n.* Acronym for **I**nternet **C**ache **P**rotocol. A networking protocol used by cache servers to locate specific Web objects in neighboring caches. Typically implemented over UDP, ICP also can be used for cache selection. ICP was developed for the Harvest research project at the University of Southern California. It has been implemented in SQUID and other Web proxy caches.

ICQ *n.* A downloadable software program developed by Mirabilis, and now owned by AOL Time-Warner Inc., that notifies Internet users when friends, family, or other selected users are also on line and allows them to communicate with one another in real time. Through ICQ, users can chat, send e-mail, exchange messages on message boards, and transfer URLs and files, as well as launch third-party programs, such as games, in which multiple people can participate. Users compile a list of other users with whom they want to communicate. All users must register with the ICQ server and have ICQ software on their computer. The name is a reference to the phrase "I seek you." *See also* instant messaging.

ICSA *n.* Acronym for **I**nternational **C**omputer **S**ecurity **A**ssociation. An education and information organization concerned with Internet security issues. Known as the NCSA (National Computer Security Association) until 1997, the ICSA provides security assurance systems and product certification; disseminates computer security information in white papers, books, pamphlets, videos, and other publications; organizes consortiums devoted to various security issues; and maintains a Web site that provides updated information on viruses and other computer security topics. Founded in 1987, the ICSA is currently located in Reston, VA.

ID *n.* Acronym for **i**ntrusion **d**etection. *See* IDS.

IDS *n.* Acronym for **i**ntrusion-**d**etection **s**ystem. A type of security management system for computers and networks that gathers and analyzes information from various areas within a computer or a network to identify possible security breaches, both inside and outside the organization. An IDS can detect a wide range of hostile attack signatures, generate alarms, and, in some cases, cause routers to terminate communications from hostile sources. *Also called:* intrusion detection. *Compare* firewall.

IDSL *n.* Acronym for **I**nternet **d**igital **s**ubscriber **l**ine. A high-speed digital communications service that provides Internet access as fast as 1.1 Mbps (megabits per second) over standard telephone lines. IDSL uses a hybrid of ISDN and digital subscriber line technology. *See also* DSL, ISDN.

IE *n.* Acronym for **i**nformation **e**ngineering. A methodology for developing and maintaining information-processing systems, including computer systems and networks, within an organization.

IEEE *n.* Acronym for **I**nstitute of **E**lectrical and **E**lectronics **E**ngineers. A society of engineering and electronics professionals based in the United States but boasting membership from numerous other countries. The IEEE (pronounced "eye triple ee") focuses on electrical, electronics, computer engineering, and science-related matters.

IEEE 1284 *n.* The IEEE standard for high-speed signaling through a bidirectional parallel computer interface. A computer that is compliant with the IEEE 1284 standard can communicate through its parallel port in five modes: outbound data transfer to a printer or similar device ("Centronics" mode), inbound transfer 4 (nibble mode) or 8 (byte mode) bits at a time, bidirectional Enhanced Parallel Ports (EPP) used by storage devices and other nonprinter peripherals, and Enhanced Capabilities Ports (ECP) used for bidirectional communication with a printer.

IEEE 1394 *n.* A nonproprietary, high-speed, serial bus input/output standard. IEEE 1394 provides a means of connecting digital devices, including personal computers and consumer electronics hardware. It is platform-independent, scalable (expandable), and flexible in supporting peer-to-peer (roughly, device-to-device) connections. IEEE 1394 preserves data integrity by eliminating the need to convert digital signals into analog signals. Created for desktop networks by Apple Computer and later developed by the IEEE 1394 working group, it is considered a low-cost interface for devices such as digital cameras, camcorders, and multimedia devices and is seen as a means of integrating personal computers and home electronics equipment. FireWire is the proprietary implementation of the standard by Apple Computer. *See also* IEEE.

IEEE 1394 connector *n.* A type of connector that enables you to connect and disconnect high-speed serial devices. An IEEE 1394 connector is usually on the back of your computer near the serial port or the parallel port. The IEEE 1394 bus is used primarily to connect high-end digital video and audio devices to your computer; however, some hard disks, printers, scanners, and DVD drives can also be connected to your computer using the IEEE 1394 connector.

IEEE 1394 port *n.* A 4- or 6-pin port that supports the IEEE 1394 standard and can provide direct connections between digital consumer electronics and computers. *See also* IEEE 1394.

IEEE 488 *n.* The electrical definition of the General-Purpose Interface Bus (GPIB), specifying the data and control lines and the voltage and current levels for the bus.

IEEE 696/S-100 *n.* The electrical definition of the S-100 bus, used in early personal computer systems that used microprocessors such as the 8080, Z-80, and 6800. The S-100 bus, based on the architecture of the Altair 8800, was extremely popular with early computer enthusiasts because it permitted installation of a wide range of expansion boards.

IEEE 802.x *n.* A series of networking specifications developed by the IEEE. The x following 802 is a placeholder for individual specifications. The IEEE 802.x specifications correspond to the physical and data-link layers of the ISO/OSI reference model, but they divide the data-link layer into two sublayers. The logical link control (LLC) sublayer applies to all IEEE 802.x specifications and covers station-to-station connections, generation of message frames, and error control. The media access control (MAC) sublayer, dealing with network access and collision detection, differs from one IEEE 802 standard to another. IEEE 802.3 is used for bus networks that use

CSMA/CD, both broadband and baseband, and the baseband version is based on the Ethernet standard. IEEE 802.4 is used for bus networks that use token passing, and IEEE 802.5 is used for ring networks that use token passing (token ring networks). IEEE 802.6 is an emerging standard for metropolitan area networks, which transmit data, voice, and video over distances of more than 5 kilometers. IEEE 802.14 is designed for bidirectional transmission to and from cable television networks over optical fiber and coaxial cable through transmission of fixed-length ATM cells to support television, data, voice, and Internet access. *See also* bus network, ISO/OSI reference model, ring network, token passing, token ring network.

IEEE 802.11 *n.* The Institute of Electrical and Electronics Engineers' (IEEE) specifications for wireless networking. These specifications, which include 802.11, 802.11a, 802.11b, and 802.11g, allow computers, printers, and other devices to communicate over a wireless local area network (LAN).

IEPG *n.* Acronym for **I**nternet **E**ngineering and **P**lanning **G**roup. A collaborative group of Internet service providers whose goal is to promote the Internet and coordinate technical efforts on it.

IESG *n. See* Internet Engineering Steering Group.

IETF *n.* Acronym for **I**nternet **E**ngineering **T**ask **F**orce. A worldwide organization of individuals interested in networking and the Internet. Managed by the IESG (Internet Engineering Steering Group), the IETF is charged with studying technical problems facing the Internet and proposing solutions to the Internet Architecture Board (IAB). The work of the IETF is carried out by various Working Groups that concentrate on specific topics, such as routing and security. The IETF is the publisher of the specifications that led to the TCP/IP protocol standard. *See also* Internet Engineering Steering Group.

IFIP *n.* Acronym for **I**nternational **F**ederation of **I**nformation **P**rocessing. An organization of societies, representing over 40 member nations, that serves information-processing professionals. The United States is represented by the Federation on Computing in the United States (FOCUS). *See also* AFIPS, FOCUS.

IGMP *n. See* Internet Group Membership Protocol.

IGP *n. See* Interior Gateway Protocol.

IGRP *n.* Acronym for **I**nterior **G**ateway **R**outing **P**rotocol. A protocol developed by Cisco Systems that allows coordination between the routing of a number of gateways. Goals of IGRP include stable routing in large networks, fast response to changes in network topology, and low overhead. *See also* communications protocol, gateway, topology.

IIOP *n.* Acronym for **I**nternet **I**nter-**O**RB **P**rotocol. A networking protocol that enables distributed programs written in different programming languages to communicate over the Internet. IIOP, a specialized mapping in the General Inter-ORB Protocol (GIOP) based on a client/server model, is a critical part of the Common Object Request Broker Architecture (CORBA). *Compare* DCOM.

IIS *n. See* Internet Information Server.

ILEC *n.* Acronym for **I**ncumbent **L**ocal **E**xchange **C**arrier. A telephone company that provides local service to its customers. *Compare* CLEC.

IM *n. See* instant messaging.

image map *n.* An image that contains more than one hyperlink on a Web page. Clicking different parts of the image links the user to other resources on another part of the Web page or a different Web page or in a file. Often an image map, which can be a photograph, drawing, or a composite of several different drawings or photographs, is used as a map to the resources found on a particular Web site. Older Web browsers support only server-side image maps, which are executed on a Web server through CGI script. However, most newer Web browsers (Netscape Navigator 2.0 and higher and Internet Explorer 3.0 and higher) support client-side image maps, which are executed in a user's Web browser. *Also called:* clickable maps. *See also* CGI script, hyperlink, Web page.

IMAP4 *n.* Acronym for **I**nternet **M**essage **A**ccess **P**rotocol **4**. The latest version of IMAP, a method for an e-mail program to gain access to e-mail and bulletin board messages stored on a mail server. Unlike POP3, a similar protocol, IMAP allows a user to retrieve messages efficiently from more than one computer. *Compare* POP3.

IMC *n. See* Internet Mail Consortium.

IMHO *n.* Acronym for **i**n **m**y **h**umble **o**pinion. IMHO, used in e-mail and in online forums, flags a statement that the writer wants to present as a personal opinion rather than as a statement of fact. *See also* IMO.

IMO *n.* Acronym for **i**n **m**y **o**pinion. A shorthand phrase used often in e-mail and Internet news and discussion groups to indicate an author's admission that a statement he or she has just made is a matter of judgment rather than fact. *See also* IMHO.

IMT-2000 *n. See* International Mobile Telecommunications for the Year 2000.

Inbox *n.* In many e-mail applications, the default mailbox where the program stores incoming messages. *See also* e-mail, mailbox. *Compare* Outbox.

incumbent local exchange carrier *n. See* ILEC.

independent content provider *n.* A business or organization that supplies information to an online information service, such as America Online, for resale to the information service's customers. *See also* online information service.

INET *n.* **1.** Short for **Internet**. **2.** An annual conference held by the Internet Society.

infection *n.* The presence of a virus or Trojan horse in a computer system. *See also* Trojan horse, virus, worm.

.info *n.* One of seven new top-level domain names approved in 2001 by the Internet Corporation for Assigned Names and Numbers (ICANN). Unlike the other new domain names, which focus on specific types of Web sites, .info is meant for unrestricted use.

infobahn *n.* The Internet. *Infobahn* is a mixture of the terms *information* and *Autobahn*, a German highway known for the high speeds at which drivers can legally travel. *Also called:* Information Highway, Information Superhighway, the Net.

infomediary *n.* A term created from the phrase *information intermediary*. A service provider that positions itself between buyers and sellers, collecting, organizing, and distributing focused information that improves the interaction of consumer and online business.

information appliance *n.* A specialized computer designed to perform a limited number of functions and, especially, to provide access to the Internet. Although devices such as electronic address books or appointment calendars might be considered information appliances, the term is more typically used for devices that are less expensive and less capable than a fully functional personal computer. Set-top boxes are a current example; other devices, envisioned for the future, would include network-aware microwaves, refrigerators, watches, and the like. *Also called:* appliance.

information center *n.* **1.** A large computer center and its associated offices; the hub of an information management and dispersal facility in an organization. **2.** A specialized type of computer system dedicated to information retrieval and decision-support functions. The information in such a system is usually read-only and consists of data extracted or downloaded from other production systems.

information engineering *n. See* IE.

Information Highway or **information highway** *n. See* Information Superhighway.

Information Industry Association *n. See* SIIA.

information packet *n. See* packet (definition 1).

information resource management *n.* The process of managing the resources for the collection, storage, and manipulation of data within an organization or system.

Information Services *n.* The formal name for a company's data processing department. *Acronym:* IS. *Also called:* Data Processing, Information Processing, Information Systems, Information Technology, Management Information Services, Management Information Systems.

Information Superhighway *n.* The existing Internet and its general infrastructure, including private networks, online services, and so on. *See also* National Information Infrastructure.

Information Technology Industry Council *n.* Trade organization of the information technology industry. The council promotes the interests of the information technology industry and compiles information on computers, software, telecommunications, business equipment, and other topics related to information technology. *Acronym:* ITIC.

information theory *n.* A mathematical discipline founded in 1948 that deals with the characteristics and the transmission of information. Information theory was originally applied to communications engineering but has proved relevant to other fields, including computing. It focuses on such aspects of communication as amount of data, transmission rate, channel capacity, and accuracy of transmission, whether over cables or within society.

information warehouse *n.* The total of an organization's data resources on all computers.

information warfare *n.* Attacks on the computer operations on which an enemy country's economic life or safety depends. Possible examples of information warfare include crashing air traffic control systems or massively corrupting stock exchange records.

Infoseek *n.* A Web search site that provides full-text results for user searches plus categorized lists of related sites. InfoSeek is powered by the Ultraseek search engine and searches Web pages, Usenet newsgroups, and FTP and Gopher sites.

infrared *adj.* Having a frequency in the electromagnetic spectrum in the range just below that of red light. Objects radiate infrared in proportion to their temperature. Infrared radiation is traditionally divided into four somewhat arbitrary categories based on its wavelength. See the table. *Acronym:* IR.

Table I.1   Infrared Radiation Categories.

near infrared	750–1500 nanometers (nm)
middle infrared	1500–6000 nm
far infrared	6000–40,000 nm
far-far infrared	40,000 nm–1 millimeter (mm)

Infrared Data Association *n. See* IrDA.

infrared device *n.* A computer, or a computer peripheral such as a printer, that can communicate by using infrared light. *See also* infrared.

infrared file transfer *n.* Wireless file transfer between a computer and another computer or device using infrared light. *See also* infrared.

infrared network connection *n.* A direct or incoming network connection to a remote access server using an infrared port. *See also* infrared port.

infrared port *n.* An optical port on a computer for interfacing with an infrared-capable device. Communication is achieved without physical connection through cables. Infrared ports can be found on some laptops, notebooks, and printers. *See also* infrared, port.

I

inline *adj.* **1.** In programming, referring to a function call replaced with an instance of the function's body. Actual arguments are substituted for formal parameters. An inline function is usually done as a compile-time transformation to increase the efficiency of the program. *Also called:* unfold, unroll. **2.** In HTML code, referring to graphics displayed along with HTML-formatted text. Inline images placed in the line of HTML text use the tag <IMG>. Text within an inline image can be aligned to the top, bottom, or middle of a specific image.

inline discussion *n.* Discussion comments that are associated with a document as a whole or with a particular paragraph, image, or table of a document. In Web browsers, inline discussions are displayed in the body of the document; in word-processing programs, they are usually displayed in a separate discussion or comments pane.

inline graphics *n.* Graphics files that are embedded in an HTML document or Web page and viewable by a Web browser or other program that recognizes HTML. By avoiding the need for separate file opening operations, inline graphics can speed the access and loading of an HTML document. *Also called:* inline image.

inline image *n.* An image that is embedded within the text of a document. Inline images are common on Web pages. *See also* inline graphics.

inline stylesheet *n.* A stylesheet included within an HTML document. Because an inline stylesheet is directly associated with an individual document, any changes made to that document's appearance will not affect the appearance of other Web site documents. *Compare* linked stylesheet.

Inmarsat *n.* Acronym for **In**ternational **Mar**itime **Sat**ellite. Organization based in London, England, that operates satellites for international mobile telecommunications services in more than 80 nations. Inmarsat provides services for maritime, aviation, and land use.

inoculate *vb.* To protect a program against virus infection by recording characteristic information about it. For example, a calculated value used to test data for the presence of errors (a checksum) on the code can be recomputed and compared with the stored original checksums each time the program is run; if any have changed, the program file is corrupt and may be infected. *See also* virus.

INS *n. See* WINS.

insider attack *n.* An attack on a network or system carried out by an individual associated with the hacked system. Insider attacks are typically the work of current or former employees of a company or organization who have knowledge of passwords and network vulnerabilities. *Compare* intruder attack.

instant messaging *n.* A service that alerts users when friends or colleagues are on line and allows them to communicate with each other in real time through private online chat areas. With instant messaging, a user creates a list of other users with whom he or she wishes to communicate; when a user from his or her list is on line, the service alerts the user and enables immediate contact with the other user. While instant messaging has primarily been a proprietary service offered by Internet service providers such as AOL and MSN, businesses are starting to employ instant messaging to increase employee efficiency and make expertise more readily available to employees.

Institute of Electrical and Electronics Engineers *n. See* IEEE.

integral modem *n.* A modem that is built into a computer, as opposed to an internal modem, which is a modem on an expansion card that can be removed. *See also* external modem, internal modem, modem.

Integrated Services Digital Network *n. See* ISDN.

Integrated Services LAN *n. See* isochronous network.

integration *n.* In computing, the combining of different activities, programs, or hardware components into a functional unit. *See also* integral modem, ISDN.

intellectual property *n.* Content of the human intellect deemed to be unique and original and to have marketplace value—and thus to warrant protection under the law. Intellectual property includes but is not limited to ideas; inventions; literary works; chemical, business, or computer processes; and company or product names and logos. Intellectual property protections fall into four categories: copyright (for literary works, art, and music), trademarks (for company and product names and logos), patents (for inventions and processes), and trade secrets (for recipes, code, and processes). Concern over defining and protecting intellectual property in cyberspace has brought this area of the law under intense scrutiny.

intelligence *n.* **1.** The ability of hardware to process information. A device without intelligence is said to be dumb; for example, a dumb terminal connected to a computer can receive input and display output but cannot process information independently. **2.** The ability of a program to monitor its environment and initiate appropriate actions to achieve a desired state. For example, a program waiting for data to be read from disk might switch to another task in the meantime. **3.** The ability of a program to simulate human thought. **4.** The ability of a machine such as a robot to respond appropriately to changing stimuli (input).

intelligent agent *n.* *See* agent (definition 2).

intelligent cable *n.* A cable that incorporates circuitry to do more than simply pass signals from one end of the cable to the other, such as to determine the characteristics of the connector into which it is plugged. *Also called:* smart cable.

Intelligent Concept Extraction *n.* A technology owned by Excite, Inc., for searching indexed databases to retrieve documents from the World Wide Web. Intelligent Concept Extraction is like other search technologies in being able to locate indexed Web documents related to one or more key words entered by the user. Based on proprietary search technology, however, it also matches documents conceptually by finding relevant information even if the document found does not contain the key word or words specified by the user. Thus, the list of documents found by Intelligent Concept Extraction can include both documents containing the specified search term and those containing alternative words related to the search term. *Acronym:* ICE.

intelligent database *n.* A database that manipulates stored information in a way that people find logical, natural, and easy to use. An intelligent database conducts searches relying not only on traditional data-finding routines but also on predetermined rules governing associations, relationships, and even inferences regarding the data. *See also* database.

Intelligent hub *n.* A type of hub that, in addition to transmitting signals, has built-in capability for other network chores, such as monitoring or reporting on network status. Intelligent hubs are used in different types of networks, including ARCnet and 10Base-T Ethernet. *See also* hub.

interactive services *n.* *See* BISDN.

interactive television *n.* A video technology in which a viewer interacts with the television programming. Typical uses of interactive television include Internet access, video on demand, and video conferencing. *See also* video conferencing.

interactive TV *n. See* iTV.

interactive video *n.* The use of computer-controlled video, in the form of a CD-ROM or videodisc, for interactive education or entertainment. *See also* interactive television.

interapplication communication *n.* The process of one program sending messages to another program. For example, some e-mail programs allow users to click on a URL within the message. After the user clicks on the URL, browser software will automatically launch and access the URL.

interconnect *n.* **1.** *See* system area network. **2.** An electrical or mechanical connection. Interconnect is the physical connection and communication between two components in a computer system.

Interior Gateway Protocol *n.* A protocol used for distributing routing information among routers (gateways) in an autonomous network—that is, a network under the control of one administrative body. The two most often used interior gateway protocols are RIP (Routing Information Protocol) and OSPF (Open Shortest Path First). *Acronym:* IGP. *See also* autonomous system, OSPF, RIP. *Compare* exterior gateway protocol.

Interior Gateway Routing Protocol *n. See* IGRP.

Interix *n.* A software application from Microsoft that allows businesses to run existing UNIX-based legacy applications while adding applications based on the Microsoft Windows operating system. Interix serves as a single enterprise platform from which to run UNIX-based, Internet-based, and Windows-based applications.

internal modem *n.* A modem constructed on an expansion card to be installed in one of the expansion slots inside a computer. *Compare* external modem, integral modem.

International Computer Security Association *n. See* ICSA.

International Federation of Information Processing *n. See* IFIP.

International Maritime Satellite *n. See* Inmarsat.

International Mobile Telecommunications for the Year 2000 *n.* Specifications set forth by the International Telecommunications Union (ITU) to establish third-generation wireless telecommunication network architecture. The specifications include faster data transmission speeds and improved voice quality. *Acronym:* IMT-2000.

International Organization for Standardization *n. See* ISO.

International Telecommunication Union *n. See* ITU.

International Telecommunication Union-Telecommunication Standardization Sector *n. See* ITU-T.

International Telegraph and Telephone Consultative Committee *n.* English-language form of the name for the Comité Consultatif International

Télégraphique et Téléphonique, a standards organization that became part of the International Telecommunication Union in 1992. *See also* CCITT, ITU-T.

Internaut *n. See* cybernaut.

internet *n.* Short for **internet**work. A set of computer networks that may be dissimilar and are joined together by means of gateways that handle data transfer and conversion of messages from the sending networks' protocols to those of the receiving network.

Internet *n.* The worldwide collection of networks and gateways that use the TCP/IP suite of protocols to communicate with one another. At the heart of the Internet is a backbone of high-speed data communication lines between major nodes or host computers, consisting of thousands of commercial, government, educational, and other computer systems, that route data and messages. One or more Internet nodes can go off line without endangering the Internet as a whole or causing communications on the Internet to stop, because no single computer or network controls it. The genesis of the Internet was a decentralized network called ARPANET created by the U.S. Department of Defense in 1969 to facilitate communications in the event of a nuclear attack. Eventually other networks, including BITNET, Usenet, UUCP, and NSFnet, were connected to ARPANET. Currently the Internet offers a range of services to users, such as FTP, e-mail, the World Wide Web, Usenet news, Gopher, IRC, telnet, and others. *Also called:* the Net. *See also* BITNET, FTP[1] (definition 1), Gopher, IRC, NSFnet, telnet[1], Usenet, UUCP, World Wide Web.

Internet2 *n.* A computer-network development project launched in 1996 by a collaborative group of 120 universities under the auspices of the University Corporation for Advanced Internet Development (UCAID). The consortium is now being led by over 190 universities working with industry and government. The goal of Internet2, whose high-speed, fiberoptic backbone was brought on line in early 1999, is the development of advanced Internet technologies and applications for use in research and education at the university level. Though not open for public use, Internet2 and the technologies and applications developed by its members are intended to eventually benefit users of the commercial Internet as well. Some of the new technologies Internet2 and its members are developing and testing include IPv6, multicasting, and quality of service (QoS). Internet2 and the Next Generation Internet (NGI) are complementary initiatives. *Compare* Internet, Next Generation Internet.

Internet access *n.* **1.** The capability of a user to connect to the Internet. This is generally accomplished through one of two ways. The first is through a dialing up of an Internet service provider or an online information services provider via a modem connected to the user's computer. This method is the one used by the majority of home computer users. The second way is through a dedicated line, such as a T1 carrier, that is connected to a local area network, to which, in turn, the user's computer is connected. The dedicated line solution is used by larger organizations, such as corporations, which either have their own node on the Internet or connect to an Internet service provider that is a node. A third way that is emerging is for users to use set-top boxes with their TVs. Generally, however, this will give a user access only to documents on the World Wide Web. *See also* ISP, LAN, modem, node (definition 2).

2. The capability of an online information service to exchange data with the Internet, such as e-mail, or to offer Internet services to users, such as newsgroups, FTP, and the World Wide Web. Most online information services offer Internet access to their users. *See also* FTP[1] (definition 1), online information service.

Internet access device *n.* A communications and signal-routing mechanism, possibly incorporating usage tracking and billing features, for use in connecting multiple remote users to the Internet.

Internet access provider *n. See* ISP.

Internet account *n.* A generic term for a registered username at an Internet Service Provider (ISP). An Internet account is accessed via username and password. Services such as dial-in PPP Internet access and e-mail are provided by ISPs to Internet account owners.

Internet address *n. See* domain name address, e-mail address, IP address.

Internet appliance *n.* **1.** *See* set-top box. **2.** *See* server appliance.

Internet Architecture Board *n.* The body of the Internet Society (ISOC) responsible for overall architectural considerations regarding the Internet. The IAB also serves to adjudicate disputes in the standards process. *Acronym:* IAB. *See also* Internet Society.

Internet Assigned Numbers Authority *n. See* IANA, ICANN.

Internet backbone *n.* One of several high-speed networks connecting many local and regional networks, with at least one connection point where it exchanges packets with other Internet backbones. Historically, the NSFnet (predecessor to the modern Internet) was the backbone to the entire Internet in the United States. This backbone linked the supercomputing centers that the National Science Foundation (NSF) runs. Today, different providers have their own backbones so that the backbone for the supercomputing centers is independent of backbones for commercial Internet providers such as MCI and Sprint. *See also* backbone.

Internet broadcasting *n.* Broadcasting of audio, or audio plus video, signals across the Internet. Internet broadcasting includes conventional over-the-air broadcast stations that transmit their signals into the Internet as well as Internet-only stations. Listeners use audio Internet software, such as RealAudio. One method of Internet broadcasting is MBONE. *See also* MBONE, RealAudio.

Internet Cache Protocol *n. See* ICP.

Internet Control Message Protocol *n. See* ICMP.

Internet Corporation for Assigned Names and Numbers *n. See* ICANN.

Internet cramming *n. See* Web cramming.

Internet Directory *n.* **1.** Online database of sites organized by category where you can search for files and information by subject, keyword, or other criteria. **2.** Storage place for information such as names, Web addresses, organizations, departments, countries, and locations. Typically, Internet Directories are used to look up e-mail addresses that are not in a local address book or a corporate-wide directory.

Internet Draft *n.* A document produced by the Internet Engineering Task Force (IETF) for purposes of discussing a possible change in standards that govern the Internet. An Internet Draft is subject to revision or replacement at any time; if not replaced or revised, the Internet Draft is valid for no more than six months. An Internet Draft, if accepted, may be developed into an RFC. *See also* IETF, RFC.

Internet Engineering and Planning Group *n. See* IEPG.

Internet Engineering Steering Group *n.* The group within the Internet Society (ISOC) that, along with the Internet Architecture Board (IAB), reviews the standards proposed by the Internet Engineering Task Force (IETF). *Acronym:* IESG.

Internet Engineering Task Force *n. See* IETF.

Internet Explorer *n.* Microsoft's Web browsing software. Introduced in October 1995, the latest versions of Internet Explorer include many features that allow you to customize your experience on the Web. Internet Explorer is also available for the Macintosh and UNIX platforms. *See also* ActiveX control, Java applet, Web browser.

Internet Foundation Classes *n.* A Java class library developed by Netscape to facilitate the creation of full-feature, mission-critical Java applications. Internet Foundation Classes (IFC) comprises user-interface objects and frameworks intended to extend Java's Abstract Window Toolkit (AWT) and includes a multifont text editor; essential application controls; and drag-and-drop, drawing/event, windowing, animation, object persistence, single-thread, and localization frameworks. *See also* Java Foundation Classes.

Internet gateway *n.* A device that provides the connection between the Internet backbone and another network, such as a LAN (local area network). Usually the device is a computer dedicated to the task or a router. The gateway generally performs protocol conversion between the Internet backbone and the network, data translation or conversion, and message handling. A gateway is considered a node on the Internet. *See also* gateway, Internet backbone, node (definition 2), router.

Internet Group Membership Protocol *n.* A protocol used by IP hosts to report their host group memberships to any immediately neighboring multicast routers. *Acronym:* IGMP.

Internet home *n. See* smart home.

Internet Information Server *n.* Microsoft's brand of Web server software, utilizing HTTP (Hypertext Transfer Protocol) to deliver World Wide Web documents. It incorporates various functions for security, allows for CGI programs, and also provides for Gopher and FTP services.

Internet Inter-ORB Protocol *n. See* IIOP.

Internet Mail Consortium *n.* An international membership organization of businesses and vendors involved in activities related to e-mail transmission over the Internet. The goals of the Internet Mail Consortium are related to the promotion and expansion of Internet mail. The group's interests range from making Internet mail

127

easier for new users to advancing new mail technologies and expanding the role played by Internet mail into areas such as electronic commerce and entertainment. For example, the Internet Mail Consortium supports two companion specifications, vCalendar and vCard, designed to facilitate electronic exchange of scheduling and personal information. *Acronym:* IMC.

Internet Naming Service *n. See* WINS.

Internet Printing Protocol *n.* A specification for transmission of documents to printers through the Internet. Development of the Internet Printing Protocol (IPP) was proposed in 1997 by members of the Internet Engineering Task Force (IETF). Intended to provide a standard protocol for Internet-based printing, IPP covers both printing and printer management (printer status, job cancellation, and so on). It is applicable to print servers and to network-capable printers.

Internet Protocol *n. See* IP.

Internet Protocol address *n. See* IP address.

Internet Protocol next generation *n. See* IPng.

Internet Protocol number *n. See* IP address.

Internet Protocol Security *n. See* IPSec.

Internet Protocol version 4 *n. See* IPv4.

Internet Protocol version 6 *n. See* IPv6.

Internet reference model *n. See* TCP/IP reference model.

Internet Relay Chat *n. See* IRC.

Internet Research Steering Group *n.* The governing body of the Internet Research Task Force (IRTF). *Acronym:* IRSG.

Internet Research Task Force *n.* A volunteer organization that is an arm of the Internet Society (ISOC) focused on making long-term recommendations concerning the Internet to the Internet Architecture Board (IAB). *Acronym:* IRTF. *See also* Internet Society.

Internet robot *n. See* spider.

Internet security *n.* A broad topic dealing with all aspects of data authentication, privacy, integrity, and verification for transactions over the Internet. For example, credit card purchases made via a World Wide Web browser require attention to Internet security issues to ensure that the credit card number is not intercepted by an intruder or copied from the server where the number is stored, and to verify that the credit card number is actually sent by the person who claims to be sending it.

Internet Security and Acceleration Server *n.* A software application from Microsoft Corporation to increase the security and performance of Internet access for businesses. Internet Security and Acceleration Server provides an enterprise firewall and high-performance Web cache server to securely manage the flow of information from the Internet through the enterprise's internal network. *Acronym:* ISA Server.

Internet Server Application Programming Interface *n. See* ISAPI.

Internet service provider *n. See* ISP.

Internet Society *n.* An international, nonprofit organization based in Reston, Virginia, comprising individuals, companies, foundations, and government agencies, that promotes the use, maintenance, and development of the Internet. The Internet Architecture Board (IAB) is a body within the Internet Society. In addition, the Internet Society publishes the *Internet Society News* and produces the annual INET conference. *Acronym:* ISOC. *See also* INET, Internet Architecture Board.

Internet Software Consortium *n.* A nonprofit organization that develops software that is available for free, via the World Wide Web or FTP, and engages in development of Internet standards such as the Dynamic Host Configuration Protocol (DHCP). *Acronym:* ISC. *See also* DHCP.

Internet SSE *n. See* SSE.

Internet Streaming Media Alliance *n. See* ISMA.

Internet synchronization *n.* **1.** The process of synchronizing data between computing and communication devices that are connected to the Internet. **2.** A feature in Microsoft Jet and Microsoft Access that allows replicated information to be synchronized in an environment in which an Internet server is configured with Microsoft Replication Manager, a tool included with Microsoft Office 2000 Developer.

Internet Talk Radio *n.* Audio programs similar to radio broadcasts but distributed over the Internet in the form of files that can be downloaded via FTP. Internet Talk Radio programs, prepared at the National Press Building in Washington, D.C., are 30 minutes to 1 hour in length; a 30-minute program requires about 15 MB of disk space. *Acronym:* ITR.

Internet telephone *n.* Point-to-point voice communication that uses the Internet instead of the public-switched telecommunications network to connect the calling and called parties. Both the sending and the receiving party need a computer, a modem, an Internet connection, and an Internet telephone software package to make and receive calls.

Internet Telephony Service Provider *n. See* ITSP.

Internet telephony *n. See* VoIP.

Internet television *n.* The transmission of television audio and video signals over the Internet.

Internet traffic distribution *n. See* ITM.

Internet traffic management *n. See* ITM.

internetwork[1] *adj.* Of or pertaining to communications between connected networks. It is often used to refer to communication between one LAN (local area network) and another over the Internet or another WAN (wide-area network). *See also* LAN, WAN.

internetwork[2] *n.* A network made up of smaller, interconnected networks.

Internetwork Packet Exchange *n. See* IPX.

129

Internetwork Packet Exchange/Sequenced Packet Exchange *n. See* IPX/SPX.

Internet World *n.* Series of international conferences and exhibitions on e-commerce and Internet technology sponsored by *Internet World* magazine. Major conferences include the world's largest Internet conferences, Internet World Spring and Internet World Fall.

Internet Worm *n.* A string of self-replicating computer code that was distributed through the Internet in November 1988. In a single night, it overloaded and shut down a large portion of the computers connected to the Internet at that time by replicating itself over and over on each computer it accessed, exploiting a bug in UNIX systems. Intended as a prank, the Internet Worm was written by a student at Cornell University. *See also* back door, worm.

InterNIC *n.* Short for NSFnet (**Inter**net) **N**etwork **I**nformation **C**enter. The organization that has traditionally registered domain names and IP addresses as well as distributed information about the Internet. InterNIC was formed in 1993 as a consortium involving the U.S. National Science Foundation, AT&T, General Atomics, and Network Solutions, Inc. (Herndon, Va.). The latter partner administers InterNIC Registration Services, which assigns Internet names and addresses.

interstitial *n.* An Internet ad format that appears in a pop-up window between Web pages. Interstitial ads download completely before appearing, usually while a Web page the user has chosen is loading. Because interstitial pop-up windows don't appear until the entire ad has downloaded, they often use animated graphics, audio, and other attention-getting multimedia technology that require longer download time.

in the wild *adj.* Currently affecting the computing public, particularly in regard to computer viruses. A virus that is not yet contained or controlled by antivirus software or that keeps reappearing despite virus detection measures is considered to be in the wild. *See also* virus.

intranet *n.* A private network based on Internet protocols such as TCP/IP but designed for information management within a company or organization. Its uses include such services as document distribution, software distribution, access to databases, and training. An intranet is so called because it looks like a World Wide Web site and is based on the same technologies, yet is strictly internal to the organization and is not connected to the Internet proper. Some intranets also offer access to the Internet, but such connections are directed through a firewall that protects the internal network from the external Web. *Compare* extranet.

intraware *n.* Groupware or middleware for use on a company's private intranet. Intraware packages typically contain e-mail, database, workflow, and browser applications. *See also* groupware, intranet, middleware.

intruder *n.* An unauthorized user or unauthorized program, generally considered to have malicious intent, on a computer or computer network. *See also* bacterium, cracker, Trojan horse, virus.

intruder attack *n.* A form of hacker attack in which the hacker enters the system without prior knowledge or access to the system. The intruder will typically use a combination of probing tools and techniques to learn about the network to be hacked. *Compare* insider attack.

Intrusion Countermeasure Electronics *n. See* ICE (definition 3).

intrusion detection *n. See* IDS.

intrusion-detection system *n. See* IDS.

IP *n.* Acronym for **I**nternet **P**rotocol. The protocol within TCP/IP that governs the breakup of data messages into packets, the routing of the packets from sender to destination network and station, and the reassembly of the packets into the original data messages at the destination. IP runs at the internetwork layer in the TCP/IP model—equivalent to the network layer in the ISO/OSI reference model. *See also* ISO/OSI reference model, TCP/IP. *Compare* TCP.

IP address *n.* Short for **I**nternet **P**rotocol **address**. A 32-bit (4-byte) binary number that uniquely identifies a host (computer) connected to the Internet to other Internet hosts, for the purposes of communication through the transfer of packets. An IP address is expressed in "dotted quad" format, consisting of the decimal values of its 4 bytes, separated with periods; for example, 127.0.0.1. The first 1, 2, or 3 bytes of the IP address identify the network the host is connected to; the remaining bits identify the host itself. The 32 bits of all 4 bytes together can signify almost 2^{32}, or roughly 4 billion, hosts. (A few small ranges within that set of numbers are not used.) *Also called:* Internet Protocol number, IP number. *See also* host, IANA, ICANN, InterNIC, IP, IP address classes, packet (definition 2). *Compare* domain name.

IP address classes *n.* Short for **I**nternet **P**rotocol **address classes**. The classes into which IP addresses were divided to accommodate different network sizes. Each class is associated with a range of possible IP addresses and is limited to a specific number of networks per class and hosts per network. See the table. *See also* Class A IP address, Class B IP address, Class C IP address, IP address.

Address Class	Range of IP Addresses	Networks per Class	Hosts per Network (maximum number)
Class A (/8)	1.x.x.x to 126.x.x.x	126	16,777,214
Class B (/16)	128.0.x.x to 191.255.x.x	16,384	65,534
Class C (/24)	192.0.0.x to 223.255.255.x	2,097,152	254

IP address classes. Each x represents the host-number field assigned by the network administrator.

IP aliasing *n. See* NAT.

ipchains *n. See* iptables.

IP Filter *n.* Short for **I**nternet **P**rotocol **Filter**. A TCP/IP packet filter for UNIX, particularly BSD. Similar in functionality to netfilter and iptables in Linux, IP Filter can be used to provide network address translation (NAT) or firewall services. *See also* firewall. *Compare* netfilter, iptables.

IP masquerading *n. See* NAT.

IP multicasting *n.* Short for **I**nternet **P**rotocol **multicasting**. The extension of local area network multicasting technology to a TCP/IP network. Hosts send and receive multicast datagrams, the destination fields of which specify IP host group addresses rather than individual IP addresses. A host indicates that it is a member of a group by means of the Internet Group Management Protocol. *See also* datagram, Internet Group Membership Protocol, IP, MBONE, multicasting.

IPng *n.* Acronym for **I**nternet **P**rotocol **n**ext **g**eneration. A revised version of the Internet Protocol (IP) designed primarily to address growth on the Internet. IPng is compatible with, but an evolutionary successor to, the current version of IP, IPv4 (IP version 4), and was approved as a draft standard in 1998 by the IETF (Internet Engineering Task Force). It offers several improvements over IPv4 including a quadrupled IP address size (from 32 bits to 128 bits), expanded routing capabilities, simplified header formats, improved support for options, and support for quality of service, authentication, and privacy. *Also called:* IPv6. *See also* IETF, IP, IP address.

IP number *n. See* IP address.

IPP *n. See* Internet Printing Protocol.

IPSec *n.* Short for **I**nternet **P**rotocol **Sec**urity. A security mechanism under development by the IETF (Internet Engineering Task Force) designed to ensure secure packet exchanges at the IP (Internet Protocol) layer. IPSec is based on two levels of security: AH (Authentication Header), which authenticates the sender and assures the recipient that the information has not been altered during transmission, and ESP (Encapsulating Security Protocol), which provides data encryption in addition to authentication and integrity assurance. IPSec protects all protocols in the TCP/IP protocol suite and Internet communications by using Layer Two Tunneling Protocol (L2TP) and is expected to ensure secure transmissions over virtual private networks (VPNs). *See also* anti-replay, communications protocol, Diffie-Hellman, ESP IEEE standard, IETF, IP, IPv6, Layer Two Tunneling Protocol, TCP/IP, packet, virtual private network.

IP Security *n. See* IPSec.

IP/SoC Conference and Exhibition *n.* Acronym for **I**ntellectual **P**roperty/**S**ystem **o**n a **C**hip **Conference and Exhibition**. Leading conference and exhibition for executives, architects, and engineers using intellectual property in the design and production of system-on-a-chip semiconductors. The event features product exhibits and forums for the exchange of information.

IP splicing *n. See* IP spoofing.

IP spoofing *n.* The act of inserting a false sender IP address into an Internet transmission in order to gain unauthorized access to a computer system. *Also called:* IP splicing. *See also* IP address, spoofing.

IP switching *n.* A technology developed by Ipsilon Networks (Sunnyvale, Calif.) that enables a sequence of IP packets with a common destination to be transmitted over a high-speed, high-bandwidth Asynchronous Transfer Mode (ATM) connection.

iptables *n.* A utility used to configure firewall settings and rules in Linux. Part of the netfilter framework in the Linux kernel, iptables replaces ipchains, a previous implementation. *See also* netfilter. *Compare* IP Filter.

IP telephony *n.* Telephone service including voice and fax, provided through an Internet or network connection. IP telephony requires two steps: conversion of analog voice to digital format by a coding/uncoding device (codec) and conversion of the digitized information to packets for IP transmission. *Also called:* Internet telephony, Voice over IP (VoIP). *See also* H.323, VoIP.

IP tunneling *n.* A technique used to encapsulate data inside a TCP/IP packet for transmission between IP addresses. IP tunneling provides a secure means for data from different networks to be shared over the Internet.

IPv4 *n.* Short for **I**nternet **P**rotocol version **4**. The current version of the Internet Protocol (IP), as compared with the next-generation IP, which is known familiarly as IPng and more formally as IPv6 (IP version 6). *See also* IP. *Compare* IPng.

IPv6 *n.* Short for **I**nternet **P**rotocol version **6**. The next-generation Internet Protocol from the Internet Engineering Task Force (IETF), IPv6 is now included as part of IP support in many products and in the major operating systems. IPv6 offers several improvements from IPv4, most significantly an increase of available address space from 32 to 128 bits, which makes the number of available addresses effectively unlimited. Usually called IPng (next generation), IPv6 also includes support for multicast and anycast addressing. *See also* anycasting, IP, IPng.

ipvs *n.* Acronym for **IP** **V**irtual **S**erver. *See* LVS.

IPX *n.* Acronym for **I**nternetwork **P**acket **E**xchange. The protocol in Novell NetWare that governs addressing and routing of packets within and between LANs. IPX packets can be encapsulated in Ethernet packets or Token Ring frames. IPX operates at ISO/OSI levels 3 and 4 but does not perform all the functions at those levels. In particular, IPX does not guarantee that a message will be complete (no lost packets); SPX has that job. *See also* Ethernet (definition 1), packet, Token Ring network. *Compare* SPX (definition 1).

IPX/SPX *n.* Acronym for **I**nternetwork **P**acket **E**xchange/**S**equenced **P**acket **E**xchange. The network and transport level protocols used by Novell NetWare, which together correspond to the combination of TCP and IP in the TCP/IP protocol suite. IPX is a connectionless protocol that handles addressing and routing of packets. SPX, which runs above IPX, ensures correct delivery. *See also* IPX, SPX (definition 1).

IR *n. See* infrared.

IRC *n.* Acronym for **I**nternet **R**elay **C**hat. A service that enables an Internet user to participate in a conversation on line in real time with other users. An IRC channel, maintained by an IRC server, transmits the text typed by each user who has joined the channel to all other users who have joined the channel. Generally, a channel is dedicated to a particular topic, which may be reflected in the channel's name. An IRC client shows the names of currently active channels, enables the user to join a channel, and then displays the other participants' words on individual lines so that the user can respond. IRC was invented in 1988 by Jarkko Oikarinen of Finland. *See also* channel (definition 2), server (definition 2).

IrDA *n.* Acronym for **I**nfrared **D**ata **A**ssociation. The industry organization of computer, component, and telecommunications vendors who have established the standards for infrared communication between computers and peripheral devices such as printers.

IRL *n.* Acronym for **i**n **r**eal **l**ife. An expression used by many online users to denote life outside the computer realm, especially in conjunction with virtual worlds such as online talkers, IRC, MUDs, and virtual reality. *See also* IRC, MUD, talker, virtual reality.

IRSG *n. See* Internet Research Steering Group.

IRTF *n. See* Internet Research Task Force.

ISAPI *n.* Acronym for **I**nternet **S**erver **A**pplication **P**rogramming **I**nterface. An easy-to-use, high-performance interface for back-end applications for Microsoft's Internet Information Server (IIS). ISAPI has its own dynamic-link library, which offers significant performance advantages over the CGI (Common Gateway Interface) specification. *See also* Internet Information Server. *Compare* CGI.

ISAPI filter *n.* A DLL file used by Microsoft Internet Information Server (IIS) to verify and authenticate ISAPI requests received by the IIS.

ISA Server *n. See* Internet Security and Acceleration Server.

ISC *n. See* Internet Software Consortium.

ISDN *n.* Acronym for **I**ntegrated **S**ervices **D**igital **N**etwork. A high-speed digital communications network evolving from existing telephone services. The goal in developing ISDN was to replace the current telephone network, which requires digital-to-analog conversions, with facilities totally devoted to digital switching and transmission, yet advanced enough to replace traditionally analog forms of data, ranging from voice to computer transmissions, music, and video. ISDN is available in two forms, known as BRI (Basic Rate Interface) and PRI (Primary Rate Interface). BRI consists of two B (bearer) channels that carry data at 64 Kbps and one D (data) channel that carries control and signal information at 16 Kbps. In North America and Japan, PRI consists of 23 B channels and 1 D channel, all operating at 64 Kbps; elsewhere in the world, PRI consists of 30 B channels and 1 D channel. Computers and other devices connect to ISDN lines through simple, standardized interfaces. *See also* BRI, channel (definition 2), PRI.

ISDN terminal adapter *n.* The hardware interface between a computer and an ISDN line. *See also* ISDN.

I seek you *n.* *See* ICQ.

ISLAN *n.* *See* isochronous network.

ISMA *n.* Acronym for Internet Streaming Media Alliance. A nonprofit organization promoting the adoption of open standards for the streaming of rich media over Internet Protocol (IP) networks. ISMA membership consists of a number of technology companies and groups including Apple Computer, Cisco Systems, IBM, Kasenna, Philips, and Sun Microsystems. *See also* Windows Media Technologies.

ISO *n.* Short for International Organization for Standardization (often incorrectly identified as an acronym for International Standards Organization), an international association of 130 countries, each of which is represented by its leading standard-setting organization—for example, ANSI (American National Standards Institute) for the United States. The ISO works to establish global standards for communications and information exchange. Primary among its accomplishments is the widely accepted ISO/OSI reference model, which defines standards for the interaction of computers connected by communications networks. *ISO* is not an acronym; rather, it is derived from the Greek word *isos*, which means "equal" and is the root of the prefix "iso-."

ISOC *n.* *See* Internet Society.

isochronous network *n.* A type of network defined in the IEEE 802.9 specification that combines ISDN and LAN technologies to enable networks to carry multimedia. *Also called:* Integrated Services LAN, ISLAN.

ISO/OSI reference model *n.* Short for International Organization for Standardization Open Systems Interconnection **reference model**. A layered architecture (plan) that standardizes levels of service and types of interaction for computers exchanging information through a communications network. The ISO/OSI reference model separates computer-to-computer communications into seven protocol layers, or levels, each building—and relying—upon the standards contained in the levels below it. The lowest of the seven layers deals solely with hardware links; the highest deals with software interactions at the application-program level. It is a fundamental blueprint designed to help guide the creation of networking hardware and software. *Also called:* OSI reference model.

ISP *n.* Acronym for Internet service provider. A business that supplies Internet connectivity services to individuals, businesses, and other organizations. Some ISPs are large national or multinational corporations that offer access in many locations, while others are limited to a single city or region. *Also called:* access provider, service provider.

ISSE *n.* *See* SSE.

IT *n.* Acronym for Information Technology. *See* Information Services.

ITM *n.* Short for Internet traffic management. The analysis and control of Internet traffic to improve efficiency and optimize for high availability. With ITM, Web traffic is distributed among multiple servers using load balancers and other devices. *See also* load balancing.

ITSP *n.* Acronym for Internet Telephony Service Provider. A business that supplies PC-to-telephone calling capabilities to individuals, businesses, and organizations. Through an ITSP, calls initiated on a PC travel over the Internet to a gateway that, in turn, sends the call to the standard public switched phone network and, eventually, to the receiving telephone. *See also* ISP, telephony.

ITU *n.* Acronym for International Telecommunication Union. An international organization based in Geneva, Switzerland, that is responsible for making recommendations and establishing standards governing telephone and data communications systems for public and private telecommunications organizations. Founded in 1865 under the name International Telegraph Union, it was renamed the International Telecommunication Union in 1934 to signify the full scope of its responsibilities. ITU became an agency of the United Nations in 1947. A reorganization in 1992 aligned the ITU into three governing bodies: the Radiocommunication Sector, the Telecommunication Standardization Sector (ITU-TSS, ITU-T, for short; formerly the CCITT), and the Telecommunication Development Sector. *See also* ITU-T.

ITU-T *n.* The standardization division of the International Telecommunication Union, formerly called Comité Consultatif International Télégraphique et Téléphonique (CCITT). The ITU-T develops communications recommendations for all analog and digital communications. *Also called:* ITU-TSS. *See also* CCITT Groups 1-4, ITU.

ITU-TSS *n. See* ITU-T.

ITU-T V series *n. See* V series.

ITU-T X series *n. See* X series.

iTV *n.* Acronym for Interactive television. A communications medium combining television with interactive services. iTV offers two-way communications between users and communications providers. From their televisions, users can order special programming, respond to programming options, and access the Internet and additional services such as instant messaging and telephone functions.

i-way *n. See* Information Superhighway.

J

J2EE *n.* Acronym for Java 2 Platform Enterprise Edition. An application server framework from Sun Microsystems, Inc., for the development of distributed applications. It includes all the previous Java APIs targeted for multi-tiered distributed enterprise information systems. The J2EE platform consists of a set of services, application programming interfaces (APIs), and protocols that provide the functionality for developing multitiered, Web-based applications. *See also* Enterprise JavaBeans, Java, Jini, JMS, JNDI, JSP, JTA, JTS, RMI-IIOP.

jabber *n.* A continuous stream of random data transmitted over a network as the result of some malfunction.

Jabber *n.* An XML-based instant messaging system. Jabber software is available for most operating systems and allows user access to other instant messaging services. Jabber is an open source application overseen by Jabber.org.

jack in *vb.* **1.** To log on to a computer. **2.** To connect to a network or BBS, especially for purposes of entering an IRC or a virtual reality simulation, such as a MUD. (To leave is to *jack out*.) *See also* IRC, MUD.

jack out *vb.* **1.** To log off a computer. **2.** To disconnect from a network or online bulletin board system. *See also* jack in, log on.

Janet *n.* Short for the Joint Academic Network. A wide area network in the United Kingdom that serves as the principal backbone for the Internet in that country. *See also* backbone (definition 1).

.jar *n.* A file name extension that identifies a compressed JAR (Java Archive) file. Note: By changing the .jar extension to .zip, you can use popular extraction tools such as PKZIP or WINZIP to look at a .jar file's contents. *See also* JAR, PKZIP, .zip.

JAR *n.* Acronym for Java Archive file. JAR files allow Java developers to efficiently deploy Java classes and their associated resources. The elements in a JAR file are compressed just as in a standard zip file. JAR files include a security mechanism and a special META-INF directory that contains administrative information about the contents of the files. Using a combination of a digital signature and the META-INF data, JAR files can be signed to ensure authenticity and security. *See also* .jar.

Java *n.* An object-oriented programming language developed by Sun Microsystems, Inc. Similar to C++, Java is smaller, more portable, and easier to use than C++ because it is more robust and it manages memory on its own. Java was also designed to be secure and platform-neutral (meaning that it can be run on any platform) through the fact that Java programs are compiled into bytecode, which is not refined to the point of relying on platform-specific instructions and runs on a computer in a special software environment known as a virtual machine. This characteristic of Java makes it a useful language for programming Web applications, since users access the

Web from many types of computers. Java is used in programming small applications, or applets, for the World Wide Web, as well as in creating distributed network applications. *See also* Java applet, Jini.

Java applet *n.* A Java class that is loaded and run by an already-running Java application such as a Web browser or an applet viewer. Java applets can be downloaded and run by any Web browser capable of interpreting Java, such as Internet Explorer, Netscape Navigator, and HotJava. Java applets are frequently used to add multimedia effects and interactivity to Web pages, such as background music, real-time video displays, animations, calculators, and interactive games. Applets can be activated automatically when a user views a page, or they may require some action on the part of the user, such as clicking on an icon in the Web page. *See also* applet, Java.

JavaBean *n.* A Java component architecture defined in the JavaBeans specification developed by Sun Microsystems. A JavaBean, or Bean, is a reusable application component—an independent code segment—that can be combined with other JavaBean components to create a Java applet or application. The JavaBean concept emphasizes the platform-independence of the Java language, in which ideally a program, once written, can run on any computing platform. JavaBeans are similar to Microsoft's ActiveX controls. ActiveX controls, however, can be developed in different programming languages but executed only on a Windows platform. JavaBeans can be developed only in the Java programming language but ideally can run on any platform. *See also* ActiveX, Java.

Java Card *n.* An application programming interface (API) from Sun Microsystems, Inc., that allows Java applets and programs to run on smart cards and other devices with limited memory. Java Card uses a Java Card Virtual Machine designed for severely memory-constrained devices. *See also* applet, Java Card Virtual Machine, smart card (definition 2).

Java Card Virtual Machine *n.* An ultra-small-footprint, highly optimized foundation of a runtime environment within the Java 2 Platform Micro Edition. Derived from the Java Virtual Machine (JVM), it is targeted at smart cards and other severely memory-constrained devices. The Java Card Virtual Machine can run in devices with memory as small as 24 KB of ROM, 16 KB of EEPROM, and 512 bytes of RAM. *See also* Java Card.

Java chip *n.* An implementation on a single integrated circuit of the virtual machine specified for execution of the Java programming language. Such chips, which are being developed by Sun Microsystems, Inc., could be used in very small devices and as controllers for appliances. *See also* Java.

Java Developer's Kit *n.* A set of software tools developed by Sun Microsystems, Inc., for writing Java applets or applications. The kit, which is distributed free, includes a Java compiler, interpreter, debugger, viewer for applets, and documentation. *Acronym:* JDK. *See also* applet, Java, Java applet.

Java Foundation Classes *n.* A Java-based set of class libraries developed by Sun Microsystems, Inc. Encompassing fundamentals of the Internet Foundation Classes created by Netscape Communications Corp., the Java Foundation Classes extend the Java Abstract Window Toolkit (AWT) by providing graphical user interface components for use in developing commercial and Internet-related Java applications. *See also* Internet Foundation Classes, Java, JavaBean.

Java IDL *n.* Short for **Java I**nterface **D**efinition **L**anguage. A Java technology that provides CORBA interoperability and connectivity capabilities for the Java platform. These capabilities enable Java applications to invoke operations on remote network services using the Object Management Group Interface Definition Language and Internet Inter-ORB Protocol. *See also* J2EE, RMI-IIOP.

JavaMail *n.* An API in the Sun Microsystems, Inc., Java platform for sending and receiving mail. A set of abstract APIs that model a mail system, JavaMail provides a platform-independent and protocol-independent framework to build Java-based e-mail client applications. *See also* e-mail, J2EE.

Java Management Application Programming Interface *n.* A set of application programming interface specifications, proposed by Sun Microsystems, Inc., to enable the Java language to be used for network management. *Acronym:* JMAPI. *See also* Java.

JavaOS *n.* An operating system designed to run applications written in the Java programming language. JavaOS was created by JavaSoft, an operating company of Sun Microsystems, Inc., to run the Java Virtual Machine (JVM) directly on microprocessors, and thus eliminate the need for a resident operating system. JavaOS is small and designed for network computers, as well as devices ranging from game machines to pagers and cellular telephones. *See also* Java.

JavaScript *n.* A scripting language developed by Netscape Communications and Sun Microsystems that is loosely related to Java. JavaScript, however, is not a true object-oriented language, and it is limited in performance compared with Java because it is not compiled. Basic online applications and functions can be added to Web pages with JavaScript, but the number and complexity of available application programming interface functions are fewer than those available with Java. JavaScript code, which is included in a Web page along with the HTML code, is generally considered easier to write than Java, especially for novice programmers. A JavaScript-compliant Web browser, such as Netscape Navigator or Internet Explorer, is necessary to run JavaScript code. *See also* HTML. *Compare* Java.

JavaServer Pages *n. See* JSP.

Java Speech Grammar Format *n.* A platform-independent grammar description format developed for use with speech recognition systems. Java Speech Grammar Format is used extensively with Voice XML and can be used with most speech recognition systems and related applications. *Acronym:* JSGF.

Java Virtual Machine *n.* The environment in which Java programs run. The Java Virtual Machine gives Java programs a software-based "computer" they can interact with. (Programs, even the most seemingly unchallenging ones designed for children or entertainment, must run within an environment from which they can use memory, display information, gather input, and so on.) Because the Java Virtual Machine is not a real computer but exists in software, a Java program can run on any physical computing platform, such as a Windows 9x computer or a Macintosh, equipped with an interpreter—usually an Internet browser—that can carry out the program's instructions and a Java Virtual Machine that provides the "hardware" on which the program can run. *Acronym:* JVM.

JDK *n.* *See* Java Developer's Kit.

jDoc *n.* A cross-platform, interactive format for display, distribution, and interaction with live Web pages. jDoc documents are small in size and can be embedded in HTML documents to offer client-side interactivity. jDoc was created by EarthStones and is an extension to Sun's Java platform.

JetSend Protocol *n.* A platform-independent communications protocol developed by Hewlett-Packard to enable direct device-to-device communication. The JetSend protocol is designed to provide JetSend-enabled devices with the ability to exchange information and data without the need for device drivers or reliance on servers or user intervention. The protocol is intended for use with printers, scanners, fax machines, and other such information "appliances" and was developed to simplify and improve interoperability between and among a wide range of devices.

JFIF *n.* Acronym for **J**PEG **F**ile **I**nterchange **F**ormat. A means of saving photographic images stored according to the Joint Photographic Experts Group image compression technique. JFIF represents a "common language" file format in that it is designed specifically to allow users to transfer JPEG images easily between different computers and applications. *See also* JPEG, TIFF JPEG.

Jini *n.* A technical specification developed by Sun Microsystems that uses a small piece (48 KB) of Java code to allow any network device with a Java Virtual Machine (JVM) to announce its availability and provide its services to any other device connected to the same network. Jini is based on the concept of creating a "federation" of self-configuring devices capable of transparently exchanging code when necessary to simplify interactions between network devices. *See also* Java.

JIT *adj.* *See* just-in-time.

JMAPI *n.* *See* Java Management Application Programming Interface.

JMS *n.* Acronym for **J**ava **M**essaging **S**ervice. In the J2EE network platform, JMS is an API for using enterprise messaging systems such as IBM MQ Series, TIBCO Rendezvous, and others. *See also* J2EE.

JNDI *n.* Acronym for **J**ava **N**aming and **D**irectory **I**nterface. A set of APIs in the J2EE platform from Sun Microsystems, Inc., that assists with the interfacing to multiple naming and directory services. *See also* J2EE.

Joint Photographic Experts Group *n. See* JPEG (definition 1).

journal *n.* A computer-based log or record of transactions that takes place in a computer or across a network. A journal could be used, for example, to record message transfers on a communications network, to keep track of system activities that alter the contents of a database, or to maintain a record of files that have been archived for storage or deleted from the system. A journal is often kept as a means of reconstructing events or sets of data should they become lost or damaged.

.jpeg *n.* The file extension that identifies graphic image files in the JPEG format. *See also* JPEG.

JPEG *n.* **1.** Acronym for **J**oint **P**hotographic **E**xperts **G**roup. An ISO/ITU standard for storing images in compressed form using a discrete cosine transform. JPEG trades off compression against loss; it can achieve a compression ratio of 100:1 with significant loss and possibly 20:1 with little noticeable loss. **2.** A graphic stored as a file in the JPEG format.

JPEG File Interchange Format *n. See* JFIF.

.jpg *n.* The file extension that identifies graphic images encoded in the JPEG File Interchange Format, as originally specified by the Joint Photographic Experts Group (JPEG). Inline graphics on World Wide Web pages are often .jpg files, such as coolgraphic.jpg. *See also* JPEG (definition 2).

JScript *n.* An interpreted, object-based scripting language that borrows from C, C++, and Java. It is Microsoft's implementation of the ECMA 262 language specification (ECMAScript Edition 3). The latest versions of JavaScript and JScript are compliant with the European Computer Manufacturing Association's ECMAScript Language Specification (ECMA 262 standard, for short).

JSP *n.* Short for **J**ava**S**erver **P**ages. A technology created by Sun Microsystems to enable development of platform-independent Web-based applications. Using HTML and XML tags and Java scriptlets, JSP helps Web site developers create cross-platform programs. JSP scriptlets run on the server, not in a Web browser, and generate dynamic content on Web pages, with the ability to integrate content from a variety of data sources, such as databases, files, and JavaBean components. Web site developers can concentrate on design and display of a Web site without the need for application development expertise. *See also* Java, JavaBean. *Compare* Active Server Pages.

JSP container *n.* Short for **J**ava**S**erver **P**ages **container**. In the J2EE platform, a JSP container provides the same services as a servlet container, such as providing network services over which requests and responses are sent, decoding requests, and formatting responses. All servlet containers must support HTTP as a protocol for requests

J

and responses, but they may also support additional request-response protocols such as HTTPS. The JSP container is also an engine that interprets and processes JSP pages into a servlet. *See also* container, HTTP, HTTPS, J2EE, servlet, servlet container.

JTA *n.* Acronym for **J**ava **T**ransaction **A**PI. In the J2EE platform, JTA specifies transactions, comments, and rollbacks used by EJBs (Enterprise JavaBeans). It is a high-level, implementation-independent protocol API that allows applications and application servers to access transactions. *See also* J2EE, JTS, rollback.

JTS *n.* Acronym for **J**ava **T**ransaction **S**ervices. In the J2EE platform, JTS specifies the implementation of a transaction manager that supports JTA and implements the Java mapping of the OMG Object Transaction Service specification at a level below the API. JTS propagates transactions using the Internet Inter-ORB Protocol (IIOP). *See also* J2EE, JTA, rollback.

JUG *n.* Acronym for **J**ava **U**ser **G**roup. A user group that meets to discuss the Java programming language and the Java platform. *See also* user group.

Jughead *n.* Acronym for **J**onzy's **U**niversal **G**opher **H**ierarchy **E**xcavation **a**nd **D**isplay. An Internet service that enables a user to locate directories in Gopherspace through a keyword search. A Jughead server indexes keywords appearing in directory titles in top-level Gopher menus but does not index the files within the directories. To access Jughead, users must point their Gopher clients to a Jughead server. *See also* Gopher, Gopherspace. *Compare* Archie, Veronica.

jump page *n.* *See* doorway page.

Jump to .NET *n.* Acronym for **J**ava **U**ser **M**igration **P**ath to Microsoft **.NET**. A set of Microsoft technologies and services that enable Java programmers to preserve, enhance, and migrate Java language projects onto the Microsoft .NET platform. It includes tools for interoperability of existing code, Java language syntax support, and automated conversion of Java source code to C#. JUMP to .NET enables programmers using the Java language to move existing code to the Microsoft .NET platform. *See also* .NET.

just-in-time *adj.* **1.** Describing a system of inventory control and industrial production management based on the Japanese *kanban* system. Under a just-in-time system, workers receive materials from suppliers "just in time" for scheduled manufacturing to take place. Line workers generally signal that they require materials by means of a card or a computerized request system. **2.** Describing an action that is taken only when it becomes necessary, such as just-in-time compilation or just-in-time object activation. **3.** Describing a compiler that compiles Java on the fly. *Acronym:* JIT. *See also* Java, on the fly.

JVM *n.* *See* Java Virtual Machine.

K

kamikaze packet *n. See* Chernobyl packet.

KB *n.* Short for **K**nowledge **B**ase. Primary source of product information for Microsoft support engineers and customers. This comprehensive collection of articles, updated daily, contains detailed how-to information, answers to technical-support questions, and known issues. *Also called:* Microsoft Knowledge Base.

Kerberos *n.* A network authentication protocol developed by MIT. Kerberos authenticates the identity of users attempting to log on to a network and encrypts their communications through secret-key cryptography. A free implementation of Kerberos is available from MIT, although it is also available in many commercial products. *Also called:* Kerberos v5 authentication protocol. *See also* authentication, cryptography, IPSec.

Kermit *n.* A file transfer protocol used in asynchronous communications between computers. Kermit is a very flexible protocol used in many software packages designed for communications over telephone lines. *Compare* Xmodem, Ymodem, Zmodem.

key *n.* **1.** On a keyboard, the combination of a plastic keycap, a tension mechanism that suspends the keycap but allows it to be pressed down, and an electronic mechanism that records the key press and key release. **2.** In database management, an identifier for a record or group of records in a datafile. **3.** In encryption and digital signatures, a string of bits used for encrypting and decrypting information to be transmitted. Encryption commonly relies on two different types of keys, a public key known to more than one person (say, both the sender and the receiver) and a private key known only to one person (typically, the sender). **4.** A metal object used with a physical lock to disable a computer system.

key binary large object *n.* A key binary large object (BLOB) provides a way to store keys outside of the cryptographic service provider (CSP) and is used to transfer keys securely from one CSP to another. A key BLOB consists of a standard header followed by data representing the key. *Acronym:* key BLOB.

key BLOB *n. See* key binary large object.

keymaster *n.* A common host name assigned by network administrators to a gateway or router. Popularized in part by the Keymaster character in the 1984 movie "Ghostbusters."

key pair *n.* A widely used encryption scheme that allows secure use of digital certificate identification. A key pair consists of a public key and a private key. The public key is shared with other individuals; the private key is known only to its owner. The public and private key form an asymmetric pair, meaning the keys on either end of a transmission are different. A message encrypted with the public key can be decrypted

K

only with the private key, and a message encrypted with the private key can be decrypted only with the public key.

keyword *n.* **1.** A characteristic word, phrase, or code that is stored in a key field and is used to conduct sorting or searching operations on records in a database. **2.** Any of the set of words that composes a given programming language or set of operating-system routines.

keyword density *n.* A measurement of the keywords on a Web page as a percentage of total text. High keyword density can increase a Web site's probability of being found by search engines, some of which use keyword density to rank a Web page's relevance to an Internet search. *See also* keyword (definition 1).

keyword-in-context *n.* An automatic search methodology that creates indexes of document text or titles. Each keyword is stored in the resulting index along with some surrounding text, usually the word or phrase that precedes or follows the keyword in the text or title. *Acronym:* KWIC.

keyword stuffing *vb. See* spamdexter.

kill file *n. See* bozo filter.

knowbot *n.* Short for **know**ledge ro**bot**. An artificial-intelligence program that follows a set of predetermined rules to perform work, such as searching for files or looking for documents that contain specific pieces of information on a network, such as the Internet. *See also* bot (definition 2).

KWIC *n. See* keyword-in-context.

K

L

L2TP *n. See* Layer Two Tunneling Protocol.

L8R *adv.* Abbreviation for later, as in "See you later," an expression often used in e-mail or Usenet groups as a closing remark.

label switching *n. See* MPLS.

label switch path *n. See* MPLS.

label switch router *n. See* MPLS.

LACP *n.* Acronym for **L**ink **A**ggregation **C**ontrol **P**rotocol. *See* link aggregation.

LAN *n.* Acronym for local area network. A group of computers and other devices dispersed over a relatively limited area and connected by a communications link that enables any device to interact with any other on the network. LANs commonly include PCs and shared resources such as laser printers and large hard disks. The devices on a LAN are known as nodes, and the nodes are connected by cables through which messages are transmitted. *See also* baseband network, broadband network, bus network, client/server architecture, communications protocol, contention, CSMA/CD, network, peer-to-peer architecture, ring network, star network. *Compare* WAN.

LANE *n.* Acronym for **LAN E**mulation. *See* ATM (definition 1), communications protocol, LAN.

LAN Manager *n.* An older LAN (local area network) technology developed by Microsoft and distributed by Microsoft, IBM (as IBM LAN Server), and other original equipment manufacturers. Superseded by TCP/IP networking protocols in Windows 9x, LAN Manager implemented the NetBEUI protocol and was notable for its small stack size. It was used to connect computers running the MS-DOS, OS/2, or UNIX operating systems to allow users to share files and system resources and to run distributed applications using a client/server architecture. *See also* client/server architecture, LAN, NetBEUI.

LANtastic *n.* A network operating system from Artisoft designed to support both peer-to-peer and client/server networks consisting of PCs running a mix of MS-DOS and Windows operating systems.

last in, first out *n.* A method of processing a queue in which items are removed in inverse order relative to the order in which they were added—that is, the last in is the first out. *Acronym: LIFO. See also* stack. *Compare* first in, first out.

last mile *n.* The connection (which may in fact be more or less than one mile) between an end user's system and that of a service provider, such as a telephone company. The "last mile" connection historically has referred to the twisted-pair copper wires used between a home and the telephone company. While this definition remains accurate, "last mile" is now often used more broadly to refer to the link between an end user's system and the high-speed Internet access technology of a service pro-vider, such as an ISP (Internet service provider). Thus, for modem users accessing the Internet through voice-grade lines, the last mile is still equivalent to the phone com-pany's twisted-pair copper wiring. However, because standard modem transmission over voice-grade lines is sometimes frustratingly slow, other last mile solutions have been designed to provide greater speed and bandwidth. These include coaxial cable (used in cable TV), fiber optics, or a radio link (such as a cellular telephone or a point-to-point link). DSL and ISDN are methods for providing high-speed last-mile data service through twisted-pair copper wires. *See also* DSL, ISDN, twisted-pair wiring. *Compare* local loop.

latency *n.* The time required for a signal to travel from one point on a network to another. *See also* ping[1] (definition 1).

layer *n.* **1.** The protocol or protocols operating at a particular level within a protocol suite, such as IP within the TCP/IP suite. Each layer is responsible for providing spe-cific services or functions for computers exchanging information over a communica-tions network (such as the layers in the ISO/OSI reference model) and information is passed from one layer to the next. Although different suites have varying numbers of levels, generally the highest layer deals with software interactions at the application level, and the lowest governs hardware-level connections between different comput-ers. See the table. *See also* ISO/OSI reference model, protocol stack, TCP/IP. **2.** In communications and distributed processing, a set of rules and standards that handles a particular class of events.

Table L.1   Layers in the ISO/OSI reference model.

ISO/OSI layer	Focus
Application (highest level)	Program-to-program transfer of information
Presentation	Text formatting and display, code conversion
Session	Establishing, maintaining, and coordinating communication
Transport	Accurate delivery, service quality
Network	Transport routes, message handling and transfer
Data-link	Coding, addressing, and transmitting information
Physical	Hardware connections

layer 4 switching *n.* In Network Address Translation (NAT), a function that han-dles incoming packets and changes the IP address and destination port to transfer them to the proper server within the private network, and then readdresses return packets leaving the private network. Because layer 4 switching controls the address on packets moving in both directions, the internal network remains transparent to the client. *See also* LVS, NAT.

layered architecture *n.* The division of a network model into multiple discrete layers, or levels, through which messages pass as they are prepared for transmission. In a layered architecture, protocols at each layer provide specific services or functions and rely on protocols in the layers above and below them for other needed services. *See also* protocol.

Layer Two Tunneling Protocol *n.* An industry-standard Internet tunneling protocol that provides encapsulation for sending Point-to-Point Protocol (PPP) frames across packet-oriented media. For IP networks, Layer Two Tunneling Protocol traffic is sent as User Datagram Protocol (UDP) messages. In Microsoft operating systems, this protocol is used in conjunction with Internet Protocol security (IPSec) as a virtual private network (VPN) technology to provide remote access or router-to-router VPN connections. Layer Two Tunneling Protocol is described in RFC 2661. *Acronym:* L2TP. *See also* IPSec, Point-to-Point Protocol, tunnel, User Datagram Protocol.

lcd *n.* In some FTP clients, the command that changes the current directory on the local system. *See also* FTP client.

LCP *n. See* Point-to-Point Protocol.

LDAP *n. See* Lightweight Directory Access Protocol.

leapfrog attack *n.* A method used by hackers to make an attack difficult to trace back to the source. In a leapfrog attack the hacker uses a User ID stolen from another source or routes information through a series of hosts to hide their identity and obscure the origin of the attack. *Also called:* network weaving.

LER *n. See* MPLS.

letterbomb *n.* An e-mail message that is intended to impair the recipient's computer use. Some sequences of control characters can lock up a terminal, files attached to the message may contain viruses or Trojan horses, and a sufficiently large message can overflow a mailbox or crash a system. *See also* e-mail[1] (definition 1), mailbox, Trojan horse, virus.

LHARC *n.* A freeware file-compression utility program introduced in 1988. With LHARC, the contents of one or more files can be compressed into a singular, smaller file, with the extension .lha. A copy of the program is required to uncompress these files. LHARC can also embed a small program with the compressed information and save everything in a single file, called a self-extracting archive, with an .exe extension. As a result, the recipient of the compressed file does not need a separate program to uncompress the file. *See also* freeware, PKZIP.

Lightweight Directory Access Protocol *n.* A network protocol designed to work on TCP/IP stacks to extract information from a hierarchical directory such as X.500. This gives users a single tool to comb through data to find a particular piece of information, such as a user name, an e-mail address, a security certificate, or other contact information. *Acronym:* LDAP. *See also* CCITT X series.

L

Lightweight Internet Person Schema *n.* In Lightweight Directory Access Protocol directories, a specification for the retrieval of such information as names and e-mail addresses. *Acronym:* LIPS. *See also* Lightweight Directory Access Protocol.

line *n.* **1.** Any wire or wires, such as power lines and telephone lines, used to transmit electrical power or signals. **2.** In communications, a connection, usually a physical wire or other cable, between sending and receiving (or calling and called) devices, including telephones, computers, and terminals. **3.** In a SONET network, a segment that runs between two multiplexers. *See also* SONET.

line adapter *n.* A device, such as a modem or network card, that connects a computer to a communications line and converts a signal to an acceptable form for transmission.

line analyzer *n.* A monitoring device used to verify the integrity of a communications line and to assist in troubleshooting.

linear bus *n. See* bus network.

line-based browser *n.* A Web browser whose display is based on text rather than graphics. A popular line-based browser is Lynx. *See also* Lynx, Web browser.

link *n. See* hyperlink.

link aggregation *n.* A technique for combining two or more Ethernet connections into one logical link, or trunk, between two devices. It is used to increase the bandwidth capacity of connections and to make these connections more resilient. The IEEE 802.3ad specification standardizes this process among different vendors using the Link Aggregation Control Protocol (LACP). *Also called:* bonding, trunking. *See also* IEEE 802.x.

Link Aggregation Control Protocol *n. See* link aggregation.

Link Control Protocol *n. See* Point-to-Point Protocol.

linked stylesheet *n.* A stylesheet existing separately from the HTML documents to which it is linked. A linked stylesheet may be used for sets of Web pages or entire Web sites requiring a uniform appearance. Since the style is defined once and linked to associated Web pages, the entire site can be changed by modifying a single stylesheet file. *Compare* inline stylesheet.

linkrot *n.* A condition affecting inadequately maintained Web pages that results in outdated, inoperative links to other Web pages.

Linux *n.* A version of the UNIX System V Release 3.0 kernel developed for PCs with 80386 and higher-level microprocessors. Developed by Linus Torvalds (for whom it is named) along with numerous collaborators worldwide, Linux is distributed free, and its source code is open to modification by anyone who chooses to work on it, although some companies distribute it as part of a commercial package with Linux-compatible utilities. The Linux kernel (or core of the operating system) works with the GNU utilities developed by the Free Software Foundation, which did not produce a kernel. It is used by some as an operating system for network servers and in the 1998/1999 timeframe began to gain increased visibility through support from vendors such as IBM and Compaq. *See also* free software, GNU, UNIX.

Lion worm *n.* A UNIX shellscript worm first detected in early 2001 that infects Linux servers using Berkeley Internet Name Domain (BIND) tools. After it has used a BIND exploit to infect a machine, Lion steals password files and other critical information and transmits them to the hacker. Lion then installs hacking tools and replaces critical files, hiding itself and opening multiple back doors for further compromise. The Lion worm was apparently launched in early 2001 by a group of Chinese hackers with a specific political agenda. In references to this worm, "Lion" may also be spelled as "1i0n".

LISTSERV *n.* One of the most popular commercial mailing list managers, marketed by L-SOFT International in versions for BITNET, UNIX, and Windows. *See also* mailing list, mailing list manager.

live *n.* Used to identify a Web site that has been published to a Web server and can be browsed by site visitors. *Also called:* going live.

Live3D *n.* A Netscape proprietary Virtual Reality Modeling Language (VRML) plug-in for Web browsers that allows users to view and interact with a virtual-reality world. *See also* VRML.

LLC *n.* Acronym for **L**ogical **L**ink **C**ontrol. In the IEEE 802.x specifications, the higher of two sublayers that make up the ISO/OSI data link layer. The LLC is responsible for managing communications links and handling frame traffic. *See also* IEEE 802.x, MAC.

Lmhosts file *n.* A local text file that lists the names of network hosts (sometimes called NetBIOS names) to IP addresses for hosts that are not located on the local subnet. *See also* IP address.

load balancing *n.* **1.** In distributed processing, the distribution of activity across two or more servers in order to avoid overloading any one with too many requests from users. Load balancing can be either static or dynamic. In the former, the load is balanced ahead of time by assigning different groups of users to different servers. In the latter, software refers incoming requests at runtime to whichever server is most capable of handling them. **2.** In client/server network administration, the process of reducing heavy traffic flows either by dividing a busy network segment into multiple smaller segments or by using software to distribute traffic among multiple network interface cards working simultaneously to transfer information to a server. **3.** In communications, the process of routing traffic over two or more routes rather than one. Such load balancing results in faster, more reliable transmissions.

local area network *n. See* LAN.

localhost *n.* The name that is used to represent the same computer on which a TCP/IP message originates. An IP packet sent to localhost has the IP address 127.0.0.1 and does not actually go out to the Internet. *See also* IP address, packet (definition 1), TCP/IP.

local loop *n.* The (end) portion of a telephone connection that runs from the subscriber to the local telephone exchange. *See also* last mile.

local newsgroups *n.* Newsgroups that are targeted toward a geographically limited area such as a city or educational institution. Posts to these newsgroups contain information that is specific to the area, concerning such topics as events, meetings, and sales. *See also* newsgroup.

LocalTalk *n.* An inexpensive cabling scheme used by AppleTalk networks to connect Apple Macintosh computers, printers, and other peripheral devices. *See also* AppleTalk.

local user profile *n.* A user profile that is created automatically on the computer the first time a user logs on to a computer. *See also* mandatory user profile, roaming user profile, user profile.

location-based service *n.* A service provided to a wireless mobile device based on the device's location. Location-based services can range from simple services, such as listing nearby restaurants, to more complex features, such as connecting to the Internet to monitor traffic conditions and find the least congested route to a destination.

lockout *n.* The act of denying access to a given resource (file, memory location, I/O port), usually to ensure that only one program at a time uses that resource.

Logical Link Control *n. See* LLC.

logical network *n.* A way to describe the topology, or layout, of a computer network. Referring to a logical (rather than physical) topology describes the way information moves through the network—for example, in a straight line (bus topology) or in a circle (ring topology). The difference between describing a network as logical or physical is sometimes subtle because the physical network (the actual layout of hardware and cabling) doesn't necessarily resemble the logical network (the path followed by transmissions). A logical ring, for example, might include groups of computers cabled octopus-like to hardware "collection points" which, in turn, are cabled to one another. In such a network, even though the physical layout of computers and connecting hardware might not visually resemble a ring, the logical layout followed by network transmissions would, indeed, be circular. *See also* bus network, ring network, star network, token ring network, topology. *Compare* physical network.

logic bomb *n.* A type of Trojan horse that executes when certain conditions are met, such as when a user performs a specific action.

login *n. See* logon.

log in *vb. See* log on.

logoff *n.* The process of terminating a session with a computer accessed through a communications line. *Also called:* logout.

log off *vb.* To terminate a session with a computer accessed through a communications line—usually a computer that is both distant and open to many users. *Also called:* log out. *Compare* log on.

logon *n.* The process of identifying oneself to a computer after connecting to it over a communications line. *Also called:* login.

log on *vb.* To gain access to a specific computer, a program, or a network by identifying oneself with a username and a password. *Also called:* log in. *Compare* log off.

logon script *n.* A file assigned to certain user accounts on a network system. A logon script runs automatically every time the user logs on. It can be used to configure a user's working environment at every logon, and it allows an administrator to influence a user's environment without managing all aspects of it. A logon script can be assigned to one or more user accounts. *Also called:* login script. *See also* user account.

logout *n. See* logoff.

log out *vb. See* log off.

LOL *n.* Acronym for laughing out loud. An interjection used in e-mail, online forums, and chat services to express appreciation of a joke or other humorous occurrence. *See also* ROFL.

long-haul *adj.* Of, pertaining to, or being a type of modem that is able to transmit over long distances. *Compare* short-haul.

LonWorks *n.* An open standard for network automation created by the Echelon Corporation and supported by the LonMark Interoperability Association. LonWorks, introduced in 1991, can be used in building, transportation, industrial, and home applications to implement a distributed control network.

loop check *n. See* echo check.

loop configuration *n.* A communications link in which multiple stations are joined to a communications line that runs in a closed loop. Generally, data sent by one station is received and retransmitted in turn by each station on the loop. The process continues until the data reaches its final destination. *See also* ring network.

Lotus cc:Mail *n. See* cc:Mail.

Lotus Domino *n.* A groupware application that transforms Lotus Notes into an application and messaging server. *See also* Lotus Notes.

Lotus Notes *n.* A groupware application introduced in 1988 by Lotus Development Corporation and now owned by IBM. Lotus Notes combines e-mail, calendar management, group scheduling, contact and task management, newsgroup access,

L

and Web browsing capability (through the integration of Microsoft Internet Explorer) in one client application. Lotus Notes also offers search capabilities across multiple formats and file types on a network or the Web.

LU *n.* Acronym for **l**ogical **u**nit. In an IBM SNA network, a point denoting the beginning or end of a communications session. *See also* SNA.

LUG *n.* Acronym for **L**inux **U**sers **G**roup. *See* user group.

lurk *vb.* To receive and read articles or messages in a newsgroup or other online conference without contributing to the ongoing exchange.

lurker *n.* A person who lurks in a newsgroup or other online conference. *See also* lurk. *Compare* netizen.

LVS *n.* Acronym for **L**inux **V**irtual **S**erver. A high-performance open source server that handles connections from clients and passes them on to a cluster of real servers. LVS receives incoming packets and forwards them to the proper back-end server. LVS is typically used to build scalable Web, mail, or other network services. *Also called:* ipvs. *See also* layer 4 switching.

Lycos *n.* A Web search engine and directory that provides summaries of pages matching search requests. In addition, the Lycos site offers categorized directories of sites, reviews of selected sites, and services for finding names, viewing maps, and so on.

Lynx *n.* A text-only Web browser program for UNIX platforms.

L

M

MAC *n.* Acronym for **M**edia **A**ccess **C**ontrol. In the IEEE 802.x specifications, the lower of two sublayers that make up the ISO/OSI data link layer. The MAC manages access to the physical network, delimits frames, and handles error control. *See also* IEEE 802.x, LLC.

MacBinary *n.* A file transfer protocol used to preserve coding for Macintosh-produced files stored in non-Macintosh computers, containing the file's resource fork (contains information such as program code, font data, digitized sound, or icons), data fork (contains user-supplied information such as the text of a word-processing document), and the Macintosh standard interface (called Finder) information block.

Mac OS *n.* Short for **Mac**intosh **o**perating **s**ystem. The name given to the Macintosh operating system, beginning with version 7.5 in September 1994, when Apple started licensing the software to other computer manufacturers. *See also* Macintosh.

macrocontent *n.* The primary text or other content of a Web page. *Compare* microcontent.

macro virus *n.* A virus that is written in a macro language associated with an application. The macro virus is carried by a document file used with that application and executes when the document is opened.

MacTCP *n.* A Macintosh extension that allows Macintosh computers to use TCP/IP. *See also* TCP/IP.

MADCAP *n.* *See* multicast address dynamic client allocation protocol.

MAE *n.* Acronym for **M**etropolitan **A**rea **E**xchange. One of the Internet exchange points operated by MCI WorldCom, through which Internet service providers (ISPs) connect in order to exchange data. The two largest MAEs, MAE East (outside Washington, D.C.) and MAE West (near San Jose, California) are major national and international network interconnect points; more than half of all traffic through the Internet travels through one or both of these points. MCI WorldCom also operates smaller, regional MAEs in Chicago, Dallas, Houston, Los Angeles, New York, Paris, and Frankfurt. *See also* backbone (definition 1), ISP.

Magellan *n.* A Web directory. Named for the Portuguese explorer, Magellan reviews and rates all Web sites it lists. Published by the McKinley Group, Magellan is now owned by Excite, Inc.

mailbomb[1] *n.* An excessively large amount of e-mail data (a very large number of messages or one very large message) sent to a user's e-mail address in an attempt to make the user's mailer program crash or to prevent the user from receiving further legitimate messages. *See also* e-mail[1] (definition 1). *Compare* letterbomb.

M

mailbomb² *vb.* To send a mailbomb to a user. One person might mailbomb a user with a single enormous message; a large number of users might mailbomb an unpopular person by simultaneously sending messages of normal size.

mailbot *n.* A program that automatically responds to e-mail messages or performs actions based on commands within the messages. A mailing list manager is one example. *See also* mailing list manager.

mailbox *n.* A disk storage area assigned to a network user for receipt of e-mail messages. *See also* e-mail¹ (definition 1).

mail digest *n. See* digest (definition 2).

mailer-daemon *n.* A program used to transport e-mail between hosts on a network. *See also* daemon.

mail header *n.* A block of text at the top of an e-mail message containing such information as the addresses of the sender and recipients, the date and time sent, the address to which a reply is to be sent, and the subject. The mail header is used by an e-mail client or program. *See also* e-mail¹ (definition 1).

mailing list *n.* A list of names and e-mail addresses that are grouped under a single name. When a user places the name of the mailing list in a mail client's To: field, the client sends the message to the machine where the mailing list resides, and that machine automatically sends the message to all the addresses on the list (possibly allowing a moderator to edit it first). *See also* LISTSERV, mailing list manager, Majordomo, moderator.

mailing list manager *n.* Software that maintains an Internet or intranet mailing list. The mailing list manager accepts messages posted by subscribers; sends copies of the messages (which may be edited by a moderator) to all the subscribers; and accepts and processes user requests, such as to subscribe or to unsubscribe to the mailing list. The most commonly used mailing list managers are LISTSERV and Majordomo. *See also* LISTSERV, mailing list, Majordomo, moderator.

mail merge *n.* A mass-mail facility that takes names, addresses, and sometimes pertinent facts about recipients and merges the information into a form letter or another such basic document.

mail reflector *n.* A newsgroup that consists simply of the messages posted to a mailing list translated into newsgroup format.

mailto *n.* A protocol designator used in the HREF of a hyperlink that enables a user to send e-mail to someone. For instance, Anne E. Oldhacker has the e-mail address aeo@baz.foo.com and an HTML document contains the code <A HREF="mailto:aeo@baz.foo.com">E-mail Anne!</A>. If a user clicks on the hyperlink "E-mail Anne!", the user's e-mail application is launched and the user can send e-mail to her without knowing her actual e-mail address. *See also* e-mail¹ (definition 1), HTML, hyperlink.

M

mainframe computer *n.* A high-level, typically large and expensive computer designed to handle intensive computational tasks. Mainframe computers are characterized by their ability to simultaneously support many users connected to the computer by terminals. The name is derived from "main frame," the cabinet originally used to house the processing unit of such computers. *See also* supercomputer.

Majordomo *n.* The name of a popular software program that manages and supports Internet mailing lists. *See also* mailing list, mailing list manager.

major geographic domain *n.* A two-character sequence in an Internet domain name address that indicates the country/region in which a host is located. The major geographic domain is the last part of the domain name address, following the subdomain and domain codes; for example, uiuc.edu.us indicates a host at the University of Illinois in the United States, whereas cam.ac.uk indicates a host at the University of Cambridge in the United Kingdom. The code .us, which indicates a domain in the United States, is usually omitted. *Also called:* country code. *See also* DNS (definition 1), domain name address.

Make Changes *n.* The Macintosh-style permission that gives users the right to make changes to a folder's contents; for example, modifying, renaming, moving, creating, and deleting files. When AppleTalk network integration translates access privileges into permissions, a user who has the Make Changes privilege is given Write and Delete permissions. *See also* permission.

malicious mobile code *n.* A virus or other destructive program that takes advantage of security weaknesses in wireless transmission systems. Malicious mobile code may affect computers, PDAs, Internet-capable digital phones, and other wireless networking devices.

malware *n.* Software created and distributed for malicious purposes, such as invading computer systems in the form of viruses, worms, or innocent-seeming plug-ins and extensions that mask other destructive capabilities. *Also called:* malicious software.

MAN *n.* Acronym for **m**etropolitan **a**rea **n**etwork. A high-speed network that can carry voice, data, and images at up to 200 Mbps or faster over distances of up to 75 km. Based on the network architecture, the transmission speed can be higher for shorter distances. A MAN, which can include one or more LANs as well as telecommunications equipment such as microwave and satellite relay stations, is smaller than a wide area network but generally operates at a higher speed. *Compare* LAN, WAN.

managed service provider *n.* A business that supplies remote access services to individuals and enterprises. Managed service providers offer remote connections, network management, user support, security, and applications hosting. *Acronym:* MSP. *Compare* ISP.

Management and Monitoring Tools *n.* Software components that include utilities for network management and monitoring, along with services that support client dialing and the updating of client phone books. Also included is the Simple Network Management Protocol (SNMP). *See also* SNMP.

M

Management Information Base *n.* A set of objects that represents various types of information about a device, used by a network management protocol (for example, SNMP) to manage the device. Because different network management services are used for different types of devices and protocols, each service has its own set of objects. *Acronym:* MIB. *See also* service, SNMP.

management information system *n.* A computer-based system for processing and organizing information so as to provide various levels of management within an organization with accurate and timely information needed for supervising activities, tracking progress, making decisions, and isolating and solving problems. *Acronym:* MIS.

mandatory user profile *n.* A user profile that is not updated when the user logs off. It is downloaded to the user's desktop each time the user logs on, and it is created by an administrator and assigned to one or more users to create consistent or job-specific user profiles. *See also* local user profile, roaming user profile, user profile.

man-in-the-middle attack *n.* A form of attack in which the intruder intercepts messages between parties in a public key exchange. Each party's messages are diverted to the intruder, who may alter them before sending them on. The parties on each end of the exchange remain unaware that their messages are being intercepted and modified. *Also called:* bucket brigade attack.

manual link *n.* A link that requires you to take action to update your data after the data in the source document changes.

MAPI *n.* Acronym for **M**essaging **A**pplication **P**rogramming **I**nterface. The Microsoft interface specification that allows different messaging and workgroup applications (including e-mail, voice mail, and fax) to work through a single client, such as the Exchange client included with Windows 95 and Windows NT.

markup language *n.* A set of codes in a text file that instructs a computer how to format the file on a printer or video display or how to index and link its contents. Examples of markup languages are Hypertext Markup Language (HTML) and Extensible Markup Language (XML), which are used in Web pages, and Standard Generalized Markup Language (SGML), which is used for typesetting and desktop publishing purposes and in electronic documents. Markup languages of this sort are designed to enable documents and other files to be platform-independent and highly portable between applications. *See also* HTML, SGML, XML.

marquee *n.* A nonstandard HTML extension that causes scrolling text to appear as part of a Web page. Currently, marquees are viewable only with Internet Explorer. *See also* HTML, Internet Explorer, Web page.

marquee component *n.* A region on a page that displays a horizontally scrolling text message.

M

master file *n.* In a set of database files, the file containing more or less permanent descriptive information about the principal subjects of the database, summary data, and one or more critical key fields. For example, customers' names, account numbers, addresses, and credit terms might be stored in a master file. *Compare* transaction file.

MathML *n.* Acronym for **Math**ematical **M**arkup Language. An XML application for describing mathematical notation and capturing both its structure and content. The goal of MathML is to enable mathematics to be served, received, and processed on the Web, just as HTML has enabled this functionality for text.

MAU *n.* Acronym for **M**ultistation **A**ccess **U**nit. A hub device in a token ring network that connects computers in a physical hub-and-spokes arrangement but uses the logical ring required in token ring networks. *Also called:* MSAU. *See also* hub, token ring network.

MBONE or **Mbone** *n.* Short for **m**ulticast back**bone**. A small set of Internet sites, each of which can transmit real-time audio and video simultaneously to all the others. MBONE sites are equipped with special software to send and receive packets at high speed using the IP one-to-many multicasting protocol. The MBONE has been used for video conferencing and even for a Rolling Stones concert in 1994. *See also* RealAudio.

MCF *n. See* Meta-Content Format.

m-commerce *n.* Short for **m**obile **commerce**. M-commerce involves the use of personal digital assistants (PDAs), digital phones, and other wireless handheld devices equipped with microbrowsers for the online buying and selling of goods. M-commerce is distinguished from other electronic commerce by the level of portability. Wireless Application Protocol (WAP) standards form the foundation of m-commerce technology, which takes advantage of smart phone capabilities with e-mail, fax, Internet, and phone in one mobile unit. *See also* microbrowser, Wireless Application Protocol.

MCP *n.* Acronym for **M**icrosoft **C**ertified **P**rofessional. A basic certification from Microsoft that verifies an individual's ability to successfully implement a Microsoft product or technology as part of a solution for an organization. The MCP certification is often used as a building block for acquiring additional certifications in specialized skill areas such as databases, programming languages, and Web development.

MCSA *n.* Acronym for **M**icrosoft **C**ertified **S**ystems **A**dministrator. A certification from Microsoft that verifies an individual's ability to implement, manage, and troubleshoot existing Microsoft Windows and Windows .NET network and system environments. *See also* MCP.

MCSD *n.* Acronym for **M**icrosoft **C**ertified **S**olution **D**eveloper. A certification from Microsoft that verifies an individual's ability to use Microsoft development tools, technologies, and platforms to design and develop business solutions. *See also* MCP.

MCSE *n.* Acronym for **M**icrosoft **C**ertified **S**ystem **E**ngineer. A certification from Microsoft that verifies an individual's ability to analyze business requirements and then design and implement business solutions with Microsoft Windows platforms and server software. *See also* MCP.

Media Access Control *n. See* MAC.

M

media filter *n.* **1.** A device used with local area networks (LANs) as an adapter between two different types of media. For example, an RJ-45 connector might be used between coaxial cable and unshielded twisted pair (UTP) cables. Media filters are similar in function to transceivers. As with many components to LANs, manufacturers often choose different names for similar products, so a LAN expert is needed to decide which media filters are required for a particular LAN. *See also* coaxial cable, LAN, transceiver, UTP. **2.** A device added to data networks to filter out electronic noise from the environment. For example, a media filter might be added to an Ethernet network based on coaxial cabling to prevent data loss from interference by nearby electronic equipment. *See also* coaxial cable, Ethernet (definition 1).

media stream *n.* A continuous sequence of audio or audio-and-video through a network.

Melissa *n.* A macro virus that affects Word files in Microsoft Office 97 and Office 2000 and first appeared in the spring of 1999. Melissa is delivered as an attachment to an e-mail with the subject line "An Important Message From *<user name>*," a message beginning "Here is that document you asked for…," or both. When the attachment is opened, the virus propagates (if Microsoft Outlook is installed) by sending itself to the first 50 e-mail addresses in the user's Outlook address book. On the infected machine, the virus also changes the registry, infects the Normal.dot Word template (which, in turn, infects new documents), and, in Office 2000, disables the Word macro virus warning. Although the Melissa virus does not destroy data, it can affect e-mail performance through the increased volume of messages. If an infected document is open at a time when the day of the month is the same as the minute value of the current time, the virus inserts the text "Twenty-two points, plus triple-word-score, plus fifty points for using all my letters. Game's over. I'm outta here" at the current location of the cursor. The virus was named after an acquaintance of the hacker who developed it.

meltdown *n.* **1.** The complete collapse of a computer network caused by a higher level of traffic than the network can support. The term refers, by analogy, to the accidental melting down of a nuclear reactor core. **2.** Colloquially, the breakdown of a person, usually in a job situation, caused by overwork, stress, or failure.

mesh network *n.* A communications network having two or more paths to any node.

message *n.* **1.** In communications, a unit of information transmitted electronically from one device to another. A message can contain one or more blocks of text as well as beginning and ending characters, control characters, a software-generated header (destination address, type of message, and other such information), and error-checking or synchronizing information. A message can be routed directly from sender to receiver through a physical link, or it can be passed, either whole or in parts, through a switching system that routes it from one intermediate station to another. *See also* frame (definition 1), frame (definition 2), header, message switching, network, packet (definition 1), packet switching, synchronous transmission. **2.** In software, a piece of

M

information passed from the application or operating system to the user to suggest an action, indicate a condition, or inform that an event has occurred. **3.** In message-based operating environments, such as Windows, a unit of information passed among running programs, certain devices in the system, and the operating environment itself.

message header *n.* A sequence of bits or bytes at the beginning of a message that usually provides a timing sequence and specifies such aspects of the message structure as its length, data format, and block identification number. *See also* header.

message of the day *n.* A daily bulletin for users of a network, multiuser computer, or other shared system. In most cases, users are shown the message of the day when they log into the system. *Acronym:* MOTD.

Message Passing Interface *n. See* MPI.

message queue *n.* An ordered list of messages awaiting transmission, from which they are taken up on a first in, first out (FIFO) basis.

Message Queuing *n.* A message queuing and routing system for Microsoft Windows that enables distributed applications running at different times to communicate across heterogeneous networks and with computers that may be off line. Message Queuing provides guaranteed message delivery, efficient routing, security, and priority-based messaging. Message Queuing was formerly known as MSMQ.

Message Security Protocol *n.* A protocol for Internet messages that is based on the use of encryption and verification to ensure security. It also allows for permissions at the server level for delivery or rejection of e-mail. *Acronym:* MSP.

message switching *n.* A technique used on some communications networks in which a message, with appropriate address information, is routed through one or more intermediate switching stations before being sent to its destination. On a typical message-switching network, a central computer receives messages, stores them (usually briefly), determines their destination addresses, and then delivers them. Message switching enables a network both to regulate traffic and to use communications lines efficiently. *Compare* circuit switching, packet switching.

message transfer agent *n. See* MTA.

messaging *n.* The use of computers and data communication equipment to convey messages from one person to another, as by e-mail, voice mail, or fax.

Messaging Application Programming Interface *n. See* MAPI.

messaging client *n.* An application program that enables its user to send or receive messages (such as e-mail or fax) to and from other users with the help of a remote server.

messaging-oriented middleware *n. See* MOM.

Meta-Content Format *n.* An open format for describing information about content of a structured body of data such as a Web page, a set of files on a Windows

M

desktop, or a relational database. Meta-Content Format might be used for indexes, data dictionaries, or price lists. *Acronym:* MCF.

metatag or **meta tag** *n.* A tag in an HTML or XML document that allows a Web-page creator to include such information as the author's name, keywords identifying content, and descriptive details (for example, non-text objects on the page). The information that is marked with metatags does not appear on the Web page when a user views it in a browser, but it can be viewed in the HTML or XML source. Metatags are included in the head of a document and are often used to assist search engines in indexing the page. *See also* HTML, source, tag, XML.

Metropolitan Area Exchange *n. See* MAE.

metropolitan area network *n. See* MAN.

mget *n.* Short for **multiple get**. A command in most FTP clients with which a user can request the transfer of several files at once. *See also* FTP[1] (definition 1).

MHTML *n.* Acronym for Multipurpose Internet Mail Extension Hypertext Markup Language, or MIME HTML. A standard method for sending an HTML document encapsulated with inline graphics, applets, linked documents, and other items referred to in the HTML document. *See also* HTML, MIME.

MIB *n. See* Management Information Base.

microbrowser *n.* An application for mobile phones that allows users to access the Internet to send and receive e-mail and browse the Web. Microbrowsers don't have the full functionality of a Web browser on a PC. For instance, microbrowsers are capable of loading only stripped-down text versions of Web pages. Most microbrowser products are built to utilize the Wireless Application Protocol (WAP) standard. *See also* Wireless Application Protocol.

microcontent *n.* Short pieces of text on a Web page that help provide an overview of the page's contents. Microcontent introduces, summarizes, or enhances the macrocontent of a Web page, and includes headings, page titles, ALT text, links, and subheads. *Compare* macrocontent.

microsite *n.* **1.** A small Web site targeted to a single message or topic and nested within a larger site. Microsites geared to promotional and sales of specific products and services may be integrated into popular Web sites by advertisers. **2.** A small Web site with a single focus. *Also called:* minisite.

Microsoft FrontPage *n.* A program you can use to create and manage Internet and intranet sites without programming; FrontPage is available as part of one of the Microsoft Office suites or as a stand-alone product.

Microsoft Internet Explorer *n. See* Internet Explorer.

Microsoft Knowledge Base *n. See* KB.

Microsoft MSN Explorer *n. See* MSN Explorer.

Microsoft MSN Messenger Service *n. See* .NET Messenger Service.

Microsoft .NET Messenger Service *n. See* .NET Messenger Service.

Microsoft Network *n. See* MSN.

Microsoft Office *n. See* Office.

Microsoft Operations Manager *n.* A server and application management solution developed by Microsoft Corporation to deliver event and performance management for the Windows 2000–based environment and .NET Enterprise Server applications. Operations management features include enterprise event log reports from across the corporate network, proactive monitoring and alert messaging, and reporting and trend analysis for problem tracking. Microsoft Operations Manager provides flexibility through sophisticated management rules, which can be customized to meet the needs of individual businesses. Microsoft Operations Manager support for management technology standards permits easy integration with other enterprise management systems.

Microsoft Outlook *n. See* Outlook.

Microsoft Project *n.* A software application developed by Microsoft Corporation to simplify the planning and management of projects. Microsoft Project includes features that help you build and manage projects, set schedules and milestones, and communicate and share ideas with team members.

Microsoft Reader *n.* A software application developed by Microsoft for downloading electronic books and other publications onto any personal computer, laptop computer, or Pocket PC handheld device. Additional features allow users to bookmark pages, highlight text, write notes, and look up definitions.

Microsoft Tech•Ed *n.* An annual training conference held by Microsoft Corporation to educate engineers and businesses using Microsoft technology. The conference provides attendees with access to information, experts, and training labs on Microsoft's latest technologies.

Microsoft Visual InterDev *n. See* Visual InterDev.

Microsoft Visual Studio *n. See* Visual Studio.

Microsoft Visual Studio .NET *n.* A complete development environment for building on the Microsoft .NET technology. Using Visual Studio .NET, developers can create secure, scalable applications and Web services quickly in the language of their choice, leveraging existing systems and skills.

Microsoft Windows *n. See* Windows.

Microsoft Windows Messenger *n. See* .NET Messenger Service.

Microsoft Windows NT *n. See* Windows NT.

Microsoft Word *n. See* Word.

M

Microsoft XML *n. See* MSXML.

middleware *n.* Software that sits between two or more types of software and translates information between them. Middleware can cover a broad spectrum of software and generally sits between an application and an operating system, a network operating system, or a database management system. Examples of middleware include Common Object Request Broker Architecture (CORBA) and other object broker programs and network control programs.

.mil *n.* In the Internet's Domain Name System, the top-level domain that identifies addresses operated by U.S. military organizations. The designation .mil appears at the end of the address. *See also* DNS (definition 1), domain (definition 3). *Compare* .com, .edu, .gov, .net, .org.

Military Network *n. See* MILNET.

MILNET *n.* Short for **Mil**itary **Net**work. A wide area network that represents the military side of the original ARPANET. MILNET carries nonclassified U.S. military traffic. *See also* ARPANET. *Compare* NSFnet.

MIME or **mime** *n.* Acronym for **M**ultipurpose **I**nternet **M**ail **E**xtensions. A protocol widely used on the Internet that extends the SMTP (Simple Mail Transfer Protocol) to permit data, such as video, sound, and binary files, to be transmitted by Internet e-mail without having to be translated into ASCII format first. This is accomplished by the use of MIME types, which describe the contents of a document. A MIME-compliant application sending a file, such as some e-mail programs, assigns a MIME type to the file. The receiving application, which must also be MIME-compliant, refers to a standardized list of documents that are organized into MIME types and subtypes to interpret the content of the file. For instance, one MIME type is *text*, and it has a number of subtypes, including *plain* and *html*. A MIME type of *text/html* refers to a file that contains text written in HTML. MIME is part of HTTP, and both Web browsers and HTTP servers use MIME to interpret e-mail files they send and receive. *See also* HTTP, HTTP server, Simple Mail Transfer Protocol, Web browser. *Compare* BinHex.

minicomputer *n.* A mid-level computer built to perform complex computations while dealing efficiently with a high level of input and output from users connected via terminals. Minicomputers also frequently connect to other minicomputers on a network and distribute processing among all the attached machines. Minicomputers are used heavily in transaction-processing applications and as interfaces between mainframe computer systems and wide area networks. *See also* mainframe computer, supercomputer, wide area network.

mirroring *n.* **1.** In a network, a means of protecting data on a network by duplicating it, in its entirety, on a second disk. Mirroring is one strategy implemented in RAID security. **2.** On the Internet, replicating a Web site or an FTP site on another server. A site is often mirrored if it is frequently visited by multiple users. This eases the net-

M

work traffic to the site, making it easier for users to gain access to the information or files on it. A site may also be mirrored in different geographic locations to facilitate downloading by users in various areas. *See also* RAID.

mirror site *n.* A file server that contains a duplicate set of files to the set on a popular server. Mirror sites exist to spread the distribution burden over more than one server or to eliminate the need to use high-demand international circuits.

misc. newsgroups *n.* Usenet newsgroups that are part of the misc. hierarchy and have the prefix *misc.* These newsgroups cover topics that do not fit into the other standard Usenet hierarchies (comp., news., rec., sci., soc., talk.). *See also* newsgroup, traditional newsgroup hierarchy, Usenet.

misuse detection *n. See* IDS.

MMDS *n.* Short for **m**ultichannel **m**ultipoint **d**istribution **s**ervice. A fixed wireless service proposed for use as an alternative when DSL or cable modem options are not practical or desirable. The MMDS spectrum was originally used for distance learning and wireless cable video services before attracting interest for fixed broadband wireless services. *See also* broadband.

MNP10 *n.* Short for **M**icrocom **N**etworking **P**rotocol, Class **10**. An industry-standard communication protocol used for modem connections over analog cellular telephone connections. The most recent version of MNP10 is MNP 10EC (EC stands for Enhanced Cellular). *See also* communications protocol.

mobile computing *n.* The process of using a computer while traveling. Mobile computing usually requires a portable computer that is battery powered, rather than a desktop system.

Mobile Explorer *n.* A modular wireless applications and services platform designed by Microsoft to power Web-enabled wireless telephones. When connected to a wireless network, Mobile Explorer provides secure mobile access to corporate or personal e-mail, corporate networks, and the Internet. It includes a multimode microbrowser, which can display Web content coded in a variety of markup languages used for small, handheld devices, including cHTML, HTML, WAP 1.1, and WML. *See also* microbrowser.

Mobile Information Server *n.* A software application developed by Microsoft to allow telecommunications carriers, enterprise customers, and business partners to securely extend Microsoft Exchange Server information, corporate intranet applications, and services to users of wireless handheld computing devices. Microsoft Information Server provides mobile users with access to personal services and data stored on the intranet, such as e-mail, document files, appointment calendars, and contacts.

mobile IP *n.* Acronym for **mobile I**nternet **P**rotocol. An Internet protocol designed to support host mobility. Mobile IP enables a host to remain connected to the Internet with the same IP address (called the home address) while moving to different loca-

M

tions. Mobile IP tracks a moving host by registering the presence of the host with a foreign agent; the home agent then forwards packets to the remote network. *See also* IP.

mobile telephone switching office *n.* Computer that controls wireless phone calls. The mobile telephone switching office controls the operation of wireless cell sites, tracks calls, and transfers signals between wireless networks and traditional wired telephone systems. *Acronym:* MTSO.

modec *n.* In telecommunications, a device that generates analog modem signals digitally. The term *modec* is a combination of the terms *modem* and *codec* (coder/decoder—or hardware that can convert audio or video signals between analog and digital forms). *See also* modem (definition 2).

modem *n.* **1.** Short for **mo**dulator/**dem**odulator. A communications device that converts between digital data from a computer or terminal and analog audio signals that can pass through a standard telephone line. Because the telephone system was designed to handle voice and other audio signals and a computer processes signals as discrete units of digital information, a modem is necessary at both ends of the telephone line to exchange data between computers. At the transmit end, the modem converts from digital to analog audio; at the receiving end, a second modem converts the analog audio back to its original digital form. In order to move a high volume of data, high-speed modems rely on sophisticated methods for "loading" information onto the audio carrier—for example, they may combine frequency shift keying, phase modulation, and amplitude modulation to enable a single change in the carrier's state to represent multiple bits of data. In addition to the basic modulation and demodulation functions, most modems also include firmware that allows them to originate and answer telephone calls. International standards for modems are specified by the International Telecommunications Union, or ITU. Despite their capabilities, modems do require communications software in order to function. *Compare* digital modem. **2.** Any communications device that acts as an interface between a computer or terminal and a communications channel. Although such a device may not actually modulate or demodulate analog signals, it may be described as a modem because modem is perceived by many users to be a black box that connects a computer to a communications line (such as a high-speed network or a cable TV system). *See also* digital modem.

modem bank *n.* A collection of modems connected to a server maintained by an ISP or the operator of a BBS or remote-access LAN. Most modem banks are configured to allow a remote user to dial a single phone number that routes calls to an available phone number on the bank. *See also* BBS (definition 1), ISP, LAN.

modem eliminator *n.* A device that enables two computers to communicate without modems. *See also* null modem.

modem ready *n. See* MR.

moderated *adj.* Subjected to review by a moderator, who may remove irrelevant or inflammatory articles or messages before redistributing them through a newsgroup, mailing list, or other messaging system.

M

moderator *n.* In some Internet newsgroups and mailing lists, a person through whom all messages are filtered before they are distributed to the members of the newsgroup or list. The moderator discards or edits any messages that are not considered appropriate. *See also* mailing list, newsgroup.

modulation *n.* **1.** The process of changing or regulating the characteristics of a carrier wave vibrating at a certain amplitude (height) and frequency (timing) so that the variations represent meaningful information. **2.** In computer communications, the means by which a modem converts digital information sent by a computer to the audio form that it sends over a telephone line.

MOM *n.* Acronym for **m**essaging-**o**riented **m**iddleware. A class of programs that translates data and messages between applications that use one format and communications services (such as NetBIOS and TCP/IP) that expect a different format.

monitoring software *n.* A program or set of programs used to oversee computer-based systems and networks for the purpose of tracking usage or identifying, reporting on, and solving problems at the earliest possible stage. Monitoring software is used in a variety of areas ranging from hardware platforms and their components to operating systems, databases, Internet/intranet access, and business applications. Typically, different tools are used to monitor individual system components, though the individual monitors might feed information to a higher-level monitor in order to encompass an entire computing environment.

MOO *n.* Short for MUD, **o**bject-**o**riented. A type of virtual environment on the Internet, similar to a game-oriented MUD but based on an object-oriented language and generally focused more on programming than on games. *See also* MUD.

.moov *n.* A file extension indicating a QuickTime MooV video file for a Macintosh computer. *See also* MooV.

MooV *n.* The file format for QuickTime movies that stores synchronized tracks for control, video, audio, and text. *See also* QuickTime.

morphing *n.* Short for meta**morph**osing. A process by which one image is gradually transformed into another, creating the illusion of a metamorphosis occurring in a short time. A common motion picture special-effects technique, morphing is available in many advanced computer animation packages.

Mosaic *n.* The first popular graphical World Wide Web browser. Released on the Internet in early 1993 by the National Center for Supercomputing Applications (NCSA) at the University of Illinois at Urbana-Champaign, Mosaic is available as freeware and shareware for Windows, Macintosh, and X Window systems. Mosaic is distinguished from other early Web browsers by its ease of use and its addition of inline images to Web documents. *Also called:* NCSA Mosaic.

Motion JPEG *n.* A standard for storing motion video, proposed by the Joint Photographic Experts Group (JPEG), that uses JPEG image compression for each frame. *See also* JPEG (definition 1). *Compare* MPEG (definition 1).

M

mousetrapping *n.* A practice employed by some Web sites in which the back and exit buttons of a visitor's Web browser are disabled and attempts to leave the site are redirected to other pages on the site or to other sites against the visitor's will. Mousetrapping is most often associated with adult-oriented Web sites. *Compare* page-jacking.

.mov *n.* A filename extension for a movie file in Apple's QuickTime format. *See also* QuickTime.

.movie *n. See* .mov.

Moving Picture Experts Group *n. See* MPEG (definition 1).

Mozilla *n.* **1.** A nickname for the Netscape Navigator (later, Netscape Communicator) Web browser, coined by the Netscape Corporation. *See also* Mosaic, Netscape Navigator. **2.** Since 1998, when the Communicator source code was released for free, for use by any interested parties, the name Mozilla has been extended as a generic reference to any Web browser based on Navigator source code.

mozilla.org *n.* The name of the group charged by the Netscape Corporation to act as a clearinghouse for Mozilla-related matters, such as questions, changes to code, bug reporting, forums, and so on.

MP3 *n.* Acronym for **M**PEG Audio Layer-**3**. A digital audio coding scheme used in distributing recorded music over the Internet. MP3 shrinks the size of an audio file by a factor of 10 to 12 without seriously degrading the quality (CD-recording level) of the sound. MP3 files are given the file extension .mp3. Although MP3 is part of the MPEG family, it is audio-only and is not the same as the now-defunct MPEG-3 standard. *See also* MPEG-3.

MP3 encoder *n. See* encoder.

.mpeg *n.* The file extension that identifies video and sound files compressed in the MPEG format specified by the Moving Pictures Experts Group. *See also* MPEG.

MPEG *n.* **1.** Acronym for **M**oving **P**icture **E**xperts **G**roup. A set of standards for audio and video compression established by the Joint ISO/IEC Technical Committee on Information Technology. The MPEG standard has different types that have been designed to work in different situations. *Compare* Motion JPEG. **2.** A video/audio file in the MPEG format. Such files generally have the extension .mpg. *See also* JPEG. *Compare* Motion JPEG.

MPEG-1 *n.* The original MPEG standard for storing and retrieving video and audio information, designed for CD-ROM technology. MPEG-1 defines a medium bandwidth of up to 1.5 Mbps, two audio channels, and noninterlaced video. *See also* MPEG (definition 1). *Compare* MPEG-2, MPEG-3, MPEG-4.

MPEG-2 *n.* An extension of the MPEG-1 standard designed for broadcast television, including HDTV. MPEG-2 defines a higher bandwidth of up to 40 Mbps, five audio channels, a wider range of frame sizes, and interlaced video. *See also* HDTV, MPEG (definition 1). *Compare* MPEG-1, MPEG-3, MPEG-4.

M

MPEG-3 *n.* Initially an MPEG standard designed for HDTV (high-definition television), but it was found that MPEG-2 could be used instead. Therefore, this standard no longer exists. *See also* HDTV, MPEG (definition 1). *Compare* MP3, MPEG-1, MPEG-2, MPEG-4.

MPEG-4 *n.* A standard currently under development designed for videophones and multimedia applications. MPEG-4 provides a lower bandwidth of up to 64 Kbps. *See also* MPEG (definition 1). *Compare* MPEG-1, MPEG-2, MPEG-3.

.mpg *n. See* .mpeg.

MPI *n.* Acronym for **M**essage **P**assing **I**nterface. A specification for message passing on workstation clusters and massively parallel processing (MPP) architectures. MPI was designed as a proposed standard by the MPI Forum, a committee of vendors and users.

MPLS *n.* Acronym for **M**ultiprotocol **L**abel **S**witching. A standards-based technique used to manage and optimize traffic flow for large-scale networks. In an MPLS network, incoming packets are assigned a label by a label edge router (LER). Label switch routers (LSRs) use these labels to forward the packets through the network along a label switch path (LSP). Each LSR removes the existing label and assigns a new one. MPLS combines the advantages of bridges (Layer 2 switching, which is used in ATM and frame relay) and routers (Layer 3 switching, which is used in IP). MPLS serves to create faster and more scalable networks to facilitate quality of service, class of service, and the use of VPNs.

MPOA *n.* Acronym for **M**ulti-**P**rotocol **O**ver **ATM**. A specification established by the ATM Forum (an industry group of Asynchronous Transfer Mode users and vendors) to integrate ATM into existing Ethernet, token ring, and TCP/IP networks. *See also* ATM (definition 1).

MPPP *n. See* Multilink Point-to-Point Protocol.

mput *n.* In many FTP clients, the command that instructs the local client to transmit multiple files to the remote server.

MR *n.* Acronym for **m**odem **r**eady. A light on the front panel of a modem indicating that the modem is ready.

MSDN *n.* Acronym for the **M**icrosoft **D**eveloper **N**etwork. An online, print, and CD-DVD resource for developers that features content and programs focused on development trends and Microsoft technologies. Some features of MSDN include technical articles and reference material; information on upcoming conferences and events; developer support through peer-to-peer interaction, information sharing, and direct interaction with Microsoft; and software subscription programs.

MSN *n.* Acronym for **M**icrosoft **N**etwork. An online service and Internet portal, launched with the introduction of Windows 95 in August 1995.

M

MSN Explorer *n.* Microsoft software that integrates the functionality of Internet Explorer, Windows Media Player, Hotmail, MSN Messenger, MSN Communities, Music Central, and other MSN content and services. *See also* MSN.

MSN Messenger Service *n. See* .NET Messenger Service.

MSXML *n.* Acronym for Microsoft **XML**. A Java-based XML parser from Microsoft that provides support for World Wide Web Consortium (W3C) standards for XML documents and applications.

MTA *n.* Acronym for **m**essage **t**ransfer **a**gent. An application process, as described in the X.400 message-handling system, responsible for delivering e-mail messages. After receiving a message, an MTA stores it temporarily and either delivers it or forwards it to another MTA. During this process, the MTA can change the message headers. *See also* X series.

MTTR *n.* Acronym for **m**ean **t**ime **t**o **r**epair. The average time interval, usually expressed in hours, that it takes to repair a failed component.

MTU *n.* Acronym for **M**aximum **T**ransmission **U**nit. The largest packet of data that can be transmitted on a network. MTU size varies, depending on the network—576 bytes on X.25 networks, for example, 1500 bytes on Ethernet, and 17,914 bytes on 16 Mbps Token Ring. Responsibility for determining the size of the MTU lies with the link layer of the network. When packets are transmitted across networks, the path MTU, or PMTU, represents the smallest packet size (the one that all networks can transmit without breaking up the packet) among the networks involved.

MUD *n.* Acronym for **m**ulti**u**ser **d**ungeon. A virtual environment on the Internet in which multiple users simultaneously participate in a role-playing game—generally a medieval fantasy, hence the "dungeon"—and interact with each other in real time. *Also called:* multiuser simulation environment.

MUD, object-oriented *n. See* MOO.

multicast address dynamic client allocation protocol *n.* An extension to the DHCP protocol standard used to support dynamic assignment and configuration of IP multicast addresses on TCP/IP-based networks. *Acronym:* MADCAP.

multicast backbone *n. See* MBONE.

multicasting *n.* The process of sending a message simultaneously to more than one destination on a network. *Compare* anycasting.

multichannel multipoint distribution service *n. See* MMDS.

multihoming *n.* **1.** In Mac OS X, an automatic network selection feature that allows one computer to maintain multiple network addresses. Multihoming may be used with a computer that is used from multiple locations, such as home and office, or to create special connection settings, such as separate systems for communication inside and outside of an intranet. **2.** The use of multiple addresses and/or multiple interfaces for a single

M

node. A multihomed host has either multiple network interfaces connected to two or more networks, or a single network interface that has been assigned multiple IP addresses. Multihoming can be used to provide redundancy to achieve quality of service.

multilayer switch *n.* A network switch that uses information from more than one ISO/OSI layer (Layer 2, Layer 3, Layer 4, and/or Layer 7) to forward traffic. *See also* ISO/OSI reference model, switch (definition 4).

Multilink Point-to-Point Protocol *n.* An Internet protocol that allows computers to establish multiple physical links to combine their bandwidths. This technology creates a virtual link with more capacity than a single physical link. *Acronym:* MPPP. *See also* PPP.

multimode phone *n.* Wireless phone that operates on both analog and digital networks. A multimode phone may be dual-mode (analog and one digital network) or tri-mode (analog and two digital networks).

multipartite virus *n.* A type of virus that combines characteristics and techniques of both boot sector and file viruses. Multipartite viruses first infect either system sectors or files and then spread quickly to infect the entire system. Because of their multiple capabilities, multipartite viruses are difficult to remove from an infected system. *Also called:* bimodal virus, bipartite virus.

multiple recipients *n.* **1.** The capability of sending e-mail to more than one user at a time by listing more than one e-mail address on a line. Delimiters such as commas or semicolons are used to separate the e-mail addresses. *See also* e-mail[1] (definition 1), mailing list. **2.** The subscribers on a mailing list. A message sent to the list is addressed to the "multiple recipients of" the list.

multiplexer *n.* A device for funneling several different streams of data over a common communications line. Multiplexers are used either to attach many communications lines to a smaller number of communications ports or to attach a large number of communications ports to a smaller number of communications lines. *Acronym:* MUX.

multipoint configuration *n.* A communications link in which multiple stations are connected sequentially to the same communications line. Typically, the communications line is controlled by a primary station, such as a computer, and the stations attached to the line are secondary.

multiport repeater *n. See* active hub.

Multiprotocol Label Switching *n. See* MPLS.

Multi-Protocol Over ATM *n. See* MPOA.

Multipurpose Internet Mail Extensions *n. See* MIME.

Multipurpose Internet Mail Extensions HTML *n. See* MHTML.

multisystem network *n.* A communications network in which two or more host computers can be accessed by network users.

M

multi-tier *n. See* three-tier client/server, two-tier client/server.

multiuser *n. See* multiuser system.

multiuser dungeon *n. See* MUD.

multiuser simulation environment *n. See* MUD.

multiuser system *n.* Any computer system that can be used by more than one person. Although a microcomputer shared by several people can be considered a multiuser system, the term is generally reserved for machines that can be accessed simultaneously by several people through communications facilities or via network terminals.

munging *n. See* address munging.

MUSE *n.* Short for **mu**ltiu**se**r simulation **e**nvironment. *See* MUD.

.museum *n.* One of seven new top-level domain names approved in 2000 by the Internet Corporation for Assigned Names and Numbers (ICANN), .museum is meant for use by museum Web sites.

MYOB *n.* Acronym for **M**ind **y**our **o**wn **b**usiness. An expression used in e-mail and newsgroups.

my two cents *n.* An expression used informally in newsgroup articles and, less frequently, e-mail messages or mailing lists, to indicate that the message is the writer's contribution to an ongoing discussion. *Also called:* $0.02. *See also* mailing list, newsgroup.

M

N

NACN *n. See* North American Cellular Network.

nagware *n.* Slang for computer shareware that, on starting or before closing, displays a prominent reminder to pay for the program. *See also* shareware.

NAK *n.* Acronym for **n**egative **ack**nowledgement. A control code, ASCII character 21 (hexadecimal 15), transmitted to a sending station or computer by the receiving unit as a signal that transmitted information has arrived incorrectly. *Compare* ACK.

NAK attack *n.* Acronym for **n**egative **ack**nowledgement **attack**. A hacker attack that uses the negative acknowledgement control code character to enter a seemingly secure system. A NAK attack uses weaknesses in the system handling NAK replies that may leave it temporarily unprotected. *See also* NAK.

.name *n.* One of seven new top-level domain names approved in 2000 by the Internet Corporation for Assigned Names and Numbers (ICANN), .name is meant for registration by individuals for personal Web sites. The seven new domain names became available for use in the spring of 2001.

Name Binding Protocol *n. See* NBP.

named anchor *n.* In HTML, a tag within a document that can act as a destination for a hyperlink. Named anchors are useful because they allow a link to a specific location within a document. *Also called:* named target. *See also* anchor, HTML, hyperlink.

named entity *n. See* character entity.

named target *n. See* named anchor.

name server *n. See* CSO name server, DNS server.

namespace *n.* **1.** A grouping of one or more names that represent individual objects within the group in a shared computing environment, such as a network. The names within a namespace are unique, are created according to the same rules, and can be resolved into a particular identifying item of information, such as an IP address or a network device. A namespace can be either flat—a single collection of unique names— or hierarchical, as is the Internet's DNS (Domain Name System), which is based on a treelike structure that is refined through successive levels beginning with the root server and the Internet's top-level domains (.com, .net, .org, and so on). In everyday terms, a namespace is comparable to a telephone book, in which each name is unique and resolves to the phone number and address of a particular individual, business, or other entity. **2.** A means of identifying elements and attributes in an XML document by assigning them a two-part name with the first part being the namespace and the second part being the functional name. A namespace identifies a set of names to prevent confusion when multiple objects with identical functional names are taken from different sources and brought together in the same XML document. Namespaces typically reference a Uniform Resource Identifier (URI) because each URI will be unique.

N

name-value pair *n.* In CGI programming, one of the data items collected from an HTML form by the browser and passed through the server to a CGI script for processing. *See also* CGI, CGI script, HTML.

naming container *n.* Any ASP.NET control that implements the INamingContainer interface. This is a marker interface that enables a control to create a new naming scope under itself so that ID attributes assigned to its child controls are unique within the entire ASP.NET page that contains the control.

NAP *n. See* Network Access Point.

Napster *n.* An Internet music search application that allows users to search for and swap MP3 files over the Web. In response to a user request for a song or an artist, Napster searches the hard drives of all other Napster users on line. When the requested item is found, the file is downloaded to the computer making the request. Napster also includes a chat room and a library of most popular items. The introduction of Napster in 1999 sparked heated debate over copyright and digital distribution issues. *See also* MP3.

narrowband *n.* A bandwidth set aside by the FCC for mobile or portable radio services, such as advanced two-way paging systems, including transmission rates between 50 bps and 64 Kbps. Narrowband formerly referred to the bandwidth from 50 to 150 bps. *See also* bandwidth, FCC. *Compare* broadband.

narrowband ISDN *n.* Name used to distinguish current ISDN lines from the developing broadband ISDN technology. *See also* broadband ISDN, ISDN.

narrowcast *vb.* To transmit data or programming to a defined or limited area or audience. A cable television company narrowcasts its programs only to subscribers, whereas network television stations *broadcast* to everyone with reception equipment in their transmission range. On the Web, content delivered to users via push technology represents a form of narrowcasting. *See also* unicast. *Compare* multicasting.

NAS *n.* Acronym for Network-Attached Storage. A platform-independent storage appliance connected to a network. NAS uses a storage unit with a built-in server that can communicate with clients over a network. NAS devices are popular for ease of maintenance, manageability, and scalability. *Compare* SAN.

NAT *n.* Acronym for Network Address Translation. The process of converting between IP addresses used within an intranet or other private network and Internet IP addresses. This approach makes it possible to use a large number of addresses within the private network without depleting the limited number of available numeric Internet IP addresses. Variations of NAT displaying similar functions include IP aliasing, IP masquerading, and Port Address Translation.

national attachment point *n. See* Network Access Point.

National Center for Supercomputing Applications *n. See* NCSA (definition 1).

National Committee for Information Technology Standards *n.* A committee formed by the Information Technology Industry Council to develop national standards for use in the information technology industry and to promote those standards for international use. *Acronym:* NCITS.

National Computer Security Association *n. See* ICSA.

National Information Infrastructure *n.* A U.S. government program to extend and oversee the development of the Information Superhighway. The National Information Infrastructure is made up of a high-bandwidth, wide area network that can carry data, fax, video, and voice transmissions to users throughout the United States. The network is being developed mostly by private carriers. Many of the services, which are aimed at enabling the efficient creation and dissemination of information, are already available on the Internet itself, including increased accessibility to quality education through distance learning and increased access to government services. *Acronym:* NII. *See also* Information Superhighway, Internet2, Next Generation Internet. *Compare* Internet.

National Institute of Standards and Technology *n.* A branch of the U.S. Commerce Department that works to develop and encourage standards for measurement, science, and technology in order to promote commerce and improve productivity in the marketplace. Prior to 1988, the National Institute of Standards and Technology was known as the National Bureau of Standards. *Acronym:* NIST.

National Science Foundation *n.* A U.S. government agency intended to promote scientific research by funding both research projects and projects that facilitate scientific communication, such as NSFnet, the former backbone of the Internet. *Acronym:* NSF. *See also* backbone (definition 1), NSFnet.

navigation bar *n.* On a Web page, a grouping of hyperlinks for getting around in that particular Web site. *See also* hyperlink.

Navigator *n. See* Netscape Navigator.

NBP *n.* Acronym for Name Binding Protocol. A protocol used on AppleTalk local area networks to translate between node names (known to users) and numeric AppleTalk addresses. NBP operates at the transport level (level 4 of the ISO/OSI reference model). *See also* AppleTalk, communications protocol, ISO/OSI reference model.

NC *n. See* network computer.

NCC *n. See* network-centric computing.

NCITS *n. See* National Committee for Information Technology Standards.

NCP *n. See* Point-to-Point Protocol.

NCSA *n.* **1.** Acronym for National Center for Supercomputing Applications. A research center located at the University of Illinois at Urbana-Champaign. NCSA was founded in 1985 as a part of the National Science Foundation, specializing in scientific visualization tasks, but is best known as the home of NCSA Mosaic, the first graphical Web browser, and of NCSA Telnet. *See also* Mosaic, NCSA Telnet. **2.** *See* ICSA.

NCSA Mosaic *n. See* Mosaic.

NCSA server *n.* The HTTP server developed by the National Center for Supercomputing Applications of the University of Illinois. This server and the CERN server were the first HTTP servers developed for the World Wide Web and are available free through downloading. *See also* HTTP server (definition 1), NCSA (definition 1). *Compare* CERN server.

NCSA Telnet *n.* A freeware telnet client program developed and distributed by the National Center for Supercomputing Applications. *See also* client (definition 2), NCSA (definition 1).

NDIS *n.* Acronym for **N**etwork **D**river **I**nterface **S**pecification, a software interface, or set of rules, designed to enable different network protocols to communicate with a variety of network adapters. Providing a standard—a common "language"—for the drivers used by network adapters, NDIS enables a single network adapter to support multiple protocols and, conversely, also enables a single protocol to work with network adapters from different vendors.

NDMP *n.* Acronym for **N**etwork **D**ata **M**anagement **P**rotocol. An open protocol for network-based backups of file servers that allows platform-independent data storage. *See also* communications protocol, file server.

NDS *n.* Acronym for **N**ovell **D**irectory **S**ervices. A feature introduced in Novell NetWare 4.0 that provides access to directories that may be located on one or more servers.

negative acknowledgement *n. See* NAK.

.net *n.* In the Internet's Domain Name System, the top-level domain that identifies addresses of network providers. The designation .net appears at the end of the address. *See also* DNS (definition 1), domain (definition 3). *Compare* .com, .edu, .gov, .mil, .org.

net.- *prefix* A prefix used to describe people and institutions on the Internet. For example, a very well respected person might be described as a net.god.

Net *n.* **1.** Short for Inter**net**. **2.** Short for Use**net**.

.NET *n.* The set of Microsoft technologies that provides tools for connecting information, people, systems, and devices. The technologies provide individuals and organizations with the ability to build, host, deploy, and use XML Web service connected solutions.

net address *n.* **1.** A World Wide Web address (URL). *See also* URL. **2.** An e-mail address. **3.** The DNS name or IP address of a machine. *See also* DNS (definition 1), IP address. **4.** The address, burned into a network adapter, that is used to uniquely identify a node on a network. *See also* network interface card.

NetBEUI *n.* Short for **NetBIOS** **E**xtended **U**ser **I**nterface. NetBEUI is a network protocol created by IBM and now used by Microsoft, HP, and Compaq. It is usually used in small, department-size local area networks (LANs) of 1 to 200 clients. It can use Token Ring source routing as its only method of routing. It is the extended version of the NetBIOS standard. *See also* communications protocol, LAN, NetBIOS.

NetBIOS *n.* An application programming interface (API) that can be used by application programs on a local area network consisting of IBM and compatible micro-

N

computers running MS-DOS, OS/2, or some version of UNIX. Primarily of interest to programmers, NetBIOS provides application programs with a uniform set of commands for requesting the lower-level network services required to conduct sessions between nodes on a network and to transmit information back and forth.

NetBIOS Extended User Interface *n. See* NetBEUI.

net boot *n. See* PXE boot.

NetBSD *n.* A free version of the BSD UNIX operating system developed as a result of a volunteer effort. NetBSD is highly interoperable, runs on many hardware platforms, and is nearly POSIX compliant. *See also* BSD UNIX, POSIX.

Netcaster *n. See* netcasting (definition 2).

netcasting *n.* **1.** Synonym for webcasting. **2.** A Netscape technology used in Netscape Netcaster that enabled a user to subscribe to channels that pushed Web content to the user's desktop without actively retrieving the information. Netscape Netcaster, which was part of previous versions of Netscape Navigator, competed with Microsoft Active Desktop. Unlike Active Desktop, which uses Microsoft's Channel Definition Format (CDF), the Netcaster push client was based on existing open standards (HTML, Java, and JavaScript). *See also* push[2] (definition 2). *Compare* Active Desktop.

.NET Compact Framework *n.* A hardware-independent environment for running programs on resource-constrained computing devices. It inherits the full .NET Framework architecture of the common language runtime, supports a subset of the .NET Framework class library, and contains classes designed exclusively for the .NET Compact Framework. Supported devices include personal data assistants (PDAs) (such as the Pocket PC), mobile phones, set-top boxes, automotive computing devices, and custom-designed embedded devices built with the Microsoft Windows CE operating system.

.NET data provider *n.* A component of ADO.NET that provides access to data from a relational database.

netfilter *n.* The packet-filtering system for Linux introduced in the 2.4 kernel. Netfilter is the first stateful firewall implemented in Linux. *See also* firewall, iptables. *Compare* IP Filter.

NetFind *n. See* AOL NetFind.

.NET Framework *n.* A platform for building, deploying, and running XML Web services and applications. It provides a highly productive, standards-based, multilanguage environment for integrating existing investments with next generation applications and services, as well as the agility to solve the challenges of deployment and operation of Internet-scale applications. The .NET Framework consists of three main parts: the common language runtime, a hierarchical set of unified class libraries, and a componentized version of ASP called ASP.NET. *See also* ASP.NET, common language runtime, .NET Framework class library.

.NET Framework class library *n.* A Common Language Specification (CLS)–compliant library of classes, interfaces, and value types that are included in the Microsoft .NET Framework SDK. This library provides access to system functionality and is designed to be the foundation on which .NET Framework applications, components, and controls are built.

.NET Framework data provider *n.* A component of ADO.NET that provides access to data from a relational data source. A .NET Framework data provider contains classes to connect to a data source, execute commands at the data source, and return query results from the data source, including the ability to execute commands within transactions. A .NET Framework data provider also contains classes to populate a DataSet with results from a data source and propagate changes in a DataSet back to the data source.

net.god *n.* A highly respected person within the Internet community.

nethead *n.* **1.** A person who uses the Internet as if addicted to it. **2.** A Grateful Dead fan who participates in the rec.music.gdead newsgroup or some other forum dedicated to that band.

netiquette *n.* Short for **net**work et**iquette**. Principles of courtesy observed in sending electronic messages, such as e-mail and Usenet postings. The consequences of violating netiquette include being flamed and having one's name placed in the bozo filter of one's intended audience. Disapproved behavior includes gratuitous personal insults; posting of large amounts of irrelevant material; giving away the plot of a movie, television show, or novel without warning; posting offensive material without encrypting it; and excessive cross-posting of a message to multiple groups without regard to whether the group members are likely to find it interesting. *See also* bozo filter, flame[2].

netizen *n.* A person who participates in online communication through the Internet and other networks, especially conference and chat services, such as Internet news or Fidonet. *Compare* lurker.

NetMeeting *n.* A software application developed by Microsoft Corporation to allow video conferencing among parties using personal computers connected via the Internet. NetMeeting allows participants in different locations to view each other, engage in text chat conversations, send and receive videos, exchange information graphically via an electronic whiteboard, share Windows-based applications, and transfer files.

.NET Messenger Service *n.* A popular instant-messaging service provided by Microsoft as part of the .NET strategy. With .NET Messenger Service, formerly called MSN Messenger Service, users can communicate using the Windows Messenger, included in Windows XP, or MSN Messenger applications. *See also* instant messaging. *Compare* AIM, ICQ, Yahoo! Messenger.

.NET My Services *n.* A suite of XML Web services for managing and protecting personal information and interactions across applications, devices, and services. Formerly code-named HailStorm, .NET My Services is based on the Microsoft .NET Passport user-authentication system. The suite of .NET My Services includes services such as .NET ApplicationSettings, .NET Calendar, .NET Contacts, .NET Devices, .NET Documents, .NET Inbox, .NET Locations, .NET Profile, and .NET Wallet. *See also* .NET, Passport.

NetPC *n.* Short for **Net**work **PC**. An industry-defined, Windows-based PC system that is small and meant to act as simply an access point. These PCs generally have very small hard drives, no disk drives, and are built to have a very low cost. Some older NetPCs can boot through remote access to a server and user server-based resources for most computing actions.

net.personality *n.* A slang term for a person who has attained some degree of celebrity on the Internet.

net.police *n.* Persons (usually self-appointed) who try to enforce their understanding of the "rules" that apply to conduct on the Internet. Their activities may be directed toward users who violate the rules of netiquette, spammers who send unsolicited advertising as e-mail or to newsgroups, or even people who post "politically incorrect" comments to newsgroups or mailing lists. *See also* netiquette, spam.

Netscape Navigator *n.* The widely used family of Web browser programs, made by Netscape Corporation. Versions of Netscape Navigator are available for the Windows and Macintosh platforms, and for many varieties of UNIX. Netscape Navigator, which is based on NCSA's Mosaic Web browser, was one of the first commercially available Web browsers. In 1999, Netscape Corporation was purchased by America Online. *See also* Mosaic, Web browser.

Netscape Netcaster *n. See* netcasting (definition 2).

Netscape Server Application Programming Interface *n. See* NSAPI.

Netspeak *n.* The set of conventions for writing English in e-mail, IRCs, and newsgroups. Netspeak is characterized by acronyms (such as IMHO or ROFL) and clarifying devices such as emotags and emoticons. Use of Netspeak should be governed by netiquette. *See also* emotag, emoticon, IMHO, IRC, netiquette, ROFL.

netspionage *n.* Corporate-sponsored hacking of a competitor's digital information for the theft of trade secrets.

Net surfing *n.* The practice of exploring the Internet without a specific goal in mind. The concept of Net surfing is similar to (and probably derived from) "channel surfing" in reference to watching television.

Net TV *n. See* Internet television.

NetWare *n.* A family of LAN (local area network) operating system products developed by Novell, Inc. Designed to run on PCs and Macintoshes, Novell NetWare allows users to share files and system resources such as hard disks and printers. *See also* network operating system.

network *n.* A group of computers and associated devices that are connected by communications facilities. A network can involve permanent connections, such as cables, or temporary connections made through telephone or other communication links. A network can be as small as a LAN (local area network) consisting of a few computers, printers, and other devices, or it can consist of many small and large computers distributed over a vast geographic area (WAN, or wide area network). *See also* ALOHAnet, Ethernet (definition 1), LAN, WAN.

Network Access Point *n.* One of the interchange points for Internet traffic, where various Internet network carriers and major ISPs exchange data. When Internet traffic originates on one network and goes to another network, it almost always passes through at least one Network Access Point, or NAP. In the United States, major NAPs include MAE East, in Vienna, Virginia, and MAE West, in San Jose, California (both operated by MCI WorldCom); the Chicago NAP (operated by Ameritech); the Pacific Bell NAP (with multiple locations in California); the Digital Internet Exchange in Palo Alto, California (operated by Digital/Compaq); and the Sprint NAP in Pennsauken, New Jersey. Additional local and regional exchange points are located in many other locations around the world. *Acronym:* NAP. *Also called:* National Attachment Point.

network adapter *n. See* network interface card.

Network Address Translation *n. See* NAT.

network administrator *n.* The person in charge of operations on a computer network. The duties of a network administrator can be broad and might include such tasks as installing new workstations and other devices, adding and removing individuals from the list of authorized users, archiving files, overseeing password protection and other security measures, monitoring usage of shared resources, and handling malfunctioning equipment. *See also* system administrator.

network architecture *n.* The underlying structure of a computer network, including hardware, functional layers, interfaces, and protocols, used to establish communication and ensure the reliable transfer of information. Network architectures are designed to provide both philosophical and physical standards for the complexities of establishing communications links and transferring information without conflict. Various network architectures exist, including the internationally accepted seven-layer ISO Open Systems Interconnection (OSI) model and IBM's Systems Network Architecture (SNA). *See also* ISO/OSI reference model, SNA.

Network-Attached Storage *n. See* NAS.

network boot *n. See* PXE boot.

network card *n. See* network interface card.

network-centric computing *n.* A computing environment in which a network server or servers represent the hub of activity. Considered the "third wave" in large-system computing after mainframe and desktop developments, network-centric computing establishes servers as the main source of computing power, to give users direct access to network-based applications and information. In network-centric computing systems, applications are not preinstalled or uninstalled locally, that is, on the desktop; they are accessed on an as-needed, "on-the-fly" basis. Thus, individual desktop computers do not have to maintain large amounts of disk storage or load and manage application programs. *See also* server.

network computer *n.* A computer designed for use on a network in which programs and storage are provided by servers. Network computers, unlike dumb terminals, have their own processing power, but their design does not include local storage and they depend on network servers for applications. *Acronym:* NC.

network congestion *n. See* congestion.

network connection *n. See* Ethernet.

network control program *n.* In a communications network that includes a mainframe computer, a program that usually resides in a communications controller and takes over communications tasks such as routing, error control, line control, and polling (checking terminals for transmissions), leaving the main computer free for other functions. *See also* communications controller.

Network Control Protocol *n. See* Point-to-Point Protocol.

network database *n.* **1.** A database that runs in a network. **2.** A database containing the address of other users in the network. **3.** In information management, a type of database in which data records can be related to one another in more than one way. A network database is similar to a hierarchical database in the sense that it contains a progression from one record to another. It differs in being less rigidly structured: any single record can point to more than one other record and, conversely, can be pointed to by one or more records. In effect, a network database allows more than one path between any two records, whereas a hierarchical database allows only one, from parent (higher-level record) to child (lower-level record).

Network Data Management Protocol *n. See* NDMP.

network device driver *n.* Software that coordinates communication between the network adapter card and the computer's hardware and other software, controlling the physical function of the network adapter card.

network directory *n.* On a local area network, a directory on a disk that is located on a computer other than the one the user is operating. A network directory differs from a network drive in that the user has access to only that directory. Whether the rest of the disk is accessible to the user depends on whether he or she has been granted access rights by the network administrator. On the Macintosh, a network directory is referred to as a shared folder. *Also called:* networked directory, shared directory. *See also* network drive, shared folder.

network drive *n.* On a local area network, a disk drive whose disk is available to other computers on the network. Access to a network drive might not be allowed to all users of the network; many operating systems contain security provisions that

N

enable a network administrator to grant or deny access to part or all of a network drive. *Also called:* networked drive. *See also* network directory.

Network Driver Interface Specification *n. See* NDIS.

networked directory *n. See* network directory.

networked drive *n. See* network drive.

networked home *n. See* smart home.

Network File System *n. See* NFS.

network information center *n. See* NIC (definition 2).

network interface card *n.* An expansion card or other device used to provide network access to a computer or other device, such as a printer. Network interface cards mediate between the computer and the physical media, such as cabling, over which transmissions travel. *Acronym:* NIC. *Also called:* network adapter, network card.

Network Kernel Extension *n. See* NKE.

network latency *n.* The time it takes for information to be transferred between computers in a network.

network layer *n.* The third of the seven layers in the ISO/OSI reference model for standardizing computer-to-computer communications. The network layer is one level above the data-link layer and ensures that information arrives at its intended destination. It is the middle of the three layers (data-link, network, and transport) concerned with the actual movement of information from one device to another. *See also* ISO/OSI reference model.

network meltdown *n. See* broadcast storm, meltdown.

network model *n.* A database structure, or layout, similar to a hierarchical model, except that records can have multiple parent records as well as multiple child records. A database management system that supports a network model can be used to simulate a hierarchical model. *See also* network database (definition 3).

network modem *n.* A modem that is shared by users of a network for calling an online service provider, an ISP, a service bureau, or other online source. *See also* ISP, service bureau.

network news *n.* The newsgroups on the Internet, especially those in the Usenet hierarchy.

Network News Transfer Protocol *n. See* NNTP.

network operating system *n.* An operating system specifically designed to support networking. A server-based network operating system provides networking support for multiple simultaneous users as well as administrative, security, and management functions. On the desktop, a network-aware operating system provides users with the ability to access network resources. Unlike a single-user operating system, a network operating system must acknowledge and respond to requests from many workstations, managing such details as network access and communications, resource allocation and sharing, data protection, and error control. *Acronym:* NOS. *Also called:* network OS.

network operation center *n.* The office in an enterprise that is responsible for maintaining network integrity and improving network efficiency while reducing system downtime. *Acronym:* NOC.

network OS *n. See* network operating system.

network protocol *n.* A set of rules and parameters that defines and enables communication through a network.

Network Query Language *n.* A scripting language for controlling intelligent agents for Web applications. *Acronym:* NQL.

network server *n. See* server.

network services *n.* **1.** In a corporate environment, the division that maintains the network and the computers. **2.** In a Windows environment, extensions to the operating system that allow it to perform network functions such as network printing and file sharing.

network software *n.* Software including a component that facilitates connection to or participation in a network.

Network Solutions, Inc. *n. See* NSI.

network structure *n.* The record organization used in a particular network model.

Network Terminator 1 *n.* An ISDN device that acts as an interface between an ISDN telephone line and one or more terminal adapters or terminal devices, such as an ISDN telephone. *Acronym:* NT-1. *See also* ISDN, ISDN terminal adapter.

Network Time Protocol *n.* An Internet protocol used to synchronize the clocks in computers connected to the Internet. *Acronym:* NTP. *See also* communications protocol.

network topology *n. See* topology.

network weaving *n. See* leapfrog attack.

NetWorld+Interop *n.* International conference and exhibition for the networking and information technology industry. NetWorld+Interop draws attendees from a variety of industries, including telecommunications, Internet services, and e-commerce. NetWorld+Interop features product exhibits, educational conferences, tutorials, and workshops.

NeuralCast Technology *n.* Technology developed by RealNetworks to improve the transmission of digital media over RealNetworks servers. NeuralCast Technology uses a variety of protocols, introduces new techniques to correct errors in streaming signals, and uses telephone and satellite transmissions to coordinate server networks to optimize digital media transmission.

neural network *n.* A type of artificial-intelligence system modeled after the neurons (nerve cells) in a biological nervous system and intended to simulate the way a brain processes information, learns, and remembers. A neural network is designed as an interconnected system of processing elements, each with a limited number of inputs and an output. These processing elements are able to "learn" by receiving weighted inputs that, with adjustment, time, and repetition, can be made to produce appropriate outputs. Neural networks are used in areas such as pattern recognition, speech analysis, and speech synthesis.

newbie *n.* **1.** An inexperienced user on the Internet. **2.** In a particularly derogatory sense, an inexperienced Usenet user who asks for information that is readily available in the FAQ. *See also* FAQ.

news *n.* The Internet protocol for retrieving files from an Internet newsgroup. You can create hyperlinks to newsgroups using news://.

news.announce.newusers *n.* A newsgroup that contains general information for new users about using Internet newsgroups.

newsfeed or **news feed** *n.* Deliveries, exchanges, or distributions of newsgroup articles to and from news servers. Newsfeeds are accomplished through cooperating news servers, which communicate via NNTP through network connections. *Also called:* feed. *See also* newsgroup, news server, NNTP.

newsgroup *n.* A forum on the Internet for threaded discussions on a specified range of subjects. A newsgroup consists of articles and follow-up posts. An article with all of its follow-up posts—which are (supposed to be) related to the specific subject named in the original article's subject line—constitutes a thread. Each newsgroup has a name that consists of a series of words, separated by periods, indicating the newsgroup's subject in terms of increasingly narrow categories, such as rec.crafts.textiles.needlework. Some newsgroups can be read and posted to only on one site; others, such as those in the seven Usenet hierarchies or those in ClariNet, circulate throughout the Internet. *See also* article, bit. newsgroups, ClariNet, follow-up, Great Renaming, local newsgroups, mail reflector, threaded discussion, traditional newsgroup hierarchy, Usenet. *Compare* mailing list.

newsmaster *n.* The person in charge of maintaining the Internet news server at a particular host. Sending e-mail to "newsmaster@domain.name" is the standard way to reach a given newsmaster.

news. newsgroups *n.* Usenet newsgroups that are part of the news. hierarchy and begin with "news." These newsgroups cover topics that deal with Usenet itself, such as Usenet policy and the creation of new Usenet newsgroups. *See also* newsgroup, traditional newsgroup hierarchy, Usenet. *Compare* comp. newsgroups, misc. newsgroups, rec. newsgroups, sci. newsgroups, soc. newsgroups, talk. newsgroups.

.newsrc *n.* The file extension that identifies a setup file for UNIX-based newsreaders. The setup file typically contains a current list of newsgroups that the user subscribes to and the articles in each newsgroup that the user has already read. *See also* newsreader.

newsreader *n.* A Usenet client program that enables a user to subscribe to Usenet newsgroups, read articles, post follow-ups, reply by e-mail, and post articles. Many Web browsers also provide these functions. *See also* article, e-mail[1] (definition 1), follow-up, newsgroup, Usenet, Web browser.

news server *n.* A computer or program that exchanges Internet newsgroups with newsreader clients and other servers. *See also* newsgroup, newsreader.

Newton *n.* A personal digital assistant (PDA) developed by Apple Computer, Inc. *See also* PDA.

Newton OS *n.* The operating system that controls the Newton MessagePad personal digital assistant (PDA). *See also* PDA.

Next Generation Internet *n.* An initiative funded by the U.S. federal government designed to develop faster, more powerful networking technologies than are available on the current global Internet. The Next Generation Internet, or NGI, was begun in 1997 under the auspices of a number of government agencies, including DARPA (Defense Advanced Research Projects Agency), NASA (National Aeronautics & Space Administration), and the NSF (National Science Foundation). Its objective is to develop advanced networking technologies and to demonstrate them on university and government test networks running 100 to 1000 times faster than the current Internet. The technologies developed are intended for eventual use by schools, businesses, and the general public. *Acronym:* NGI. *Compare* Internet, Internet2.

NFS *n.* Acronym for **N**etwork **F**ile **S**ystem. A distributed file system that allows users to access remote files and directories on a network as if they were local. NFS is compatible with Microsoft Windows and UNIX-based systems, including Linux and Mac OS X.

NGI *n. See* Next Generation Internet.

NIC *n.* **1.** *See* network interface card. **2.** Acronym for **n**etwork **i**nformation **c**enter. An organization that provides information about a network and other support to users of the network. The principal NIC for the Internet is InterNIC. Intranets and other private networks may have their own NICs. *See also* InterNIC.

NIC handle *n. See* handle.

nickname *n.* A name used in the destination field of an e-mail editor in place of one or more complete network addresses. For example "Fred" might be a nickname for fred@history.washington.edu. If the nickname has been established within the program, a user need only type "Fred" instead of the entire address, or perhaps "history faculty" instead of all the individual faculty addresses. *See also* alias.

NIDS *n.* Acronym for **n**etwork-based **i**ntrusion-**d**etection **S**ystem. A type of intrusion detection system (IDS) that analyzes the individual packets moving across a network. NIDS can detect packets that a firewall might not catch. *See also* IDS.

NII *n. See* National Information Infrastructure.

N

Nimda worm *n.* A persistent worm that can slow or freeze mail servers, take control of Web pages, and infect systems through several different means. The Nimda worm spreads as an attached file through e-mail, through an Internet scan for vulnerable Web servers, through a JavaScript on an infected Web page, or through network sharing. The Nimda worm first appeared in 2001, with several variants following the original version.

NIS *n.* Acronym for **N**etwork **I**nformation **S**ervice. *See* Yellow Pages (definition 1).

NIST *n. See* National Institute of Standards and Technology.

nixpub *n.* A list of ISPs (Internet service providers) available in the newsgroups comp.bbs.misc and alt.bbs. *See also* ISP.

NKE *n.* Acronym for **N**etwork **K**ernel **E**xtension. A modification or extension of the Mac OS X networking infrastructure. NKEs may be loaded or unloaded dynamically, without recompiling the kernel or without the need to reboot the system. NKEs allow the creation and configuration of protocol stacks and modules that may monitor or modify network traffic or add other networking features to the kernel.

NNTP *n.* Acronym for **N**etwork **N**ews **T**ransfer **P**rotocol. A de facto protocol standard on the Internet used to distribute news articles and query news servers.

NOC *n. See* network operation center.

node *n.* **1.** A junction of some type. **2.** In networking, a device, such as a client computer, a server, or a shared printer, that is connected to the network and is capable of communicating with other network devices. **3.** In tree structures, a location on the tree that can have links to one or more nodes below it. Some authors make a distinction between node and element, with an element being a given data type and a node comprising one or more elements as well as any supporting data structures. *See also* tree.

noise *n.* **1.** Any interference that affects the operation of a device. **2.** Unwanted electrical signals, produced either naturally or by the circuitry, that distort or degrade the quality or performance of a communications channel.

nondedicated server *n.* A computer on a network that can function as both a client and a server; typically, a desktop machine on a peer-to-peer network. *Compare* dedicated server.

North American Cellular Network *n.* Telecommunications network that enables wireless phone users in North America to send and receive calls when roaming outside their service area. *Acronym:* NACN.

NOS *n. See* network operating system.

Novell Directory Services *n. See* NDS.

Novell NetWare *n. See* NetWare.

NQL *n. See* Network Query Language.

NSAPI *n.* Acronym for Netscape Server Application Programming Interface. A specification for interfaces between the Netscape HTTP server and other application programs. NSAPI can be used to provide access to application programs from a Web browser through a Web server. *See also* HTTP server (definition 1), Web browser.

NSF *n. See* National Science Foundation.

NSFnet *n.* Short for the National Science Foundation Network. A WAN (wide area network), developed by the National Science Foundation to replace ARPANET for civilian purposes. NSFnet served as a major backbone for the Internet until mid-1995. Backbone services in the United States for the Internet are now provided by commercial carriers. *See also* ARPANET, backbone (definition 1).

NSFnet Network Information Center *n. See* InterNIC.

NSI *n.* Acronym for Network Solutions, Inc. The organization responsible, since 1992, for registering top-level Internet domain names and maintaining the authoritative ("A") database of top-level domains replicated daily on 12 other root servers on the Internet. In 1998, with the privatization of Internet administration, the functions performed by NSI (under cooperative agreement with the U.S. National Science Foundation) became the responsibility of ICANN, a new, nonprofit organization. NSI remains active, but its association with the U.S. government entered the "ramping down" phase in 1998/1999. *See also* IANA, ICANN.

NT-1 *n. See* Network Terminator 1.

NT file system *n. See* NTFS.

NTFS *n.* Acronym for NT file system. An advanced file system designed for use specifically with the Windows NT operating system. It supports long file names, full security access control, file system recovery, extremely large storage media, and various features for the Windows NT POSIX subsystem. It also supports object-oriented applications by treating all files as objects with user-defined and system-defined attributes. *See also* FAT file system, HPFS, POSIX.

NTLM authentication protocol *n.* A challenge/response authentication protocol. The NTLM authentication protocol was the default for network authentication in Windows NT version 4.0 and earlier and Windows Millennium Edition (Windows Me) and earlier. The protocol continues to be supported in Windows 2000 and Windows XP but no longer is the default. *See also* Kerberos.

NTP *n.* Acronym for Network Time Protocol. A protocol used for synchronizing the system time on a computer to that of a server or other reference source such as a radio, satellite receiver, or modem. NTP provides time accuracy within a millisecond on local area networks and a few tens of milliseconds on wide area networks. NTP configurations may utilize redundant servers, diverse network paths, and cryptographic authentication to achieve high accuracy and reliability.

N

NuBus *n.* A high-performance expansion bus used in Macintosh computers, offering high bandwidth and multiple bus controllers. Invented at the Massachusetts Institute of Technology (MIT), NuBus was eventually licensed to Texas Instruments and other companies.

null modem *n.* A way of connecting two computers via a cable that enables them to communicate without the use of modems. A null modem cable accomplishes this by crossing the sending and receiving wires so that the wire used for transmitting by one device is used for receiving by the other and vice versa.

NWLink *n.* An implementation of the Internetwork Packet Exchange (IPX), Sequenced Packet Exchange (SPX), and NetBIOS protocols used in Novell networks. NWLink is a standard network protocol that supports routing and can support NetWare client-server applications, where NetWare-aware Sockets-based applications communicate with IPX/SPX Sockets-based applications. *See also* IPX/SPX, NetBIOS, RIPX.

O

OAGI *n.* Acronym for **O**pen **A**pplications **G**roup, **I**nc. A nonprofit consortium of software vendors and businesses created to develop and define XML-based interoperability specifications and standards among enterprise-scale applications. The OAGI was formed in 1995 by a small number of business enterprise software companies and organizations and has grown to more than sixty member companies.

OAGIS *n.* Acronym for **O**pen **A**pplications **G**roup **I**ntegration **S**pecification. A set of XML-based specifications and standards designed to promote B2B e-commerce by providing interoperability between enterprise-scale applications and between companies. OAGIS includes business document specifications and definitions, business process scenarios, and templates for business forms such as invoices and requisitions. OAGIS is overseen by the Open Applications Group, Inc., a nonprofit consortium of software vendors and customers. *See also* OAGI.

OASIS *n.* Acronym for **O**rganization for the **A**dvancement of **S**tructured **I**nformation **S**tandards. A consortium of technology companies formed to develop guidelines for use of XML (Extensible Markup Language) and related information standards.

Oberon *n.* An extensible object-oriented language based on Modula-2, whose later versions support the .NET Framework. *Also called:* Active Oberon for .NET.

object *n.* **1.** Short for object code (machine-readable code). **2.** In object-oriented programming, a variable comprising both routines and data that is treated as a discrete entity. **3.** In graphics, a distinct entity. For example, a bouncing ball might be an object in a graphics program. **4.** A single, runtime instance of object type that the operating system defines. Objects visible in user mode include event, file, I/O completion port, key, object directory, port, process, section, semaphore, symbolic link, thread, timer, and token objects. Many user-mode objects are implemented through the use of a corresponding kernel-mode object. Kernel-mode-only objects include adapter, APC, controller, device, device queue, DPC, driver, interrupt, mutex, and stream file objects.

object linking and embedding *n. See* OLE.

object request broker *n. See* ORB.

OC3 *n.* Short for **o**ptical **c**arrier **3**. One of several optical signal circuits used in the SONET high-speed fiberoptic data transmission system. OC3 carries a signal of 155.52 Mbps, the minimum transmission speed for which SONET and the European standard, SDH, are fully interoperable. *See also* SONET.

OCX *n.* Short for **OLE c**ustom control. A software module based on OLE and COM technologies that, when called by an application, produces a control that adds some desired feature to the application. OCX technology is portable across platforms, works on both 16-bit and 32-bit operating systems, and can be used with many applications. It is the successor to VBX (Visual Basic custom control) technology, which supported

O

only Visual Basic applications, and is the basis for ActiveX controls. OCXs have, in fact, been superseded by ActiveX controls, which are much smaller and therefore work much better over the Internet. *See also* ActiveX control, COM (definition 2), OLE, Visual Basic.

ODBC *n.* Acronym for **O**pen **D**ata**b**ase **C**onnectivity. In the Microsoft WOSA (Windows Open System Architecture) structure, an interface providing a common language for Windows applications to gain access to a database on a network. *See also* WOSA.

ODBC driver *n.* Short for **O**pen **D**ata**b**ase Connectivity **driver**. A program file used to connect to a particular database. Each database program, such as Access or dBASE, or database management system, such as SQL Server, requires a different driver.

ODBMG *n. See* Object Database Management Group.

odd parity *n. See* parity.

ODI *n.* Acronym for **O**pen **D**ata-link **I**nterface. A specification developed by Novell to enable a network interface card (NIC) to support multiple protocols, such as TCP/IP and IPX/SPX. ODI also simplifies development of device drivers by eliminating concern about the particular protocol to be used in transferring information over the network. ODI is comparable in some ways to the Network Driver Interface Specification, or NDIS. *See also* NDIS, network adapter.

ODMA *n.* Acronym for **O**pen **D**ocument **M**anagement API. A specification for a standard application program interface that enables desktop applications, such as Microsoft Word, to interact seamlessly with specialized document management systems (DMS) installed on network servers. The ODMA specification is the property of the Association for Information & Image Management (AIIM). *See also* application programming interface, document management system.

OFC *n. See* Open Financial Connectivity.

Office *n.* Microsoft's family of individual and business application software suites for the Windows and Macintosh platforms. Office is built around three core products: Word for word processing, Excel for spreadsheets, and Outlook for e-mail and collaboration. Office XP, the most recent version for the Windows platform, is available in several versions: the Office XP Standard or Standard for Students and Teachers version, which includes Word, Excel, Outlook, and PowerPoint; the Office XP Professional version, which adds Access; Office XP Developer, which includes Word, Excel, Outlook, PowerPoint, Access, FrontPage, Microsoft's new SharePoint Team Services collaboration and team Web solution, and Developer Tools; and finally, Office XP Professional Special Edition, which offers all the programs in Office XP Professional plus FrontPage, SharePoint Team Services, Publisher, and IntelliMouse Explorer. Office v. X for Mac is the most recent version for the Macintosh and includes Word, Entourage (for e-mail and collaboration), Excel, and PowerPoint. See the table.

Table 0.1   Application Specifications

Product	Function	Platform
Word	Word processing	Windows, Macintosh
Excel	Spreadsheets	Windows, Macintosh
Outlook	E-mail, collaboration	Windows
Entourage	E-mail, collaboration	Macintosh
Publisher	Desktop publishing	Windows
Access	Database management	Windows
PowerPoint	Presentation graphics	Windows, Macintosh
FrontPage	Web site creation	Windows
SharePoint Team Services	Team Web solution	Windows

office automation *n.* The use of electronic and communications devices, such as computers, modems, and fax machines and any associated software, to perform office functions mechanically rather than manually.

offline *adj.* **1.** In reference to a computing device or a program, unable to communicate with or be controlled by a computer. *Compare* online (definition 1). **2.** In reference to one or more computers, being disconnected from a network. *Compare* online (definition 2). **3.** Colloquially, a reference to moving a discussion between interested parties to a later, more appropriate, time. For example, "We can talk about this offline. Let's get back on topic now."

offline navigator *n.* Software designed to download e-mail, Web pages, or newsgroup articles or postings from other online forums and save them locally to a disk, where they can be browsed without the user paying the cost of idle time while being connected to the Internet or an online information service. *Also called:* offline reader.

offline reader *n. See* offline navigator.

offline storage *n.* A storage resource, such as a disk, that is not currently available to the system.

offload *vb.* To assume part of the processing demand from another device. For example, some LAN-attached gateways can offload TCP/IP processing from the host machine, thereby freeing up significant processing capacity in the CPU. *See also* gateway, host, TCP/IP.

OLE *n.* Acronym for **o**bject **l**inking and **e**mbedding. A technology for transferring and sharing information among applications. When an object, such as an image file created with a paint program, is linked to a compound document, such as a spreadsheet or a document created with a word processing program, the document contains only a reference to the object; any changes made to the contents of a linked object will be seen in the compound document. When an object is embedded in a compound document, the document contains a copy of the object; any changes made to the contents of the original object will not be seen in the compound document unless the embedded object is updated.

OLE Database *n.* An application programming interface developed by Microsoft for accessing databases. OLE Database is an open specification that can interface with all types of data files on a computer network. *Acronym:* OLE DB.

O

OLTP *n.* Acronym for online transaction processing. A system for processing transactions as soon as the computer receives them and updating master files immediately in a database management system. OLTP is useful in financial record keeping and inventory tracking. *See also* database management system, transaction processing. *Compare* batch processing.

OM-1 *n. See* OpenMPEG Consortium.

one-to-many replication *n.* A server configuration allowing replication of data from one or more large servers to a greater number of smaller servers.

one-way trust *n.* A type of trust relationship in which only one of the two domains trusts the other domain. For example, domain A trusts domain B and domain B does not trust domain A. All one-way trusts are nontransitive. *See also* transitive trust, two-way trust.

onion routing *n.* An anonymous communication technique first developed by the U.S. Navy, in which a message is wrapped in layers of encryption and passed through several intermediate stations to obscure its point of origin. In onion routing, data packets are sent through a complex network of routers, each of which opens an anonymous connection to the next, until it reaches its destination. When the packet is received by the first onion router, it is encrypted once for each additional router it will pass through. Each subsequent onion router unwraps one layer of encryption until the message reaches its destination as plain text.

online *adj.* **1.** In reference to a computing device or a program, activated and ready for operation; capable of communicating with or being controlled by a computer. *Compare* offline (definition 1). **2.** In reference to one or more computers, connected to a network. *Compare* offline (definition 2). **3.** In reference to a user, currently connected to the Internet, an online service, or a BBS or using a modem to connect to another modem. **4.** In reference to a user, being able to connect to the Internet, an online service, or a BBS by virtue of having an account that gives one access.

online community *n.* **1.** All users of the Internet and World Wide Web collectively. **2.** A local community that places political forums on line for the discussion of local government or issues of public concern. **3.** Members of a specific newsgroup, mailing list, MUD, BBS, or other online forum or group. *See also* BBS (definition 1), mailing list, MUD, newsgroup.

online game *n.* A game that is meant to be played while connected to the Internet, intranet, or other network, with one or more other people simultaneously connected. Online games allow gamers to interact with other players without having their physical presence necessary. *See also* computer game.

online information service *n.* A business that provides access to databases, file archives, conferences, chat groups, and other forms of information through dial-up, or dedicated communications links, or through the Internet. Most online information services also offer access to the Internet connections along with their own proprietary services. The largest consumer online information services in the U.S. are America Online, CompuServe, and MSN.

Online Privacy Alliance *n. See* OPA.

online service *n. See* online information service.

online transaction processing *n. See* OLTP.

on the fly *adv.* Doing a task or process as needed without suspending or disturbing normal operations. For example, it is often said that an HTML document can be edited on the fly because its content can be revised without the need to completely shut down or re-create the Web site on which it resides. *See also* HTML document, Web site.

OPA *n.* Acronym for **O**nline **P**rivacy **A**lliance. An organization of over eighty Internet companies and trade associations created to be the voice of the industry on digital privacy issues. The OPA stresses the need for consumer trust and encourages online businesses to post privacy policies. The OPA created a set of guidelines for privacy policies that have become the industry standard.

Open Applications Group, Inc. *n. See* OAGI.

Open Data-link Interface *n. See* ODI.

OpenDoc *n.* An object-oriented application programming interface (API) that enables multiple independent programs (component software) on several platforms to work together on a single document (compound document). Similar to OLE, Open-Doc allows images, sound, video, other documents, and other files to be embedded or linked to the document. OpenDoc is supported by an alliance that includes Apple, IBM, the Object Management Group, and the X Consortium. *See also* application programming interface. *Compare* ActiveX, OLE.

Open Document Management API *n. See* ODMA.

Open Financial Connectivity *n.* The Microsoft specification for an interface between electronic banking services and Microsoft Money personal finance software. *Acronym:* OFC.

OpenMPEG Consortium *n.* An international organization of hardware and software developers for promoting the use of the MPEG standards. *Acronym:* OM-1. *See also* MPEG.

Open Profiling Standard *n.* An Internet personalization and privacy specification submitted for consideration to the World Wide Web Consortium by Netscape Communications Corporation, Firefly Network, Inc., and VeriSign, Inc. Open Profiling Standard (OPS) enables users to customize online services while protecting their

O

privacy. To achieve personalization and privacy concomitantly, OPS is based on the concept of a Personal Profile, which is stored on the individual's computer and contains the user's unique identification, demographic and contact data, and possibly content preferences. This information remains under the user's control and can be released wholly or in part to the requesting site. *Acronym:* OPS. *See also* cookie, digital certificate.

Open Shortest Path First *n. See* OSPF.

open source *n.* The practice of making the source code (program instructions) for a software product freely available, at no cost, to interested users and developers, even though they were not involved in creating the original product. The distributors of open source software expect and encourage users and outside programmers to examine the code in order to identify problems, and to modify the code with suggested improvements and enhancements. Widely used open source products include the Linux operating system and the Apache Web server.

open standard *n.* A publicly available set of specifications describing the characteristics of a hardware device or software program. Open standards are published to encourage interoperability and thereby help popularize new technologies. *See also* standard (definition 2).

open system *n.* **1.** In communications, a computer network designed to incorporate all devices—regardless of the manufacturer or model—that can use the same communications facilities and protocols. **2.** In reference to computer hardware or software, a system that can accept add-ons produced by third-party suppliers.

Open Systems Interconnection reference model *n. See* ISO/OSI reference model.

Opera *n.* A Web browser developed by Opera Software S/A. Opera is notable for its strict W3C standards support. Opera is often chosen by Web developers to test Web sites for W3C compliance. *See also* W3C, Web browser.

OPS *n. See* Open Profiling Standard.

optimize *vb.* **1.** In Web design functions, to reduce the file size of a photo or graphic to allow faster loading. Files are typically optimized through a combination of means such as reducing overall image quality and fine-tuning color information. **2.** To fine-tune an application for improved performance.

Orange Book *n.* **1.** A U.S. Department of Defense standards document entitled "Trusted Computer System Evaluation Criteria, DOD standard 5200.28-STD, December, 1985," which defines a system of ratings from A1 (most secure) to D (least secure), indicating the ability of a computer system to protect sensitive information. *Compare* Red Book (definition 1). **2.** A specifications book written by the Sony and Philips Corporations, covering the compact disc write-once formats (CD-R, PhotoCD). *Compare* Green Book, Red Book (definition 2).

ORB *n.* Acronym for **o**bject **r**equest **b**roker. In client/server applications, an interface to which the client makes a request for an object. The ORB directs the request to the server containing the object and then returns the resulting values to the client. *See also* clientc, CORBA.

.org *n.* In the Internet's Domain Name System, the top-level domain that identifies addresses operated by organizations that do not fit any of the other standard domains. For instance, the Public Broadcasting System (PBS) is neither a commercial, for-profit corporation (.com) nor an educational institution with enrolled students (.edu), so it has the Internet address pbs.org. The designation .org appears at the end of the address. *See also* DNS (definition 1), domain (definition 3). *Compare* .com, .edu, .gov, .mil, .net.

Organization for the Advancement of Structured Information Standards *n. See* OASIS.

OSI *n. See* ISO/OSI reference model.

OSI protocol stack *n.* The set of protocols based on—and corresponding to—the ISO/OSI reference model.

OSI reference model *n. See* ISO/OSI reference model.

OSPF *n.* Acronym for **O**pen **S**hortest **P**ath **F**irst. A routing protocol for IP networks, such as the Internet, that allows a router to calculate the shortest path to each node for sending messages. The router sends information on the nodes it is linked to, called link-state advertisements, to other routers on the network to accumulate link-state information to make its calculations. *See also* communications protocol, node (definition 2), path (definition 1), router.

OTOH *n.* Acronym for **o**n **t**he **o**ther **h**and. A shorthand expression often used in e-mail, Internet news, and discussion groups.

Outbox *n.* In many e-mail applications, the default mailbox where the program stores outgoing messages. *See also* e-mail[1] (definition 1), mailbox. *Compare* Inbox.

Outlook *n.* Microsoft's messaging and collaboration application software. A member of the Microsoft Office suite, Outlook includes e-mail, an integrated calendar, and contact-management and task-management features, and it also provides support for building customized tools, such as special-purpose forms, for collaborative functions.

output *n.* The results of processing, whether sent to the screen or printer, stored on disk as a file, or sent to another computer in a network.

overwriting virus *n.* A type of virus that overwrites the host file it has infected, destroying the original data. *Also called:* overwrite virus.

P

P2P or **P-to-P** *n.* An Internet-based networking option in which two or more computers connect directly to each other to communicate and share files without use of a central server. Interest in P2P networking blossomed with the introduction of Napster and Gnutella. Short for Peer-to-Peer. *See also* peer-to-peer architecture, peer-to-peer communications.

P3P *n.* Acronym for **P**latform for **P**rivacy **P**references. An open W3C protocol that allows Internet users to control the type of personal information that is collected by the Web sites they visit. P3P uses User Agents built into browsers and Web applications to allow P3P-enabled Web sites to communicate privacy practices to users before they log on to the Web site. P3P compares the Web site's privacy policies with the user's personal set of privacy preferences, and it reports any disagreements to the user.

packet *n.* **1.** A unit of information transmitted as a whole from one device to another on a network. **2.** In packet-switching networks, a transmission unit of fixed maximum size that consists of binary digits representing both data and a header containing an identification number, source and destination addresses, and sometimes error-control data. *See also* packet switching.

packet assembler and disassembler *n. See* packet assembler/disassembler.

packet assembler/disassembler *n.* An interface between non-packet-switching equipment and a packet-switching network. *Acronym:* PAD.

packet filtering *n.* The process of controlling network access based on IP addresses. Firewalls will often incorporate filters that allow or deny users the ability to enter or leave a local area network. Packet filtering is also used to accept or reject packets such as e-mail, based on the origin of the packet, to ensure security on a private network. *See also* firewall, IP address, packet (definition 1).

packet flooding *n.* A technique employed in a number of DoS (denial of service) attacks in which a flood of packets of data are sent to a target server, overwhelming the computer and rendering it unable to respond to legitimate network requests. Examples of specific types of packet flooding include smurf attacks and SYN flood attacks. *See also* DoS, packet, smurf attack, SYN flood.

packet header *n.* The portion of a data packet that precedes the body (data). The header contains data, such as source and destination addresses and control and timing information, that is needed for successful transmission.

Packet Internet Groper *n. See* ping[1] (definition 1).

packet sniffer *n.* A hardware and/or software device that examines every packet sent across a network. To work, a packet sniffer must be installed in the same network block as the network it is intended to sniff. Designed as a problem-solving tool to isolate problems degrading network performance, packet sniffers have become security risks on some networks because crackers can use them to capture nonencrypted user IDs, passwords, credit card numbers, e-mail addresses, and other confidential information. *See also* cracker, packet. *Compare* monitoring software.

packet switching *n.* A message-delivery technique in which small units of information (packets) are relayed through stations in a computer network along the best route available between the source and the destination. A packet-switching network handles information in small units, breaking long messages into multiple packets before routing. Although each packet may travel along a different path, and the packets composing a message may arrive at different times or out of sequence, the receiving computer reassembles the original message correctly. Packet-switching networks are considered to be fast and efficient. To manage the tasks of routing traffic and assembling/disassembling packets, such a network requires some intelligence from the computers and software that control delivery. The Internet is an example of a packet-switching network. Standards for packet switching on networks are documented in the International Telecommunication Union (ITU) recommendation X.25. *Compare* circuit switching.

Packet Switching Exchange *n.* An intermediary switching station in a packet-switching network.

PAD *n. See* packet assembler/disassembler.

page banner *n.* A section of a Web page containing a graphic element and text, such as the page title. Page banners are usually displayed at the top of a Web page. Page banners can also be used to link to other Web sites for advertising purposes. *Also called:* banner.

page-jacking *n.* A deceptive practice that detours Web visitors from legitimate sites generated as search engine results to copycat Web pages, from which they will be redirected to pornographic or other unwanted sites. Page-jacking is accomplished by copying the contents and metatags of a Web page, altering its title and content so that, on search results, it displays before the original, and then submitting the copied page to search engines. When clicking on the link to the copied site, the visitor will instead be redirected to an unwanted and unrelated site. *See also* metatag. *Compare* mousetrapping.

PAP *n.* **1.** Acronym for **P**assword **A**uthentication **P**rotocol. A method for verifying the identity of a user attempting to log on to a Point-to-Point Protocol (PPP) server. PAP is used if a more rigorous method, such as the Challenge Handshake Authentication Protocol (CHAP), is not available or if the user name and password that the user submitted to PAP must be sent to another program without encryption. **2.** Acronym for **P**rinter **A**ccess **P**rotocol. The protocol in AppleTalk networks that governs communication between computers and printers.

parallel port *n.* An input/output connector that sends and receives data 8 bits at a time, in parallel, between a computer and a peripheral device such as a printer, scanner, CD-ROM, or other storage device. The parallel port, often called a Centronics interface after the original design standard, uses a 25-pin connector called a DB-25 connector that includes three groups of lines: four for control signals, five for status signals, and eight for data. *See also* IEEE 1284. *Compare* serial port.

parallel server *n.* A computer system that implements some form of parallel processing to improve its performance as a server. *See also* SMP server.

parity *n.* The quality of sameness or equivalence, in the case of computers usually referring to an error-checking procedure in which the number of 1s must always be the same—either even or odd—for each group of bits transmitted without error. If parity is checked on a per-character basis, the method is called vertical redundancy checking, or VRC; if checked on a block-by-block basis, the method is called longitudinal redundancy checking, or LRC. In typical modem-to-modem communications, parity is one of the parameters that must be agreed upon by sending and receiving parties before transmission can take place. See the table. *See also* parity bit, parity check, parity error.

Table P.1 Types of Parity.

Type	Description
Even parity	The number of 1s in each successfully transmitted set of bits must be an even number.
Odd parity	The number of 1s in each successfully transmitted set of bits must be an odd number.
No parity	No parity bit is used.
Space parity	A parity bit is used and is always set to 0.
Mark parity	A parity bit is used and is always set to 1.

parity bit *n.* An extra bit used in checking for errors in groups of data bits transferred within or between computer systems. With PCs, the term is frequently encountered in modem-to-modem communications, in which a parity bit is often used to check the accuracy with which each character is transmitted, and in RAM, where a parity bit is often used to check the accuracy with which each byte is stored.

parity check *n.* The use of parity to check the accuracy of transmitted data. *See also* parity, parity bit.

parity error *n.* An error in parity that indicates an error in transmitted data or in data stored in memory. If a parity error occurs in communications, all or part of a message must be retransmitted; if a parity error occurs in RAM, the computer usually halts. *See also* parity, parity bit.

partnership *n.* The settings on a desktop computer and Windows CE device that allow information to be synchronized, as well as copied or moved between the computer and device. The mobile device can have partnerships with up to two desktop computers. *See also* synchronization (definition 6).

pASP *n. See* pocket Active Server Pages.

passivation *n.* In Sun Microsystems's J2EE network platform, the process of "turning off" an Enterprise JavaBean (EJB) by caching it from memory to secondary storage. *See also* Enterprise JavaBeans, J2EE. *Compare* activation.

passive hub *n.* A type of hub used on ARCnet networks that passes signals along but has no additional capability. *See also* ARCnet. *Compare* active hub, Intelligent hub.

passive node *n.* A network node that "listens" for transmissions but is not actively involved in passing them along the network; typical of a node on a bus network. *See also* bus network, node (definition 2).

Passport *n.* A suite of personal identification services from Microsoft that consolidates user names, passwords, and other information. With the Passport single sign-in service, a user enters one name and password at any Passport site on the Internet; after signing in to one Passport site, a user can sign in to others without reentering the information. Passport also provides a server-based wallet service that stores credit card and billing information, a Kids Passport service, and a public-profile service. Passport is one of the foundation services of the Microsoft .NET initiative. *See also* .NET, .NET My Services, single sign-on, wallet.

pass-through *adj.* **1.** In general, a reference to something that acts as an intermediary between other entities. For example, a pass-through proxy server allows external access to an internal (protected) server by passing requests from the requesting client to the server without allowing direct access. **2.** Pertaining to a device or connector that moves a signal or set of signals from the input to the output without making any changes. For example, a peripheral device such as a SCSI adapter might have a pass-through parallel I/O port for connecting a printer through the same connector.

password *n.* The string of characters entered by a user to verify his or her identity to the network. The system compares the code against a stored list of authorized passwords and users. If the code is legitimate, the system allows the user access at whatever security level has been approved for the owner of the password. Ideally a password is a combination of text, numbers, and punctuation or other characters that cannot be guessed at or easily cracked by intruders.

password attack *n.* An attack on a computer or network in which a password is stolen and decrypted or is revealed by a password dictionary program. The compromised password opens the network to the hacker and may also be used to reveal additional network passwords. *See also* password sniffing.

Password Authentication Protocol *n. See* PAP (definition 1).

password protection *n.* The use of passwords as a means of allowing only authorized users access to a computer system or its files.

password shadowing *n.* A security system in which an encrypted password is stored in a separate "shadow" file, and its place is taken by a token representing the password. Password shadowing is used as protection from password attacks. *See also* password attack, password sniffing.

P

password sniffing *n.* A technique employed by hackers to capture passwords by intercepting data packets and searching them for passwords. *Also called:* packet sniffing.

path *n.* **1.** In communications, a link between two nodes in a network. **2.** A route through a structured collection of information, as in a database, a program, or files stored on disk. **3.** In programming, the sequence of instructions a computer carries out in executing a routine. **4.** In information processing, such as the theory underlying expert (deductive) systems, a logical course through the branches of a tree of inferences leading to a conclusion. **5.** In file storage, the route followed by the operating system through the directories in finding, sorting, and retrieving files on a disk. **6.** In graphics, an accumulation of line segments or curves to be filled or drawn.

PBX *n.* Acronym for **P**rivate **B**ranch E**x**change. An automatic telephone switching system that enables users within an organization to place calls to each other without going through the public telephone network. Users can also place calls to outside numbers.

PCIX *n.* **1.** Acronym for **P**eripheral **C**omponent **I**nterconnect E**x**tended. A computer bus technology developed by IBM, Compaq, and Hewlett-Packard that allows data to be transferred at greater speeds. PCIX increases the speed of data from 66 MHz to 133 MHz, but it will not run faster than the connected peripherals or computer processor will allow. PCI and PCIX peripherals are compatible with one another. *Also called:* PCI-X. **2.** Acronym for **P**ermission-based **C**ustomer **I**nformation E**x**change. A framework for the organization and exchange of information between customer and vendor. PCIX allows different companies to map information into a customer-friendly, permission-based format without changing internal database structures.

PCS *n. See* Personal Communications Services.

PCT *n.* **1.** Acronym for **p**rogram **c**omprehension **t**ool. A software engineering tool that facilitates the process of understanding the structure and/or functionality of computer programs. **2.** Acronym for **P**rivate **C**ommunications **T**echnology, a protocol standard drafted by Microsoft and submitted to the IETF for consideration. PCT, like the Netscape-designed SSL (Secure Sockets Layer), supports authentication and encryption for securing privacy in Internet communications. **3.** Acronym for **P**ersonal **C**ommunications **T**echnology. An enhanced version of Secure Sockets Layer (SSL).

PDA *n.* Acronym for **P**ersonal **D**igital **A**ssistant. A lightweight palmtop computer designed to provide specific functions like personal organization (calendar, note taking, database, calculator, and so on) as well as communications. More advanced models also offer multimedia features. Many PDA devices rely on a pen or other pointing device for input instead of a keyboard or mouse, although some offer a keyboard too small for touch typing to use in conjunction with a pen or pointing device. For data storage, a PDA relies on flash memory instead of power-hungry disk drives. *See also* pen computer.

PDC *n. See* Primary Domain Controller.

.pdf *n.* The file extension that identifies documents encoded in the Portable Document Format developed by Adobe Systems. To display or print a .pdf file, the user should obtain the freeware Adobe Acrobat Reader. *See also* Portable Document Format.

PDS *n.* **1.** Acronym for **P**rocessor **D**irect **S**lot. An expansion slot in Macintosh computers that is connected directly to the CPU signals. There are several kinds of PDS slots with different numbers of pins and different sets of signals, depending on which CPU is used in a particular computer. **2.** Acronym for **P**arallel **D**ata **S**tructure. A hidden file, located in the root directory of a disk that is shared under AppleShare, that contains access privilege information for folders.

Peachy virus *n.* A virus, first detected in 2001, that was the first to attempt to spread itself through PDF files. The Peachy virus takes advantage of an Adobe Acrobat feature that enables users to embed files in PDF documents. The embedded Peachy virus file infects the computer of a user who downloads the PDF file and then opens the file in Adobe Acrobat.

peer *n.* Any of the devices on a layered communications network that operate on the same protocol level. *See also* network architecture.

peer-to-peer architecture *n.* A network of two or more computers that use the same program or type of program to communicate and share data. Each computer, or *peer*, is considered equal in terms of responsibilities and each acts as a server to the others in the network. Unlike a client/server architecture, a dedicated file server is not required. However, network performance is generally not as good as under client/server, especially under heavy loads. *Also called:* peer-to-peer network. *See also* peer, peer-to-peer communications, server. *Compare* client/server architecture.

peer-to-peer communications *n.* Interaction between devices that operate on the same communications level on a network based on a layered architecture. *See also* network architecture.

peer-to-peer network *n. See* peer-to-peer architecture.

PEM *n. See* Privacy Enhanced Mail.

pen computer *n.* Any of a class of computers whose primary input device is a pen (stylus) instead of a keyboard. A pen computer is usually a smaller, handheld device and has a flat semiconductor-based display such as an LCD display. It requires either a special operating system designed to work with the pen input device or a proprietary operating system designed to work with a specific-purpose device. The pen computer is the primary model for an emerging class of computers known as personal digital assistants (PDAs). *See also* PDA.

permission *n.* In a networked or multiuser computer environment, the ability of a particular user to access a particular resource by means of his or her user account. Permissions are granted by the system administrator or other authorized person. Several levels of access can be given: read only, read and write (view and change), or read, write, and delete. *Also called:* Access permission.

permission class *n.* A class that defines access to a resource or defines an identity by supporting authorization checks.

P

permission object *n.* An instance of a permission class that represents access rights to resources or identity. A permission object can be used to specify a request, a demand, or a grant of permission.

permissions log *n.* A file on a network or multiuser computer environment where permissions for users are stored. When a user attempts to access a resource on the system, the permissions log is checked to see whether the user has permission to use it.

Per Seat Licensing *n.* A licensing mode that requires a separate Client Access License for each client computer, regardless of whether all the clients access the server at the same time. *See also* client. *Compare* Per Server Licensing.

Per Server Licensing *n.* A licensing mode that requires a separate Client Access License for each concurrent connection to the server, regardless of whether there are other client computers on the network that do not happen to connect concurrently. *Compare* Per Seat Licensing.

persistent link *n. See* hot link.

Personal Communications Services *n.* Term used by the United States Federal Communications Commission (FCC) to cover a range of wireless, all-digital communications technologies and services, including cordless phones, voice mail, paging, faxing, and personal digital assistants (PDAs). Personal Communications Services, or PCS, is divided into narrowband and broadband categories. Narrowband, which operates in the 900 MHz band of frequencies, provides paging, data messaging, faxing, and one- and two-way electronic messaging capabilities. Broadband, which operates in the 1850 MHz to 1990 MHz range and is considered the next-generation PCS, enables two-way voice, data, and video communications. The cellular phone technologies known as GSM (Global System for Mobile Communications), CDMA (Code Division Multiple Access), and TDMA (Time Division Multiple Access) are included in the PCS category. *Acronym:* PCS. *Compare* Code Division Multiple Access, Global System for Mobile Communications, TDMA.

personal digital assistant *n. See* PDA.

personal identification number *n. See* PIN.

personal information manager *n. See* PIM.

personalization technology *n.* An e-commerce marketing technique in which Web sites and services analyze the interests of individual customers. The e-business then uses this information to deliver services, product offerings, and advertising that match each customer's personal interests.

Personal Web Server *n.* Microsoft applications that allow a computer running the Windows family of operating systems to function as a Web server for publishing personal Web pages and intranet sites. Personal Web Server is available as part of Microsoft Windows NT 4.0 Option Pack (NTOP), Windows 98, and Windows 95 OEM Service Release 2. FrontPage Personal Web Server is available as part of FrontPage 1.1, FrontPage 97, FrontPage 98, and FrontPage 2000.

PGP *n.* Acronym for **P**retty **G**ood **P**rivacy. A program for public key encryption, using the RSA algorithm, developed by Philip Zimmermann. PGP software is available in unsupported free versions and supported commercial versions. *See also* privacy, public key encryption, RSA encryption.

phage virus *n.* A destructive virus that affects the Palm operating system (OS). Phage copies itself, overwriting application files and destroying them. Once the first host file is infected, Phage will spread to all available files. Phage may be spread from one Palm device to another by beaming or connection with a docking station. Phage was one of the first viruses created specifically to affect handheld wireless devices and the first to impact the Palm OS.

P

phoneline networking *n.* The use of telephone wiring for connecting computers and other devices in a small network, such as a home network. *See also* HomePNA.

Photoshop *n.* Adobe software product for digital image editing and enhancement, photo retouching, and color management of graphic images. Photoshop includes such features as multiple undo, text editing with formatting control, and enhanced color management and controls. The program supports numerous Web and graphics file formats and runs on both the Windows and Power Macintosh platforms.

PHP *n.* Acronym for **PHP: H**ypertext **P**reprocessor. An open source scripting language used with HTML documents to execute server-side interactive functions. PHP runs on all major operating systems and is primarily used with Linux and UNIX Web servers or on Windows servers with add-on software. PHP may be embedded in a Web page and used to access and present database information. An HTML document that contains a PHP script usually has a .php filename extension. Originally PHP stood for "Personal Home Page," with later versions standing for "PHP Hypertext Preprocessor" or simply PHP. The syntax of PHP is fairly simple and very similar to that of Perl, with some aspects of Bourne shell, JavaScript, and C. It can also be regarded as a technology (server-side environment for ported script engines, like ASP).

phreak¹ *n.* A person who breaks into, or *cracks*, telephone networks or other secured systems. In the 1970s, the telephone system used audible tones as switching signals, and *phone phreaks* used homebrew hardware to match the tones and steal long-distance service. *See also* homebrew. *Compare* cracker, hacker (definition 2).

phreak² *vb.* To break into, or *crack*, phone networks or computer systems. *See also* homebrew. *Compare* hack.

physical layer *n.* The first, or lowest, of the seven layers in the ISO/OSI reference model for standardizing computer-to-computer communications. The physical layer is totally hardware-oriented and deals with all aspects of establishing and maintaining a physical link between communicating computers. Among specifications covered on the physical layer are cabling, electrical signals, and mechanical connections. *See also* ISO/OSI reference model.

physical network *n.* One of two ways of describing the topology, or layout, of a computer network; the other is logical network. A physical network refers to the actual configuration of the hardware forming a network—that is, to the computers, connecting hardware, and especially the cabling patterns that give the network its shape. Basic physical layouts include the bus, ring, and star topologies. *See also* bus network, logical network, ring network, star network.

picoJava *n.* A microprocessor developed by Sun Microsystems, Inc., that executes Java code. *See also* Java.

PICS *n. See* Platform for Internet Content Selection.

Pilot *n.* A series of popular handheld personal digital assistants (PDAs) designed by Palm and based on the Palm OS operating system. Palm introduced its first Pilot model in 1996, followed in 1997 by the PalmPilot, and thereafter by a series of other Palm handheld models.

PIM *n.* Acronym for **p**ersonal **i**nformation **m**anager. An application that usually includes an address book and organizes unrelated information, such as notes, appointments, and names, in a useful way.

PIN *n.* Acronym for **p**ersonal **i**dentification **n**umber. A unique code number used to gain access to personal information or assets via an electronic device. PINs are used by a variety of electronic services such as automated bank tellers, Internet sites, and wireless phone services.

pine *n.* Acronym for **p**ine **is** **n**ot **e**lm, or for **P**rogram for **I**nternet **N**ews and **E**-mail. One of the most commonly encountered programs for reading and composing e-mail on character-based UNIX systems. The pine program was developed as an improved version of elm at the University of Washington. *Compare* elm.

ping¹ *n.* **1.** Acronym for **P**acket **I**nter**n**et **G**roper. A protocol for testing whether a particular computer is connected to the Internet by sending a packet to its IP address and waiting for a response. The name actually comes from submarine active sonar, where a sound signal—called a "ping"—is broadcast, and surrounding objects are revealed by their reflections of the sound. **2.** A UNIX utility that implements the ping protocol.

ping² *vb.* **1.** To test whether a computer is connected to the Internet using the ping utility. **2.** To test which users on a mailing list are current by sending e-mail to the list asking for a response.

Ping of Death *n.* A form of Internet vandalism that entails sending a packet that is substantially larger than the usual 64 bytes over the Internet via the ping protocol to a remote computer. The size of the packet causes the computer to crash or reboot. *See also* packet (definition 2), ping¹ (definition 1).

ping packet *n.* An "are you there" message transmitted by a Packet Internet Groper program. A ping packet is sent from one node to the IP (Internet Protocol) address of a network computer to determine whether that node is able to send and receive transmissions. Many shareware and freeware ping utilities for PCs are available for download from the Internet. *See also* ping[1] (definition 1), packet[1] (definition 1).

ping pong *n.* **1.** In communications, a technique that changes the direction of transmission so that the sender becomes the receiver and vice versa. **2.** In information processing and transfer, the technique of using two temporary storage areas (buffers) rather than one to hold both input and output.

ping-pong buffer *n.* A double buffer in which each part is alternately filled and flushed, resulting in a more or less continuous stream of input and output data. *See also* ping pong (definition 2).

pink contract *n.* A non-standard addendum to a contract with an Internet service provider (ISP), specifically offering the client the opportunity to send unsolicited commercial e-mail and put up spam-related Web sites. *See also* spam.

PKUNZIP *n.* A shareware utility program that uncompresses files compressed by the PKZIP shareware utility program. PKUNZIP is generally made available with PKZIP; distribution of PKUNZIP for commercial purposes is not permitted without obtaining permission from its publisher, PKware, Inc. *See also* PKZIP.

PKZIP *n.* A widely used shareware utility program for compressing files. Developed by PKware, Inc., in 1989 and available from a wide variety of sources, PKZIP can combine one or more files into a compressed output file having the extension .zip. A companion utility program, PKUNZIP, is required to uncompress the compressed files. *See also* PKUNZIP, shareware.

Platform for Internet Content Selection *n.* A specification for rating and labeling Internet content. Originally developed by the World Wide Web Consortium to enable parents, teachers, administrators, and other caretakers to control the material to which children have online access, its use has expanded to include the protection of privacy and intellectual property. PICS is not itself a system for rating Internet content. Rather, it specifies the format conventions to be used by rating systems in devising labels that can be read by PICS-compatible software. *Acronym:* PICS.

Platform for Privacy Preference Project *n. See* P3P.

Platform for Privacy Preferences *n. See* P3P.

PlayStation *n.* Sony Corporation's console computer entertainment gaming system. PlayStation 2, the latest version, is a 128-bit system that features a 300-Mhz processor, 32 MB of Direct RDRAM main memory, and a floating-point performance of 6.2 GFLOPS. PlayStation 2 also offers the capability to play CDs and DVDs. *See also* computer game, console game. *Compare* Dreamcast, GameCube, Xbox.

plug and play *n.* **1.** Generally, a reference to the ability of a computer system to automatically configure a device added to it. Plug and play capability exists in Macintoshes based on the NuBus and, since Windows 95, on PC-compatible computers. **2.** When capitalized and, especially, when abbreviated PnP, a set of specifications developed by Intel and Microsoft that allows a PC to configure itself automatically to work with peripherals such as monitors, modems, and printers. A user can plug in a peripheral and "play" it without manually configuring the system. A Plug and Play PC requires both a BIOS (basic input/output system) that supports Plug and Play and a Plug and Play expansion card. *Abbreviation:* PnP.

plug-in *n.* **1.** A small software program that plugs into a larger application to provide added functionality. **2.** A software component that plugs into the Netscape Navigator. Plug-ins permit the Web browser to access and execute files embedded in HTML documents that are in formats the browser normally would not recognize, such as many animation, video, and audio files. Most plug-ins are developed by software companies who have proprietary software in which the embedded files are created. *Compare* helper application.

PMML *n.* Acronym for **P**redictive **M**odel **M**arkup **L**anguage. An XML-based language that enables sharing of defined predictive models between compliant vendor applications.

PNG *n.* Acronym for **P**ortable **N**etwork **G**raphics. A file format for bitmapped graphic images, designed to be a replacement for the GIF format, without the legal restrictions associated with GIF. *See also* GIF.

PNNI *n.* Short for **P**rivate **N**etwork-to-**N**etwork **I**nterface. A routing protocol used in ATM networks that provides switches with the ability to communicate changes in the network. Through PNNI, switches can be informed of changes to the network as they occur and can then use the information to make appropriate routing decisions. *See also* ATM.

PnP *n. See* plug and play (definition 2).

pocket Active Server Pages *n.* A scaled-down version of the Active Server Pages optimized for server-side Mobile Channels scripting. *Acronym:* pASP.

pocket Excel *n.* A scaled-down version of Microsoft Excel for the Pocket PC.

Pocket PC *n.* A personal handheld computing device based on specifications designed by Microsoft and running the Microsoft Windows for Pocket PC operating system. Pocket PCs maintain the look of a Windows operating system display screen and offer compact versions of many of the applications that run on Windows-powered personal computers. A number of manufacturers produce Pocket PCs, including Hewlett-Packard, Compaq, and Casio.

pocket Word *n.* A scaled-down version of Microsoft Word for the Pocket PC.

PointCast *n.* An Internet service that delivers and displays a personalized set of news articles to individual users. Unlike the World Wide Web and other Internet applications, PointCast is a *push* technology, where the server automatically uploads data without a specific command from the client. *See also* server (definition 2).

point of presence *n.* **1.** A point in a wide area network to which a user can connect with a local telephone call. **2.** A point at which a long distance telephone carrier connects to a local telephone exchange or to an individual user. *Acronym:* POP.

point of sale *n. See* POS.

point-to-point configuration *n.* A communications link in which dedicated links exist between individual origins and destinations, as opposed to a point-to-multipoint configuration, in which the same signal goes to many destinations (such as a cable TV system), or a switched configuration, in which the signal moves from the origin to a switch that routes the signal to one of several possible destinations. *Also called:* point-to-point connection.

point-to-point connection *n. See* point-to-point configuration.

point-to-point message system *n.* In Sun Microsystems's J2EE network platform, a messaging system that uses message queues to store asynchronous, formatted data for coordinating enterprise applications. Each message is addressed to a specific queue, and client applications retrieve messages from the queues. *See also* asynchronous, J2EE.

Point-to-Point Protocol *n. See* PPP.

point-to-point tunneling *n.* A means of setting up secure communications over an open, public network such as the Internet. *See also* PPTP.

Point-to-Point Tunneling Protocol *n. See* PPTP.

pop *vb.* To fetch the top (most recently added) element of a stack, removing that element from the stack in the process. *Compare* push[2] (definition 1).

POP *n. See* point of presence, Post Office Protocol.

POP3 *n.* Acronym for **P**ost **O**ffice **P**rotocol 3. This is the current version of the Post Office Protocol standard in common use on TCP/IP networks. *See also* Post Office Protocol, TCP/IP.

port *n.* **1.** An interface through which data is transferred between a computer and other devices (such as a printer, mouse, keyboard, or monitor), a network, or a direct connection to another computer. The port appears to the CPU as one or more memory addresses that it can use to send or receive data. Specialized hardware, such as in an add-on circuit board, places data from the device in the memory addresses and sends data from the memory addresses to the device. Ports may also be dedicated solely to input or to output. Ports typically accept a particular type of plug used for a specific purpose. For example, a serial data port, a keyboard, and a high-speed network port all use different connectors, so it's not possible to plug a cable into the wrong port. *Also called:* input/output port. **2.** port number.

port 25 blocking *n.* An anti-spam technique adopted by many ISPs to prevent bulk mailings of unsolicited commercial e-mail. Spammers may try to use SMTP

P

servers to relay a single commercial e-mail to multiple recipients. Port 25 blocking filters prevent this spam distribution method. Although it is a popular remedy for some spam problems, port 25 blocking may cause problems for legitimate users of non-compatible e-mail programs.

Portable Document Format *n.* The Adobe specification for electronic documents that use the Adobe Acrobat family of servers and readers. *Acronym:* PDF. *See also* .pdf.

Portable Network Graphics *n. See* PNG.

portal *n.* A Web site that serves as a gateway to the Internet. A portal is a collection of links, content, and services designed to guide users to information they are likely to find interesting—news, weather, entertainment, commerce sites, chat rooms, and so on. Excite, MSN.com, Netscape NetCenter, and Yahoo! are examples of portals. *See also* home page (definition 1), Web site.

portmapper *n.* A service used by Remote Procedure Call (RPC) to assign port numbers. RPC doesn't follow the Well-Known Ports port designations, and only Portmapper is assigned a permanent port number. Because hackers may gain access to portmapper communication, various portmapper security tools are often used to prevent theft of information. *See also* remote procedure call.

port number *n.* A number that enables IP packets to be sent to a particular process on a computer connected to the Internet. Some port numbers, called "well-known" port numbers, are permanently assigned; for example, e-mail data under SMTP goes to port number 25. A process such as a telnet session receives an "ephemeral" port number when it starts; data for that session goes to that port number, and the port number goes out of use when the session ends. A total of 65,535 port numbers are available for use with TCP, and the same number are available for UDP. *See also* IP, Simple Mail Transfer Protocol, socket (definition 1), TCP, UDP. *Compare* IP address.

POS *n.* Acronym for **p**oint **o**f **s**ale. The place in a store at which goods are paid for. Computerized transaction systems, such as those in use at automated supermarkets, use scanners for reading tags and bar codes, electronic cash registers, and other special devices to record purchases at this point.

POSIT *n.* Acronym for **P**rofiles for **O**pen **S**ystems **I**nternetworking **T**echnology. A set of nonmandatory standards for U.S. government network equipment. POSIT, which recognizes the prevalence of TCP/IP, is the successor to GOSIP. *See also* GOSIP, TCP/IP.

POSIX *n.* Acronym for **P**ortable **O**perating **S**ystem **I**nterface for UNIX. An Institute of Electrical and Electronics Engineers (IEEE) standard that defines a set of operating-system services. Programs that adhere to the POSIX standard can be easily ported from one system to another. POSIX was based on UNIX system services, but it was created in a way that allows it to be implemented by other operating systems. *See also* service (definition 2).

post¹ *n. See* article.

post[2] *vb.* **1.** To submit an article in a newsgroup or other online conference or forum. The term is derived from the "posting" of a notice on a physical bulletin board. *See also* newsgroup. **2.** To place a file on a server on a network or on a Web site.

postmaster *n.* The logon name (and therefore the e-mail address) of an account that is responsible for maintaining e-mail services on a mail server. When an account holder is having trouble with e-mail, a message to postmaster or "postmaster@machine.org.domain.name" will usually reach a human who can solve the problem.

P

post office *n.* The server and associated storage and mail handling services that provide the centralized location for collection and distribution of e-mail over a network.

Post Office Protocol *n.* A protocol for servers on the Internet that receive, store, and transmit e-mail and for clients on computers that connect to the servers to download and upload e-mail. *Acronym:* POP.

PPP *n.* Acronym for **P**oint-to-**P**oint **P**rotocol. A widely used data link protocol for transmitting TCP/IP packets over dial-up telephone connections, such as between a computer and the Internet. PPP, which supports dynamic allocation of IP addresses, provides greater protection for data integrity and security and is easier to use than SLIP, at a cost of greater overhead. PPP itself is based on a Link Control Protocol (LCP) responsible for setting up a computer-to-computer link over telephone lines and a Network Control Protocol (NCP) responsible for negotiating network-layer details related to the transmission. It was developed by the Internet Engineering Task Force in 1991. *Compare* SLIP.

PPPoE *n.* Acronym for **P**oint-to-**P**oint **P**rotocol **o**ver **E**thernet. A specification for connecting users on an Ethernet network to the Internet through a broadband connection, such as a single DSL line, wireless device, or cable modem. Using PPPoE and a broadband modem, LAN users can gain individual authenticated access to high-speed data networks. By combining Ethernet and Point-to-Point Protocol (PPP), PPPoE provides Internet service providers (ISPs) with the ability to manipulate a limited number of IP addresses by assigning an address only when the user is connected to the Internet. PPPoE is an efficient way to create a separate connection for each user to a remote server. When the Internet connection is broken, the IP address becomes available to be assigned to another user.

PPTP *n.* Acronym for **P**oint-to-**P**oint **T**unneling **P**rotocol. An extension of the Point-to-Point Protocol used for communications on the Internet. PPTP was developed by Microsoft to support virtual private networks (VPNs), which allow individuals and organizations to use the Internet as a secure means of communication. PPTP supports encapsulation of encrypted packets in secure wrappers that can be transmitted over a TCP/IP connection. *See also* virtual network.

presence technology *n.* An application, such as instant messaging, which finds specific users when they are connected to the network and which may alert interested users to each other's presence. Third-generation wireless networks will integrate presence technology with digital cell phones, PDAs, pagers, and other communications and entertainment devices.

presentation layer *n.* The sixth of the seven layers in the ISO/OSI reference model for standardizing computer-to-computer communications. The presentation layer is responsible for formatting information so that it can be displayed or printed. This task generally includes interpreting codes (such as tabs) related to presentation, but it can also include converting encryption and other codes and translating different character sets. *See also* ISO/OSI reference model.

Pretty Good Privacy *n. See* PGP.

PRI *n.* Acronym for **P**rimary **R**ate **I**nterface. One of two ISDN transmission rate services (the other is the basic rate interface, BRI). PRI has two variations. The first, which operates at 1.536 Mbps, transmits data over 23 B channels and sends signaling information at 64 Kbps over one D channel in the United States, Canada, and Japan. The second, which operates at 1.984 Mbps, transmits data over 30 B channels and sends signaling information at 64 Kbps over one D channel in Europe and Australia. *See also* BRI, ISDN.

Primary Domain Controller *n.* **1.** In Windows NT, a database providing a centralized administration site for resources and user accounts. The database allows users to log onto the domain, rather than onto a specific host machine. A separate account database keeps track of the machines in the domain and allocates the domain's resources to users. **2.** In any local area network, the server that maintains the master copy of the domain's user accounts database and that validates logon requests. *Acronym:* PDC.

Printer Access Protocol *n. See* PAP (definition 2).

printer port *n.* A port through which a printer can be connected to a personal computer. On PC-compatible machines, printer ports are usually parallel ports and are identified in the operating system by the logical device name LPT. On many newer PCs, the parallel port on the case of the CPU has a printer icon beside it to identify it as a printer port. Serial ports can also be used for some printers (logical device name COM), although configuration is generally required. On Macintoshes, printer ports are usually serial ports and are also used to connect Macs to an AppleTalk network. *See also* AppleTalk, parallel port, serial port.

printer server *n. See* print server.

print server *n.* A workstation that is dedicated to managing printers on a network. The print server can be any station on the network. *Also called:* printer server.

privacy *n.* The concept that a user's data, such as stored files and e-mail, is not to be examined by anyone else without that user's permission. A right to privacy is not generally recognized on the Internet. Federal law protects only e-mail in transit or in temporary storage, and only against access by Federal agencies. Employers often claim a right to inspect any data on their systems. To obtain privacy, the user must take active measures such as encryption. *See also* encryption, PGP, Privacy Enhanced Mail. *Compare* security.

Privacy Enhanced Mail *n.* An Internet standard for e-mail systems that use encryption techniques to ensure the privacy and security of messages. *Acronym:* PEM. *See also* encryption, standard. *Compare* PGP.

privacy policy *n.* Public statement delineating how a Web site uses the information it gathers from visitors to the site. Some Web sites sell this information to third parties or use the information for marketing purposes. Other sites have strict policies limiting how that information may be used.

private channel *n.* In Internet relay chat (IRC), a channel reserved for the use of a certain group of people. Private channel names are hidden from view by the public at large. *Also called:* secret channel. *See also* IRC.

Private Communications Technology *n.* See PCT (definition 2).

private folders *n.* In a shared network environment, those folders on a user's computer that are not accessible by other users on the network. *Compare* public folders.

private key *n.* One of two keys in public key encryption. The user keeps the private key secret and uses it to encrypt digital signatures and to decrypt received messages. *See also* public key encryption. *Compare* public key.

Private Network-to-Network Interface *n.* See PNNI.

privatization *n.* Generally, the process of turning something over from government to commercial industry control. In the context of computer science and the Internet, the term refers to the government's turning over of various Internet backbones to private industry—for example, control of NSFnet was passed from the government to private business in 1992—and to the government's more recent (1998) privatization of responsibility for domain names and addresses, which was shifted from IANA and NSI/InterNIC to a new organization known as ICANN. *See also* IANA, ICANN, InterNIC.

privileges *n.* See access privileges.

.pro *n.* One of seven new top-level domain names approved in 2000 by the Internet Corporation for Assigned Names and Numbers (ICANN), .pro is meant for use in Web sites relating to professions such as physicians, accountants, and lawyers. Six of the new domains became available for use in the spring of 2001; negotiations are still underway for the final registry agreement for the .pro domain.

Procmail *n.* An open-source e-mail-processing utility for Linux and other UNIX-based computers and networks. Procmail can be used to create mail servers and mailing lists, filter mail, sort incoming mail, preprocess mail, and perform other mail-related functions.

Prodigy *n.* An Internet service provider (ISP) that offers Internet access and a wide range of related services. Prodigy was founded by IBM and Sears as a proprietary online service, was acquired by International Wireless in 1996, and in 1999 entered into a partnership with SBC Communications. The addition of SBC's Internet customer base made Prodigy the third largest ISP in the United States.

Prodigy Information Service *n.* An online information service founded by IBM and Sears. Like its competitors America Online and CompuServe, Prodigy offers access to databases and file libraries, online chat, special interest groups, e-mail, and Internet connectivity. *Also called:* Prodigy.

P

Project 802 *n.* The IEEE project to define networking standards that resulted in the 802.x specifications. *See also* IEEE, IEEE 802.x.

Project Gutenberg *n.* A project that makes the texts of books that are in the public domain available over the Internet. The files for the books are in plain ASCII, to make them accessible to as many people as possible. Project Gutenberg, based at the University of Illinois at Urbana-Champaign, can be reached at mrcnext.cso.uiuc.edu via FTP or through the Web page http://www.promo.net/pg/. *See also* ASCII.

promiscuous-mode transfer *n.* In network communications, a transfer of data in which a node accepts all packets regardless of their destination address.

proprietary *adj.* Of, pertaining to, or characteristic of something that is privately owned. Generally, the term refers to technology that has been developed by a particular corporation or entity, with specifications that are considered by the owner to be trade secrets. Proprietary technology may be legally used only by a person or entity purchasing an explicit license. Also, other companies are unable to duplicate the technology, both legally and because its specifications have not been divulged by the owner. *Compare* public domain.

proprietary software *n.* A program owned or copyrighted by an individual or a business and available for use only through purchase or by permission of the owner. *Compare* open source, public-domain software.

protocol *n. See* communications protocol.

protocol analyzer *n.* A management tool designed to identify and diagnose computer network problems. A protocol analyzer looks at LAN (local area network) or WAN (wide area network) traffic and finds protocol errors, connection delays, and other network faults. The protocol analyzer can filter and decode traffic, suggest solutions to problems, provide graphical reports, and show traffic by protocol and percent utilization. *See also* communications protocol.

protocol layer *n. See* layer.

protocol stack *n.* The set of protocols that work together on different levels to enable communication on a network. For example, TCP/IP, the protocol stack on the Internet, incorporates more than 100 standards including FTP, IP, SMTP, TCP, and Telnet. *See also* ISO/OSI reference model. *Compare* protocol suite.

protocol suite *n.* A set of protocols designed, usually by one vendor, as complementary parts of a protocol stack. *Compare* protocol stack.

proxy server *n.* A firewall component that manages Internet traffic to and from a local area network (LAN) and can provide other features, such as document caching and access control. A proxy server can improve performance by supplying frequently requested data, such as a popular Web page, and can filter and discard requests that the owner does not consider appropriate, such as requests for unauthorized access to proprietary files. *See also* firewall.

PSE *n. See* Packet Switching Exchange.

PSN *n.* Acronym for packet-switching network. *See* packet switching.

PSTN *n. See* Public Switched Telephone Network.

pub *n. See* /pub.

/pub *n.* Short for public. A directory in an anonymous FTP archive that is accessible by the public and that generally contains files available for free download. *See also* anonymous FTP.

public directory *n.* A directory on an FTP server that is accessible by anonymous users for the purpose of retrieving or storing files. Often the directory is called /pub. *See also* anonymous FTP, FTP (definition 1), FTP server.

public domain *n.* The set of all creative works, such as books, music, or software, that are not covered by copyright or other property protection. Works in the public domain can be freely copied, modified, and otherwise used in any manner for any purpose. Much of the information, texts, and software on the Internet is in the public domain, but putting a copyrighted work on the Internet does not put it in the public domain. *Compare* proprietary.

public-domain software *n.* A program donated for public use by its owner or developer and freely available for copying and distribution. *Compare* free software, freeware, proprietary software, shareware.

public files *n.* Files with no access restrictions.

public folders *n.* The folders that are made accessible on a particular machine or by a particular user in a shared networking environment. *Compare* private folders.

public key *n.* One of two keys in public key encryption. The user releases this key to the public, who can use it for encrypting messages to be sent to the user and for decrypting the user's digital signature. *See also* public key encryption. *Compare* private key.

public key cryptography *n. See* public key encryption.

public key encryption *n.* An asymmetric scheme that uses a pair of keys for encryption: the public key encrypts data, and a corresponding secret key decrypts it. For digital signatures, the process is reversed: the sender uses the secret key to create a unique electronic number that can be read by anyone possessing the corresponding public key, which verifies that the message is truly from the sender. *See also* private key, public key.

public rights *n.* In the context of the Internet, the extent to which members of the public are permitted to use (and to place) information on the Internet under intellectual property law. *See also* fair use, public domain, public-domain software.

Public Switched Telephone Network *n.* The public telephone system.

pull *vb.* The process of retrieving data from a network server. *Compare* push[2] (definition 2). *See* pop.

push[1] *n.* A technology developed in relation to the World Wide Web, designed to provide end users with personalized Web access by having a site actively "push" requested information to the user's desktop, either automatically or at specified intervals. Push was developed as a means of relieving users from having to actively retrieve ("pull") information from the Web. It is not, as yet, especially popular.

push[2] *vb.* **1.** To add a new element to a stack, a data structure generally used to temporarily hold pieces of data being transferred or the partial result of an arithmetic operation. *See also* stack. *Compare* pop. **2.** In networks and the Internet, to send data or a program from a server to a client at the instigation of the server. *Compare* pull.

pwd *n.* Acronym for **p**rint **w**orking **d**irectory. The UNIX command for displaying the current directory.

PXE boot *n.* Acronym for **P**reboot E**x**ecution **E**nvironment **boot**. A BIOS-supported technology used to boot a PC remotely. To power on a PC and boot it from the network, PXE must be enabled in the BIOS, and the NIC in the PC must be PXE compliant. PXE boot is specified in the Intel Wired for Management (WfM) standard. *Also called:* network boot.

Q

QOS or **QoS** *n. See* quality of service.

quality of service *n.* **1.** Generally, the handling capacity of a system or service; the time interval between request and delivery of a product or service to the client or customer. **2.** In computer technology, the guaranteed throughput (data transfer rate) level.

queue *n.* A multi-element data structure from which (by strict definition) elements can be removed only in the same order in which they were inserted; that is, it follows a first in, first out (FIFO) constraint. There are also several types of queues in which removal is based on factors other than order of insertion—for example, some priority value assigned to each element. *See also* element. *Compare* stack.

queuing *n.* In networking, the process of buffering data in preparation for transmission. *See also* fair queuing; first in, first out; last in, first out; weighted fair queuing.

QuickTime *n.* Software components developed by Apple for creating, editing, publishing, and viewing multimedia content. QuickTime, which supports video, animation, graphics, 3-D, VR (virtual reality), MIDI, music, sound, and text, has been part of the Mac OS since version 7 of the operating system and is used in many Macintosh applications. Windows applications can also run QuickTime files but require the installation of special player software. QuickTime is often used on the Web to provide Web pages with video and animation. Most Web browsers support plug-ins for running these types of files. QuickTime is also part of the new MPEG-4 specification. *See also* MPEG-4.

quit *n.* **1.** An FTP command that instructs the server to drop the current connection with the client from which it received the command. **2.** A command in many applications for exiting the program.

R

RADIUS *n.* Acronym for **R**emote **A**uthentication **D**ial-**I**n **U**ser **S**ervice protocol. A proposed Internet protocol in which an authentication server provides authorization and authentication information to a network server to which a user is attempting to link. *See also* authentication, communications protocol, server (definition 2).

RADSL *n.* Acronym for **r**ate-**a**daptive **a**symmetric **d**igital **s**ubscriber line. A flexible, high-speed version of ADSL (asymmetric digital subscriber line) that is capable of adjusting transmission speed (bandwidth) based on signal quality and length of the transmission line. As the signal quality improves or deteriorates while a transmission line is being used, the transmission speed is adjusted accordingly. *See also* ADSL, xDSL.

RAID *n.* Acronym for **r**edundant **a**rray of **i**ndependent (or **i**nexpensive) **d**isks. A data storage method in which data is distributed across a group of computer disk drives that function as a single storage unit. All the information stored on each of the disks is duplicated on other disks in the array. This redundancy ensures that no information will be lost if one of the disks fails. RAID is generally used on network servers where data accessibility is critical and fault tolerance is required. There are various defined levels of RAID, each offering differing trade-offs among access speed, reliability, and cost. *See also* parity bit, server (definition 1).

RARP *n.* Acronym for **R**everse **A**ddress **R**esolution **P**rotocol. A TCP/IP protocol for determining the IP address (or logical address) of a node on a local area network connected to the Internet, when only the hardware address (or physical address) is known. While RARP refers only to finding the IP address and ARP technically refers to the opposite procedure, ARP is commonly used for both senses. *See also* ARP.

RAS *n.* **1.** *See* remote access server, Remote Access Service. **2.** Acronym for **r**eliability, **a**vailability, **s**erviceability. *See* high availability.

rate-adaptive asymmetric digital subscriber line *n.* *See* RADSL.

RDF *n.* *See* Resource Description Framework.

Reader *n.* *See* Microsoft Reader.

read notification *n.* An e-mail feature providing feedback to the sender that a message has been read by the recipient.

RealAudio *n.* Streaming audio technology developed by RealNetworks, Inc., for distributing radio and FM-quality sound files over the Internet in real time. RealAudio is based on two components: client software for decompressing the sound on the fly and server software for delivering it. The client software is free, distributed either as a downloadable program or as part of browser software. *See also* RealPlayer, RealVideo, stream, streaming.

RealPlayer *n.* An Internet media player and browser plug-in developed by RealNetworks, Inc., that supports playback of RealAudio and RealVideo, as well as certain other formats, after installation of appropriate plug-ins. The current version allows RealPlayer users to surf for media content directly from the player or through a Web browser. *See also* RealAudio, RealVideo.

RealSystem G2 *n.* An open, standards-based platform for delivery of streaming audio and video over the Internet and other TCP/IP networks developed by RealNetworks, Inc. RealSystem G2 was introduced by RealNetworks in its audio and video players, servers, and development tools in 1998. Among other features, RealSystem G2 scales to different bandwidths, includes streaming that adjusts delivery to available bandwidth, and supports SMIL (Synchronized Multimedia Integration Language) for multimedia presentations. *See also* RealPlayer, RealVideo, SMIL, streaming.

RealSystem Producer *n.* A software application developed by RealNetworks that converts most types of video and sound files into RealMedia formats for use as streaming media over the Internet or within a corporate intranet.

RealSystem Server *n.* Software developed by RealNetworks to enable a server to broadcast streaming media. Several versions of RealSystem Server are available, designed to meet needs ranging from small intranet servers to large proxy servers.

real-time conferencing *n. See* teleconferencing.

Real-Time Control Protocol *n.* A scalable transport control protocol that works with the Real-Time Protocol (RTP) to monitor real-time transmissions to multiple participants over a network—for example, during videoconferencing. The Real-Time Control Protocol, or RTCP, transmits packets of control information at regular intervals and is used to determine how well information is being delivered to recipients. *Acronym:* RTCP. *See also* Real-Time Protocol, Real-Time Streaming Protocol, Resource Reservation Setup Protocol.

real-time operating system *n.* An operating system designed for the needs of a process-controlled environment. A real-time operating system recognizes that responses must be made and tasks handled instantly, with no lag time. Real-time operating systems are typically used as embedded systems in devices and applications requiring time-critical reaction, such as telecommunications, air traffic control, and robotic functions. *Acronym:* RTOS.

Real-Time Protocol *n.* An Internet-standard network transport protocol used in delivering real-time data, including audio and video. The Real-Time Protocol, or RTP, works with both unicast (single sender, single recipient) and multicast (single sender, multiple recipients) services. RTP is often used in conjunction with the Real-Time Control Protocol (RTCP), which monitors delivery. *Acronym:* RTP. *See also* Real-Time Control Protocol, Real-Time Streaming Protocol, stream.

real-time streaming *n.* The process of delivering a streaming media file via a specialized streaming media server using real-time streaming protocol (RTSP). With real-time streaming, the file itself actually plays on the streaming media server, even though it is viewed on the computer that opened the file. Real-time streaming transmits at a higher bandwidth than HTTP streaming. It is often used to broadcast live events, such as concerts or keynote conference addresses. *See also* HTTP streaming.

Real-Time Streaming Protocol *n.* A control protocol for the delivery of streamed multimedia data over Internet Protocol (IP) networks. The Real-Time Streaming Protocol, or RTSP, was developed by Columbia University, Progressive Networks, and Netscape and has been submitted as a proposed standard to the IETF (Internet Engineering Task Force). RTSP is designed to deliver real-time, live, or stored audio and video efficiently over a network. It can be used either for groups of recipients or for on-demand delivery to a single recipient. *Acronym:* RTSP. *See also* Advanced Streaming Format, Real-Time Protocol, Resource Reservation Setup Protocol, stream.

RealVideo *n.* The streaming technology developed by RealNetworks, Inc., for distributing video over intranets and the Internet. RealVideo transmits video from a server in encoded (compressed) form. The video and accompanying sound are viewed on the client end with the help of a software player. RealVideo works with both IP and IP multicasting and, as with RealAudio, does not require transmission of complete files before playback can begin. *See also* RealAudio, RealPlayer, streaming.

receipt notification *n.* An e-mail feature providing feedback to the sender that a message has been received by the recipient.

rec. newsgroups *n.* Usenet newsgroups that are part of the rec. hierarchy and whose names have the prefix *rec.* These newsgroups cover topics devoted to discussions of recreational activities, hobbies, and the arts. *See also* newsgroup, traditional newsgroup hierarchy, Usenet. *Compare* comp. newsgroups, misc. newsgroups, news. newsgroups, sci. newsgroups, soc. newsgroups, talk. newsgroups.

Recreational Software Advisory Council *n.* An independent, nonprofit organization established in the fall of 1994 by a group of six trade organizations, led by the Software Publishers Association. The Council's goal was to create a new, objective content-labeling rating system for recreational software and other media such as the Internet. *Acronym:* RSAC.

Red Book *n.* **1.** The standards documents of the U.S. National Security Agency entitled "Trusted Network Interpretation of the Trusted Computer System Evaluation Criteria (NCSC-TG-005)" and "Trusted Network Interpretation (NCS-TG-011)." These documents define a system of ratings from A1 (most secure) to D (nonsecure), indicating the ability of a computer network to protect sensitive information. *Compare* Orange Book (definition 1). **2.** A specifications book written by the Sony Corporation and Philips Corporation and endorsed by ISO, covering audio compact discs. *Compare* Green Book, Orange Book (definition 2). **3.** Telecommunications standards published by the CCITT.

reflective routing *n.* In wide area networks, the process of using a reflector to distribute data, thereby reducing the load of the network server. *See also* reflector.

reflector *n.* A program that sends messages to a number of users upon receipt of a signal from a single user. A common type of reflector is an e-mail reflector, which forwards any e-mail sent to it to the multiple recipients currently on its list. *See also* multiple recipients. *Compare* mail reflector.

region code *n.* Codes on DVD movie titles and DVD-ROM drives that prevent playback of certain DVDs in certain geographical regions. Region codes are part of the DVD specification. *See also* CSS, deCSS.

relative URL *n.* Short for **relative** **u**niform **r**esource **l**ocator. A form of URL in which the domain and some or all directory names are omitted, leaving only the document name and extension (and perhaps a partial list of directory names). The indicated file is found in a location relative to the pathname of the current document. *Acronym:* RELURL. *See also* URL.

reliability, availability, serviceability *n. Acronym:* RAS. *See* high availability.

R

RELURL *n. See* relative URL.

remailer *n.* A service that will forward e-mail while concealing the e-mail address of the originator of the message. Remailers may be used by individuals who wish to retain their privacy or avoid unsolicited commercial e-mail (UCE). Remailers may also be used to hide the identities of individuals and businesses sending spam or malicious or fraudulent e-mail.

remote *adj.* Not in the immediate vicinity, as a computer or other device located in another place (room, building, or city) and accessible through some type of cable or communications link.

remote access *n.* The use of a remote computer.

remote access server *n.* A host on a LAN (local area network) that is equipped with modems to enable users to connect to the network over telephone lines. *Acronym:* RAS.

Remote Access Service *n.* Windows software that allows a user to gain remote access to the network server via a modem. *Acronym:* RAS. *See also* remote access.

Remote Authentication Dial-In User Service *n. See* RADIUS.

Remote Installation Services *n.* Software services that allow an administrator to set up new client computers remotely, without having to visit each client. The target clients must support remote booting. *Acronym:* RIS.

remote login *n.* The action of logging in to a computer at a distant location by means of a data communications connection with the computer that one is presently using. After remote login, the user's own computer behaves like a terminal connected to the remote system. On the Internet, remote login is done primarily by rlogin and telnet. *See also* rlogin[1] (definition 1), telnet[1].

remote monitoring *n. See* RMON.

remote network monitoring *n. See* RMON.

Remote PC *n. See* remote system.

remote procedure call *n.* In programming, a call by one program to a second program on a remote system. The second program generally performs a task and returns the results of that task to the first program. *Acronym:* RPC.

remote system *n.* The computer or network that a remote user is accessing via a modem. *See also* remote access. *Compare* remote terminal.

remote terminal *n.* A terminal that is located at a site removed from the computer to which it is attached. Remote terminals rely on modems and telephone lines to communicate with the host computer. *See also* remote access. *Compare* remote system.

rename *n.* A command in most file transfer protocol (FTP) clients and in many other systems that allows the user to assign a new name to a file or files.

repeater *n.* A device used on communications circuits that decreases distortion by amplifying or regenerating a signal so that it can be transmitted onward in its original strength and form. On a network, a repeater connects two networks or two network segments at the physical layer of the ISO/OSI reference model and regenerates the signal.

repeating Ethernet *n. See* repeater.

replay attack *n.* An attack in which a valid message is intercepted and then repeatedly retransmitted, either for fraudulent purposes or as part of a larger attack scheme.

replication *n.* In a distributed database management system, the process of copying the database (or parts of it) to the other parts of the network. Replication allows distributed database systems to remain synchronized. *See also* distributed database, distributed database management system.

Request to Send *n. See* RTS.

Research Libraries Information Network *n.* The combined online catalog of the Research Libraries Group, which includes many of the major research libraries in the United States. *Acronym:* RLIN.

resolution *n.* The process of translation between a domain name address and an IP address. *See also* DNS, IP address.

resolve *vb.* **1.** To match one piece of information to another in a database or lookup table. **2.** To find a setting in which no hardware conflicts occur. **3.** To convert a logical address to a physical address or vice versa. **4.** To convert an Internet domain name to its corresponding IP address. *See also* DNS, IP address.

resource *n.* Any part of a computer system or a network, such as a disk drive, printer, or memory, that can be allotted to a program or a process while it is running.

resource allocation *n.* The process of distributing a computer system's facilities to different components of a job in order to perform the job.

Resource Description Framework *n.* A specification developed by the World Wide Web Consortium (W3C) to define a flexible infrastructure for organizing and managing metadata (data about data) across the Web and the Internet. The Resource Description Framework is intended to provide a framework based on XML (eXtensible Markup Language) that can standardize the way applications exchange metadata (or metacontent). Possible uses include search engines, content rating systems, and other areas in which exchange of information about data is valuable. *Acronym:* RDF. *See also* XML.

resource file *n.* A file that consists of resource data and the resource map that indexes it. *See also* resource.

Resource Reservation Setup Protocol *n.* A communications protocol designed to allow for "bandwidth on demand." A remote receiver requests that a certain amount of bandwidth be reserved by the server for a data stream; the server sends back a message (similar to the RSVP sent in reply to an invitation) indicating whether or not the request has been granted. *Acronym:* RSVP (Resource Reservation Setup Protocol).

R

resource sharing *n.* The act of making files, printers, and other network resources available for use by others.

retro virus *n.* A type of virus that avoids detection by attacking or disabling antivirus programs. *Also called:* anti-anti-virus.

return from the dead *vb.* To regain access to the Internet after having been disconnected.

Reverse Address Resolution Protocol *n. See* RARP.

Reverse ARP *n. See* RARP.

reverse path forwarding *n.* A technique that makes routing decisions through a TCP/IP network by using the source address of a datagram rather than the destination address. Reverse path forwarding is used in broadcast and multicast applications because it reduces redundant transmissions to multiple recipients. *Acronym:* RPF. *See also* datagram, TCP/IP.

RFC *n.* Acronym for **R**equest **f**or **C**omments. A document in which a standard, a protocol, or other information pertaining to the operation of the Internet is published. The RFC is actually issued, under the control of the IAB, *after* discussion and serves as the standard. RFCs can be obtained from sources such as InterNIC.

Rich Text Format *n.* An adaptation of DCA (Document Content Architecture) that is used for transferring formatted text documents between applications, even those applications running on different platforms, such as between IBM and compatibles and Macintoshes. *Acronym:* RTF. *See also* DCA.

RIFF *n.* Acronym for **R**esource **I**nterchange **F**ile **F**ormat. Developed jointly by IBM and Microsoft, RIFF is a broad-based specification designed to be used in defining standard formats for different types of multimedia files. A tagged-file specification,

RIFF relies on headers that "tag" individual data elements in a file, identifying them by type and length. Because tags identify data elements, the RIFF specification can be extended to cover new types of elements while continuing to support older applications, which can simply ignore new, unrecognized elements they encounter in a file. AVI (Audio Video Interleaved) is one such file format.

ring network *n.* A LAN (local area network) in which devices (nodes) are connected in a closed loop, or ring. Messages in a ring network pass around the ring from node to node in one direction. When a node receives a message, it examines the destination address attached to the message. If the address is the same as the node's, the node accepts the message; otherwise, it regenerates the signal and passes the message along to the next node in the ring. Such regeneration allows a ring network to cover larger distances than star and bus networks. The ring can also be designed to bypass any malfunctioning or failed node. Because of the closed loop, however, adding new nodes can be difficult. *Also called:* ring topology. *See also* token passing, token ring network. *Compare* bus network, star network.

ring topology *n. See* ring network.

rip *vb.* To convert audio data from a compact disc into a WAV file or other digital format, typically in preparation for further encoding as an MP3 file. *See also* MP3.

RIP *n.* Acronym for **R**outing **I**nformation **P**rotocol. An Internet protocol, defined in RFC 1058, that defines the exchange of routing table information. Through RIP, each router on a network sends its routing table to its nearest neighbor every 30 seconds. Under RIP, routing is determined by the number of hops between source and destination. RIP is an interior gateway protocol (a protocol used by gateways for exchanging routing information). Because it is not the most efficient of routing protocols, it is being replaced by the more efficient Open Shortest Path First (OSPF) protocol. *See also* Bellman-Ford distance-vector routing algorithm, communications protocol, Interior Gateway Protocol, OSPF.

RIPE *n.* Acronym for **R**eseaux **IP** **E**uropéens. A voluntary organization of ISPs (Internet service providers) dedicated to the goal of a smoothly functioning, pan-European Internet network. Most of the work performed by RIPE is handled by discrete working groups that deal with issues such as management of the RIPE database and technical networking questions. RIPE also provides services that include registering domain names within top-level Internet domains and assigning IP (Internet Protocol) addresses. Member organizations of RIPE are supported by the RIPE NCC (Network Coordination Centre), based in Amsterdam, The Netherlands. *See also* American Registry for Internet Numbers.

ripper *n.* Digital audio technology that converts audio data from a compact disc into a WAV file or other digital format. An encoder then converts this file into a file (typically an MP3 file) that can be played back by software known as a player. *See also* encoder, MP3.

RIPX *n.* A protocol used by routers to exchange information between routers on an IPX network and by hosts to determine the best routers to use when forwarding IPX traffic to a remote IPX network. *Also called:* RIP for IPX. *See also* communications protocol, IPX, NWLink, router.

RIS *n. See* Remote Installation Services.

Rivest-Shamir-Adleman encryption *n. See* RSA encryption.

RLIN *n. See* Research Libraries Information Network.

rlogin[1] *n.* **1.** A protocol used to log in to a networked computer in which the local system automatically supplies the user's login name. *See also* communications protocol, logon. *Compare* telnet[1]. **2.** A UNIX command in BSD UNIX that enables a user to log in to a remote computer on a network using the rlogin protocol. *See also* BSD UNIX.

rlogin[2] *vb.* To connect to a networked computer using the rlogin protocol.

RLSD *n.* Acronym for **R**eceived **L**ine **S**ignal **D**etect. *See* DCD.

RMI-IIOP *n.* Acronym for **R**emote **M**ethod **I**nvocation over **I**nternet Inter-ORB Protocol. A subsystem of the Java 2 Platform, Enterprise Edition (J2EE). It provides the ability to write CORBA applications for the Java platform without learning the CORBA Interface Definition Language (IDL). RMI-IIOP includes the full functionality of a CORBA Object Request Broker and allows the programming of CORBA servers and applications via the RMI application programming interface (API). RMI-IIOP is useful for developers using Enterprise Java Beans (EJBs), since the remote object model for an EJB is RMI-based. *Also called:* RMI over IIOP. *See also* CORBA, Enterprise JavaBeans, J2EE.

RMON *n.* Acronym for **r**emote **mon**itoring or **r**emote network **mon**itoring. A protocol that enables network information to be monitored and analyzed at a central site. The nine management information bases (MIBs) defined by RMON provide statistics about network traffic. *See also* MIB. *Compare* SNMP.

roaming user profile *n.* A server-based user profile that is downloaded to the local computer when a user logs on; it is updated both locally and on the server when the user logs off. A roaming user profile is available from the server when logging on to a workstation or server computer. When logging on, the user can use the local user profile if it is more current than the copy on the server. *See also* local user profile, mandatory user profile, user profile.

robopost *vb.* To post articles to newsgroups automatically, usually by means of a bot. *See also* bot (definition 3), newsgroup, post.

robot *n.* **1.** A machine that can sense and react to input and cause changes in its surroundings with some degree of intelligence, ideally without human supervision. Although robots are often designed to mimic human movements in carrying out their work, they are seldom humanlike in appearance. Robots are commonly used in manufacturing products such as automobiles and computers. **2.** *See* bot, spider.

ROFL *n.* Acronym for rolling on the floor, laughing. An expression, used mostly in newsgroups and online conferences, to indicate one's appreciation of a joke or other humorous circumstance. *Also called:* ROTFL.

role-playing game *n.* A game that is played on line, such as MUD, in which participants take on the identities of characters who interact with each other. These games often have a fantasy or science fiction setting and a set of rules that all players need to follow. Role-playing games may be similar to adventure games in terms of story line, but also feature management and decision making for the character assumed during the course of the game. *Acronym:* RPG. *See also* MUD.

rollback *n.* **1.** A return to a previous stable condition, as when the contents of a hard disk are restored from a backup after a destructive hard disk error. **2.** The point in an online transaction when all updates to any databases involved in the transaction are reversed.

root *n.* The main or uppermost level in a hierarchically organized set of information. The root is the point from which subsets branch in a logical sequence that moves from a broad focus to narrower perspectives. *See also* tree.

root account *n.* On UNIX systems, the account having control over the operation of a computer. The system administrator uses this account for system maintenance. *Also called:* superuser. *See also* system administrator.

root name *n.* In MS-DOS and Windows, the first part of a filename. In MS-DOS and earlier versions of Windows, the maximum length of the root name was eight characters; in Windows NT and later versions of Windows, the root name may be as long as 255 characters.

root name server *n. See* root server.

root server *n.* A computer with the ability to locate DNS servers containing information about top-level Internet domains, such as com, org, uk, it, jp, and other country domains, in the Internet's Domain Name System (DNS) hierarchy. Beginning with the root server and continuing through referrals to name servers at lower levels of the hierarchy, the DNS is able to match a "friendly" Internet address, such as microsoft.com, with its numerical counterpart, the IP address. Root servers thus contain the data needed for referrals to name servers at the highest level of the hierarchy. There are 13 root servers in the world, located in the United States, the United Kingdom, Sweden, and Japan. *Also called:* root name server. *See also* DNS (definition 1), DNS server, top-level domain.

root web *n.* The default, top-level web provided by a Web server. To access the root web, you supply the URL of the server without specifying a page name or subweb.

ROT13 encryption *n.* A simple encryption method in which each letter is replaced with the letter of the alphabet 13 letters after the original letter, so that A is replaced by N, and so forth; N, in turn, is replaced by A, and Z is replaced by M.

ROT13 encryption is not used to protect messages against unauthorized readers; rather, it is used in newsgroups to encode messages that a user may not want to read, such as sexual jokes or spoilers. Some newsreaders can automatically perform ROT13 encryption and decryption at the touch of a key.

ROTFL *n. See* ROFL.

routable protocol *n.* A communications protocol that is used to route data from one network to another by means of a network address and a device address. TCP/IP is an example of a routable protocol.

router *n.* An intermediary device on a communications network that expedites message delivery. On a single network linking many computers through a mesh of possible connections, a router receives transmitted messages and forwards them to their correct destinations over the most efficient available route. On an interconnected set of LANs (local area networks)—including those based on differing architectures and protocols—using the same communications protocols, a router serves the somewhat different function of acting as a link between LANs, enabling messages to be sent from one to another. *See also* bridge, gateway.

R

Routing Information Protocol *n. See* RIP (definition 1).

routing table *n.* In data communications, a table of information that provides network hardware (bridges and routers) with the directions needed to forward packets of data to locations on other networks. The information contained in a routing table differs according to whether it is used by a bridge or a router. A bridge relies on both the source (originating) and destination addresses to determine where and how to forward a packet. A router relies on the destination address and on information in the table that gives the possible routes—in hops or in number of jumps—between itself, intervening routers, and the destination. Routing tables are updated frequently as new or more current information becomes available. *See also* bridge, hop, internetwork, router.

RPC *n. See* remote procedure call.

RPF *n. See* reverse path forwarding.

RPG *n. See* role-playing game.

RS-232-C standard *n.* An accepted industry standard for serial communications connections. Adopted by the Electrical Industries Association, this Recommended Standard (RS) defines the specific lines and signal characteristics used by serial communications controllers to standardize the transmission of serial data between devices. The letter *C* denotes that the current version of the standard is the third in a series. *See also* CTS, DSR, DTR, RTS, RXD, TXD.

RS-422/423/449 *n.* Standards for serial communications with transmission distances over 50 feet. RS-449 incorporates RS-422 and RS-423. Macintosh serial ports are RS-422 ports. *See also* RS-232-C standard.

RSA *n.* A widely used public/private key algorithm. It is the default cryptographic service provider (CSP) for Microsoft Windows. It was patented by RSA Data Security, Inc., in 1977. *See also* cryptographic service provider.

RSAC *n. See* Recreational Software Advisory Council.

RSA encryption *n.* Short for **R**ivest-**S**hamir-**A**dleman **encryption**. The public key encryption algorithm, introduced by Ronald Rivest, Adi Shamir, and Leonard Adleman in 1978, on which the PGP (Pretty Good Privacy) encryption program is based. *See also* PGP, public key encryption.

RSVP *n. See* Resource Reservation Setup Protocol.

RTCP *n. See* Real-Time Control Protocol.

RTF *n. See* Rich Text Format.

R

RTFM *n.* Acronym for **r**ead **t**he **f**laming (or **f**riendly) **m**anual. A common answer to a question in an Internet newsgroup or product support conference that is adequately explained in the instruction manual. (The F in this acronym is not necessarily assumed to represent polite language.) *Also called:* RTM.

RTM *n.* Acronym for **r**ead **t**he **m**anual. *See* RTFM.

RTOS *n. See* real-time operating system.

RTP *n. See* Real-Time Protocol.

RTS *n.* Acronym for **R**equest **t**o **S**end. A signal sent, as from a computer to its modem, to request permission to transmit; the signal is often used in serial communications. RTS is a hardware signal sent over pin 4 in RS-232-C connections. *See also* RS-232-C standard. *Compare* CTS.

RTSP *n. See* Real-Time Streaming Protocol.

RXD *n.* Short for Receive (**rx**) **D**ata. A line used to carry received serial data from one device to another, such as from a modem to a computer. Pin 3 is the RXD line in RS-232-C connections. *See also* RS-232-C standard. *Compare* TXD.

S

Samba *n.* A popular freeware program that provides file and print services, authentication and authorization, name resolution, and service announcement (browsing). As a file server, Samba enables the sharing of files, printers, and other resources on a UNIX Samba server with Windows clients over a network. Based on the Server Message Block (SMB) protocol, Samba originally was developed as a Network File System (NFS) for UNIX by Andrew Tridgell. *See also* NFS, SMB.

SAN *n. See* storage area network.

sandbox *n.* **1.** Java Virtual Machine security area for downloaded (remote or untrusted) applets, an area in which such applets are confined and prevented from accessing system resources. Confinement to the sandbox prevents downloaded applets from carrying out potentially dangerous operations, maliciously or otherwise. They have to "play" inside the sandbox, and any attempt to "escape" is thwarted by the Java Security Manager. **2.** Slang for the research and development department at many software and computer companies. *See also* applet, Java Virtual Machine.

SAOL *n.* Acronym for **S**tructured **A**udio **O**rchestra **L**anguage. Part of the MPEG-4 standard, SAOL describes a set of tools for producing computer music, audio for computer games, streaming Internet sound or music, and other multimedia applications. SAOL is a flexible computer language for describing music synthesis and integrating synthetic sound with recorded sound in an MPEG-4 bit stream. *See also* bit stream, MPEG-4, streaming (definition 1).

SAP *n. See* Service Advertising Protocol.

SASL *n.* Acronym for **S**imple **A**uthentication and **S**ecurity **L**ayer. An authentication support mechanism for use with connection-based protocols. SASL allows a client to request identification from a server and negotiate use of an added security layer for authentication during subsequent client/server interaction.

SAX *n.* Acronym for **S**imple **A**PI for **X**ML. An event-driven application program interface (API) used to interpret an XML file. SAX works with an XML parser, providing an interface between the parser and an XML application. SAX is used as an alternative to the more complex object-based Document Object Model (DOM) interface. *See also* DOM.

sci. newsgroups *n.* Usenet newsgroups that are part of the sci. hierarchy and begin with "sci." These newsgroups are devoted to discussions of scientific research and applications, except for computer science, which is discussed in the comp. newsgroups. *See also* newsgroup, traditional newsgroup hierarchy, Usenet. *Compare* comp. newsgroups, misc. newsgroups, news. newsgroups, rec. newsgroups, soc. newsgroups, talk. newsgroups.

SCP *n.* Acronym for **S**imple **C**ontrol **P**rotocol. A lightweight peer-to-peer networking protocol for devices that have limited processing and memory resources and operate over limited-bandwidth networks such as powerline carrier (PLC) systems. Products using SCP can interoperate with products using the Universal Plug and Play (UPnP), CEBus, and Home Plug & Play (HPnP) standards. Developed by a team of companies including Microsoft and General Electric, SCP enables the interaction between UPnP devices, devices based on Internet Protocol (IP), and non-IP-capable devices such as coffeemakers and alarm clocks. SCP, which was designed as a stand-alone protocol, can be used in residential, commercial, industrial, and utility applications. *See also* UPnP networking.

screen name *n.* A name under which an America Online user is known. The screen name may be the same as the user's real name. *See also* America Online.

screen phone *n.* A type of Internet appliance combining a telephone with an LCD display screen, a digital fax modem, and a computer keyboard, with ports for a mouse, printer, and other peripheral devices. Screen phones can be used as regular telephones for voice communications and can also be used as terminals to gain access to the Internet and other online services.

script *n.* A program consisting of a set of instructions to an application or a utility program. The instructions usually use the rules and syntax of the application or utility. On the World Wide Web, scripts are commonly used to customize or add interactivity to Web pages.

scriptlet *n.* A reusable Web page based on the features of Dynamic HTML (DHTML) that can be created with HTML text and a scripting language and then inserted as a control in another Web page or in an application. Developed by Microsoft and introduced in Internet Explorer version 4, scriptlets are implemented as .htm files that give developers a relatively easy, object-based means of creating components that reflect the Web metaphor and that can be used to add interactivity and functionality—for example, animation, color changes, pop-up menus, or drag-and-drop capability—to Web pages without requiring repeated trips to the server. *Also called:* Microsoft Scripting Component. *See also* dynamic HTML. *Compare* applet.

SCSI *n.* Acronym for **S**mall **C**omputer **S**ystem **I**nterface, a standard high-speed parallel interface defined by the X3T9.2 committee of the American National Standards Institute (ANSI). A SCSI (pronounced "scuzzy") interface is used to connect microcomputers to SCSI peripheral devices, such as many hard disks and printers, and to other computers and local area networks. *Also called:* SCSI-1, SCSI I.

SCSI-1 *n. See* SCSI.

SCSI-2 *n.* An enhanced ANSI standard for SCSI (Small Computer System Interface) buses. Compared with the original SCSI standard (now called SCSI-1), which can transfer data 8 bits at a time at up to 5 MB per second, SCSI-2 offers increased data width, increased speed, or both. A SCSI-2 disk drive or host adapter can work with SCSI-1 equipment at the older equipment's maximum speed. *Also called:* SCSI II. *See also* Fast SCSI, Fast/Wide SCSI, SCSI, Wide SCSI. *Compare* UltraSCSI.

SCSI bus *n.* A parallel bus that carries data and control signals from SCSI devices to a SCSI controller. *See also* bus, SCSI device.

SCSI chain *n.* A set of devices on a SCSI bus. Each device (except the host adapter and the last device) is connected to two other devices by two cables, forming a daisy chain. *See also* daisy chain, SCSI.

SCSI connector *n.* A cable connector used to connect a SCSI device to a SCSI bus. *See also* bus, SCSI device.

SCSI device *n.* A peripheral device that uses the SCSI standard to exchange data and control signals with a computer's CPU. *See also* SCSI.

SCSI ID *n.* The unique identity of a SCSI device. Each device connected to a SCSI bus must have a different SCSI ID. A maximum of eight SCSI IDs can be used on the same SCSI bus. *See also* bus, SCSI device.

SCSI network *n.* A set of devices on a SCSI bus, which acts like a local area network. *See also* SCSI.

SCSI port *n.* **1.** A SCSI host adapter within a computer, which provides a logical connection between the computer and all of the devices on the SCSI bus. *See also* SCSI. **2.** A connector on a device for a SCSI bus cable. *See also* SCSI.

SDH *n.* *See* Synchronous Digital Hierarchy.

S

SDLC *n.* Acronym for **S**ynchronous **D**ata **L**ink **C**ontrol, the data transmission protocol most widely used by networks conforming to IBM's Systems Network Architecture (SNA). SDLC is similar to the HDLC (High-level Data Link Control) protocol developed by the International Organization for Standardization (ISO). *See also* HDLC.

SDMI *n.* *See* Secure Digital Music Initiative.

SDSL *n.* Acronym for **s**ymmetric (or **s**ingle-line) **d**igital **s**ubscriber **l**ine, a digital telecommunications technology that is a variation of HDSL. SDSL uses one pair of copper wires rather than two pairs of wires and transmits at 1.544 Mbps. *Compare* ADSL.

search engine *n.* **1.** A program that searches for keywords in documents or in a database. **2.** On the Internet, a program that searches for keywords in files and documents found on the World Wide Web, newsgroups, Gopher menus, and FTP archives. Some search engines are used for a single Internet site, such as a dedicated search engine for a Web site. Others search across many sites, using such agents as spiders to gather lists of available files and documents and store these lists in databases that users can search by keyword. Examples of the latter type of search engine are Lycos and Excite. Most search engines reside on a server. *See also* agent (definition 2), FTP, Gopher or gopher, newsgroup, spider, World Wide Web.

secondary service provider *n.* An Internet service provider that provides a Web presence but not direct connectivity. *See also* ISP.

second-level domain *n.* The level immediately beneath the top-level domain in the Internet's DNS hierarchy. *See also* domain (definition 3).

secure channel *n.* A communications link that has been protected against unauthorized access, operation, or use by means of isolation from the public network, encryption, or other forms of control. *See also* encryption.

Secure Digital Music Initiative *n.* A coalition of companies from the recording, electronics, and information technology industries founded in February 1999 for the purpose of developing an open standard for the secure distribution of music in digital form. The Secure Digital Music Initiative specification is designed to provide consumers with flexibility and convenient access to electronically distributed music (that is, over the Internet) while also protecting the rights of artists. *Acronym:* SDMI. *See also* MP3, Windows Media Technologies.

Secure Electronics Transactions protocol *n.* Protocol for conducting secure transactions over the Internet, the result of a joint effort by GTE, IBM, MasterCard, Microsoft, Netscape, SAIC, Terisa Systems, VeriSign, and Visa. *Acronym:* SET.

Secure Hash Algorithm *n. See* SHA.

Secure HTTP *n. See* S-HTTP, HTTPS.

Secure Hypertext Transfer Protocol *n. See* S-HTTP.

Secure/Multipurpose Internet Mail Extensions *n. See* S/MIME.

Secure Password Authentication *n.* A feature that allows a server to confirm the identity of the person logging on. *Acronym:* SPA.

secure site *n.* A Web site having the capability of providing secure transactions, ensuring that credit card numbers and other personal information will not be accessible to unauthorized parties.

Secure Sockets Layer *n. See* SSL.

Secure Transaction Technology *n.* The use of the SSL (Secure Sockets Layer), S-HTTP (Secure HTTP), or both in online transactions, such as form transmission or credit card purchases. *Acronym:* STT. *See also* S-HTTP, SSL.

secure wide area network *n.* A set of computers that communicate over a public network, such as the Internet, but use security measures, such as encryption, authentication, and authorization, to prevent their communications from being intercepted and understood by unauthorized users. *Acronym:* S/WAN. *See also* authentication, authorization, encryption, virtual private network (definition 1).

security *n.* The technologies used to make a service resistant to unauthorized access to the data that it holds or for which it is responsible. A major focus of computer security, especially on systems that are accessed by many people or through communications lines, is the prevention of system access by unauthorized individuals.

security log *n.* A log, generated by a firewall or other security device, that lists events that could affect security, such as access attempts or commands, and the names of the users involved. *See also* firewall.

self-extracting archive *n. See* self-extracting file.

self-extracting file *n.* An executable program file that contains one or more compressed text or data files. When a user runs the program, it uncompresses the compressed files and stores them on the user's hard drive.

sendmail *n.* A popular open-source UNIX-based implementation of the Simple Mail Transfer Protocol (SMTP) for delivering e-mail. Written in 1981 by Eric Allman at the University of California at Berkeley, sendmail was the first Internet message transfer agent (MTA).

send statement *n.* In SLIP and PPP scripting languages, a statement that tells the program that dials an Internet service provider's number (a *dialer program*) to send certain characters. *See also* ISP, PPP, SLIP.

Sequenced Packet Exchange *n. See* SPX (definition 1).

Serial Line Internet Protocol *n. See* SLIP.

serial port *n.* An input/output location (channel) that sends and receives data to and from a computer's central processing unit or a communications device one bit at a time. Serial ports are used for serial data communication and as interfaces with some peripheral devices, such as mice and printers.

Serial Storage Architecture *n. See* SSA.

server *n.* **1.** On a local area network (LAN), a computer running administrative software that controls access to the network and its resources, such as printers and disk drives, and provides resources to computers functioning as workstations on the network. **2.** On the Internet or other network, a computer or program that responds to commands from a client. For example, a file server may contain an archive of data or program files; when a client submits a request for a file, the server transfers a copy of the file to the client. *See also* application server (definitions 1 and 2), client/server architecture. *Compare* client.

server appliance *n.* A device designed to deliver one or more specific network services in a single turnkey package that includes both hardware and software. All necessary programs are preinstalled on a server appliance, which has minimal, simplified options and controls. Server appliances can be used to complement or replace traditional servers on a network and can provide such services as file and printer sharing and Internet connectivity. *Also called:* appliance. *See also* information appliance.

server-based application *n.* A program that is shared over a network. The program is stored on the network server and can be used at more than one client machine at a time.

server cluster *n.* A group of independent computer systems, known as nodes, working together as a single system to ensure that mission-critical applications and resources remain available to clients. A server cluster is the type of cluster that Cluster service implements. *See also* cluster.

server control *n. See* ASP.NET server control.

server error *n.* A failure to complete a request for information through HTTP that results from an error at the server rather than an error by the client or the user. Server errors are indicated by HTTP status codes beginning with 5. *See also* HTTP.

server farm *n.* A centralized grouping of network servers maintained by an enterprise or, often, an Internet service provider (ISP). A server farm provides a network with load balancing, scalability, and fault tolerance. Individual servers may be connected in such a way that they appear to represent a single resource.

serverlet *n. See* servlet.

Server Message Block *n. See* SMB.

server push-pull *n.* A combination of Web client/server techniques individually called "server push" and "client pull." In server push, the server loads data to the client, but the data connection stays open. This allows the server to continue sending data to the browser as necessary. In client pull, the server loads data to the client, but the data connection does not stay open. The server sends an HTML directive to the browser telling it to reopen the connection after a certain interval to get more data or possibly to open a new URL. *See also* HTML, server (definition 2), URL.

server-side include *n.* A mechanism for including dynamic text in World Wide Web documents. Server-side includes are special command codes that are recognized and interpreted by the server; their output is placed in the document body before the document is sent to the browser. Server-side includes can be used, for example, to include the date/time stamp in the text of the file. *Acronym:* SSI. *See also* server (definition 2).

service *n.* **1.** A customer-based or user-oriented function, such as technical support or network provision. **2.** In reference to programming and software, a program or routine that provides support to other programs, particularly at a low (close to the hardware) level. **3.** In networking, specialized, software-based functionality provided by network servers—for example, directory services that provide the network equivalent of "phone books" needed for locating users and resources.

Service Advertising Protocol *n.* A method used by a service-providing node in a network (such as a file server or application server) to notify other nodes on the network that it is available for access. When a server boots, it uses the protocol to advertise its service; when the same server goes off line, it uses the protocol to announce that it is no longer available. *Acronym:* SAP. *See also* server (definition 1).

service provider *n. See* ISP.

servlet or **servelet** *n.* A small Java program that runs on a server. The term is a companion to applet, a Java program that usually runs on the client. Servlets perform lightweight Web services, such as redirecting a Web user from an outdated address to the correct page—tasks traditionally handled by CGI (Common Gateway Interface) applications. Because servlets are automatically threaded and highly responsive, they execute quickly, thereby reducing system overhead. *Also called:* serverlet. *See also* applet, CGI.

servlet container *n*. In Sun Microsystems's J2EE network platform, a container that decodes requests, formats responses, and provides the network services over which requests and responses are sent. All servlet containers must support HTTP as a protocol for requests and responses, but they may also support additional request-response protocols such as HTTPS. *See also* container (definition 3), HTTP, HTTPS.

session *n*. **1.** The time during which a program is running. In most interactive programs, a session is the time during which the program accepts input and processes information. **2.** In communications, the time during which two computers maintain a connection. **3.** A specific protocol layer in the ISO/OSI reference model that manages communication between remote users or processes. *See also* ISO/OSI reference model, session layer.

session bean *n*. In the Java programming language and J2EE network platform, an enterprise bean that is created by a client and usually exists only for the duration of a single client/server session. It performs operations, such as calculations or accessing a database, for the client. While a session bean may be transactional, it is not recoverable should a system crash occur. Session bean objects can either be stateless or can maintain conversational state across methods and transactions. If a session bean maintains state, the Enterprise JavaBean (EJB) container manages this state if the object must be removed from memory. However, the session bean object itself must manage its own persistent data. *See also* EJB.

session layer *n*. The fifth of seven layers in the ISO/OSI reference model. The session layer handles the details that must be agreed on by the two communicating devices. *See also* ISO/OSI reference model.

SET protocol *n*. *See* Secure Electronics Transactions protocol.

.sgm *n*. The MS-DOS/Windows 3.*x* file extension that identifies files encoded in Standard Generalized Markup Language (SGML). Because MS-DOS and Windows 3.*x* cannot recognize file extensions longer than three letters, the .sgml extension is truncated to three letters in those environments. *See also* SGML.

.sgml *n*. The file extension that identifies files encoded in Standard Generalized Markup Language. *See also* SGML.

SGML *n*. Acronym for **S**tandard **G**eneralized **M**arkup **L**anguage. An information management standard adopted by the International Organization for Standardization (ISO) in 1986 as a means of providing platform- and application-independent documents that retain formatting, indexing, and linked information. SGML provides a grammarlike mechanism for users to define the structure of their documents and the tags they will use to denote the structure in individual documents. *See also* ISO.

SHA *n*. Acronym for **S**ecure **H**ash **A**lgorithm. A technique that computes a 160-bit condensed representation of a message or data file, called a *message digest*. The SHA is used by the sender and the receiver of a message in computing and verifying a digital signature, for security purposes. *See also* digital signature.

S

share *vb.* To make files, directories, or folders accessible to other users over a network.

shared directory *n. See* network directory.

shared folder *n.* On a Macintosh computer connected to a network and running System 6.0 or higher, a folder that a user has made available to others on the network. A shared folder is analogous to a network directory on a PC. *See also* network directory.

shared medium *n.* The communications medium shared by network nodes; essentially, the network bandwidth.

shared memory *n.* **1.** Memory accessed by more than one program in a multitasking environment. **2.** A portion of memory used by parallel-processor computer systems to exchange information.

shared name *n. See* strong name.

shared network directory *n. See* network directory.

shared resource *n.* **1.** Any device, data, or program used by more than one device or program. **2.** On a network, any resource made available to network users, such as directories, files, and printers.

S

SharePoint team Web site *n.* A customizable Web site with features that help a team work together. The default site has pages for document libraries, announcements, and team events. Only members, specified by the site creator, can use the site.

shareware *n.* Copyrighted software that is distributed on a try-before-you-buy basis. Users who want to continue using the program after the trial period are encouraged to send a payment to the program's author. *Compare* free software, freeware, public-domain software.

Shockwave *n.* A format for multimedia audio and video files within HTML documents, created by Macromedia, which markets a family of Shockwave servers and plug-in programs for Web browsers. *See also* HTML.

shopping cart *n.* In e-commerce programs, a file in which an online customer stores information on potential purchases until ready to order. Usually represented on screen with a drawing of a shopping cart, the virtual shopping cart provides a recognizable point of reference to users new to the e-commerce experience. *See also* e-commerce.

short-haul *adj.* Of or pertaining to a communications device that transmits a signal over a communications line for a distance less than approximately 20 miles. *Compare* long-haul.

short message service *n.* Service for wireless phones that allows users to send and receive brief messages consisting of text and numbers. *Acronym:* SMS.

shout *vb.* To use ALL CAPITAL LETTERS for emphasis in e-mail or a newsgroup article. Excessive shouting is considered a violation of netiquette. A word can be more acceptably emphasized by placing it between *asterisks* or _underscores_. *See also* netiquette.

shovelware *n.* A commercially sold CD-ROM containing a miscellaneous assortment of software, graphic images, text, or other data that could otherwise be obtained at little or no cost, such as freeware or shareware from the Internet and BBSs or public-domain clip art. *See also* BBS (definition 1), freeware, shareware.

SHS virus *n.* Any of a class of viruses that infect a user's system by hiding in files with an .shs extension. These viruses typically spread through e-mail attachments. A widely distributed e-mail warning cautions readers to beware of the "SHS virus," but no one specific virus by that name exists.

SHTML *n.* Short for server-parsed **HTML**. Hypertext Markup Language (HTML) text that contains embedded server-side include commands. SHTML documents are fully read, parsed, and modified by the server before being passed to the browser. *See also* HTML, server-side include.

S-HTTP or **SHTTP** *n.* Acronym for Secure Hypertext Transfer Protocol. An extension to HTTP that supports various encryption and authentication measures to keep all transactions secure from end to end. S-HTTP is designed to ensure the security of individual transmissions over the Internet and has been approved as a standard by the Internet Engineering Task Force (IETF). S-HTTP should not be confused with HTTPS, a Netscape-developed technology based on SSL (Secure Sockets Layer). HTTPS is also designed to ensure secure transmissions, but does so between communicating computers rather than on a message-by-message basis. *Also called:* Secure HTTP. *See also* SSL.

.sig *n.* A file extension for a signature file for e-mail or Internet newsgroup use. The contents of this file are automatically appended to e-mail correspondence or newsgroup articles by their respective client software. *See also* signature file (definition 1).

SIG *n.* Acronym for special interest group. An e-mail online discussion group or a group of users who meet and share information, especially one of the groups supported by the Association for Computing Machinery (ACM), such as SIGGRAPH for computer graphics.

signature *n.* **1.** A sequence of data used for identification, such as text appended to an e-mail message or a fax. **2.** A unique number built into hardware or software for authentication purposes.

signature block *n.* A block of text that an e-mail client or a newsreader automatically places at the end of every message or article before the message or article is transmitted. Signature blocks typically contain the name, e-mail address, and affiliation of the person who created the message or article.

signature file *n.* **1.** A file that contains information inserted by a user and automatically appended to e-mail correspondence or newsgroup articles by client software. A signature file typically contains the name or nickname of the user and might include such information as the user's e-mail address, Web page, company, or job title. **2.** A file that updates an antivirus program so that the program recognizes signatures of new viruses and removes the viruses from the user's computer. *See also* antivirus program, virus signature.

sign off *vb. See* log off.

sign on *vb. See* log on.

SIIA *n.* Acronym for **S**oftware & **I**nformation **I**ndustry **A**ssociation. A nonprofit trade association representing over 1200 high-tech companies worldwide and charged with watching over the interests of the software and digital content industry. The SIIA was formed in 1999 when the Software Publishers Association (SPA) merged with the Information Industry Association (IIA). The SIIA focuses on three areas: providing information and forums in which to distribute information to the high-tech industry; protection in the form of an antipiracy program geared to help members enforce their copyrights; and promotion and education.

Silicon Alley *n.* The Manhattan, New York, metropolitan area. Originally the term referred to the area of Manhattan below 41st Street, which had a heavy concentration of technology companies, but it now includes the entire island, reflecting the number of businesses involved in computer technology in that area. The name was inspired by Silicon Valley, the area of northern California that is home to many technology firms. *See also* Silicon Valley.

Silicon Valley *n.* The region of California south of San Francisco Bay, otherwise known as the Santa Clara Valley, roughly extending from Palo Alto to San Jose. Silicon Valley is a major center of electronics and computer research, development, and manufacturing.

Silicorn Valley *n.* Clusters of high-tech companies headquartered in small cities in the Midwestern United States, particularly in areas of rural Iowa.

SIM *n. See* Society for Information Management.

SIM card *n.* Short for **S**ubscriber **I**dentity **M**odule **card**. A smart card designed for use with GSM (Global System for Mobile Communications) mobile phones. SIM cards contain chips that store a subscriber's personal identifier (SIM PIN), billing information, and data (names, phone numbers). *See also* Global System for Mobile Communications, smart card (definition 2).

Simple API for XML *n. See* SAX.

Simple Authentication and Security Layer *n. See* SASL.

Simple Control Protocol *n. See* SCP.

Simple Mail Transfer Protocol *n.* A TCP/IP protocol for sending messages from one computer to another on a network. This protocol is used on the Internet to route e-mail. *Acronym:* SMTP. *See also* communications protocol, TCP/IP. *Compare* CCITT X series, Post Office Protocol.

Simple Network Management Protocol *n. See* SNMP.

Simple Object Access Protocol *n. See* SOAP.

simplex *n.* Communication that takes place only from sender to receiver. *Compare* duplex[2], half-duplex[2].

single attachment station *n.* An FDDI node that connects to the primary ring through a concentrator. *Compare* dual attachment station.

single-line digital subscriber line *n. See* SDSL.

single sign-on *n.* A system enabling a user to enter one name and password to log on to different computer systems or Web sites. Single sign-on is also available for enterprise systems so a user with a domain account can log on to a network once, using a password or smart card, and thereby gain access to any computer in the domain. *See also* domain, smart card (definition 1).

SirCam worm *n.* A malicious worm that combines fast infection with the potential to deliver multiple malicious payloads. SirCam spreads through multiple means, both by mailing infected personal files from a compromised disk to other potential victims and through Windows network shares on unprotected machines. One time in 20 SirCam deletes the contents of the infected drive, and one time in 50 it fills all free space on the disk with trash data. SirCam was discovered in mid-2001 and has reappeared regularly since that time.

.sit *n.* The file extension for a Macintosh file compressed with StuffIt. *See also* StuffIt.

SLIP *n.* Acronym for Serial Line Internet Protocol. A data link protocol that allows transmission of TCP/IP data packets over dial-up telephone connections, thus enabling a computer or a LAN (local area network) to be connected to the Internet or some other network. It is an older, less secure protocol than the PPP (Point-to-Point Protocol) and does not support dynamic allocation of IP addresses. A newer form of SLIP, known as CSLIP (Compressed SLIP), optimizes transmission of long documents by compressing header information. *See also* IP. *Compare* PPP.

SLIP emulator *n.* Software that mimics a SLIP connection in UNIX shell accounts that do not offer a direct SLIP connection. Many Internet service providers (ISPs) are UNIX based and offer shell accounts to users for Internet access. Like a SLIP connection, the SLIP emulator allows the user to avoid dealing with the ISP's UNIX environment directly when accessing the Internet and to use Internet applications such as graphical Web browsers. *See also* ISP, SLIP.

slotted-ring network *n.* A ring network allowing data to be transmitted between data stations in one direction. A slotted-ring network transfers data in predefined time slots (fixed-length portions of a data frame) in the transmission stream over one transmission medium. *See also* ring network. *Compare* token ring network.

Small Business Server *n.* A software application developed by Microsoft Corporation to increase the efficiency of Web-based services for small businesses with 50 or fewer personal computers. Small Business Server provides shared Internet access, features for building Web-based customer management and customer communications tools, and additional features that increase productivity by streamlining employee access to files and applications over the Web.

Small Computer System Interface *n. See* SCSI.

Small Office/Home Office *n. See* SOHO.

smart *adj.* A synonym for intelligent. *See* intelligence.

smart cable *n. See* intelligent cable.

smart card *n.* **1.** In computers and electronics, a circuit board with built-in logic or firmware that gives it some kind of independent decision-making ability. **2.** In banking and finance, a credit card that contains an integrated circuit that gives it a limited amount of intelligence and memory.

smart card reader *n.* A device that is installed in computers to enable the use of smart cards for enhanced security features. *See also* smart card (definition 2).

smart device *n.* An electronic device capable of being networked and remotely controlled in a smart home. Smart devices can include appliances, lighting, heating and cooling systems, entertainment systems, and security systems. *See also* home automation, home network (definition 1), smart home.

smart home *n.* A home or building wired for networking and home automation. In a smart home, occupants control smart devices programmatically or on command using a home-networking communications protocol. *Also called:* automated home, digital home, e-home, Internet home, networked home, smart house, wired home. *See also* home automation, home network (definition 1).

smartphone *n.* A hybrid between a wireless telephone and a personal digital assistant (PDA). Smartphones integrate wireless telephones with many of the personal organizational functions of PDAs, such as calendar, calculator, database, e-mail, wireless Web access, note taking, and other programs common to lightweight palm-style computers. Smartphones may rely on a stylus, keypad, or both for data entry or may use voice recognition technology. *See also* cell, PDA, pen computer, wireless phone.

SmartSuite *n.* A suite of business application programs sold by Lotus Development. Lotus SmartSuite includes six programs: Lotus 1-2-3 spreadsheet, Lotus WordPro word processor, Lotus Approach database, Lotus Freelance Graphics presentation software, Lotus Organizer time-management software, and Lotus FastSite Internet/intranet publishing tool. SmartSuite Millennium Edition 9.7 supports collaboration, Web publishing, use of Internet/intranet resources, and customizable document and project organizers. SmartSuite competes with Microsoft Office and WordPerfect Office.

SMB *n.* Acronym for **S**erver **M**essage **B**lock. A file-sharing protocol designed to allow networked computers to transparently access files that reside on remote systems over a variety of networks. The SMB protocol defines a series of commands that pass information between computers. SMB uses four message types: session control, file, printer, and message. *See also* LAN Manager, NetBIOS, Samba.

SMDS *n.* Acronym for **S**witched **M**ultimegabit **D**ata **S**ervices. A very high-speed, connectionless, packet-switched data transport service that connects LANs (local area networks) and WANs (wide area networks).

SMIL *n.* Acronym for **S**ynchronized **M**ultimedia **I**ntegration **L**anguage. A markup language that enables separate elements, including audio, video, text, and still images, to be accessed separately and then integrated and played back as a synchronized multimedia presentation. Based on XML (eXtensible Markup Language), SMIL allows Web authors to define the objects in the presentation, describe their locations onscreen, and determine when they will be played back. The language is based on statements that can be entered with a text editor and was developed under the auspices of the World Wide Web Consortium (W3C). *See also* markup language, XML.

smiley *n.* *See* emoticon.

S/MIME *n.* Acronym for **S**ecure/**M**ultipurpose **I**nternet **M**ail **E**xtensions. An Internet e-mail security-oriented protocol that adds public key encryption and support for digital signatures to the widely used MIME e-mail protocol. *See also* public key encryption.

SMIS *n.* Acronym for **S**ociety for **M**anagement **I**nformation **S**ystems. *See* Society for Information Management.

SMP *n.* Acronym for **s**ymmetric **m**ultiprocessing. A computer architecture in which multiple processors share the same memory, which contains one copy of the operating system, one copy of any applications that are in use, and one copy of the data. Because the operating system divides the workload into tasks and assigns those tasks to whichever processors are free, SMP reduces transaction time. *See also* architecture.

SMP server *n.* Short for **s**ymmetric **m**ultiprocessing **server**. A computer that is designed with the SMP architecture to improve its performance as a server in client/server applications. *See also* SMP.

SMS *n.* *See* short message service, Systems Management Server.

SMTP *n.* *See* Simple Mail Transfer Protocol.

smurf attack *n.* A form of denial-of-service attack on an Internet server that sends simultaneous echo request packets ("ping" packets) to one or more broadcast IP addresses (such as an IRC server), each of which in turn relays the request to as many as 255 individual host computers, with the address of the attack's victim as the forged (spoofed) source address. When the hosts return echo packets to the apparent source of the request, the volume of the responses is enough to disable the network. *See also* denial of service attack, spoofing.

SNA *n.* Acronym for **S**ystems **N**etwork **A**rchitecture. A network model devised by IBM to enable IBM products, including mainframes, terminals, and peripherals, to communicate and exchange data. SNA started out as a five-layer model and was later extended with two additional layers to correspond more closely to the ISO/OSI reference model. More recently, the SNA model was modified to include minicomputers and microcomputers in a specification known as APPC (Advanced Program to Program Communications). *See also* APPC. *Compare* ISO/OSI reference model.

snail mail *n.* A popular phrase on the Internet for referring to mail services provided by the U.S. Postal Service and similar agencies in other countries. The term has its origins in the fact that regular postal mail is slow compared with e-mail.

sneaker *n.* An individual employed by a company or organization to test their security by breaking into the employer's network. Information gathered by the sneaker can be used to repair network security weaknesses. *See also* tiger team.

sneakernet *n.* Transfer of data between computers that are not networked together. The files must be written onto floppy disks on the source machine, and a person must physically transport the disks to the destination machine.

sniffer *n. See* packet sniffer.

SNMP *n.* Acronym for Simple Network Management Protocol. The network management protocol of TCP/IP. In SNMP, agents, which can be hardware as well as software, monitor the activity in the various devices on the network and report to the network console workstation. Control information about each device is maintained in a structure known as a management information block. *See also* agent (definition 4), TCP/IP.

SOAP *n.* Acronym for Simple Object Access Protocol. A simple, XML-based protocol for exchanging structured and type information on the Web. The protocol contains no application or transport semantics, which makes it highly modular and extensible.

Society for Information Management *n.* A professional society based in Chicago for information systems executives, formerly the Society for Management Information Systems. *Acronym:* SIM.

Society for Management Information Systems *n. See* Society for Information Management.

socket *n.* **1.** An identifier for a particular service on a particular node on a network. The socket consists of a node address and a port number, which identifies the service. For example, port 80 on an Internet node indicates a Web server. *See also* port number, sockets API. **2.** The receptacle part of a connector, which receives a plug. **3.** A receptacle on a PC motherboard into which a microprocessor is plugged. A socket-mounted microprocessor, such as the Pentium, connects to the motherboard through numerous pins on the underside. Newer Intel microprocessors, such as the Pentium II and later, plug into the motherboard through an edge connector along the side of the chip.

sockets API *n.* An application programming interface implemented to create and use sockets in client/server networking. The most common sockets API is the University of California at Berkeley UNIX/BSD implementation (Berkeley Sockets API), which is the basis for Winsock. *See also* socket (definition 1).

soc. newsgroups *n.* Usenet newsgroups that are part of the soc. hierarchy and have the prefix soc. These newsgroups are devoted to discussions of current events and social issues. Soc. newsgroups are one of the seven original Usenet newsgroup hierarchies. The other six are comp., misc., news., rec., sci., and talk. *See also* newsgroup, traditional newsgroup hierarchy, Usenet.

softmodem *n. See* software-based modem.

software *n.* Computer programs; instructions that make hardware work. Two main types of software are system software (operating systems), which controls the workings of the computer, and applications, such as word processing programs, spreadsheets, and databases, which perform the tasks for which people use computers. Two additional categories, which are neither system nor application software but contain elements of both, are network software, which enables groups of computers to communicate, and language software, which provides programmers with the tools they need to write programs. In addition to these task-based categories, several types of software are described based on their method of distribution. These include packaged software (canned programs), sold primarily through retail outlets; freeware and public domain software, which are distributed free of charge; shareware, which is also distributed free of charge, although users are requested to pay a small registration fee for continued use of the program; and vaporware, software that is announced by a company or individuals but either never makes it to market or is very late. *See also* freeware, network software, shareware.

Software & Information Industry Association *n. See* SIIA.

software-based modem *n.* A modem that uses a general-purpose, reprogrammable digital signal processor chip and RAM-based program memory rather than a dedicated chip with the modem functions burned into the silicon. A software-based modem can be reconfigured to update and change the modem's features and functions.

software handshake *n.* A handshake that consists of signals transmitted over the same wires used to transfer the data, as in modem-to-modem communications over telephone lines, rather than signals transmitted over special wires. *See also* handshake.

SOHO *n.* Acronym for **S**mall **O**ffice/**H**ome **O**ffice, a term used for home-based and small businesses. The fast-growing SOHO market has sparked a concomitant expansion in computer software and hardware products designed specifically to meet the needs of self-employed individuals or small businesses. *See also* distributed workplace, telecommuter.

Solaris *n.* A distributed UNIX-based computing environment created by Sun Microsystems, Inc., widely used as a server operating system. Versions of Solaris exist for SPARC computers, 386 and higher Intel platforms, and the PowerPC.

SOM *n.* **1.** Acronym for **S**ystem **O**bject **M**odel. A language-independent architecture from IBM that implements the CORBA standard. *See also* CORBA. **2.** Acronym for self-organizing map. A form of neural network in which neurons and their connections are added automatically as needed to develop the desired mapping from input to output.

SONET *n.* Acronym for **S**ynchronous **O**ptical **Net**work. A high-speed network that provides a standard interface for communications carriers to connect networks based on fiberoptic cable. SONET is designed to handle multiple data types (voice, video, and so on). It transmits at a base rate of 51.84 Mbps, but multiples of this base rate go as high as 2.488 Gbps (gigabits per second).

spam¹ *vb.* To distribute unwanted, unrequested mail widely on the Internet by posting a message to too many recipients or too many newsgroups. The act of distributing such mail, known as spamming, angers most Internet users and has been known to invite retaliation, often in the form of return spamming that can flood and possibly disable the electronic mailbox of the original spammer.

spam² *n.* **1.** An unsolicited e-mail message sent to many recipients at one time, or a news article posted simultaneously to many newsgroups. Spam is the electronic equivalent of junk mail. In most cases, the content of a spam message or article is not relevant to the topic of the newsgroup or the interests of the recipient; spam is an abuse of the Internet in order to distribute a message to a huge number of people at minimal cost. **2.** An unsolicited e-mail message from a business or individual that seeks to sell the recipient something. *Also called:* UCE, unsolicited commercial e-mail.

spam blocking *n.* *See* address munging.

spambot *n.* A program or device that automatically posts large amounts of repetitive or otherwise inappropriate material to newsgroups on the Internet. *See also* bot (definition 3), robopost, spam¹.

spamdexter *n.* An individual who lures users to spam-related Web sites by loading the site with hundreds of hidden copies of popular keywords, even if those words have no relation to the Web site. Because the keywords appear so many times, the spamdexter's site will appear near the top of search result and indexing lists. The term spamdexter was created by combining the words *spam* and *index*. *Also called:* keyword stuffing.

sparse infector *n.* A type of virus or other malicious code that delivers its payload only when certain predetermined conditions are met. A sparse infector might hide on an infected computer until a certain date or until a certain number of files or applications have been run. By restricting their active phases to only certain situations, sparse infectors are more likely to avoid detection.

special interest group *n.* *See* SIG.

spew *vb.* On the Internet, to post an excessive number of e-mail messages or newsgroup articles.

spider *n.* An automated program that searches the Internet for new Web documents and indexes their addresses and content-related information in a database, which can be examined for matches by a search engine. Spiders are generally considered to be a type of bot, or Internet robot. *Also called:* crawler. *See also* bot (definition 3), search engine (definition 2).

Spirale virus *n. See* Hybris virus.

spoofing *n.* The practice of making a transmission appear to come from an autho-rized user. For example, in IP spoofing, a transmission is given the IP address of an authorized user in order to obtain access to a computer or network. *See also* IP address.

Springboard *n.* Handspring Inc.'s expansion platform for its line of Visor handheld personal digital assistants. The term describes both the 68-pin Springboard socket incorporated into the Visor, as well as a series of add-on Springboard modules that fit into the socket. Add-on modules include features such as multimedia, games, e-books, additional memory storage, and a wireless phone module. *See also* Visor.

SPX *n.* **1.** Acronym for **S**equenced **P**acket **E**xchange. The transport level (ISO/OSI level 4) protocol used by Novell NetWare. SPX uses IPX to transfer the packets, but SPX ensures that messages are complete. *See also* ISO/OSI reference model. *Compare* IPX. **2.** Acronym for **simplex**. *See* simplex.

SSA *n.* Acronym for **S**erial **S**torage **A**rchitecture. An interface specification from IBM in which devices are arranged in a ring topology. In SSA, which is compatible with SCSI devices, data can be transferred at up to 20 megabytes per second in each direction. *See also* SCSI device.

SSE *n.* Short for **S**treaming **SIMD E**xtensions. A set of 70 new instructions imple-mented in Intel's Pentium III microprocessor. SSE, more formally called Internet SSE (ISSE), uses SIMD (single-instruction, multiple-data) operations to accelerate floating point calculations. Designed to improve performance in visual areas such as real-time 3-D and graphics rendering, SSE also provides support for development of such applications as real-time video and speech recognition.

SSL *n.* Acronym for **S**ecure **S**ockets **L**ayer. A protocol developed by Netscape Com-munications Corporation for ensuring security and privacy in Internet communications. SSL supports authentication of client, server, or both, as well as encryption during a communications session. While primary purpose of SSL is to enable secure electronic financial transactions on the World Wide Web, it is designed to work with other Inter-net services as well. This technology, which uses public key encryption, is incorporated into the Netscape Navigator Web browser and Netscape's commerce servers. *See also* commerce server, open standard, public key encryption, PCT. *Compare* S-HTTP.

SSO *n. See* single sign-on.

stack *n.* A region of reserved memory in which programs store status data such as procedure and function call addresses, passed parameters, and sometimes local vari-ables. *See also* pop, push[2] (definition 1).

staging web *n.* A local Web site maintained on a file system or local Web server that currently cannot be browsed by site visitors. These Web sites allow authors and workgroups to make changes or updates to Web sites before they are published.

staging Web server *n.* A Web server where you publish and test your Web site before putting it on a production server. A staging Web server cannot be browsed by an Internet or intranet audience.

stale link *n.* A hyperlink to an HTML document that has been deleted or moved, rendering the hyperlink useless. *See also* HTML document, hyperlink.

standard *n.* **1.** A technical guideline advocated by a recognized noncommercial or government organization that is used to establish uniformity in an area of hardware or software development. The standard is the result of a formal process, based on specifications drafted by a cooperative group or committee after an intensive study of existing methods, approaches, and technological trends and developments. The proposed standard is later ratified or approved by a recognized organization and adopted over time by consensus as products based on the standard become increasingly prevalent in the market. Standards of this type are numerous, including the ASCII character set, the RS-232-C standard, and the SCSI interface. *See also* ANSI, RS-232-C standard, SCSI. **2.** A de facto technical guideline for hardware or software development that occurs when a product or philosophy is developed by a single company and, through success and imitation, becomes so widely used that deviation from the norm causes compatibility problems or limits marketability. This type of highly informal standard setting is exemplified by Hayes-compatible modems and IBM PC–compatible computers.

standard disclaimer *n.* A phrase placed in an e-mail message or news article that is intended to replace the statement required by some businesses and institutions that the contents of the message or article do not necessarily represent the opinions or policies of the organization from whose e-mail system the message originated.

Standard Generalized Markup Language *n. See* SGML.

star bus *n.* A network topology in which nodes connect to hubs in a star pattern, but the hubs are connected by a bus trunk. Star bus is a combination of star and bus topologies.

star network *n.* A LAN (local area network) in which each device (node) is connected to a central computer in a star-shaped configuration (topology); commonly, a network consisting of a central computer (the hub) surrounded by terminals. *Compare* bus network, ring network.

starting point *n.* A World Wide Web document designed to help users begin navigating the Web. A starting point often contains tools such as search engines and hyperlinks to selected Web sites. *See also* hyperlink, search engine (definition 2), World Wide Web.

star topology *n.* A network configuration based on a central hub, from which nodes radiate in a star-shaped pattern. *See also* topology.

start page *n. See* home page (definition 2).

star-wired ring *n.* A network topology in which hubs and nodes connect to a central hub in typical star fashion, but the connections within the central hub form a ring. Star-wired ring is a combination of star and ring topologies.

static buffer *n.* A secondary sound buffer that contains an entire sound; these buffers are convenient because the entire sound can be written once to the buffer. *See also* streaming buffer.

static routing *n.* Routing based on a fixed forwarding path. Unlike dynamic routing, static routing does not adjust to changing network conditions. *Compare* dynamic routing.

static Web page *n.* Web page that displays the same content to all viewers. Usually written in hypertext markup language (HTML), a static Web page displays content that changes only if the HTML code is altered. *See also* dynamic Web page.

station *n.* **1.** In the IEEE 802.11 wireless LAN specification, a single, often mobile, node. **2.** *See* workstation.

sticky *adj.* In reference to a Web site, properties such as targeted content or services that increase the amount of time users choose to spend at the site and increase user's desire to return to the site repeatedly.

storage area network *n.* A high-speed network that provides a direct connection between servers and storage, including shared storage, clusters, and disaster-recovery devices. A storage area network, or SAN, includes components such as hubs and routers that are also used in local area networks (LANs), but it differs in being something of a "subnetwork" dedicated to providing a high-speed connection between storage elements and servers. Most SANs rely on fiber-channel connections that deliver speeds up to 1000 Mbps and can support up to 128 devices. SANs are implemented to provide the scalability, speed, and manageability required in environments that demand high data availability. *Acronym:* SAN. *Also called:* system area network.

storm *n.* On a network, a sudden, excessive burst of traffic. Storms are often responsible for network outages.

STP *n.* Acronym for **s**hielded **t**wisted **p**air. A cable consisting of one or more twisted pairs of wires and a sheath of foil and copper braid. The twists protect the pairs from interference by each other, and the shielding protects the pairs from interference from outside. Therefore, STP cable can be used for high-speed transmission over long distances. *See also* twisted-pair cable. *Compare* UTP.

stream *n.* Any data transmission, such as the movement of a file between disk and memory, that occurs in a continuous flow. Manipulating a data stream is a programming task. Consumers, however, are likely to encounter references to streams and streaming in connection to the Internet, which has increased reliance on stream techniques to enable users (even those with slower equipment) to access large multimedia files—especially those containing audio and video components—and to display or play them before all the data has been transferred.

streaming *n.* **1.** On the Internet, the process of delivering information, especially multimedia sound or video, in a steady flow that the recipient can access as the file is being transmitted. **2.** In magnetic tape storage devices, a low-cost technique to control the motion of the tape by removing tape buffers. Although streaming tape compromises start/stop performance, it achieves highly reliable storage and retrieval of data, and is useful when a steady supply of data is required by a particular application or computer.

streaming buffer *n.* A small sound buffer that can play lengthy sounds because the application dynamically loads audio data into the buffer as it plays. For example, an application could use a buffer that can hold 3 seconds of audio data to play a 2-minute sound. A streaming buffer requires much less memory than a static buffer. *See also* static buffer.

Streaming Server *n.* A server technology designed by Apple Computer to send streaming QuickTime media files over the Internet. Built on RTP and RTSP standard Internet protocols, Streaming Server can set up a QuickTime streaming media Web broadcasting station capable of streaming digital videos and music files to more than 3000 users via the Internet. Streaming Server may be used with Mac OS X and other UNIX-based operating systems. *Also called:* Darwin Streaming Server, QuickTime Streaming Server.

strong name *n.* A name that consists of an assembly's identity: its simple text name, version number, and often the culture information strengthened by a public key and a digital signature generated over the assembly. Assemblies with the same strong name are expected to be identical.

STT *n. See* Secure Transaction Technology.

StuffIt *n.* A file compression program originally written for the Apple Macintosh, used for storing a file on one or more disks. Originally shareware, StuffIt is now a commercial product for Macs and PCs that supports multiple compression techniques and allows file viewing. StuffIt files can be uncompressed using a freeware program, StuffIt Expander.

style sheet *n.* **1.** A file of instructions used to apply character, paragraph, and page layout formats in word processing and desktop publishing. **2.** A text file containing code to apply semantics such as page layout specifications to an HTML document. *See also* HTML document.

stylus *n.* A pointing device, similar to a pen, used to make selections, usually by tapping, and to enter information on the touch-sensitive surface.

subdirectory *n.* A directory (logical grouping of related files) within another directory.

subdomain *n.* A domain, often representing an administrative or other organizational subgroup within a second-level domain. *See also* domain.

subject tree *n.* A type of World Wide Web index that is organized by subject categories, many of which are broken down into subcategories, or "branches." An example of a World Wide Web subject tree is Yahoo! *See also* Yahoo!

subnet *n.* **1.** In general, a network that forms part of a larger network. **2.** In terms of the ISO/OSI reference model, the subnet comprises the layers below the transport layer—that is, the network, data link, and physical layers.

subnet mask *n.* *See* address mask.

subnetting *n.* The division of a network into subnets to improve network security and performance. *See also* subnet (definition 1). *Compare* supernetting.

subnetwork *n.* A network that is part of another, larger network.

subscribe *vb.* **1.** To add a newsgroup to the list of such groups from which a user receives all new articles. **2.** To add a name to a LISTSERV distribution list. *See also* LISTSERV.

subscription site *n.* E-commerce Web site that provides information or services to customers who pay a subscription fee.

S

subweb *n.* A named subdirectory of the root Web site that is a complete FrontPage-based Web site. Each subweb can have independent administration, authoring, and browsing permissions from the root Web site and other subwebs.

suite *n.* **1.** A set of application programs sold as a package, usually at a lower price than that of the individual applications sold separately. A suite for office work, for example, might contain a word processing program, a spreadsheet, a database management program, and a communications program. **2.** *See* protocol suite.

SunOS *n.* Short for **Sun O**perating **S**ystem. A variety of the UNIX operating system used on workstations from Sun Microsystems, Inc.

supercomputer *n.* A large, extremely fast, and expensive computer used for complex or sophisticated calculations.

supernetting *n.* The aggregation of multiple network addresses of the same class into a single block. *See also* classless interdomain routing, IP address classes. *Compare* subnetting.

superserver *n.* A network server with especially high capabilities for speed and data storage. *See also* server (definition 1).

superuser *n.* A UNIX user account with root (i.e., unrestricted) access privileges, usually that of a system administrator. *See also* root account, system administrator, user account.

surf *vb.* To browse among collections of information on the Internet, in newsgroups, in Gopherspace, and especially on the World Wide Web. As in channel surfing while watching television, users ride the wave of what interests them, jumping from topic to topic or from one Internet site to another. *Also called:* cruise.

SVG *n.* Acronym for **S**calable **V**ector **G**raphics. An XML-based language for device-independent description of two-dimensional graphics. SVG images maintain their appearance when printed or when viewed with different screen sizes and resolutions. SVG is a recommendation of the World Wide Web Consortium (W3C).

S/WAN *n. See* secure wide area network.

switch *n.* **1.** A circuit element that has two states: on and off. **2.** A control device that allows the user to choose one of two or more possible states. **3.** In communications, a computer or electromechanical device that controls routing and operation of a signal path. **4.** In networking, a device capable of forwarding packets directly to the ports associated with particular network addresses. *See also* bridge, router. **5.** In operating systems such as MS-DOS, an argument used to control the execution of a command or an application, typically starting with a slash character (/).

switch box *n.* An enclosure that contains a selector switch. When a user selects a switch setting, the signal passing through the box may be directed either from a single input to one of multiple outputs, or from the selected input to a single output. Switch boxes are often used to connect multiple peripherals, such as printers, to a single port.

switched configuration *n.* A communications link in which a signal moves from the origin to a switch that routes the signal to one of several possible destinations. *Compare* point-to-point configuration.

switched Ethernet *n.* An Ethernet network run through a high-speed switch instead of an Ethernet hub. A switched Ethernet involves dedicated bandwidth of 10 Mbps between stations rather than a shared medium. *See also* Ethernet (definition 1), switch (definition 3).

switched network *n.* A communications network that uses switching to establish a connection between parties, such as the dial-up telephone system.

Switched T1 *n.* A circuit-switched form of T1 communications. *See also* T1.

switching *n.* A communications method that uses temporary rather than permanent connections to establish a link or to route information between two parties. In the dial-up telephone network, for example, a caller's line goes to a switching center, where the actual connection is made to the called party. In computer networks, message switching and packet switching allow any two parties to exchange information. In both instances, messages are routed (switched) through intermediary stations that together serve to connect the sender and the receiver.

switching hub *n.* A central device (switch) that connects separate communication lines in a network and routes messages and packets among the computers on the network. The switch functions as a hub, or PBX, for the network. *See also* hub, packet (definition 1), PBX, switch (definition 3), switched Ethernet, switched network.

switching speed *n.* In a packet-switching telecommunications technology, such as ATM, the speed at which data packets are sent through the network. Switching speed is generally measured in kilobits or megabits per second. *See also* ATM (definition 1), packet switching.

symmetric digital subscriber line *n. See* SDSL.

symmetric multiprocessing *n. See* SMP.

symmetric multiprocessing server *n. See* SMP server.

synchronization *n.* **1.** In networking, a communications transmission in which multibyte packets of data are sent and received at a fixed rate. *See also* packet (definition 1). **2.** In networking, the matching of timing between computers on the network. All of the computers are generally assigned identical times to facilitate and coordinate communications. **3.** In a computer, the matching of timing between components of the computer so that all are coordinated. For instance, operations performed by the operating system are generally synchronized with the signals of the machine's internal clock. **4.** In application or database files, version comparisons of copies of the files to ensure they contain the same data. **5.** In multimedia, precise real-time processing. Audio and video are transmitted over a network in synchronization so that they can be played back together without delayed responses. **6.** In handheld computing, the process of updating or backing up the data on a handheld computer to the linked software applications on a desktop computer. Data changes made on the desktop computer may also be copied to the handheld during synchronization. *See also* partnership.

Synchronized Multimedia Integration Language *n. See* SMIL.

synchronous *adj.* Occurring at the same time. In computer transmissions, a reference to activity governed by a clock or by synchronized timing.

synchronous communications *n.* Computer-to-computer communications in which transmissions are synchronized by timing between the sending and receiving machines.

Synchronous Data Link Control *n. See* SDLC.

Synchronous Digital Hierarchy *n.* An ITU recommendation implemented in Europe and similar in most respects to the SONET standard used in North America and Japan. *See also* SONET.

Synchronous Optical Network *n. See* SONET.

synchronous protocol *n.* A set of guidelines developed to standardize synchronous communications between computers, usually based on either bit stream transmission or recognized character codes. Examples include the character-oriented binary synchronous (BISYNC) protocol and the bit-oriented High-level Data Link Control (HDLC) and Synchronous Data Link Control (SDLC) protocols. *See also* BISYNC, HDLC, SDLC.

S

SYN flood *n.* A method of overwhelming a host computer on a network, especially the Internet, by sending the host a high volume of SYN (synchronization) packets requesting a connection, but never responding to the acknowledgement packets returned by the host. A SYN flood is a form of denial of service attack. *See also* denial of service attack. *Compare* Ping of Death.

sysadmin *n.* The usual logon name or e-mail address for the system administrator of a UNIX-based system. *See also* system administrator.

sysop *n.* Short for **sys**tem **op**erator. The overseer of a bulletin board system (BBS) or a small multiuser computer system.

system *n.* Any collection of component elements that work together to perform a task. Examples are a hardware system consisting of a microprocessor, its allied chips and circuitry, input and output devices, and peripheral devices; an operating system consisting of a set of programs and data files; or a database management system used to process specific kinds of information.

system administrator *n.* The person responsible for administering use of a multiuser computer system, communications system, or both. A system administrator performs such duties as assigning user accounts and passwords, establishing security access levels, allocating storage space, and watching for unauthorized access to prevent virus or Trojan horse programs from entering the system. *Also called:* sysadmin. *See also* superuser, Trojan horse, virus. *Compare* sysop.

system area network *n. See* storage area network.

system operator *n. See* sysop.

Systems Management Server *n.* A Microsoft BackOffice component that provides services for centralized network management. *Acronym:* SMS.

Systems Network Architecture *n. See* SNA.

T

T1 or **T-1** *n.* A high-speed communications line that can handle digital communications and Internet access at the rate 1.544 Mbps (megabits per second). Although originally designed by AT&T to carry multiple voice calls over standard twisted-pair telephone wiring, this high-bandwidth telephone line can also transmit text and images. T1 speed is attained through multiplexing 24 separate 64 Kbps channels into a single data stream. T1 lines are commonly used by larger organizations for Internet connectivity. *Also called:* T-1 carrier. *See also* T-carrier. *Compare* fractional T1, T2, T3, T4.

T.120 standard *n.* A family of International Telecommunications Union (ITU) specifications for multipoint data communications services within computer applications, such as conferencing and multipoint file transfer.

T2 or **T-2** *n.* A T-carrier that can handle 6.312 Mbps (megabits per second) or 96 voice channels. *See also* T-carrier. *Compare* T1, T3, T4.

T3 or **T-3** *n.* A T-carrier that can handle 44.736 Mbps (megabits per second) or 672 voice channels. *See also* T-carrier. *Compare* T1, T2, T4.

T4 or **T-4** *n.* A T-carrier that can handle 274.176 Mbps (megabits per second) or 4032 voice channels. *See also* T-carrier. *Compare* T1, T2, T3.

TACACS *n.* Acronym for **T**erminal **A**ccess **C**ontroller **A**ccess **C**ontrol **S**ystem. A network access technique in which users log into a single centralized server that contains a database of authorized accounts. After the access server authenticates the user, it forwards the login information to the data server requested by the user. *See also* authentication, server (definition 2).

tag *n.* **1.** In programming, one or more characters containing information about a file, record type, or other structure. **2.** In certain types of data files, a key or an address that identifies a record and its storage location in another file. **3.** In markup languages such as SGML and HTML, a code that identifies an element in a document, such as a heading or a paragraph, for the purposes of formatting, indexing, and linking information in the document. In both SGML and HTML, a tag is generally a pair of angle brackets that contain one or more letters and numbers. Usually one pair of angle brackets is placed before an element, and another pair is placed after, to indicate where the element begins and ends. For example, in HTML, <I>hello world</I> indicates that the phrase "hello world" should be italicized. *See also* <>, element, emotag, HTML, SGML.

Tagged Image File Format *n. See* TIFF.

tag switching *n.* A multilayer Internet switching technology developed by Cisco Systems that integrates routing and switching.

talk[1] *n.* The UNIX command that, when followed by another user's name and address, is used to generate a request for a synchronous chat session on the Internet. *See also* chat[1] (definition 1).

talk[2] *vb. See* chat[2].

talker *n.* An Internet-based synchronous communication mechanism most commonly used to support multiuser chat functions. Such systems typically provide specific commands for movement through separate *rooms*, or chat areas, and allow users to communicate with other users in real time through text messages, indicate simple gestures, use a bulletin board system (BBS) for posting comments, and send internal e-mail. *See also* BBS (definition 1), chat[1] (definition 1).

talk. newsgroups *n.* Usenet newsgroups that are part of the talk. hierarchy and have the prefix talk. as part of their names. These newsgroups are devoted to debate and discussion of controversial topics. Talk. newsgroups are one of the seven original Usenet newsgroup hierarchies. The other six are comp., misc., news., rec., sci., and soc. *See also* newsgroup, traditional newsgroup hierarchy, Usenet.

TANSTAAFL *n.* Acronym for **T**here **a**in't **n**o **s**uch **t**hing **a**s **a** **f**ree **l**unch. An expression used on the Internet in e-mail, chat sessions, mailing lists, newsgroups, and other online forums; derived from *The Moon Is a Harsh Mistress*, a science-fiction classic by Robert A. Heinlein. *See also* chat[1] (definition 1), e-mail[1] (definition 1), mailing list, newsgroup.

tap[1] *n.* A device that can be attached to an Ethernet bus to enable a computer to be connected.

tap[2] *vb.* To use a stylus to quickly touch a device screen to perform an activity. Tapping is analogous to clicking with a mouse.

TAPI *n.* Acronym for **T**elephony **A**pplication **P**rogramming **I**nterface. In the Windows Open Systems Architecture (WOSA), a programming interface that gives Windows client applications access to a server's voice services. TAPI facilitates interoperability between personal computers and telephone equipment. *Also called:* Telephony API. *See also* application programming interface, WOSA. *Compare* TSAPI.

.tar *n.* The file extension that identifies uncompressed UNIX archives in the format produced by the tar program.

tar[1] *n.* Acronym for **tape ar**chive. A UNIX utility for making a single file out of a set of files that a user wishes to store together. The resulting file has the extension .tar. Unlike PKZIP, tar does not compress files, so compress or gzip is usually run on the .tar file to produce a file with extensions .tar.gz or .tar.Z. *See also* gzip, PKZIP. *Compare* untar[1].

tar[2] *vb.* To make a single file out of a set of files using the tar utility. *See also* PKZIP. *Compare* untar[2].

T-carrier *n.* A long-distance, digital communications line provided by a common carrier. Multiplexers at either end merge several voice channels and digital data streams for transmission and separate them when received. T-carrier service, introduced by AT&T in 1993, is defined at several capacity levels: T1, T2, T3, and T4. In addition to voice communication, T-carriers are used for Internet connectivity. *See also* T1, T2, T3, T4.

TCB *n.* Acronym for **T**rusted **C**omputing **B**ase. The complete set of security mechanisms that create security on a network. The TCB includes all the hardware, software, and firmware components that are responsible for system security.

TCO *n. See* total cost of ownership.

TCP *n.* Acronym for **T**ransmission **C**ontrol **P**rotocol. The protocol within TCP/IP that governs the breakup of data messages into packets to be sent via IP (Internet Protocol), and the reassembly and verification of the complete messages from packets received by IP. A connection-oriented, reliable protocol (reliable in the sense of ensuring error-free delivery), TCP corresponds to the transport layer in the ISO/OSI reference model. *See also* ISO/OSI reference model, packet, TCP/IP. *Compare* UDP.

TCP/IP *n.* Acronym for **T**ransmission **C**ontrol **P**rotocol/**I**nternet **P**rotocol. A protocol suite (or set of protocols) developed by the U.S. Department of Defense for communications over interconnected, sometimes dissimilar, networks. It is built into the UNIX system and has become the de facto standard for data transmission over networks, including the Internet.

TCP/IP reference model *n.* A networking model designed around the concept of internetworking—the exchange of information among different networks, often built on different architectures. The TCP/IP reference model, often called the Internet reference model, consists of four layers, the most distinctive of which is the internetwork that deals with routing messages and that has no equivalent in the ISO/OSI reference model or the SNA model. *Compare* ISO/OSI reference model, SNA.

TCP/IP stack *n.* The set of TCP/IP protocols. *See also* protocol stack, TCP/IP.

TDMA *n.* Short for **T**ime **D**ivision **M**ultiple **A**ccess. A multiplexing technology used to divide a single cellular phone channel into multiple subchannels. TDMA works by allocating separate time slots to each user. It is implemented in D-AMPS (Digital Advanced Mobile Phone Service), which relies on TDMA to divide each of the 30 analog AMPS channels into 3 separate subchannels, and GSM (Global System for Mobile Communications). *See also* Global System for Mobile Communications.

Teardrop attack *n.* An Internet-based attack that breaks a message into a series of IP fragments with overlapping offset fields. When these fragments are reassembled at their destination, the fields don't match, causing the system to hang, reboot, or crash.

telco *n.* Short for **tel**ephone **co**mpany. A term generally used in reference to a telephone company's provision of Internet services.

telecom closet *n. See* wiring closet.

telecommunications *n.* The transmission and reception of information of any type, including data, television pictures, sound, and facsimiles, using electrical or optical signals sent over wires or fibers or through the air.

telecommunications closet *n. See* wiring closet.

telecommute *vb.* To work in one location (often at home) and communicate with a main office at a different location through a personal computer equipped with a modem and communications software.

telecommuter *n.* A member of the workforce who conducts business outside the traditional office setting, collaborating with business associates and colleagues through communications and computer technologies. Some workers telecommute full-time; others part-time. The telecommuting ranks include self-employed home workers, small-business entrepreneurs, and employees of large corporations or organizations. *See also* distributed workplace, SOHO.

teleconferencing *n.* The use of audio, video, or computer equipment linked through a communications system to enable geographically separated individuals to participate in a meeting or discussion. *See also* video conferencing.

telematics *n.* In communications technology, the linking of computers and telecommunications. Telematics technology is becoming standard in the automotive industry, with dashboard navigation systems, roadside assistance, entertainment, Internet, and cellular services available in vehicles.

telephony *n.* Telephone technology—voice, fax, or modem transmissions based on either the conversion of sound into electrical signals or wireless communication via radio waves.

Telephony API *n. See* TAPI.

Telephony Service Provider *n.* A modem driver that enables access to vendor-specific equipment through a standard device driver interface. *Acronym:* TSP. *See also* Telephony Service Provider Interface.

Telephony Service Provider Interface *n.* The external interface of a service provider to be implemented by vendors of telephony equipment. A telephony service provider accesses vendor-specific equipment through a standard device driver interface. Installing a service provider allows Windows CE–based applications that use elements of telephony to access the corresponding telephony equipment. *Acronym:* TSPI. *See also* Telephony Service Provider.

teleprocess *vb.* To use a terminal or computer and communications equipment to access computers and computer files located elsewhere. *Teleprocess* is a term originated by IBM. *See also* distributed processing, remote access.

teleprocessing monitor *n. See* TP monitor.

teleworker *n.* A businessperson who substitutes information technologies for work-related travel. Teleworkers include home-based and small business workers who use computer and communications technologies to interact with customers and/or colleagues. *See also* distributed workplace, SOHO.

telnet[1] *n.* **1.** A client program that implements the Telnet protocol. **2.** A protocol in the TCP/IP suite that enables individuals to log on to and use a remote computer as if they were sitting at a terminal directly connected to the machine.

telnet[2] *vb.* To access a remote computer over the Internet using the Telnet protocol. *See also* telnet[1].

Telnet *n.* A protocol that enables an Internet user to log on to and enter commands on a remote computer linked to the Internet, as if the user were using a text-based terminal directly attached to that computer. Telnet is part of the TCP/IP suite of protocols.

terminal *n.* **1.** In networking, a device consisting of a video adapter, a monitor, and a keyboard. The adapter and monitor and, sometimes, the keyboard are typically combined in a single unit. A terminal does little or no computer processing on its own; instead, it is connected to a computer with a communications link over a cable. Terminals are used primarily in multiuser systems and today are not often found on single-user personal computers. *See also* terminal emulation. **2.** In electronics, a point that can be physically linked to something else, usually by a wire, to form an electrical connection.

terminal adapter *n.* The correct name for an ISDN modem, which connects a PC to an ISDN line but does not modulate or demodulate signals as a typical modem does.

terminal emulation *n.* The imitation of a terminal by using software that conforms to a standard, such as the ANSI standard for terminal emulation. Terminal-emulation software is used to make a microcomputer act as if it were a particular type of terminal while it is communicating with another computer, such as a mainframe.

terminal server *n.* In a LAN (local area network), a computer or a controller that allows terminals, microcomputers, and other devices to connect to a network or host computer, or to devices attached to that particular computer. *See also* LAN, terminal.

terminal session *n.* The period of time spent actively using a terminal. *See also* session.

test post *n.* A newsgroup article that contains no actual message but is used simply as a means of checking the connection. *See also* article, newsgroup.

TFTP *n. See* Trivial File Transfer Protocol.

theme *n.* A set of coordinated graphic elements applied to a document or Web page, or across all pages in a Web site. Themes can consist of designs and color schemes for fonts, link bars, and other page elements.

The World—Public Access UNIX *n.* One of the oldest public access Internet service providers, based in Boston. In 1990, The World began offering full dial-up Internet access to the public. Other services include World Wide Web access, Usenet, SLIP/PPP support, telnet, FTP, IRC, Gopher, and e-mail. In 1995, The World began supporting local dial-up access via UUNET. *See also* ISP.

thick Ethernet *n. See* 10Base5.

ThickNet *n. See* 10Base5.

ThickWire *n. See* 10Base5.

253

thin client *n.* A software layer of a small client for a centrally managed, network terminal. The thin client allows the user access to server-hosted applications and data.

thin Ethernet *n. See* 10Base2.

ThinNet *n. See* 10Base2.

thin server *n.* A client/server architecture in which most of an application is run on the client machine, which is called a fat client, with occasional data operations on a remote server. Such a configuration yields good client performance, but complicates administrative tasks, such as software upgrades. *See also* client/server architecture, fat client, thin client. *Compare* fat server.

thin system *n. See* thin server.

ThinWire *n. See* 10Base2.

thread *n.* **1.** In programming, a process that is part of a larger process or program. **2.** In a tree data structure, a pointer that identifies the parent node and is used to facilitate traversal of the tree. **3.** In electronic mail and Internet newsgroups, a series of messages and replies related to a specific topic.

threaded discussion *n.* In a newsgroup or other online forum, a series of messages or articles in which replies to an article are nested directly under it, instead of the articles being arranged in chronological or alphabetical order. *See also* newsgroup, thread (definition 3).

threaded newsreader *n.* A newsreader that displays posts in newsgroups as threads. Replies to a post appear directly after the original post, rather than in chronological or any other order. *See also* newsreader, post, thread (definition 3).

three-nines availability *n.* The availability of a system 99.9% of the time. Three-nines availability equates to approximately 526 minutes of downtime in a standard 365-day year. *See also* high availability.

three-tier client/server *n.* A client/server architecture in which software systems are structured into three tiers or layers: the user interface layer, the business logic layer, and the database layer. Layers may have one or more components. For example, there can be one or more user interfaces in the top tier, each user interface may communicate with more than one application in the middle tier at the same time, and the applications in the middle tier may use more than one database at a time. Components in a tier may run on a computer that is separate from the other tiers, communicating with the other components over a network. *See also* client/server architecture. *Compare* two-tier client/server.

throughput *n.* **1.** The data transfer rate of a network, measured as the number of bits per second transmitted. **2.** A measure of the data processing rate in a computer system.

thumbnail *n.* A miniature version of an image or electronic version of a page that is generally used to allow quick browsing through multiple images or pages. For example,

Web pages often contain thumbnails of images (which can be loaded much more quickly by the Web browser than the full-size image). Many of these thumbnails can be clicked to load the complete version of the image.

TIA *n.* Acronym for **t**hanks **i**n **a**dvance. On the Internet, a popular sign-off to a request of some sort. *Also called:* aTdHvAaNnKcSe.

Tier 1 *n.* An Internet Network Access Point that provides access to and interconnection among major national and international network backbone providers, such as MCI WorldCom, Sprint, BBN, and IBM. *See also* Network Access Point. *Compare* Tier 2.

Tier 2 *n.* A regional Internet Network interchange location where local ISPs exchange data. By using a Tier 2 exchange point, ISPs in the same area can move data between their users without the need to transport that data over long distances. For example, if a user in Singapore connects to a Web site in the same city through a local Tier 2 exchange point, it is not necessary to move the data through a major Network Access Point, or NAP, in Japan or North America. Tier 2 locations generally have much smaller capacities than the national and international Tier 1 NAPs. *See also* Network Access Point. *Compare* Tier 1.

.tif or **.tiff** *n.* The file extension that identifies bitmap images in Tagged Image File Format (TIFF). *See also* TIFF.

TIFF or **TIF** *n.* Acronym for **T**agged **I**mage **F**ile **F**ormat or **T**ag **I**mage **F**ile **F**ormat. A standard file format commonly used for scanning, storage, and interchange of gray-scale graphic images. TIFF may be the only format available for older programs (such as older versions of MacPaint), but most modern programs are able to save images in a variety of other formats, such as GIF or JPEG. *Compare* GIF, JPEG.

TIFF JPEG *n.* Acronym for **T**agged **I**mage **F**ile Format **JPEG**. A means of saving photographic images compressed according to the JPEG (Joint Photographic Experts Group) standard. TIFF JPEG saves more information about an image than does the lower-end JFIF (JPEG File Interchange Format), but TIFF JPEG files are limited in portability because of differences in implementation among applications. *See also* JFIF, JPEG.

tiger team *n.* A group of users, programmers, or hackers who are charged with finding flaws in networks, applications, or security procedures. Tiger teams may be hired or may be composed of volunteers, and may have a single, short-term goal or may be used for a number of investigative purposes over a longer period of time. The term "tiger team" was originally used by the military to describe infiltration groups, and was first used in the computer industry to refer to hackers hired to expose flaws in network security.

time and date stamp *n.* *See* time stamp.

Time Division Multiple Access *n.* *See* TDMA.

time out or **timeout** or **time-out** *n.* An event that indicates that a predetermined amount of time has elapsed without some other expected event taking place. The time-out event is used to interrupt the process that had been waiting for the other expected event. For example, a dial-up remote system might allow the user 60 seconds to log in after making a connection. If the user fails to enter a valid login name and password within this time, the computer breaks the connection, thus protecting itself against crackers as well as freeing a phone line that may have gone dead.

time server *n.* A computer that periodically synchronizes the time on all computers within a network. This ensures that the time used by network services and local functions remains accurate.

timestamp *n.* A certification by a trusted third party specifying that a particular message existed at a specific time and date. In a digital context, trusted third parties generate a trusted timestamp for a particular message by having a timestamping service append a time value to a message and then digitally signing the result. *See also* digital signature, service.

time stamp *n.* A time signature that is added by a program or system to files, e-mail messages, or Web pages. A time stamp indicates the time and usually the date when a file or Web page was created or last modified or when an e-mail message was sent or received. Most time stamps are created by programs and are based on the time kept by the system clock of a computer on which the program resides. Commercial time stamp services are available on the Web or by e-mail, and offer proof of posting certificates to corroborate the time and date a message was sent. *Also called:* date and time stamp, date stamp, time and date stamp.

time-synchronization service *n.* A program used to ensure that all systems on a network use a common time. Time-synchronization services on the Internet typically update real-time clocks to Universal Time Coordinate (UTC) using Network Time Protocol (NTP). Windows Time Synchronization Service (Win32Time) is a time-synchronization service. *See also* Network Time Protocol, Universal Time Coordinate.

Time to Live *n.* A header field for a packet sent over the Internet indicating how long the packet should be held. *Acronym:* TTL. *See also* header, packet (definition 1).

timing attack *n.* An attack on a cryptographic system that exploits the fact that different cryptographic operations take slightly different amounts of time to process. The attacker exploits these slight time differences by carefully measuring the amount of time required to perform private key operations. Taking these measurements from a vulnerable system can reveal the entire secret key. Cryptographic tokens, network-based cryptosystems, and other applications where attackers can make reasonably accurate timing measurements are potentially at risk from this form of attack.

Tinkerbell program *n.* A program used to monitor network traffic and alert security administrators when connections are made from a predetermined list of sites and individuals. A Tinkerbell program acts as a low-level security reporting feature.

TLA *n.* Acronym for three-letter acronym. An ironic term, usually used in jest on the Internet in e-mail, newsgroups, and other online forums, referring to the large number of acronyms in computer terminology, particularly those consisting of three letters.

TLD *n. See* top-level domain.

TLS *n.* Acronym for **T**ransport **L**ayer **S**ecurity. A standard protocol that is used to provide secure Web communications on the Internet or intranets. It enables clients to authenticate servers or, optionally, servers to authenticate clients. It also provides a secure channel by encrypting communications. TLS is the latest and a more secure version of the SSL protocol. *See also* authentication, communications protocol, SSL.

token *n.* **1.** A unique structured data object or message that circulates continuously among the nodes of a token ring and describes the current state of the network. Before any node can send a message, it must first wait to control the token. *See also* token bus network. **2.** Any nonreducible textual element in data that is being parsed—for example, the use in a program of a variable name, a reserved word, or an operator. Storing tokens as short codes shortens program files and speeds execution.

token bus *n.* The IEEE 802.4 specification for token-passing networks based on a bus or tree topology. Token bus networks were designed primarily for manufacturing but the specification also corresponds to the ARCnet architecture used for LANs.

token bus network *n.* A LAN (local area network) formed in a bus topology (stations connected to a single, shared data highway) that uses token passing as a means of regulating traffic on the line. On a token bus network, a token governing the right to transmit is passed from one station to another, and each station holds the token for a brief time, during which it alone can transmit information. The token is transferred in order of priority from an "upstream" station to the next "downstream" station, which might or might not be the next station on the bus. In essence, the token "circles" through the network in a logical ring rather than a physical one. Token bus networks are defined in the IEEE 802.4 standards. *See also* bus network, IEEE 802.x, token passing. *Compare* token ring network.

token passing *n.* A method of controlling network access through the use of a special signal, called a *token*, that determines which station is allowed to transmit. The token, which is actually a short message or a small packet, is passed from station to station around the network. Only the station with the token can transmit information. *See also* token bus network, token ring network. *Compare* contention, CSMA/CD.

token ring *n.* Spelled with lowercase *t* and *r*, the IEEE specification 802.5 for token ring networks. *See also* token ring network.

Token Ring *n. See* Token Ring network.

token ring network *n.* A LAN (local area network) formed in a ring (closed loop) topology that uses token passing as a means of regulating traffic on the line. On a token ring network, a token governing the right to transmit is passed from one station to the next in a physical circle. If a station has information to transmit, it "seizes" the token, marks it as being in use, and inserts the information. The "busy" token, plus message, is then passed around the circle, copied when it arrives at its destination, and eventually returned to the sender. The sender removes the attached message and then passes the freed token to the next station in line. Token ring networks are defined in the IEEE 802.5 standards. *See also* IEEE 802.x, ring network, token passing. *Compare* token bus network.

Token Ring network *n.* A token-passing, ring-shaped local area network (LAN) developed by IBM that operates at 4 megabits (4 million bits) per second. With standard telephone wiring, the Token Ring network can connect up to 72 devices; with shielded twisted-pair (STP) wiring, the network supports up to 260 devices. Although it is based on a ring (closed loop) topology, the Token Ring network uses star-shaped clusters of up to eight workstations connected to a wiring concentrator (Multistation Access Unit, or MSAU), which, in turn, is connected to the main ring. The Token Ring network is designed to accommodate microcomputers, minicomputers, and mainframes; it follows the IEEE 802.5 standards for token ring networks. *See also* ring network, STP, token passing.

top-level domain *n.* In the domain-name system of Internet addresses or DNS hierarchy, any of the broadest category of names, under which all domain names fit. Top-level domains for sites in the United States include .com, .edu, .gov, .net, and .org. *See also* DNS (definition 1).

topology *n.* The configuration or layout of a network formed by the connections between devices on a LAN (local area network) or between two or more LANs. *See also* bus network, LAN, ring network, star network, token ring network, tree network.

top posting *n.* In e-mail and newsgroup discussions, placing new material before material quoted from earlier posts rather than after. Because top-posted messages are read out of chronological order, top-posting is considered an undesirable practice.

total bypass *n.* A communications network that uses satellite transmission to bypass both local and long-distance telephone links.

total cost of ownership *n.* Specifically, the cost of owning, operating, and maintaining a single PC; more generally, the cost to businesses and organizations of setting up and maintaining complex and far-reaching networked computer systems. Total cost of ownership includes the up-front costs of hardware and software added to later costs of installation, personnel training, technical support, upgrades, and repairs. Industry initiatives designed to lower the total cost of ownership include centralized network management and administration, as well as hardware solutions in the form of network-based computers with or without local storage and expansion capability. *Acronym:* TCO.

TP *n. See* transaction processing.

TP monitor *n.* Short for teleprocessing **monitor** or transaction processing **monitor**. A program that controls the transfer of data between terminals (or clients) and a mainframe (or one or more servers) so as to provide a consistent environment for one or more online transaction processing (OLTP) applications. A TP monitor may also control the appearance of the screen displays and check input data for proper format. *See also* client, mainframe computer, OLTP, server (definition 1).

traceroute *n.* A utility that shows the route a packet takes through a network to arrive at a remote host. A traceroute also reports the IP addresses of all intermediate hosts or routers and the time required for the packet to reach each of them. *See also* IP address, packet.

traditional newsgroup hierarchy *n.* The seven standard newsgroup categories in Usenet: comp., misc., news., rec., sci., soc., and talk. Newsgroups can be added within the traditional hierarchy only following a formal voting process. *See also* comp. newsgroups, misc. newsgroups, newsgroup, news. newsgroups, rec. newsgroups, sci. newsgroups, soc. newsgroups, talk. newsgroups, Usenet. *Compare* alt. newsgroups.

traffic *n.* The load carried by a communications link or channel.

traffic management *n. See* ITM.

traffic shaping *n.* A technique for allocating bandwidth and preventing packet loss by enforcing prioritization policies on the transmission of data over a network. *Also called:* bandwidth shaping. *See also* bandwidth management, bandwidth reservation, token passing.

trailer *n.* Information, typically occupying several bytes, at the tail end of a block (section) of transmitted data and often containing error-checking data useful for confirming the accuracy and status of the transmission. *Compare* header.

T

trailing edge *n.* The latter part of an electronic signal. When a digital signal switches from on to off, the transition is the trailing edge of the signal.

transaction *n.* A discrete activity within a computer system, such as an entry of a customer order or an update of an inventory item. Transactions are usually associated with database management, order entry, and other online systems.

transactional e-mail *n.* A form of Web-based marketing in which goods and services are sold to consumers directly from an e-mail message. Unlike traditional e-mail marketing that requires the e-mail recipient to visit the seller's Web site, transactional e-mail allows an entire sales transaction to be completed from within the marketing e-mail. To take advantage of transactional e-mail buying options, the recipient must view the e-mail message in HTML format.

transaction file *n.* A file that contains the details of transactions, such as items and prices on invoices. It is used to update a master database file. *See also* transaction. *Compare* master file.

transaction log *n. See* change file.

transaction processing *n.* A processing method in which transactions are executed immediately after they are received by the system. *Acronym:* TP. *See also* transaction. *Compare* batch processing.

transaction processing monitor *n. See* TP monitor.

Transaction Tracking System *n. See* TTS (definition 2).

transceiver *n.* Short for **trans**mitter/re**ceiver**. A device that can both transmit and receive signals. On LANs (local area networks), a transceiver is the device that connects a computer to the network and that converts signals to and from parallel and serial form.

transceiver cable *n.* A cable that is used to connect a host adapter within a computer to a LAN (local area network). *See also* LAN.

transfer *vb.* To move data from one place to another, especially within a single computer. *Compare* transmit.

transfer rate *n.* The rate at which a circuit or a communications channel transfers information from source to destination, as over a network or to and from a disk drive. Transfer rate is measured in units of information per unit of time—for example, bits per second or characters per second—and can be measured either as a raw rate, which is the maximum transfer speed, or as an average rate, which includes gaps between blocks of data as part of the transmission time.

transitive trust *n.* The standard type of trust relationship between Windows domains in a domain tree or forest. When a domain joins an existing forest or domain tree, a transitive trust is automatically established. Transitive trusts are always two-way relationships. This series of trusts, between parent and child domains in a domain tree and between root domains of domain trees in a forest, allows all domains in a forest to trust each other for the purposes of authentication. For example, if domain A trusts domain B and domain B trusts domain C, then domain A trusts domain C. *See also* domain, one-way trust, two-way trust.

transmission channel *n. See* channel.

Transmission Control Protocol *n. See* TCP.

Transmission Control Protocol/Internet Protocol *n. See* TCP/IP.

transmit *vb.* To send information over a communications line or a circuit. Computer transmissions can take place in the following ways: asynchronous (variable timing) or synchronous (exact timing); serial (essentially, bit by bit) or parallel (byte by byte; a group of bits at once); duplex or full-duplex (simultaneous two-way communication), half-duplex (two-way communication in one direction at a time), or simplex (one-way communication only); and burst (intermittent transmission of blocks of information). *Compare* transfer.

transmitter *n.* Any circuit or electronic device designed to send electrically encoded data to another location.

transparent *adj.* **1.** In computer use, of, pertaining to, or characteristic of a device, function, or part of a program that works so smoothly and easily that it is invisible to the user. For example, the ability of one application to use files created by another is transparent if the user encounters no difficulty in opening, reading, or using the second program's files or does not even know the use is occurring. **2.** In communications, of, pertaining to, or characteristic of a mode of transmission in which data can include any characters, including device-control characters, without the possibility of misinterpretation by the receiving station. For example, the receiving station will not end a transparent transmission until it receives a character in the data that indicates end of transmission. Thus, there is no danger of the receiving station ending communications prematurely. **3.** In computer graphics, of, pertaining to, or characteristic of the lack of color in a particular region of an image so that the background color of the display shows through.

transport layer *n.* The fourth of the seven layers in the International Organization for Standardization's Open Systems Interconnection (OSI) reference model for standardizing computer-to-computer communications. The transport layer is one level above the network layer and is responsible for both quality of service and accurate delivery of information. Among the tasks performed on this layer are error detection and correction. *See also* ISO/OSI reference model.

Transport Layer Security *n. See* TLS.

trapdoor *n. See* back door.

tree *n.* A data structure containing zero or more nodes that are linked together in a hierarchical fashion. If there are any nodes, one node is the root; each node except the root is the child of one and only one other node; and each node has zero or more nodes as children. *See also* node (definition 3), root.

tree network *n.* A topology for a local area network (LAN) in which one machine is connected to one or more other machines, each of which is connected to one or more others, and so on, so that the structure formed by the network resembles that of a tree. *See also* bus network, distributed network, ring network, star network, token ring network, topology.

tree view *n.* A hierarchical representation of the folders, files, disk drives, and other resources connected to a computer or network. For example, Windows Explorer uses a tree view to display the resources that are attached to a computer or a network. *See also* resource.

tri-band phone *n.* A wireless phone designed for international travel. Tri-band phones broadcast on the personal communication service (PCS) frequency used in North America as well as PCS frequencies used in other regions of the world.

trigger[1] *n.* **1.** In a database, an action that causes a procedure to be carried out automatically when a user attempts to modify data. A trigger can instruct the database system to take a specific action, depending on the particular change attempted. Incorrect, unwanted, or unauthorized changes can thereby be prevented, helping to maintain the integrity of the database. **2.** A function built into a virus or worm that controls the release of a malicious payload or similar event. The trigger may be activated at a predetermined time or date or in response to a user-initiated event, such as opening a specific program or file. In some cases, the trigger may reset itself repeatedly until the virus is neutralized.

trigger² *vb.* To activate a function or program, such as the release of a virus payload, in response to a specific event, date, or time.

tri-mode phone *n.* A wireless phone that broadcasts on 1900 MHz personal communication service (PCS), 800 MHz digital cellular networks, and 800 MHz analog networks.

Trivial File Transfer Protocol *n.* A simplified version of File Transfer Protocol (FTP) that provides basic file transfer with no user authentication and is often used to download the initial files needed to begin an installation process. *Acronym:* TFTP. *See also* communications protocol.

Trojan horse *n.* A destructive program disguised as a game, utility, or application. When run, a Trojan horse does something harmful to the computer system while appearing to do something useful. *See also* virus, worm.

troll *vb.* To post a message in a newsgroup or other online conference in the hopes that somebody else will consider the original message so outrageous that it demands a heated reply. A classic example of trolling is an article in favor of torturing cats posted in a pet lovers' newsgroup. *See also* YHBT.

trunk *n.* **1.** In communications, a channel connecting two switching stations. A trunk usually carries a large number of calls at the same time. **2.** In networking, the cable forming the main communications path on a network. On a bus network, the single cable to which all nodes connect. *See also* backbone.

trunking *n.* *See* link aggregation.

Trusted Computing Base *n.* *See* TCB.

trust relationship *n.* A logical relationship established between domains to allow pass-through authentication, in which a trusting domain honors the logon authentications of a trusted domain. User accounts and global groups defined in a trusted domain can be given rights and permissions in a trusting domain, even though the user accounts or groups don't exist in the trusting domain's directory. *See also* authentication, domain, group, permission, user account.

TSAPI *n.* Acronym for **T**elephony **S**ervices **A**pplication **P**rogramming **I**nterface. The set of standards for the interface between a large telephone system and a computer network server, developed by Novell and AT&T and supported by many telephone equipment manufacturers and software developers. *Compare* TAPI.

TSP *n.* *See* Telephony Service Provider.

TTFN *n.* Acronym for **T**a **t**a **f**or **n**ow. An expression sometimes used in Internet discussion groups, such as Internet Relay Chat (IRC), to signal a participant's temporary departure from the group. *See also* IRC.

TTL *n.* *See* Time to Live.

TTS *n.* **1.** Acronym for **T**ext-to-**S**peech. The process of converting digital text into speech output. TTS is used extensively in fax, e-mail, and other services for the blind, and for telephone-based informational and financial services. **2.** Acronym for **T**ransaction **T**racking **S**ystem. A feature developed to protect databases from corruption caused by incomplete transactions. TTS monitors attempted transactions and in the event of a hardware or software failure, TTS will cancel the update and back out to maintain database integrity.

tunnel *vb.* To encapsulate or wrap a packet or a message from one protocol in the packet for another. The wrapped packet is then transmitted over a network via the protocol of the wrapper. This method of packet transmission is used to avoid protocol restrictions. *See also* communications protocol, packet (definition 2).

tunneling *n.* A method of transmission over internetworks based on differing protocols. In tunneling, a packet based on one protocol is wrapped, or encapsulated, in a second packet based on whatever differing protocol is needed in order for it to travel over an intermediary network. In effect, the second wrapper "insulates" the original packet and creates the illusion of a tunnel through which the wrapped packet travels across the intermediary network. In real-life terms, tunneling is comparable to "encapsulating" a present (the original packet) in a box (the secondary wrapper) for delivery through the postal system.

tunnel server *n.* A server or router that terminates tunnels and forwards traffic to the hosts on the target network. *See also* host, router, server, tunnel.

turnaround time *n.* **1.** The elapsed time between submission and completion of a job. **2.** In communications, the time required to reverse the direction of transmission in half-duplex communication mode. *See also* half-duplex[2].

turnpike effect *n.* The communications equivalent of gridlock; a reference to bottlenecks caused by heavy traffic over a communications system or network.

twisted-pair cable *n.* A cable made of two separately insulated strands of wire twisted together. It is used to reduce signal interference introduced by a strong radio source such as a nearby cable. One of the wires in the pair carries the sensitive signal, and the other wire is grounded.

twisted-pair wiring *n.* Wiring consisting of two insulated strands of copper twisted around one another to form a cable. Twisted-pair wiring comes in two forms, unshielded twisted pair (UTP) and shielded twisted pair (STP), the latter named for an extra protective sheath wrapped around each insulated pair of wires. Twisted-pair wiring can consist of a single pair of wires or, in thicker cables, two, four, or more pairs of wires. Twisted-pair wiring is typical of telephone cabling. *Compare* coaxial cable, fiberoptic cable.

two-nines availability *n.* The availability of a system 99% of the time. Two-nines availability equates to approximately 87.6 hours of downtime in a standard 365-day year. *See also* high availability.

two-tier client/server *n.* A client/business logic layer and the database layer. Fourth-generation languages (4GL) have helped to popularize the two-tier client/server architecture. *Compare* three-tier client/server.

two-way trust *n.* A type of trust relationship in which both of the domains in the relationship trust each other. In a two-way trust relationship, each domain has established a one-way trust with the other domain. For example, domain A trusts domain B and domain B trusts domain A. Two-way trusts can be transitive or nontransitive. All two-way trusts between Windows domains in the same domain tree or forest are transitive. *See also* domain, one-way trust, transitive trust.

TXD *n.* Short for Transmit (**tx**) **D**ata. A line used to carry transmitted data from one device to another, as from computer to modem; in RS-232-C connections, pin 2. *See also* RS-232-C standard. *Compare* RXD.

.txt *n.* A file extension that identifies ASCII text files. In most cases, a document with a .txt extension does not include any formatting commands, so it is readable in any text editor or word processing program. *See also* ASCII.

Tymnet *n.* A public data network available in over 100 countries, with links to some online services and Internet service providers.

typosquatter *n.* A form of cybersquatter that takes advantage of typographical errors to snare Web surfers. The typosquatter registers variations of popular trade-marked domain names that contain the most likely spelling errors (for example: JCPenny). A user who makes a mistake typing in a Web site address will be taken to the typosquatter's site, which typically is loaded with banner and pop-up ads. The typosquatter is paid by the number of users who see the ads. *See also* cybersquatter.

U

UA *n. See* user agent.

UART *n.* Acronym for **u**niversal **a**synchronous **r**eceiver-**t**ransmitter. A module, usually composed of a single integrated circuit, that contains both the receiving and transmitting circuits required for asynchronous serial communication. A UART is the most common type of circuit used in personal computer modems. *Compare* USRT.

UCAID *n.* Acronym for **U**niversity **C**orporation for **A**dvanced **I**nternet **D**evelopment. An organization created to provide guidance in advanced networking development within the university community. UCAID is responsible for the development of the Abilene fiber-optic backbone network that will interconnect over 150 universities into the Internet2 project.

UCE *n.* Acronym for **u**nsolicited **c**ommercial **e**-mail. *See* spam.

UCITA *n.* Acronym for **U**niform **C**omputer **I**nformation **T**ransactions **A**ct. Legislation proposed or enacted in several states that will set legal standards and control systems for dealing with computer information. UCITA is a model law intended as an amendment to the Uniform Commercial Code to cover new technology-related issues. One of UCITA's main provisions is a standard for mass market software shrinkwrap and clickwrap agreements (an electronic version of an End-User License Agreement).

UDDI *n.* Acronym for **U**niversal **D**escription, **D**iscovery, and **I**ntegration. A platform-independent framework functioning like a directory (similar to a telephone book) that provides a way to locate and register Web services on the Internet. The UDDI specification calls for three elements: white pages, which provide business contact information; yellow pages, which organize Web services into categories (for example, credit card authorization services); and green pages, which provide detailed technical information about individual services. The UDDI also contains an operational registry, which is available today.

UDP *n.* Acronym for **U**ser **D**atagram **P**rotocol. The connectionless protocol within TCP/IP that corresponds to the transport layer in the ISO/OSI reference model. UDP converts data messages generated by an application into packets to be sent via IP, but it is "unreliable" because it does not establish a path between sender and receiver before transmitting and does not verify that messages have been delivered correctly. UDP is more efficient than TCP, so it is used for various purposes, including SNMP; the reliability depends on the application that generates the message. *See also* communications protocol, ISO/OSI reference model, packet, SNMP, TCP/IP. *Compare* IP, TCP.

UDT *n.* Acronym for **u**niform **d**ata **t**ransfer. The service used in the OLE extensions to Windows that allows two applications to exchange data without either program knowing the internal structure of the other.

UKnet *n.* **1.** The University of Kentucky's campus network. **2.** In the United Kingdom, an Internet service provider (ISP) based at the University of Kent. *See also* ISP.

UltimateTV *n.* A television digital recording technology developed by Microsoft. UltimateTV can record up to 35 hours of DIRECTV broadcasts. Because the television signal is recording on UltimateTV's hard drive, viewers can pause a live show, rewind scenes, and watch previously shown parts of the show in slow or fast motion while UltimateTV records the remainder of the show live.

UltraSCSI *n.* An extension of the SCSI-2 standard that doubles the transfer speed of Fast-SCSI to allow a transfer rate of 20 megabytes per second (MBps) on an 8-bit connection and 40 MBps on a 16-bit connection. *See also* SCSI, SCSI-2.

Ultra Wide SCSI *n. See* UltraSCSI.

UML *n.* Acronym for **U**nified **M**odeling **L**anguage. A language developed by Grady Booch, Ivar Jacobson, and Jim Rumbaugh of Rational Software that can be used for specifying, building, and documenting software and non-software systems, such as business models. UML notation provides a common foundation for object-oriented design by providing descriptions of modeling concepts including object class, associations, interface, and responsibility. The UML standard is supported by software developers and vendors and overseen by the Object Management Group (OMG).

UMTS *n.* Acronym for **U**niversal **M**obile **T**elecommunications **S**ystem. Third-generation wireless communications standard developed to provide a consistent set of packet-based voice, text, video, and multimedia capabilities to users in any communications environment worldwide. When UMTS reaches full implementation, users will be able maintain computer and phone Internet connections from anywhere in the world.

UNC *n.* Acronym for **U**niversal **N**aming **C**onvention or, sometimes, **U**niform **N**aming **C**onvention. The system of naming files among computers on a network so that a file on a given computer will have the same pathname when accessed from any of the other computers on the network. For example, if the directory *c:\path1\path2\...pathn* on computer *servern* is shared under the name *pathdirs*, a user on another computer would open *\\servern\pathdirs\filename.ext* to access the file *c:\path1\path2\...pathn\ filename.ext* on *servern*. *See also* URL, virtual path.

Undernet *n.* An international network of Internet Relay Chat (IRC) servers created in 1992 as an alternative to the larger and more chaotic main IRC network. For information about connecting to Undernet, see http://www.undernet.org. *See also* IRC.

Unibus *n.* A bus architecture introduced by Digital Equipment Corporation in 1970.

unicast *vb.* To transmit between a single sender and a single receiver over a network. A two-way, point-to-point transmission, unicast is typical of network communications. *Compare* anycasting, narrowcast.

Unicode *n.* A 16-bit character encoding standard developed by the Unicode Consortium between 1988 and 1991. By using 2 bytes to represent each character, Unicode enables almost all the written languages of the world to be represented using a single character set. (By contrast, 8-bit ASCII is not capable of representing all the combinations of letters and diacritical marks that are used just with the Roman alphabet.) Approximately 39,000 of the 65,536 possible Unicode character codes have been assigned to date, 21,000 of them being used for Chinese ideographs. The remaining combinations are open for expansion. *Compare* ASCII.

unified messaging *n.* The integration of various communications technologies such as voicemail, fax, and e-mail into a single service. Unified messaging is designed to be a time-saving tool to provide users with a single package with which they can receive, organize, and respond to messages in a variety of media.

Unified Modeling Language *n. See* UML.

Uniform Computer Information Transactions Act *n. See* UCITA.

Uniform Data Transfer *n. See* UDT.

Uniform Memory Access *n. See* SMP.

Uniform Naming Convention *n. See* UNC.

Uniform Resource Citation *n.* A description of an object on the World Wide Web, consisting of pairs of attributes and their values, such as the Uniform Resource Identifiers (URIs) of associated resources, author names, publisher names, dates, and prices. *Acronym:* URC.

Uniform Resource Identifier *n.* A character string used to identify a resource (such as a file) from anywhere on the Internet by type and location. The set of Uniform Resource Identifiers includes Uniform Resource Names (URNs) and Uniform Resource Locators (URLs). *Acronym:* URI. *See also* relative URL, Uniform Resource Name, URL.

Uniform Resource Locator *n. See* URL.

Uniform Resource Name *n.* A scheme for uniquely identifying resources that might be available on the Internet by name, without regard to where they are located. The specifications for the format of Uniform Resource Names are still under development by the Internet Engineering Task Force (IETF). They include all Uniform Resource Identifiers (URIs) having the schemes urn:, fpi:, and path:; that is, those that are not Uniform Resource Locators (URLs). *Acronym:* URN. *See also* IETF, Uniform Resource Identifier, URL.

UniForum *n.* **1.** The International Association of Open System Professionals, an organization of UNIX users and administrators. **2.** A series of UNIX trade shows sponsored by UniForum and managed by Softbank COMDEX, Inc. *See also* COMDEX.

Unimodem *n.* **1.** The universal modem driver, provided with Windows CE, that translates Telephony Service Provider Interface (TSPI) calls into AT commands and sends the commands to a virtual device driver that talks to the modem. **2.** A universal modem that supports standard modem AT commands. Windows CE currently supports only PCMCIA modems.

uninterruptible power supply *n. See* UPS.

unique user *n.* An individual visitor to a Web site. Tracking unique users is important in ascertaining the success of a given Web site because it indicates how many different visitors access the site, as opposed to the number of hits—visits by the same or different individuals—the site receives. *Also called:* unique visitor.

unique visitor *n. See* unique user.

United States of America Standards Institute *n.* The former name of the American National Standards Institute. *See also* ANSI.

Universal Description, Discovery, and Integration *n. See* UDDI.

Universal Mobile Telecommunications System *n. See* UMTS.

Universal Naming Convention *n. See* UNC.

Universal Plug and Play *n. See* UPnP.

Universal Plug and Play Forum *n. See* UPnP Forum.

Universal Plug and Play networking *n. See* UPnP networking.

Universal Product Code *n. See* UPC.

Universal Resource Locator *n. See* URL.

universal serial bus *n. See* USB.

Universal Server *n.* **1.** Software from Oracle Corporation that supplies information from its database in a variety of forms, such as text, sound, and video, in response to HTTP requests. **2.** Database software from Informix that works with snap-in software modules to handle user needs for specific data types and ways of processing.

universal synchronous receiver-transmitter *n. See* USRT.

Universal Time Coordinate *n.* For all practical purposes, the same as Greenwich Mean Time, which is used for the synchronization of computers on the Internet. *Acronym:* UTC. *Also called:* coordinated universal time format.

University Corporation for Advanced Internet Development *n. See* UCAID.

UNIX *n.* A multiuser, multitasking operating system. Originally developed by Ken Thompson and Dennis Ritchie at AT&T Bell Laboratories from 1969 through 1973 for use on minicomputers, UNIX has evolved into a complex, powerful operating system that, because it is written in the C language, is more portable—that is, less machine-specific—than many other operating systems. UNIX has been released in a wide variety of versions, or flavors, including System V (developed by AT&T for commercial release; many current flavors on based on it), BSD UNIX (freeware developed at the University of California Berkeley, which has spun off many related flavors), AIX (a version of System V adapted by IBM to run on RISC-based workstations), A/UX (a graphical version for the Macintosh), Linux (a newer version that runs on the Intel chip), and SunOS (based on BSD UNIX and available on Sun workstations). Many flavors of UNIX are available free. With some flavors, the source code is also free, making it an instrumental part of the open source movement. UNIX is widely used as a network operating system, especially in conjunction with the Internet. *See also* BSD UNIX, Linux, open source.

UNIX shell account *n.* A shell account providing command-line access to a UNIX system.

UNIX shell scripts *n.* Sequences of UNIX commands stored as files that can be run as programs. In MS-DOS, batch (.bat) files provide similar capabilities.

UNIX-to-UNIX Copy *n. See* UUCP.

UNIX wizard *n.* A particularly expert and helpful UNIX programmer. Some companies actually use this phrase as a job title. The newsgroup comp.unix.wizards provides answers to many user questions.

unknown host *n.* A response to a request for a connection to a server that indicates that the network is unable to find the specified address. *See also* server (definition 1).

unknown recipients *n.* A response to an e-mail message that indicates that the mail server is unable to identify one or more of the destination addresses.

unmoderated *adj.* Of, pertaining to, or characteristic of a newsgroup or mailing list in which all articles or messages received by the server are automatically available or distributed to all subscribers. *Compare* moderated.

unread *adj.* **1.** Of, pertaining to, or being an article in a newsgroup that a user has not yet received. Newsreader client programs distinguish between "read" and "unread" articles for each user and download only unread articles from the server. **2.** Of, pertaining to, or being an e-mail message that a user has received but has not yet opened in an e-mail program.

unreliable protocol *n.* A communications protocol that makes a "best effort" attempt to deliver a transmission but does not provide for verifying that the transmission arrives without error.

unshielded cable *n.* Cable that is not surrounded with a metal shield. If the wires in an unshielded cable are not at least twisted around each other in pairs, the signals they carry have no protection from interference by external electromagnetic fields. Consequently, unshielded cable should be used only over very short distances. *Compare* coaxial cable, twisted-pair cable, UTP.

unshielded twisted pair *n. See* UTP.

unshielded twisted-pair wiring *n. See* UTP.

unsolicited commercial e-mail *n. See* spam.

unsubscribe *vb.* **1.** In a newsreader client program, to remove a newsgroup from the list of newsgroups to which one subscribes. *See also* newsgroup. **2.** To remove oneself as a recipient on a mailing list. *See also* mailing list.

untar¹ *n.* A utility, available for systems in addition to UNIX, for separating the individual files out of an archive assembled using the UNIX *tar* program. *Compare* tar¹.

untar² *vb.* To separate the individual files out of an archive assembled with the UNIX *tar* program. *Compare* tar².

unzip *vb.* To uncompress an archive file that has been compressed by a program such as compress, gzip, or PKZIP.

up *adj.* Functioning and available for use; used in describing computers, printers, communications lines on networks, and other such hardware.

UPC *n.* Acronym for Universal Product Code. A system of numbering commercial products using bar codes. A UPC consists of 12 digits: a number system character, a five-digit number assigned to the manufacturer, a five-digit product code assigned by the manufacturer, and a modulo 10 check digit.

uplink *n.* The transmission link from an earth station to a communications satellite.

upload¹ *n.* **1.** In communications, the process of transferring a copy of a file from a local computer to a remote computer by means of a modem or network. **2.** The copy of the file that is being or has been transferred.

upload² *vb.* To transfer a copy of a file from a local computer to a remote computer. *Compare* download.

UPnP *n.* Acronym for Universal Plug and Play. A Microsoft initiative which prompted the creation of the UPnP Forum for interconnecting computers, appliances, networks, and services. UPnP extends conventional Plug and Play to include devices connected to networks. It allows peripheral devices to discover and connect to other devices and to enumerate the characteristics of those devices. UPnP is intended to be an element of home networking, in which PCs, appliances, and the services they provide are linked together.

UPnP Device Architecture *n.* A specification developed by the Universal Plug and Play (UPnP) Forum that defines the structure of UPnP networking. The UPnP Device Architecture, formerly known as the DCP Framework, provides information about discovery, description, control, eventing, and presentation in a UPnP network. *See also* UPnP networking.

UPnP Forum *n.* A consortium of companies and individuals that oversees Universal Plug and Play (UPnP) specifications, protocols, logos, sample implementations, test suites, white papers, and other UPnP-related efforts. *See also* UPnP, UPnP Device Architecture, UPnP networking.

UPnP networking *n.* The peer-to-peer networking of intelligent machines, appliances, wireless devices, computers, and other devices according to the Universal Plug and Play (UPnP) Device Architecture. UPnP networking uses control points, devices, services, and protocols including GENA, SOAP, SSDP, standard TCP/IP, and other Internet protocols. *See also* UPnP Device Architecture.

UPS *n.* Acronym for **u**ninterruptible **p**ower **s**upply. A device, connected between a computer (or other electronic equipment) and a power source (usually an outlet receptacle), that ensures that electrical flow to the computer is not interrupted because of a blackout and, in most cases, protects the computer against potentially damaging events, such as power surges and brownouts. All UPS units are equipped with a battery and a loss-of-power sensor; if the sensor detects a loss of power, it switches over to the battery so that the user has time to save his or her work and shut off the computer. *See also* blackout, brownout.

upstream[1] *n.* The direction in which information is delivered from a client to a (Web) server. *Compare* downstream[1].

upstream[2] *adj.* **1.** The location of a server in relation to another server. *Compare* downstream[2] (definition 1). **2.** The direction in which data moves *from* an individual computer *to* the remote network. With certain communications technologies, such as ADSL, cable modems, and high-speed 56-Kbps modems, data flows upstream more slowly than downstream. For example, a 56-Kbps modem can deliver data at a 56-Kbps maximum only downstream; upstream, it delivers data at either 28.8 or 33.6 Kbps. *Compare* downstream[2] (definition 2).

uptime *n.* The amount or percentage of time a computer system or associated hardware is functioning and available for use. *Compare* downtime.

urban legend *n.* A widely distributed story that remains in circulation in spite of the fact that it is not true. Many urban legends have been floating around the Internet and other online services for years, including the request for cards for the sick boy in England (he's long since recovered and grown up), the cookie or cake recipe that cost $250 (it's a myth), and the Good Times or Penpal Greetings virus, which will infect your computer when you read an e-mail message (it does not exist). *See also* Good Times virus.

URC *n. See* Uniform Resource Citation.

URI *n. See* Uniform Resource Identifier.

URL *n.* Acronym for **U**niform **R**esource **L**ocator. An address for a resource on the Internet. URLs are used by Web browsers to locate Internet resources. A URL specifies the protocol to be used in accessing the resource (such as http: for a World Wide Web page or ftp: for an FTP site), the name of the server on which the resource resides (such as //www.whitehouse.gov), and, optionally, the path to a resource (such as an HTML document or a file on that server). *See also* FTP[1] (definition 1), HTML, HTTP, path (definition 1), server (definition 2), virtual path (definition 1), Web browser.

URN *n. See* Uniform Resource Name.

usage analysis *n.* Data collected to evaluate how a Web site is being used, such as visitor user names, how often each page was visited, and the types of Web browsers used.

USB *n.* Acronym for **u**niversal **s**erial **b**us. A serial bus with a data transfer rate of 12 megabits per second (Mbps) for connecting peripherals to a microcomputer. USB can

U

connect up to 127 peripherals, such as external CD-ROM drives, printers, modems, mice, and keyboards, to the system through a single, general-purpose port. This is accomplished by daisy chaining peripherals together. USB is designed to support the ability to automatically add and configure new devices and the ability to add such devices without having to shut down and restart the system (hot plugging). USB was developed by Intel, Compaq, DEC, IBM, Microsoft, NEC, and Northern Telecom. It competes with DEC's ACCESS.bus for lower-speed applications. *See also* bus, daisy chain. *Compare* ACCESS.bus.

U.S. Department of Defense *n.* The military branch of the United States government. The Department of Defense developed ARPANET, the origin of today's Internet and MILNET, through its Advanced Research Projects Agency (ARPA). *See also* ARPANET, Internet, MILNET.

Usenet or **UseNet** or **USENET** *n.* A worldwide network of UNIX systems that has a decentralized administration and is used as a bulletin board system by special-interest discussion groups. Usenet, which is considered part of the Internet (although Usenet predates it), comprises thousands of newsgroups, each devoted to a particular topic. Users can post messages and read messages from others in these newsgroups in a manner similar to users on dial-in BBSs. Usenet was originally implemented using UUCP (UNIX-to-UNIX Copy) software and telephone connections; that method remains important, although more modern methods, such as NNTP and network connections, are more commonly used. *See also* BBS (definition 1), newsgroup, newsreader, NNTP, UUCP.

Usenet User List *n.* A list maintained by the Massachusetts Institute of Technology that contains the name and e-mail address of everyone who has posted to the Usenet. *See also* Usenet.

user account *n.* On a secure or multiuser computer system, an established means for an individual to gain access to the system and its resources. Usually created by the system's administrator, a user account consists of information about the user, such as password, rights, and permissions. *See also* group, logon, user profile.

user agent *n.* In the terminology established by the ISO/OSI reference model for LANs (local area networks), a program that helps a client connect with a server. *Acronym:* UA. *See also* agent (definition 3), ISO/OSI reference model, LAN.

user control *n.* In ASP.NET: A server control that is authored declaratively using the same syntax as an ASP.NET page and is saved as a text file with an .ascx extension. User controls allow page functionality to be partitioned and reused. Upon first request, the page framework parses a user control into a class that derives from System.Web.UI.UserControl and compiles that class into an assembly, which it reuses on subsequent requests. User controls are easy to develop due to their page-style authoring and deployment without prior compilation. In Windows Forms: A composite control that provides consistent behavior and user interface within or across applications. The user control can be local to one application or added to a library and compiled into a DLL for use by multiple applications.

User Datagram Protocol *n. See* UDP.

user group *n.* A group of people drawn together by interest in the same computer system or software. User groups, some of which are large and influential organizations, provide support for newcomers and a forum where members can exchange ideas and information.

username *n.* The name by which a user is identified to a computer system or network. During the logon process, the user must enter the username and the correct password. If the system or network is connected to the Internet, the username generally corresponds to the leftmost part of the user's e-mail address (the portion preceding the @ sign, as in username@company.com). *See also* e-mail address, logon.

user name *n.* The name by which a person is known and addressed on a communications network. *See also* alias.

user profile *n.* A computer-based record maintained about an authorized user of a multiuser computer system. A user profile is needed for security and other reasons; it can contain such information as the person's access restrictions, mailbox location, type of terminal, and so on. *See also* user account.

USnail *n.* **1.** Slang for the United States Postal Service. USnail, a term used on the Internet, is a reference to how slow the postal service is in comparison to e-mail. **2.** Mail delivered by the United States Postal Service. *See also* snail mail.

/usr *n.* A directory in a computer system that contains subdirectories owned or maintained by individual users of the computer system. These subdirectories can contain files and additional subdirectories. Typically, /usr directories are used in UNIX systems and can be found on many FTP sites. *See also* FTP site.

USRT *n.* Acronym for **u**niversal **s**ynchronous **r**eceiver- **t**ransmitter. A module, usually composed of a single integrated circuit, that contains both the receiving and transmitting circuits required for synchronous serial communication. *Compare* UART.

UTC *n. See* Universal Time Coordinate.

UTF-8 *n.* Acronym for **U**CS **T**ransformation **F**ormat **8**. A character set for protocols evolving beyond the use of ASCII. The UTF-8 protocol provides for support of extended ASCII characters and translation of UCS-2, an international 16-bit Unicode character set. UTF-8 enables a far greater range of names than can be achieved using ASCII or extended ASCII encoding for character data. *See also* ASCII, Unicode.

UTP *n.* Acronym for **u**nshielded **t**wisted **p**air. A cable containing one or more twisted pairs of wires without additional shielding. UTP is more flexible and takes up less space than shielded twisted-pair (STP) cable but has less bandwidth. *See also* twisted-pair cable. *Compare* STP.

.uu *n.* The file extension for a binary file that has been translated into ASCII format using uuencode. *Also called:* .uud. *See also* ASCII.

U

UUCP *n.* Acronym for UNIX-to-UNIX Copy. A set of software programs that facilitates transmission of information between UNIX systems using serial data connections, primarily the public switched telephone network. *See also* uupc.

UUID *n.* Acronym for **u**niversally **u**nique **id**entifier. A 128-bit value that uniquely identifies objects such as OLE servers, interfaces, manager entry-point vectors, and client objects. Universally unique identifiers are used in cross-process communication, such as remote procedure calling (RPC) and OLE. *Also called:* GUID.

uupc *n.* The version of UUCP for IBM PCs and PC-compatibles running DOS, Windows, or OS/2. This version is a collection of programs for copying files to, logging in to, and running programs on remote networked computers. *See also* UUCP.

U

V

V.120 *n.* The ITU-T (formerly CCITT) standard that governs serial communications over ISDN lines. Data is encapsulated using a protocol similar to the Lightweight Directory Access Protocol (LDAP), and more than one connection may be multiplexed on a communications channel. *See also* communications channel, communications protocol, International Telecommunication Union, ISDN, Lightweight Directory Access Protocol, standard (definition 1), V series.

V.32terbo *n.* A modem protocol developed by AT&T for 19,200-bps modems, with fallback to the speeds supported by the ITU-T (formerly CCITT) V.32 standard. This protocol is proprietary to AT&T and was not adopted by CCITT or ITU-T. In the V series, V.34 takes the place of V.32terbo. *See also* International Telecommunication Union, V series.

V.34 *n.* Data transmission standard that provides for up to 28,800 bits per second (bps) communications over telephone lines. It defines a full-duplex (two-way) modulation technique and includes error-correcting and negotiation. *See also* V.90.

V.42 *n.* The ITU-T (formerly CCITT) recommendation specifying procedures for error correction in data communications equipment (DCEs) designed for asynchronous-to-synchronous conversion. *See also* V series.

V.42bis *n.* The ITU-T (formerly CCITT) recommendation specifying procedures for data compression in data-circuit terminating equipment utilizing error-correction operations. *See also* V series.

V.90 *n.* Data transmission standard that provides for up to 56,000 bits per second (bps) communications over telephone lines. The transmission speed from the client-side modem for uploads is 33,600 bps. The transmission speed for downloads from the host-side modem such as an Internet service provider (ISP) or a corporate network is up to 56,000 bps, with an average speed of 40,000 to 50,000 bps. When the host-side modem does not support this standard, the alternative is V.34. *See also* client, host, ISP, modem, V.34.

validation server controls *n.* A set of server controls, included with ASP.NET, that verify user input. The input is checked as it comes from HTML server controls and Web server controls (for example, a Web page form) against programmer-defined requirements. Validation controls perform input checking in server code. If the user is working with a browser that supports DHTML, the validation controls can also perform validation using client script. *See also* ASP.NET server control, HTML server control, Web server control.

value-added network *n.* A communications network that offers additional services, such as message routing, resource management, and conversion facilities, for computers communicating at different speeds or using different protocols. *Acronym:* VAN.

vampire tap *n.* A type of transceiver used on Ethernet networks that is equipped with sharp metal prongs that pierce the insulation on thicknet cable to make contact with the copper core over which signals travel.

VAN *n. See* value-added network.

vBNS *n.* Short for **v**ery high-speed **B**ackbone **N**etwork **S**ervice. A network connecting several supercomputer centers and reserved for high-performance, high-bandwidth scientific applications requiring massive computing power. The vBNS was developed by the National Science Foundation and MCI Telecommunications. It began operation in 1995, reaching speeds of 2.4 Gbps, using MCI's network of advanced switching and fiberoptic transmission technologies. Later, vBNS expanded to provide backbone services for Internet2.

VBS/VBSWG virus *n.* Acronym for **V**isual **B**asic Script/**V**isual **B**asic Script **W**orm **G**enerator **virus**. Any virus created using the VBSWG virus creation toolkit. The tools available in VBSWG worm kit allow individuals to write viruses without having significant computer knowledge. Homepage and the Anna Kournikova virus are examples of VBS/VBSWG viruses.

vCalendar *n.* A specification defining the format for applications to exchange scheduling information. The vCalendar specification is based on existing industry standards, including international standards for representing dates and times, and permits the exchange of schedules and "to-do" lists of the sort users commonly enter into personal calendars. Like the companion vCard specification for electronic business cards, it was created by the Versit consortium founded by Apple, AT&T, IBM, and Siemens. Handed off to the Internet Mail Consortium (IMC) in 1996, vCalendar is supported by numerous hardware and software vendors. *See also* vCard.

V

vCard *n.* A specification for creating an electronic business card (or personal-information card) and for the card itself. Designed to be exchanged through applications such as e-mail and teleconferencing, a vCard includes information such as name, address, telephone and fax number(s), and e-mail address. It can also include time-zone, geographic location, and multimedia data such as photographs, company logos, and sound clips. Based on the ITU's X.500 directory services specification, vCard was developed by Versit, a consortium whose principal members include Apple, AT&T, IBM, and Siemens. The specification is under the guidance of the Internet Mail consortium Version 3.0 of the vCard specification has been approved as a proposed standard by the IETF. A companion specification known as vCalendar supports electronic exchange of scheduling information. *See also* vCalendar, X series.

VCOMM *n.* The communications device driver in Windows 9x that provides the interface between Windows-based applications and drivers on one side, and port drivers and modems on the other.

VDSL *n.* Short for **v**ery-high-speed **d**igital **s**ubscriber **l**ine. The high-speed version of the xDSL (digital subscriber line) communication technologies, all of which operate over existing phone lines. VDSL can deliver up to 52 Mbps downstream, but it is effective only within about 4500 to 5000 feet of the central exchange. The data delivery rate is, in fact, related to the distance the signal must travel. To attain a rate of 52 Mbps, for example, the subscriber must be within 1000 feet of the exchange office. At a distance of 3000 feet, the data rate drops to about 26 Mbps; and at 5000 feet, the data rate drops to about 13 Mbps. *See also* central office, xDSL.

Vector Markup Language *n. See* VML.

Veronica *n.* Acronym for very easy rodent-oriented Netwide index to computerized archives. An Internet service developed at the University of Nevada that searches for Gopher archives by keywords. Users can enter Boolean operators, such as AND, OR, and XOR, to help narrow or expand their search. If any matching archives are found, they are listed on a new Gopher menu. *See also* Gopher. *Compare* Archie, Jughead.

very-high-rate digital subscriber line *n. See* VDSL.

V.everything *n.* A marketing term used by some modem manufacturers to describe modems that comply with both the ITU-T (formerly CCITT) V.34 standard and the various proprietary protocols that were used before the standard was adopted, such as V.Fast Class. A V.everything modem should be compatible with any other modem that operates at the same speed. *See also* V.Fast Class, V series.

V.Fast Class *n.* A de facto modulation standard for modems implemented by Rockwell International prior to approval of the V.34 protocol, which is the standard. Although both V.Fast Class and V.34 are capable of 28.8-Kbps transmission, V.Fast Class modems cannot communicate with V.34 modems without an upgrade. *Acronym:* V.FC. *See also* V series.

VFAT *n.* Acronym for Virtual File Allocation Table. The file system driver software used under the Windows 9x Installable File System Manager (IFS) for accessing disks. VFAT is compatible with MS-DOS disks but runs more efficiently. VFAT uses 32-bit code, runs in protected mode, uses VCACHE for disk caching, and supports long filenames.

video conferencing *n.* Teleconferencing in which video images are transmitted among the various geographically separated participants in a meeting. Originally done using analog video and satellite links, today video conferencing uses compressed digital images transmitted over wide area networks or the Internet. A 56K communications channel supports freeze-frame video; with a 1.544-Mbps (T1) channel, full-motion video can be used. *See also* 56K, desktop conferencing, T1, teleconferencing. *Compare* data conferencing.

video server *n.* A server designed to deliver digital video-on-demand and other broadband interactive services to the public over a wide area network.

Vines *n.* A UNIX-based networking operating system from Banyan Systems.

virgule *n.* The forward slash (/) character.

virtual community *n. See* online community.

virtual hosting *n.* A form of hosting that provides a Web server, communication, and other services to customers for their own Web sites. In addition to hardware, software, and communication, virtual hosting can include assistance with domain name registration, e-mail addresses, and other Web-related issues. *See also* host, hosting.

Virtual Interface Architecture *n.* An interface specification that defines a standard low-latency, high-bandwidth means of communication between clusters of servers in a System Area Network (SAN). Developed by Compaq, Intel, Microsoft, and more than 100 industry groups, the Virtual Interface Architecture is processor and operating system independent. By reducing the time required for message-passing between applications and the network, it seeks to reduce overhead and thus deliver enterprise-level scalability for mission-critical applications. *Acronym:* VIA. *Also called:* VI Architecture. *See also* cluster, system area network.

virtual LAN *n.* Short for **virtual** local area network. A local area network consisting of groups of hosts that are on physically different segments but that communicate as though they were on the same wire. *See also* LAN.

virtual name space *n.* The set of all hierarchical sequences of names that can be used by an application to locate objects. One such sequence of names defines a path through the virtual name space, regardless of whether the hierarchy of names reflects the actual arrangement of objects around the system. For example, the virtual name space of a Web server consists of all possible URLs on the network on which it runs. *See also* URL.

virtual network *n.* A part of a network that appears to a user to be a network of its own. For example, an Internet service provider can set up multiple domains on a single HTTP server so that each one can be addressed with its company's registered domain name. *See also* domain name, HTTP server (definition 1), ISP.

virtual path *n.* **1.** A sequence of names that is used to locate a file and that has the same form as a pathname in the file system but is not necessarily the actual sequence of directory names under which the file is located. The part of a URL that follows the server name is a virtual path. For example, if the directory *c:\bar\sinister\forces\distance* on the server *miles* is shared on the local area network at *foo.com* under the name *\\miles\baz* and contains the file *elena.html*, that file may be returned by a Web request for *http://miles.foo.com/baz/elena.html*. **2.** In Asynchronous Transfer Mode (ATM), a set of virtual channels that are switched together as a unit through the network. *See also* ATM (definition 1).

virtual private network *n.* **1.** Nodes on a public network such as the Internet that communicate among themselves using encryption technology so that their messages are as safe from being intercepted and understood by unauthorized users as if the nodes were connected by private lines. **2.** A WAN (wide area network) formed of permanent virtual circuits (PVCs) on another network, especially a network using tech-

V

nologies such as ATM or frame relay. *Acronym:* VPN. *See also* ATM (definition 1), frame relay.

virtual reality *n.* A simulated 3-D environment that a user can experience and manipulate as if it were physical. The user sees the environment on display screens, possibly mounted in a special pair of goggles. Special input devices, such as gloves or suits fitted with motion sensors, detect the user's actions. *Acronym:* VR.

virtual root *n.* The root directory that a user sees when connected to an Internet server, such as an HTTP or FTP server. The virtual root is actually a pointer to the physical root directory, which may be in a different location, such as on another server. The advantages of using a virtual root include being able to create a simple URL for the Internet site and to move the root directory without affecting the URL. *Also called:* v-root. *See also* server (definition 2), URL.

virtual server *n.* A virtual machine that resides on an HTTP server but has the appearance to the user of being a separate HTTP server. Several virtual servers can reside on one HTTP server, each capable of running its own programs and each with individualized access to input and peripheral devices. Each virtual server has its own domain name and IP address and appears to the user as an individual Web site. Some Internet service providers use virtual servers for those clients who want to use their own domain names. *See also* domain name, HTTP server (definition 2), IP address.

virtual storefront *n.* A company's point of presence on the Web, providing opportunities for online sales. *Also called:* electronic storefront.

virus *n.* An intrusive program that infects computer files by inserting in those files copies of itself. The copies are usually executed when the file is loaded into memory, allowing the virus to infect still other files, and so on. Viruses often have damaging side effects—sometimes intentionally, sometimes not. For example, some viruses can destroy a computer's hard disk or take up memory space that could otherwise be used by programs. *See also* Good Times virus, Trojan horse, worm.

V

virus signature *n.* A portion of unique computer code contained in a virus. Antivirus programs search for known virus signatures to identify infected programs and files. *See also* virus.

visit *n.* A session during which a person views one or more pages in a Web site.

visitor *n.* A person who views a Web page or Web site.

Visor *n.* A product line of handheld personal digital assistants (PDAs) developed by Handspring Corporation. Features include an address list, an appointments calendar, a to-do list, and memos. Visor also features a 68-pin Springboard socket that allows plug-ins of additional devices offered by Handspring. *See also* Springboard.

Visual Basic *n.* A trademarked name owned by Microsoft Corporation for a high-level, visual-programming version of Basic. Visual Basic was designed for building Windows-based applications.

Visual C++ *n.* A Microsoft application development system for the programming language C++ that runs under MS-DOS and Windows. Visual C++ is a visual programming environment. *Compare* Visual Basic, Visual J++.

Visual Café *n.* The Java-based suite of software development tools from Symantec Corporation. Visual Café is available in several product packages. The Standard Edition, intended for beginning Java programmers, includes an integrated editor, debugger, and compiler, as well as a JavaBean library, wizards, and utilities. The Professional Edition provides a larger library of JavaBeans and more sophisticated tools for development and debugging. The Database Edition, as the name indicates, adds support for database functionality. The Enterprise Suite provides a high-end environment for development of enterprise applications. *See also* Java.

Visual FoxPro Database and Command Language *n.* A Microsoft product for developing database applications that includes a rich object-oriented programming language derived from the Xbase language.

Visual InterDev *n.* Microsoft's integrated development environment for Web applications. Visual InterDev includes tools for end-to-end (design through deployment) development, as well as integrated tools for database programming and design. The first version of Microsoft Visual InterDev was released in 1997.

Visual J++ *n.* Microsoft's Java visual programming environment, which can be used to create applets and applications in the Java language. *See also* applet, Java, Java applet.

Visual SourceSafe *n.* A project-oriented version control system designed by Microsoft to manage software and Web site development. Visual SourceSafe stores files in a secure repository that provides easy access to authorized users and tracks all changes made to files. Visual SourceSafe works with any type of file produced by any development language, authoring tool, or application.

Visual Studio *n.* Microsoft's suite of software development tools for rapid development of business applications and components. Visual Studio is provided in two editions. The Professional Edition, for professional programmers, includes the Visual Basic and Visual C++ languages, Visual FoxPro for database development, Visual InterDev for Web development, and Visual J++ for Java development. The Enterprise Edition, for enterprise-level development, also includes Visual SourceSafe (a team-based source code control system) and the Developer Edition of Microsoft BackOffice Server.

Visual Studio .NET *n.* A development environment for creating XML Web services and applications on the Microsoft .NET platform. *See also* .NET, .NET My Services.

VLAN *n. See* virtual LAN.

VML *n.* Acronym for **V**ector **M**arkup **L**anguage. An XML-based specification for the exchange, editing, and delivery of 2-D vector graphics on the Web. An application of XML (Extensible Markup Language), VML uses XML tags and cascading style sheets to create and place vector graphics, such as circles and squares, in an XML or

HTML document, such as a Web page. These graphics, which are rendered in the native operating system, can include color and are editable in a variety of graphics programs. *See also* cascading style sheets, XML.

VoATM *n.* Short for **V**oice **o**ver **A**synchronous **T**ransfer **M**ode. The transmission of voice and other telephony over an ATM network. *See also* ATM, VoFR, VoIP.

VoFR *n.* Short for **V**oice **o**ver **F**rame **R**elay. Voice transmission over a frame relay network. *See also* frame relay, VoATM, VoIP.

voice-capable modem *n.* A modem that can support voice messaging applications along with its data-handling functions.

voice chat *n.* A feature offered by Internet service providers (ISPs) that allows users to converse with each other directly through an Internet connection. *See also* Internet telephone.

voice mail *n.* A system that records and stores telephone messages in a computer's memory. Unlike a simple answering machine, a voice mail system has separate mailboxes for multiple users, each of whom can copy, store, or redistribute messages.

voice messaging *n.* A system that sends and receives messages in the form of sound recordings.

voice modem *n.* A modulation/demodulation device that supports a switch to change between telephony and data transmission modes. Such a device might contain a built-in loudspeaker and microphone for voice communication, but more often it uses the computer's sound card. *See also* modem, telephony.

voice navigation *n.* The use of spoken commands to control a Web browser. Voice navigation is a feature of some plug-in applications that embellish Web browsers to allow the user to navigate the Web by means of his or her voice. *See also* Web browser.

voice-net *n.* A term used on the Internet to refer to the telephone system, often preceding the user's telephone number in an e-mail signature.

Voice over Asynchronous Transfer Mode *n.* *See* VoATM.

Voice over Frame Relay *n.* *See* VoFR.

Voice over IP *n.* *See* VoIP.

VoIP *n.* Acronym for **V**oice **o**ver **IP**. The use of the Internet Protocol (IP) for transmitting voice communications. VoIP delivers digitized audio in packet form and can be used for transmitting over intranets, extranets, and the Internet. It is essentially an inexpensive alternative to traditional telephone communication over the circuit-switched Public Switched Telephone Network (PSTN). VoIP covers computer-to-computer, computer-to-telephone, and telephone-based communications. For the sake of compatibility and interoperability, a group called the VoIP Forum promotes product development based on the ITU-T H.323 standard for transmission of multimedia over the Internet. *Also called:* Internet telephony. *See also* H.323.

V

VON *n.* Acronym for **v**oice **o**n the **n**et. A broad category of hardware and software technology for real-time voice and video transmission over the Internet. The term was coined by Jeff Pulver, who formed a group called the VON Coalition, which opposes regulation of VON technology and promotes VON to the public.

VPN *n. See* virtual private network.

VRML *n.* Acronym for **V**irtual **R**eality **M**odeling **L**anguage. A scene description language for creating 3-D interactive Web graphics similar to those found in some video games, allowing the user to "move around" within a graphic image and interact with objects. VRML, a subset of Silicon Graphics' Inventor File Format (ASCII), was created in 1994. VRML files can be created in a text editor, although CAD packages, modeling and animation packages, and VRML authoring software are the tools preferred by most VRML authors. VRML files reside on an HTTP server; links to these files can be embedded in HTML documents, or users can access the VRML files directly. To view VRML Web pages, users need a VRML-enabled browser or a VRML plug-in for Internet Explorer or Netscape Navigator. *See also* HTML document, HTTP server (definition 1).

v-root *n. See* virtual root.

V series *n.* The series of ITU-T (formerly CCITT) recommendations relating to modems and modem communications over the public phone system, including signaling, coding, and circuit characteristics. See the table.

Table V.1   Recommendations in the V Series for Modem Communications.

Recommendation Number	What It Covers
V.17	14,000-bps two-wire modems used for facsimile applications
V.21	300-bps modems used with dial-up lines; full-duplex transmission; not the same as Bell 103 (in North America)
V.22	1200-bps modems used with dial-up and leased lines; full-duplex transmission; not the same as Bell 212A (in North America)
V.22bis	2400-bps modems used with dial-up and leased lines; full-duplex transmission
V.23	600/1200-bps synchronous or asynchronous modems used with dial-up and leased lines; half-duplex transmission
V.26	2400-bps modems used with four-wire leased lines; full-duplex transmission
V.26bis	1200/2400-bps modems used with dial-up lines; full-duplex transmission
V.26ter	2400-bps modems used with dial-up and two-wire leased lines; DPSK modulation; fallback to 1200 bps; echo canceling to remove phone-line echo; full-duplex transmission
V.27	4800-bps modems used with leased lines; manual equalizer; full-duplex transmission

Table V.1 Recommendations in the V Series for Modem Communications.

Recommendation Number	What It Covers
V.27bis	2400/4800-bps modems used with leased lines; automatic equalizer; full-duplex transmission
V.27ter	2400/4800-bps modems used with dial-up lines; full-duplex transmission
V.29	9600-bps modems used with point-to-point leased circuits; half-duplex transmission or full-duplex transmission
V.32	9600-bps modems used with dial-up lines; echo canceling to remove phone-line echo; full-duplex transmission
V.32bis	4800/7200/9600/12,000/14,400-bps modems used with dial-up lines; echo canceling; full-duplex transmission
V.33	12,000/14,400-bps modems used with four-wire leased lines; synchronous; QAM modulation; time-division multiplexing; full-duplex transmission
V.34	28,800-bps modems; full-duplex transmission
V.35	Group band modems, which combine the bandwidth of more than one telephone circuit
V.54	Operation of loop test devices in modems
V.56	Network transmission model for evaluating modem performance over standard voice-grade telephone connections
V.56bis	Network transmission model for evaluating modem performance over two-wire voice-grade connections
V.56ter	Network transmission model for evaluating modem performance over two-wire, 4-kilohertz duplex modems
V.61	4800-bps modems operating at voice plus data rate or 14,000-bps modems operating at data-only rate over standard switched telephone circuits or on point-to-point, two-wire phone circuits

V

W

w³ *n. See* World Wide Web.

W3 *n. See* World Wide Web.

W3C *n.* Abbreviation for the World Wide Web Consortium, a standards body based in the United States, Europe, and Japan. The W3C is dedicated (in part) to encouraging the development of open Web standards, such as the HTML and XML document markup languages, to promote interoperability and assist the Web in achieving its potential.

WAI *n.* Acronym for **W**eb **A**ccessibility **I**nitiative. A set of guidelines released by the World Wide Web Consortium (W3C) in May 1999. The WAI is intended to promote Web accessibility for users with disabilities by setting Web design and compatibility guidelines that help assure Web access and usability for all users.

WAIS *n.* Acronym for **W**ide **A**rea **I**nformation **S**erver. A UNIX-based document search and retrieval system on the Internet that can be used to search over 400 WAIS libraries, such as Project Gutenberg, for indexed files that match keywords entered by the user. WAIS can also be used on an individual Web site such as a search engine. WAIS, developed by Thinking Machines Corporation, Apple Computer, and Dow Jones, uses the Z39.50 standard to process natural language queries. The list of documents returned by WAIS often contains numerous false matches. Users need a WAIS client to use a WAIS server. *See also* Project Gutenberg, search engine, Z39.50 standard.

WAIS client *n.* The program needed for accessing the WAIS system to search its databases. A WAIS client program must be installed on a user's own machine or accessed from a computer with such a program already installed. Many freeware and shareware WAIS programs for various operating systems, including UNIX, MS-DOS, OS/2, and Windows, are available for download on the Internet. To look for documents in a WAIS database, the user selects the database(s) to search and types a query containing keywords to search for. The WAIS client sends this query to the server, communicating with the server via the Z39.50 protocol. The server processes the request using indexes and returns a list of document headlines matching the query to the client. The user can then choose which document to retrieve, send that request to the server, and receive the complete document in return. *See also* WAIS.

WAIS database *n. See* WAIS.

waisindex *n.* **1.** A UNIX utility for building an index to text files for access using WAIS (Wide Area Information Server) query software. **2.** A URL for accessing WAIS. The URL takes the form wais://*hostport/database*[? *search*].

WAIS library *n.* A WAIS (Wide Area Information Server) database. A WAIS library is a comprehensive collection of online documents on a specific topic—for example, Project Gutenberg's collection of public-domain literary and historical texts available over the Internet, and the Dow Jones Information Service collection of business and financial information products. Because the hundreds of WAIS free libraries currently accessible are updated and maintained by volunteers, the quality of topic coverage is uneven. *See also* WAIS, WAIS client, Project Gutenberg.

WAIS server or **waisserver** *n. See* WAIS.

wallet *n.* In electronic commerce, a software program that contains a user's address and credit card information for use in paying for online purchases. When the wallet is opened at the electronic checkout, it identifies the user to the merchant's server and allows the user to authorize the appropriate debit to a credit card.

WAN *n.* Acronym for **w**ide **a**rea **n**etwork. A geographically widespread network, one that relies on communications capabilities to link the various network segments. A WAN can be one large network, or it can consist of a number of linked LANs (local area networks).

wanderer *n.* A person who frequently uses the World Wide Web. Many of these people make indexes of what they find.

WAP *n. See* Wireless Application Protocol.

war dialer *n.* A computer program that calls a range of phone numbers to identify those numbers that make a connection to a computer modem. War dialers are typically used by hackers to search for vulnerable computers and, once a connection is made, the war dialers may automatically probe the computer for potential weaknesses. Early war dialer programs called demon dialers were used to crack telephone systems in the 1970s and 1980s.

warez *n.* Illegal copies of computer software distributed through the Internet and other online channels, such as bulletin boards and FTP servers. The spelling is part of the tendency among some online groups to use odd symbols and intentional misspellings. *Compare* freeware, shareware.

WBEM *n.* Acronym for **W**eb-**B**ased **E**nterprise **M**anagement. A protocol that links a Web browser directly to a device or an application that monitors a network. *See also* communications protocol.

W

web *n.* A set of interlinked documents in a hypertext system. The user enters the web through a home page. *See also* World Wide Web.

Web *n. See* World Wide Web.

Web Accessibility Initiative *n. See* WAI.

Web address *n. See* URL.

Web application *n.* A set of clients and servers that cooperate to provide the solution to a problem.

Web architect *n.* An individual who analyzes the purpose of a Web site and forms a plan for assembling and integrating the hardware, software, and other technical resources necessary to make the site function properly.

Web author *n.* A person who creates content for the World Wide Web. A Web author might be a writer who produces text for a designer to include in a Web page, or a Web designer who writes the text and also adds graphic elements and prepares the HTML code.

Web-Based Enterprise Management *n. See* WBEM.

Web browser *n.* Software that lets a user view HTML documents and access files and software related to those documents. Originally developed to allow users to view or browse documents on the World Wide Web, Web browsers can blur the distinction between local and remote resources for the user by also providing access to documents on a network, an intranet, or the local hard drive. Web browser software is built on the concept of hyperlinks, which allow users to point and click with a mouse in order to jump from document to document in whatever order they desire. Most Web browsers are also capable of downloading and transferring files, providing access to newsgroups, displaying graphics embedded in the document, playing audio and video files associated with the document, and executing small programs, such as Java applets or ActiveX controls included by programmers in the documents. Helper applications or plug-ins are required by some Web browsers to accomplish one or more of these tasks. *Also called:* browser. *See also* ActiveX control, helper application, hyperlink, Internet Explorer, Java applet, Lynx, Mosaic, Netscape Navigator, plug-in.

Web bug *n.* A small, nearly undetectable graphic that links to a Web page and is embedded in a document for use as an eavesdropping device. A Web bug usually takes the form of a 1-by-1-pixel transparent GIF file, so it is nearly invisible. This file is placed in a Web page, Microsoft Word file, or other document that users will access. The application in which the document is opened immediately links to the Web to download and display the embedded graphic. Information about the user, including IP address, browser, referrer, and time viewed, is passed to the author of the file when the application retrieves the invisible graphic information.

W

Webby Award *n.* Award bestowed annually by the International Academy of Digital Arts and Sciences to Web sites. The academy bestows awards to Web sites in more than 20 categories, which include technical achievement, humor, and best community site.

Web cam or **webcam** *n.* A video camera whose output appears on a Web page, usually updated on a regular and frequent schedule. Web cams are used to display weather and traffic conditions, to allow customers and other users to observe current activities at the site owner's business or home (for example, at a day care center), for promotional purposes, and as a form of "gee whiz, look at this!" entertainment.

webcast[1] *n.* Live or delayed audio or video programming delivered to users over the Web. Downloading these broadcasts requires a user to have the appropriate video or audio application, such as RealPlayer. The necessary application is usually available from the webcaster without cost.

webcast[2] *vb.* To produce and disseminate Web-based audio, video, and text programming.

webcaster *n.* A company or organization that produces and disseminates Web-based audio, video, and text programming.

webcasting *n.* Popular term for broadcasting information via the World Wide Web, using push and pull technologies to move selected information from a server to a client. An emergent technology in 1997, webcasting was developed to provide users with customized content—for example, sports, news, stocks, and weather—that can be updated both regularly and automatically. Webcasting gives users the ability to specify the type of content they want to see, and it gives content providers a means of delivering such information directly to the user's desktop. *Also called:* netcasting. *See also* pull, push[2] (definition 2).

Web clipping *n.* A Web service that delivers brief snippets of information to hand-held Web-enabled devices, such as wireless phones and personal digital assistants. Rather than opening a Web site and browsing for information, Web clipping allows a customer to request specific types of information from a service. The Web clipping service then downloads the information to the handheld device.

web CLUT *n. See* browser CLUT.

Web container *n.* A container that implements the Web component contract of Sun Microsystems's Java 2 Platform Enterprise Edition (J2EE) network architecture. This contract specifies a run time environment for Web components that includes security, concurrency, life cycle management, transaction, deployment, and other services. Provided by a Web or J2EE server, a Web container provides the same services as a JavaServer Pages (JSP) container and provides a federated view of the J2EE platform APIs. *See also* application programming interface, container (definition 3), J2EE, JSP container, servlet container.

Web cramming *n.* A common form of fraud in which Internet Service Providers (ISPs) add charges to the monthly bill for fictitious services or for services the customer had been told were free.

WebCrawler *n.* A World Wide Web search engine operated by America Online. *See also* search engine.

W

WebDAV *n.* Short for **Web D**istributed **A**uthoring and Versioning. A set of extensions to the HTTP protocol that allows users to collaboratively edit, publish, and manage resources on the World Wide Web. WebDAV-enabled additions to HTTP include document writing, editing, and publishing tools and search, storage, and file sharing options.

Web development *n.* The design and coding of World Wide Web pages.

Web directory *n.* A list of Web sites, giving the URL and a description of each. *See also* URL.

Web Distributed Authoring and Versioning *n. See* WebDAV.

Web Forms *n.* The ASP.NET page framework, which consists of programmable Web pages (called Web Forms pages) that contain reusable server controls. *See also* ASP.NET server control.

Web hosting *n. See* hosting.

Web index *n.* A Web site intended to enable a user to locate other resources on the Web. The Web index may include a search facility or may merely contain individual hyperlinks to the resources indexed.

Weblication *n.* Slang for Web application. *See* Web application.

Weblog or **weblog** or **web log** *n.* A Web site that has regularly updated content reflecting the interests of the site's host. Often, but not always, the content is in journal form, has highlights of news and information from other Web sites, and is presented from a personal point of view. On some sites, the Weblog is a collaboration between visitors to the site. The high-tech-oriented Slashdot.org is frequently cited as being among the best-known Weblogs.

Webmaster or **webmaster** *n.* A person responsible for creating and maintaining a World Wide Web site. A Webmaster is often responsible for responding to e-mail, ensuring the site is operating properly, creating and updating Web pages, and maintaining the overall structure and design of the site. *Also called:* webmistress, webweaver.

webmistress *n. See* Webmaster.

webographics *n.* Demographics of Web users specifically focusing on surfing and online shopping habits and on other related information, such as connection method, browser, and platform.

WebPad *n.* A class of wireless Internet appliances offering full Internet and personal digital assistant (PDA) functions. A WebPad features a larger LCD screen than other handheld communications devices and resembles a tablet.

Web page *n.* A document on the World Wide Web. A Web page consists of an HTML file, with associated files for graphics and scripts, in a particular directory on a particular machine (and thus identifiable by a URL). Usually a Web page contains links to other Web pages. *See also* URL.

W

Web page embedding *n.* Embedding a digital streaming media player directly onto a Web page using HTML code. Rather than displaying a hyperlink to the media file, Web page embedding uses browser plug-ins to present the media player as a visual element in the layout of the Web page.

Web phone *n. See* Internet telephone.

Web Presence Provider *n.* A Web hosting and Internet service provider who manages the Web server hardware and software required to make a Web site available on the Internet. *Acronym:* WPP.

Web rage *n.* **1.** Anger or frustration related to the use or operation of the Internet. **2.** An intemperate, rude, or angry posting on the Internet; a flame. **3.** The latest fad to gain popularity among Web users.

websafe palette *n. See* browser CLUT.

Web server *n. See* HTTP server.

Web server control *n.* An ASP.NET server control that belongs to the System.Web.UI.WebControls namespace. Web server controls are richer and more abstract than HTML server controls. A Web server control has an <asp:ControlName> prefix on an ASP.NET page. *See also* ASP.NET server control, HTML server control, namespace.

Web services *n.* A modular collection of Web protocol–based applications that can be mixed and matched to provide business functionality through an Internet connection. Web services can be used over the Internet or an intranet to create products, business processes, and B2B interactions. Web services use standard Internet protocols such as HTTP, XML, and SOAP to provide connectivity and interoperability between companies.

Web Services Description Language *n. See* WSDL.

Web site *n.* A group of related HTML documents and associated files, scripts, and databases that is served up by an HTTP server on the World Wide Web. The HTML documents in a Web site generally cover one or more related topics and are interconnected through hyperlinks. Most Web sites have a home page as their starting point, which frequently functions as a table of contents for the site. Many large organizations, such as corporations, will have one or more HTTP servers dedicated to a single Web site. However, an HTTP server can also serve several small Web sites, such as those owned by individuals. Users need a Web browser and an Internet connection to access a Web site. *See also* home page, HTML, HTTP server (definition 1), Web browser.

Web Storage System *n.* The storage component of Exchange 2000 Server and SharePoint Portal servers, which integrates Web server, database, file system, and workgroup functionality. The Web Storage System lets you store and share many types of data in a single integrated system. *Acronym:* WSS.

Web switch *n.* A network device—a switch—designed to optimize Web traffic routing by using the information embedded in HTTP requests to route the requests to the most appropriate servers, no matter where they are located. Web switches are intended to address issues of speed, scalability, and performance for high-volume Web sites. *See also* switch.

W

Web terminal *n.* A system containing a central processing unit (CPU), RAM, a high-speed modem or other means of connecting to the Internet, and powerful video graphics, but no hard disk, intended to be used solely as a client to the World Wide Web rather than as a general-purpose computer. *Also called:* network computer.

Web-to-host *n.* A service that allows remote users to access programs and data on legacy or mainframe systems through a Web browser. Web-to-host packages typically include a combination of services such as emulation support, legacy access, centralized management, host services, and security options, with some degree of customization possible. *See also* mainframe computer.

WebTV *n.* A system that provides consumers with the ability to access the Web as well as send and receive e-mail on a television by means of a set-top box equipped with a modem. Users must have an ISP (Internet service provider) and subscribe to the WebTV Network. Developed by WebTV Networks, WebTV was purchased by Microsoft in 1996.

webweaver *n. See* Webmaster.

webzine *n.* An electronic publication distributed primarily through the World Wide Web, rather than as an ink-on-paper magazine. *See also* e-zine.

weighted fair queuing *n.* A technique used to improve quality of service that prioritizes each session flow passing through a network device. With weighted fair queuing, high-bandwidth traffic is given a smaller proportion of network capacity than low-bandwidth traffic. *Acronym:* WFQ. *Compare* fair queuing.

welcome page *n. See* home page.

WELL *n.* Acronym for **W**hole **E**arth 'Lectronic **L**ink. A conferencing system based in San Francisco, California, that is accessible through the Internet and through dial-up access points in many major cities. The WELL attracts many computer professionals, along with other people who enjoy participating in one of the Internet's most successful virtual communities. Because of the number of journalists and other prominent people who participate in the WELL, it has substantial influence beyond its own relatively small number of subscribers.

well-formed *n.* An XML or HTML document that follows all the rules of syntax outlined in the protocol's specification. A well-formed XML or HTML document can be read by all Web browsers without difficulty.

WEP *n.* Acronym for **W**ired **E**quivalent **P**rivacy. An encryption algorithm system included as part of the 802.11 standard, developed by the Institute of Electrical and Electronics Engineers as a security measure to protect wireless LANs from casual eavesdropping. WEP uses a shared secret key to encrypt packets before transmission between wireless LAN devices and monitors packets in transit to detect attempts at modification. WEP offers both 40-bit and 128-bit hardware-based encryption options.

WFQ *n. See* weighted fair queuing.

whatis *n.* **1.** A UNIX utility for obtaining a summary of a keyword's documentation. **2.** An Archie command for locating software whose description contains desired words.

What You See Is What You Get *adj. See* WYSIWYG.

Whistler *n.* The code name for Microsoft Windows XP that was used during its development cycle. New visual and operational features are designed to make Windows XP easy for the home user to operate. Features include real-time voice, video and application sharing, enhanced mobility, added support for digital photos and video, and download and playback of high-quality audio and video content. Like Microsoft Windows 2000, Windows XP was developed from Windows NT, consolidating consumer and business operating systems into a single code base.

whiteboard *n.* Software that allows multiple users across a network to work together on a document that is simultaneously displayed on all the users' screens, as though they are all gathered around a physical whiteboard.

Whiteboard *n.* Microsoft NetMeeting feature that opens a separate window in which multiple users can simultaneously review, create, and update graphic information. The Whiteboard is object-oriented, not pixel-oriented, allowing participants to manipulate the contents by clicking and dragging with the mouse. In addition, they can use a remote pointer or highlighting tool to point out specific contents or sections of shared pages. The NetMeeting Whiteboard is T.126 compliant and is interoperable with other T.126-compatible whiteboards.

white hat *n.* A hacker who operates without malicious intent. A white hat will not break into a system with the intention of doing damage. White hats may be employed to provide security against other hackers. *See also* hacker. *Compare* black hat.

white pages *n. See* DIB.

whois *n.* **1.** An Internet service, provided by some domains, that enables a user to find e-mail addresses and other information for users listed in a database at that domain. **2.** A UNIX command to access the whois service. **3.** A command that displays a list of all users logged onto a Novell network.

whois client *n.* A program (such as the UNIX whois command) that enables a user to access databases of usernames, e-mail addresses, and other information. *See also* whois (definition 1).

whois server *n.* Software that provides the usernames and e-mail addresses from a database (often listing people who have accounts at an Internet domain) to users who request the information using whois clients. *See also* whois (definition 1).

Whole Earth 'Lectronic Link *n. See* WELL.

WID *n.* Acronym for **W**ireless **I**nformation **D**evice. Smart phone or other handheld wireless device capable of multiple communications functions, including e-mail and Internet access.

Wide Area Information Server *n. See* WAIS.

wide area network *n. See* WAN.

wideband transmission *n. See* broadband network.

Wide SCSI *n.* A form of the SCSI-2 interface that can transfer data 16 bits at a time at up to 20 megabytes per second. The Wide SCSI connector has 68 pins. *Also called:* Wide SCSI-2. *See also* SCSI, SCSI-2. *Compare* Fast SCSI, Fast/Wide SCSI.

Wide SCSI-2 *n. See* Wide SCSI.

Windows *n.* An operating system introduced by Microsoft Corporation in 1983. Windows is a multitasking graphical user interface environment that runs on MS-DOS–based computers (Windows 3.x. and Windows for Workgroups), and as a self-contained operating

W

system for desktop computers (Windows 9x and Windows Me), workstations (Windows NT Workstation, Windows 2000 Professional), and network servers (Windows NT Server, Windows NT Enterprise Edition, Windows 2000 Server, and Windows 2000 Advanced Server). The most recent versions of Windows are Windows XP Home (home and entertainment use) and Professional (advanced computing, businesses, large organizations). The next generation of Windows server products will be the Windows .NET Server family. Windows provides a standard graphical interface based on drop-down menus, windowed regions on the screen, and a pointing device such as a mouse.

Windows 9x *n.* The architecture upon which Windows 95 and Windows 98 were built.

Windows 2000 *n.* A Microsoft operating system, the successor to Windows NT, designed for business rather than consumer use. Like its predecessor, Windows 2000 is a multithreaded, multitasking 32-bit operating system. Implemented in desktop and several server versions, Windows 2000 focuses overall on improved ease of use, networking, management, reliability, scalability, and security. See the table.

Table W.1 ATA Specifications.

Version	Designed For	Features
Windows 2000 Professional	Business desktop	Improvements in: Ease of use; security, performance, and reliability; support for mobile computing
Windows 2000 Server	Small to medium-sized deployments—workgroups, branch offices, departmental application, file, print servers	Two-way symmetric multiprocessing (SMP); ActiveDirectory; management tools; Kerberos and PKI security; COM+; Windows Terminal Support; improved Internet services
Windows 2000 Advanced Server	Mid-range departmental and application deployments	Windows 2000 Server features, plus four-way SMP; load balancing; clustering; high-performance sorting; 64-GB physical memory
Windows 2000 Datacenter Server	Large operations—data warehouses, online transaction processing (OLTP), science and engineering simulations, enterprise solutions	Windows 2000 Advanced Server features, plus 16-way SMP

Windows 2000 Advanced Server *n.* Microsoft's network server for larger organizations. Designed to replace Windows NT 4 Enterprise Edition, it supports up to four-way SMP, large physical memories, and database-intensive work. It integrates clustering and load balancing support. *See also* SMP, Windows.

Windows 2000 Datacenter Server *n.* Microsoft's network server for larger organizations. Considered the most powerful and functional server operating system ever offered by Microsoft, it supports up to 16-way SMP and up to 64 GB of physical memory (depending on system architecture). Like Windows 2000 Advanced Server, it provides both clustering and load balancing services as standard features. It is optimized for large data warehouses, econometric analysis, large-scale simulations in science and engineering, OLTP, and server consolidation projects. *See also* OLTP, SMP, Windows.

Windows 2000 Professional *n.* Microsoft's mainstream desktop operating system for businesses of all sizes. Designed to replace Windows NT Workstation 4, which many people are using today as the standard business desktop, Windows 2000 Professional builds upon the interface and kernel in NT 4. It also includes improved security, state-of-the-art features for mobile users, industrial-strength reliability, and better performance.

Windows 2000 Server *n.* Microsoft's network server for small to medium businesses. Designed to replace Windows NT 4 Server, Windows 2000 Server offers improved functionality and supports new systems with up to two-way symmetric multiprocessing (SMP).

Windows CE *n.* A small operating system from Microsoft designed for use with handheld and palm-size PCs and in embedded systems, such as the AutoPC. Windows CE, which has a user interface that is similar to Windows 9x and Windows NT, includes scaled-down versions of several Microsoft applications, including Excel, Word, Internet Explorer, Schedule+, and an e-mail client.

Windows Distributed interNet Applications Architecture *n. See* Windows DNA.

Windows DNA *n.* Short for Microsoft **Windows D**istributed inter**N**et **A**pplications Architecture. A framework introduced in 1997 as a means of integrating client/server and Web technologies in the creation of scalable, multitier applications delivered over an enterprise network. Windows DNA is based on a number of technologies, among them COM (Component Object Model), ActiveX, and dynamic HTML.

W

Windows Explorer *n.* A utility in Windows that enables the user to locate and open files and folders. Windows Explorer resembles the File Manager of Windows 3.1. The user can select folders from a list displayed on the left side of the screen and access files in a selected folder from a list displayed on the right side of the screen.

Windows Foundation Classes *n.* A Java class library for developing Java applications to run in the Windows environment. Designed by Microsoft to make it easy to write code for the Windows platform using the powerful Java programming language, the Windows Foundation Classes represent an object-oriented framework that encapsulates and unifies the Microsoft Win32 API and Dynamic HTML programming models. This framework enables developers to link Java code directly to Windows APIs. *Acronym:* WFC. *See also* Java, Java Foundation Classes.

Windows IP Configuration *n. See* Winipcfg.

Windows Me *n.* Released in 2000, the Windows Millennium Edition (Windows Me) operating system designed for home users as an upgrade from Windows 95 or Windows 98. Windows Me offers an improved home user experience including making it easier for users to share and manipulate digital photos, music, and videos, enhanced home networking capabilities, a rich Internet experience with support for broadband connections, different Internet communication tools, and online gaming.

Windows Media Player *n.* A client/control that receives a stream from a Windows Media server or local content for playback. It can run as a stand-alone client executable program. Windows Media Player can also be embedded in a Web page, a C++ program, or a Microsoft Visual Basic program that uses the client ActiveX control.

Windows Media server *n.* A server on which Windows Media Services has been installed.

Windows Media Services *n.* A digital media platform that runs on a server, such as Windows 2000, to support streaming media, such as video and audio.

Windows Media Technologies *n.* Microsoft technologies for the creation, delivery, and playing of streaming audio and video over a network, including both intranets and the Internet. Windows Media Technologies, downloadable from the Microsoft Web site, support both live and on-demand (delivered from storage) content and are based on files delivered in Advanced Streaming Format (ASF). Three major components—Windows Media Tools, Windows Media Services, and Windows Media Player—comprise Windows Media Technologies. See the table. *See also* Advanced Streaming Format. *Compare* RealSystem G2.

Table W.2   ATA Specifications.

Component	Purpose	Features
Windows Media Tools	Content creation	ASF authoring and editing tools, including tools for converting files from other formats (WAV, AVI, MPEG, and MP3) to ASF.
Windows Media Services	Content delivery	Tools for real-time and on-demand content delivery, administration tools, and Windows Media Rights Manager for piracy control.
Windows Media Player for PC platforms, Windows Media Player for Macintosh, Windows Media Player for UNIX	Content playback	ASF player for audio, audio plus still images, and full-motion video. Also supports other multimedia data, including RealAudio.

Windows Messenger *n. See* .NET Messenger Service.

Windows Metafile Format *n.* A graphics file format used by Windows to store vector graphics in order to exchange graphics information between applications and to store information between sessions. *Acronym:* WMF.

Windows Movie Maker *n.* Software from Microsoft for capturing, editing, and arranging audio and video source material to create movies. *Acronym:* WMM.

Windows .NET Server *n.* The next generation of Windows servers. Built on Windows 2000, the Windows .NET Server family includes the functionality, dependability, scalability, and security options to serve as the computing foundation for businesses of all sizes. The flexible computing architecture, built on industry standards, allows businesses to create robust and innovative applications, improve collaboration across the organization, and connect securely with customers.

Windows NT *n.* An operating system released by Microsoft Corporation in 1993. The Windows NT operating system, sometimes referred to as simply NT, is the high-end member of a family of operating systems from Microsoft. It is a completely self-contained operating system with a built-in graphical user interface. Windows NT is a 32-bit, preemptive multitasking operating system that features networking, symmetric multiprocessing, multithreading, and security. It is a portable operating system that can run on a variety of hardware platforms including those based on the Intel 80386, i486, and Pentium microprocessors and MIPS microprocessors; it can also run on multiprocessor computers. Windows NT supports up to 4 gigabytes of virtual memory and can run MS-DOS, POSIX, and OS/2 (character-mode) applications. *See also* Windows.

Windows NT Advanced Server *n.* A superset of Windows NT that provides centralized, domain-based network management and security. Windows NT Advanced Server also offers advanced hard disk fault-tolerance features, such as mirroring and additional connectivity. *See also* Windows NT.

Windows NT Embedded *n.* A version of the Microsoft Windows NT operating system designed for devices and other products that have embedded systems. Windows NT Embedded, released in 1999, targets devices in the midrange to high end of the embedded device industry, including high-speed copiers, patient monitors, private branch exchanges (PBXs), and point-of-sale terminals. Windows NT Embedded features include headless operation (with no keyboard, mouse, or display devices needed), diskless operation, and remote management infrastructure. *See also* Windows NT.

Windows Open Services Architecture *n. See* WOSA.

Windows Open System Architecture *n. See* WOSA.

Windows Script Host *n.* The language-independent scripting host for Microsoft Windows platforms. Windows Script Host is a tool that allows users to run VBScript, JScript, or any other scripting language to automate common tasks and to create macros and logon scripts.

W

Windows Sockets *n. See* Winsock.

Windows terminal *n.* A thin-client solution from Microsoft, designed to enable terminals and minimally configured computers to display Windows applications even if they are not, in themselves, capable of running Windows software. Windows terminals work in conjunction with Windows NT Server, Terminal Server edition. *See also* thin client.

Windows XP *n.* A member of the Microsoft Windows family of operating systems. Windows XP was released in 2001 in two versions: Windows XP Home Edition for home use and Windows XP Professional for advanced home computing, businesses, and larger organizations. Windows XP features a new visual design that simplifies navigation and search capabilities, improved file management, additional media and Web publishing capabilities, an improved system for device discovery and installation, and advanced features for mobile computing.

Winipcfg *n.* Short for **Win**dows **IP** **C**onfiguration. A Windows 9x utility that enables users to access information about their TCP/IP (Transmission Control Protocol/Internet Protocol) and network adapter card settings. Running the Winipcfg program (winipcfg.exe) opens the IP Configuration window, which reveals the physical address, IP address, subnet mask, and default gateway settings of the primary TCP/IP adapter (or settings of multiple adapters if more than one is installed). This information is also helpful for troubleshooting. *See also* TCP/IP.

WINS *n.* Acronym for **W**indows **I**nternet **N**aming **S**ervice. A Windows NT Server method for associating a computer's host name with its address. *Also called:* INS, Internet Naming Service. *Compare* DNS (definition 1).

Winsock *n.* Short for **Win**dows **Sock**ets. An application programming interface standard for software that provides a TCP/IP interface under Windows. The Winsock standard developed out of a Birds of a Feather (BOF) discussion that arose among software vendors at a UNIX conference in 1991; it has gained the general support of software developers, including Microsoft. *See also* application programming interface, BOF, socket (definition 1), sockets API, TCP/IP.

W

wired *adj.* **1.** Of, pertaining to, or characteristic of an electronic circuit or hardware grouping in which the configuration is determined by the physical interconnection of the components (as opposed to being programmable in software or alterable by a switch). *See also* hardwired (definition 1). **2.** Knowledgeable about Internet resources, systems, and culture. **3.** Having access to the Internet.

Wired Equivalent Privacy *n. See* WEP.

wired home *n. See* smart home.

wireless *adj.* Of, pertaining to, or characteristic of communications that take place without the use of interconnecting wires or cables, such as by radio, microwave, or infrared light.

Wireless Application Protocol *n.* A specification for a global standard for enabling digital cellular phones and other wireless devices to access Internet and other information services. The Wireless Application Protocol, or WAP, is supported by an organization known as WAP Forum, which includes such members as Motorola, Nokia, L. M. Ericsson, and Unwired Planet. The goal of the forum is to create an open standard that works with different wireless technologies. *Acronym:* WAP.

wireless communication *n.* Communication between a computer and another computer or device without wires. The form of wireless communication provided as part of the Windows operating system uses infrared light to transmit files. Radio frequencies, as used by cellular and cordless telephones, are another form of wireless communication. *See also* infrared, infrared device, infrared port.

Wireless Information Device *n. See* WID.

wireless Internet *n.* Version of the Internet designed for use on wireless phones and handheld devices with small display screens, limited memory, and slower data transmission speeds than a personal computer. Most wireless Internet sites offer content as basic text with limited graphics.

wireless LAN *n.* A LAN (local area network) that sends and receives data via radio, infrared optical signaling, or some other technology that does not require a physical connection between individual nodes and the hub. Wireless LANs are often used in office or factory settings where a user must carry a portable computer from place to place. *Also called:* WLAN.

Wireless Markup Language *n. See* WML.

Wireless Multimedia Forum *n. See* WMF (definition 2).

wireless phone *n.* Telephone that operates by means of radio waves without a wire connection. A base station (cell tower) relays the phone's signal to a wireless carrier's network, where it is transmitted to another wireless phone or to a wired telephone network.

Wireless Services server component *n.* A component that allows a content provider or carrier to configure and schedule any number of information acquisition/encoding/transmission components to create a data stream to be transmitted by a carrier to a device. The server component builds on an open architecture to allow new server components to be installed in any part of the stream at any time.

Wireless Transaction Protocol *n.* A lightweight request/reply transaction protocol for devices with limited resources over networks with low to medium bandwidth. It is not called the Wireless Transport Protocol or the Wireless Transfer Protocol. *Acronym:* WTP.

Wireless Transport Layer Security *n. See* WTLS.

wiring closet *n.* A room or location in a building where telecommunications and/or networking equipment such as hubs, switches, and routers are installed. *Also called:* data closet, telecom closet, telecommunications closet.

W

wizard *n.* **1.** Someone who is adept at making computers perform their "magic." A wizard is an outstanding and creative programmer or a power user. *Compare* UNIX wizard. **2.** A participant in a multiuser dungeon (MUD) who has permission to control the domain, even to delete other players' characters. *See also* MUD.

wizzywig *n. See* WYSIWYG.

WLAN *n. See* wireless LAN.

.wmf *n.* A file extension that identifies a vector image encoded as a Microsoft Windows Metafile.

WMF *n.* **1.** *See* Windows Metafile Format. **2.** Acronym for **W**ireless **M**ultimedia **F**orum. A consortium of technology companies formed to promote open standards for wireless streaming products. WMF members include Cisco Systems, Intel, and the Walt Disney Internet Group. *See also* ISMA.

WML *n.* Acronym for **W**ireless **M**arkup **L**anguage. A markup language developed for Web sites that are accessed with microbrowsers on Wireless Application Protocol (WAP)–enabled devices. A Web site written with WML would be viewable on handheld devices with small screens, such as cell phones. *See also* markup language, microbrowser, Wireless Application Protocol.

WMLScript *n.* A scripting language derived from the JavaScript language for use in the development of Wireless Markup Language (WML).

Word *n.* Microsoft's word processing software, available for the Windows and Macintosh platforms. In addition to extensive editing, formatting, and customization features, Word provides such tools as automatic text completion and correction. The most recent version, Word 2002 (part of Office XP) adds Web functionality—for example, the ability to save documents in HTML format. The first version, Microsoft Word for MS-DOS 1.00, was introduced in 1983.

WordPerfect Office *n.* A suite of business application programs from Corel Corporation. The basic (Standard Edition) WordPerfect Office suite includes the WordPerfect word processor, Quattro Pro spreadsheet, Corel Presentations presentation software, CorelCENTRAL personal information manager, Microsoft Visual Basic for Applications scripting tools, and Trellix Web publisher. A home and small-business package, the Voice-Powered Edition, adds speech recognition and publishing products; a business and corporate package, the Professional Edition, adds database and Internet tools to all of the preceding.

workgroup *n.* A group of users working on a common project and sharing computer files, typically over a LAN (local area network). *See also* groupware.

workgroup computing *n.* A method of working electronically in which various individuals on the same project share resources and access to files using a network arrangement, such as a local area network, enabling them to coordinate their separate tasks. This is accomplished through using software designed for workgroup computing. *See also* groupware.

workstation *n.* **1.** A combination of input, output, and computing hardware that can be used for work by an individual. **2.** A powerful stand-alone computer of the sort used in computer-aided design and other applications requiring a high-end, usually expensive, machine with considerable calculating or graphics capability. **3.** A microcomputer or terminal connected to a network.

World Wide Web *n.* The total set of interlinked hypertext documents residing on HTTP servers all around the world. Documents on the World Wide Web, called pages or Web pages, are written in HTML (Hypertext Markup Language), identified by URLs (Uniform Resource Locators) that specify the particular machine and pathname by which a file can be accessed, and transmitted from server to end user under HTTP (Hypertext Transfer Protocol). Codes, called tags, embedded in an HTML document associate particular words and images in the document with URLs so that a user can access another file, which may be halfway around the world, at the press of a key or the click of a mouse. These files may contain text (in a variety of fonts and styles), graphics images, movie files, and sounds as well as Java applets, ActiveX controls, or other small embedded software programs that execute when the user activates them by clicking a link. A user visiting a Web page also may be able to download files from an FTP site and send messages to other users via e-mail by using links on the Web page. The World Wide Web was developed by Timothy Berners-Lee in 1989 for the European Laboratory for Particle Physics, or Conseil Européen pour le Recherche Nucléaire, in French (CERN). *Acronym:* WWW. *Also called:* w[3], W3, Web. *See also* ActiveX control, HTML, HTTP, HTTP server (definition 2), Java applet, URL.

World Wide Web Consortium *n. See* W3C.

worm *n.* A program that propagates itself across computers, usually by creating copies of itself in each computer's memory. A worm might duplicate itself in one computer so often that it causes the computer to crash. Sometimes written in separate segments, a worm is introduced surreptitiously into a host system either as a prank or with the intent of damaging or destroying information. *See also* bacterium, Internet Worm, Trojan horse, virus.

W

WOSA *n.* Acronym for **W**indows **O**pen **S**ervices **A**rchitecture, also known as **W**indows **O**pen **S**ystem **A**rchitecture. A set of application programming interfaces from Microsoft that is intended to enable Windows-based applications from different vendors to communicate with each other, such as over a network. The interfaces within the WOSA standard include Open Database Connectivity (ODBC), the Messaging Application Programming Interface (MAPI), the Telephony Application Programming Interface (TAPI), Windows Sockets (Winsock), and Microsoft Remote Procedure Calls (RPC). *See also* MAPI, ODBC, remote procedure call, TAPI, Winsock.

.wrl *n.* File extension required for saving all Virtual Reality Modeling Language (VRML) documents; for example, cube.wrl. *See also* VRML.

WSDL *n.* Acronym for **W**eb **S**ervices **D**escription **L**anguage. An XML format developed to allow for better interoperability among Web services and development tools. WSDL describes network services as collections of communication endpoints capable of exchanging messages and is extensible to allow description of endpoints and their messages regardless of what message formats or network protocols are used to communicate.

WTLS *n.* Acronym for **W**ireless **T**ransport **L**ayer **S**ecurity. A security protocol that provides encryption and authentication services for the Wireless Application Protocol (WAP). The WTLS layer uses data integrity, authentication, and encryption mechanisms to provide end-to-end security and privacy for wireless transactions. WTLS is based on Transport Layer Security (TLS), a Secure Socket Layer equivalent used with Internet applications. *See also* Wireless Application Protocol.

WWW *n. See* World Wide Web.

WYSIWYG *adj.* Acronym for **W**hat **Y**ou **S**ee **I**s **W**hat **Y**ou **G**et, pronounced "wizzywig." Allowing a user to view a document as it will appear in the final product, and to directly edit the text, graphics, or other elements within that view. A WYSIWYG language is often easier to use than a markup language, which provides no immediate visual feedback regarding the changes being made. *Compare* markup language.

W

X

X10 *n.* A popular communications protocol for powerline carrier (PLC) systems that uses existing electrical wiring in a home or building for home networking. X10 uses RF signals to communicate between transmitters and receivers. *See also* home automation, home network.

X.200 *n. See* X series.

X.25 *n.* A recommendation published by the ITU-T (formerly CCITT) international communications standards organization that defines the connection between a terminal and a packet-switching network. X.25 incorporates three definitions: the electrical connection between the terminal and the network, the transmission or link-access protocol, and the implementation of virtual circuits between network users. Taken together, these definitions specify a synchronous, full-duplex terminal-to-network connection. Packet format, error control, and other features are equivalent to portions of the HDLC (High-level Data Link Control) protocol defined by the International Organization for Standardization (ISO). *See also* CCITT X series, HDLC, packet switching, virtual circuit.

X3D *n.* Acronym for **3D XML**. An XML-based 3-D graphics specification incorporating the behavior capabilities of the Virtual Reality Modeling Language (VRML). X3D is compatible with existing VRML content and tools and supports full integration with other XML-based technologies. The X3D specification was developed and administered by the Web 3D Consortium.

X.400 *n. See* X series.

X.445 *n. See* X series.

X.500 *n. See* X series.

X.509 *n. See* X series.

X.75 *n. See* X series.

Xbox *n.* A video game console developed by Microsoft Corporation and released in 2001. Powered by an Intel 733-MHz processor, the Xbox delivers increased graphics capability over previously released game consoles and provides extensive storage capacity for gaming information. Peripherals plug into four game controller ports. An Ethernet port enables online gaming via a broadband connection. *See also* computer game, console game, GameCube, PlayStation. *Compare* Dreamcast.

X Consortium *n.* The body, composed of several hardware firms, that governed the standards for the X Window System. The Open Group's X Project Team now has responsibility for the X Window System. *See also* X Window System.

xDSL *n.* An umbrella term for all of the digital subscriber line (DSL) technologies, which use a variety of modulation schemes to pack data onto copper wires. The *x* is a

X

placeholder for the first or first two letters of a member technology, which might be ADSL, HDSL, IDSL, RADSL, or SDSL. *See also* DSL.

Xerox Network System *n. See* XNS.

Xerox PARC *n.* Short for **X**erox **P**alo **A**lto **R**esearch **C**enter. Xerox's research and development facility in Palo Alto, California. Xerox PARC is the birthplace of such innovations as the local area network (LAN), the laser printer, and the graphical user interface (GUI).

XFDL *n.* Short for **E**xtensible **F**orms **D**escription **L**anguage, a document description language introduced and submitted to the World Wide Web Committee in 1998 by the Canadian Internet forms company UWI.Com. XFDL is an XML-based language for describing complex forms, such as legal and government documents. It is designed to allow for interactivity yet remain consistent with Internet standards.

XHTML *n.* Short for **E**xtensible **H**yper**t**ext **M**arkup **L**anguage. A markup language incorporating elements of HTML and XML. Web sites designed using XHTML can be more readily displayed on handheld computers and digital phones equipped with microbrowsers. XHTML was released for comments by the World Wide Web Consortium (W3C) in September 1999. *See also* HTML, microbrowser, XML.

XLANG *n.* A derivative XML language that describes the logical sequencing of business processes, as well as the implementation of the business process by using various application services.

XLink *n.* An XML language that provides a set of attributes that are used to create links between resources. XLink provides complex extended linking, link behavior, and management capabilities. XLink is able to describe links that connect sets of resources, point to multiple targets, or serve multiple roles within an XML document.

XLL *n.* Acronym for e**X**tensible **L**inking **L**anguage. Broad term intended to denote the family of XML linking/pointing/addressing languages, which include XLink, XPointer, and XPath.

XMI *n.* **1.** Acronym for **XML M**etadata **I**nterchange Format. An object-based model for exchanging program data across the Internet. XMI is sponsored by IBM, Unisys, and others and was submitted as a proposed standard to the Object Management Group (OMG); it is now one of OMG's recommended technologies. XMI is designed to allow for storing and sharing programming information and exchanging data among tools, applications, and storage locations through a network or the Internet so that software developers can collaborate on applications, even if they are not all using the same development tools. **2.** As XMI *bus*, a 64-bit parallel bus supported on certain DEC and AlphaServer processors. An XMI bus is capable of transferring data, exclusive of addressing overhead, at 100 Mbps.

XML *n.* Acronym for e**X**tensible **M**arkup **L**anguage, a condensed form of SGML (Standard Generalized Markup Language). XML lets Web developers and designers create customized tags that offer greater flexibility in organizing and presenting information than is possible with the older HTML document coding system. XML is defined as a language standard published by the W3C and supported by the industry. *See also* SGML.

XML attribute *n.* Information added to a tag to provide more information about the tag, such as <ingredient quantity="2"units="cups">flour</ingredient>.

XML element *n.* Information delimited by a start tag and an end tag in an eXtensible Markup Language (XML) document. An example would be <Lastname> Davalio</LastName>.

XML entities *n.* Combinations of characters and symbols that replace other characters when an XML document is parsed, usually those that have other meanings in XML. For example, &lt; represents the < symbol, which is also the opening bracket for a tag.

XML Metadata Interchange Format *n. See* XMI (definition 1).

XML-RPC *n.* Acronym for e**X**tensible **M**arkup **L**anguage-**R**emote **P**rocedure **C**all. A set of XML-based implementations that allows cross-platform and cross-programming language procedure calls over the Internet. XML-RPC permits complex data structures to be transmitted, processed, and returned between different operating systems running in different environments.

XML Schema *n.* A specification providing a common base for data description and validation in XML environments. XML schema replaces Document Type Definition (DTD) by defining a greater set of data types with more explicit data descriptions. XML schema has been developed as an open, vendor-neutral format to enhance information exchange and e-commerce over the Internet. It is also a standard for the description and encoding of data.

XML Schema Description Language *n. See* XSDL.

XML stylesheet *n.* Contains formatting rules that are applied to an XML file referencing the stylesheet. The standard set of rules for XML stylesheets is the Extensible Stylesheet Language (XSL). *See also* XSL.

XML Web services *n.* Units of application logic providing data and services to other applications. Applications access XML Web services via standard Web protocols and data formats such as HTTP, XML, and SOAP, independent of how each XML Web service is implemented. XML Web services combine the best aspects of component-based development and the Web and are a cornerstone of the Microsoft .NET programming model.

Xmodem *n.* A file transfer protocol used in asynchronous communications that transfers information in blocks of 128 bytes.

Xmodem 1K *n.* A version of the Xmodem file transfer protocol designed for larger, longer-distance file transfers. Xmodem 1K transmits information in 1-kilobyte (1024-byte) blocks and uses a more reliable form of error checking. *See also* Xmodem.

Xmodem-CRC *n.* An enhanced version of the Xmodem file transfer protocol that incorporates a 2-byte cyclical redundancy check (CRC) to detect transmission errors.

XMT *n.* Short for trans**mit**. A signal used in serial communications.

XNS *n.* Acronym for **X**erox **N**etwork **S**ystem. A set of protocols assigned to five numbered layers (0 through 4) that form a suite designed to handle packaging and delivery of network transmissions.

XON/XOFF *n.* An asynchronous communications protocol in which the receiving device or computer uses special characters to control the flow of data from the transmitting device or computer. When the receiving computer cannot continue to receive data, it transmits an XOFF control character that tells the sender to stop transmitting; when transmission can resume, the computer signals the sender with an XON character. *Also called:* software handshake. *See also* handshake.

XOR encryption *n.* Short for Exclusive-**OR encryption**. A simple encryption scheme using the "exclusive-or" concept, in which a decision is based on only one of two conditions being met. Using a provided key, XOR encryption performs an exclusive-or process on each byte of data to be encrypted. Because XOR encryption is not a strong security tool used alone, it is typically used as an additional level of security for Internet transmission of sensitive information.

XPath *n.* An XML language for addressing items in an XML document by specifying a path through the document structure. XPath is used by XPointer and XSLT to locate and identify XML document data. XPath is also considered a query language complement to XQuery. XPath is more supported than XQuery even though there is no approved standard yet for either. *See also* XPointer.

XPointer *n.* An XML language used to locate data within an XML document based on data property descriptions, such as attributes, location, and content. XPointer references the internal structure of a document, allowing links to be made to occurrences of a word, character set, content attribute, or other element, rather than to a specific point within the document. *See also* XPath.

X

XQuery *n.* Short for e**X**tensible **Query** Language. Designed to be a functional query language that is broadly applicable to a variety of XML data types derived from Quilt, XPath, and XQL. Both Ipedo and Software AG implement their own versions of the W3C's proposed specification for the XQuery language. *Also called:* XML Query, XQL.

XSD *n.* Acronym for e**X**tensible **S**chema **D**efinition. A prefix used by convention to indicate a W3C schema namespace.

XSDL *n.* Acronym for **X**ML **S**chema **D**escription Language. A World Wide Web Consortium (W3C) recommendation for representing XML structure. XSDL is capable of describing complex XML-based data structures, and provides options not available with Document Type Definitions (DTDs), including namespace support, XML datatypes, and improved extensibility and data type support.

X series *n.* A set of recommendations adopted by the International Telecommunication Union Telecommunication Standardization Sector (ITU-T), formerly the CCITT, and International Organization for Standardization (ISO) for standardizing equipment and protocols used in both public access and private computer networks. See the table.

Table X.1   Recommendations in X Series for Network Communications.

Recommendation Number	What It Covers
X.25	Interface required to connect a computer to a packet-switched network such as the Internet
X.75	Protocols for connecting two public data networks
X.200	Seven-layer set of protocols known as the ISO/OSI reference model for standardizing computer-to-computer connections
X.400	Format at the ISO/OSI application layer for e-mail messages over various network transports, including Ethernet, X.25, and TCP/IP. Gateways must be used to translate e-mail messages between the X.400 and Internet formats
X.445	Asynchronous Protocol Specification, which governs the transmission of X.400 messages over dial-up telephone lines
X.500	Protocols for client/server systems that maintain and access directories of users and resources in X.400 form
X.509	Digital certificates

XSL *n.* Acronym for **Ex**tensible **S**tylesheet **L**anguage. A World Wide Web Consortium (W3C) standard stylesheet language for XML documents. XSL determines how data in an XML document is displayed on the Web. XSL controls what data will be displayed, in what format, and in what type size and style. XSL contains two major extensions: XSL Transformations (XSLT), a language used to convert XML documents to HTML or other document types, and XSL Formatting Objects (XSL-FO), a language for specifying formatting semantics. *See also* XSL-FO, XSLT.

X

XSL-FO *n.* Acronym for **Ex**tensible **S**tylesheet **L**anguage **F**ormatting **O**bjects. An XML-based markup language for specifying formatting semantics. XSL-FO allows format and style information to be applied to an XML document and can be used with XSLT to produce source documents. *See also* XSL.

XSLT *n.* Acronym for **E**xtensible **S**tylesheet **L**anguage **T**ransformations. A language used in transforming an existing XML document into a restructured XML document. Formalized as a W3C Recommendation in 1999, XSLT is primarily intended for use as part of XSL. XSL describes the styling of a document in terms of XSLT transformations into an XML document. *See also* XML, XSL.

X terminal *n.* An intelligent display device, connected to an Ethernet network, that performs operations on request from client applications in an X Window System. *See also* Ethernet (definition 1), X Window System.

XUL *n.* A standards-based interface description language that provides a standard way to exchange data describing a program's user interface. XUL balances simplicity, flexibility, and ease of use with precise layout control. XUL was developed by Netscape and Mozilla and is used with XML, CSS, DOM, and HTML.

X Windows *n. See* X Window System.

X Window System *n.* A nonproprietary standardized set of display-handling routines, developed at MIT. Most often encountered on UNIX workstations, the X Window System is independent of hardware and operating system. An X Window System client calls on the server, which is located on the user's workstation, to provide a window in which the client can generate a display of text or graphics. *Also called:* X Windows. *See also* X Consortium.

X

Y

Yahoo! *n.* The first major online Web-based directory and search engine for Internet resources, which can be found at http://www.yahoo.com. *See also* search engine (definition 2).

Yahoo! Mail *n.* A popular Web-based e-mail service provided for free by Yahoo! Inc. *Compare* Hotmail.

Yahoo! Messenger *n.* A popular instant-messaging application provided for free by Yahoo! Inc. on a variety of operating systems. *See also* instant messaging. *Compare* AIM, ICQ, .NET Messenger Service.

Yanoff list *n.* The informal name of the Internet services list created and maintained by Scott Yanoff. The Yanoff list was one of the earliest directories of Internet services and resources. It is located at http://www.spectracom.com/islist/.

Yellow Pages *n.* **1.** The former name of a UNIX utility, provided by SunSoft (Sun Microsystems system software), that maintains a central database of names and locations of the resources on a network. The Yellow Pages enables processes on any node to locate resources by name. This utility is now known formally as NIS (Network Information Service). **2.** InterNIC Registration Services' database of domain names and their IP addresses. *See also* domain name, IP address. **3.** Any of several Internet business directory services. Some are print publications, some are strictly electronic, and some are both.

Yettie *n.* Short for **Y**oung, **E**ntrepreneurial **T**ech-based **T**wenty-something or **Y**oung, **E**ntrepreneurial **T**echnocrat. A person who works in a technology or Internet-related field and who embraces technological change and opportunity. Yettie is intended to be a successor to the older term "yuppie."

YHBT *n.* Acronym for **y**ou **h**ave **b**een **t**rolled. An expression used in e-mail and newsgroups to indicate that the receiver has taken a deliberately set bait. *See also* troll.

YHL *n.* Acronym for **y**ou **h**ave **l**ost. An expression used in e-mail and newsgroups, often following YHBT. *See also* YHBT.

Ymodem *n.* A variation of the Xmodem file transfer protocol that includes the following enhancements: the ability to transfer information in 1-kilobyte (1024-byte) blocks, the ability to send multiple files (batch file transmission), cyclical redundancy checking (CRC), and the ability to abort transfer by transmitting two CAN (cancel) characters in a row. *See also* Xmodem.

Y

Z

Z39.50 standard *n.* A specification for a query language based on SQL (structured query language). It is used by WAIS, among other Internet services, to search for files through the use of keywords and is widely used for remote access to library catalogs. *See also* WAIS.

zombie *n.* A computer that has become the unwilling host of a DDoS (distributed denial of services) attack program and that is controlled by remote signals from the attacker. To create a zombie, a hacker utilizes security vulnerabilities to crack a Web, mail, news, or application server and plant hidden DDoS tools such as Trinoo and Tribal Flood Network. Later, at a signal from the attacker, the server becomes a zombie that will participate in a coordinated attack on other servers. *See also* DDoS, hacker.

zone *n.* **1.** On a LAN (local area network), a subgroup of users within a larger group of interconnected networks. **2.** In Macintosh programming, a portion of memory that is allocated and reallocated by the memory manager facility as memory is requested and released by applications and by other parts of the operating system.

zone transfer *n.* The process whereby a secondary DNS server obtains information about a zone or domain from the primary server. *See also* zone (definition 1).

.zoo *n.* The file extension that identifies compressed archive files created with the zoo file compression utility. *See also* zoo210.

zoo210 *n.* Version 2.1 of zoo, a program for creating compressed archive files (whose names have the extension .zoo). The algorithm for zoo210 is based on that of LHARC. Implementations of zoo210 are available for UNIX and Intel systems. *See also* LHARC.

zoo virus *n.* A virus that is kept in an isolated environment for the benefit of anti-virus research and training. Zoo viruses are not found outside the labs of anti-virus companies.

Zope *n.* An open source application server for publishing objects on the Internet. Zope provides tools to integrate data and content from multiple sources into complete Web applications and can be used in conjunction with XML-RPC to form a system for remotely scriptable Web objects. Zope runs on UNIX, Windows NT and later, and most other major operating systems. *See also* XML-RPC.

Z

Appendix A
Instant Messaging
Emoticons and Acronyms

Instant messaging, chat, and other Internet communications formats have led to a variety of shorthand indicators and clarifiers meant to enhance the user experience.

Emotags

Emotags were first used in e-mail and newsgroups to clarify a message for the reader. Typically, emotags consist of a word or words in brackets or parentheses, such as *<joke>*, and appear right after or both before and after the text they refer to.

Smileys

The most common emoticons are faces and expressions composed of standard keyboard punctuation marks and symbols, and which are viewed sideways. These are known as "smileys" in reference to the first emoticons, which represented a smile, such as: : -). Smileys are indicators of the emotional "tone of voice" intended by the writer.

Smileys

Text	Meaning	Text	Meaning
:-)	smile	8-I or 8-l	in suspense
(-:	left-handed smile	l:-l	excessively rigid
:o)	smile with a large nose (or clown smiley)	:-]	obnoxious
:)	smile with no nose	l-)	bored (or asleep)
:->	smirk (or wry smile)	l-I	asleep
:-}	wry smile (or leer)	I^o	snoring
:-t	unsmiley	l-O	yawning
:*)	just clowning around (or inebriated)	:-"	whistling (or pursing lips)
:-))))	extreme happiness (or sarcastic happiness)	:-s	incoherent statement
:-D	very happy (or laughing)	:-#	just said the wrong thing (or braces)
(-D	laughing hard	:-!	foot in mouth
:-) :-) :-)	loud guffaw	:-() or :-D	big mouth
:'-)	laughing and crying	(:-$ or :-(*)	ill
%-)	amused (and possibly confused)	(:~) or :-')	ill with a cold
:-/	chagrined (or skeptical)	:-R	ill with the flu

Smileys *(continued)*

Text	Meaning	Text	Meaning
:-I	indifferent	%+l or %+{	lost a fight
:~)	touched (or ill with a cold)	X-(	unconscious (or dead)
(:-(	sad (or bald and sad)	<:-)	dunce
:-(	frown (or unhappy)	*:o)	bozo
:-c	very unhappy	@;-)	flirt
:-((((	extremely unhappy (or sarcastic unhappiness)	X:-)	child
:-<	forlorn	:>)	big nose
>:-(	annoyed	&:-)	curly hair (or girl smiley)
:-[	pouting	#:-)	matted hair
(:-& or %-(	angry	8-)	wearing glasses
>:-<	very angry	8:-)	glasses on forehead (or little girl, or hair in curlers)
~ :-(	very angry (or fuming mad)	B-)	wearing horn-rimmed glasses (or sunglasses)
%-(or :/)	not amused	B-]	wearing cool sunglasses
:-l	expressionless	O:-)	angel
:-l or :-(	have an ordinary day	&8-l	nerd
:-e	disappointed	c:-) or (:-)	bald
:-X	lips are sealed (or not saying a word)	:-{	has a moustache
:-v	talking	:-)} or :-)#	has a beard
:-I	hmmm	:-Q or :-I	smoker
:-8(	condescending stare	:-d~	heavy smoker
:-O	shouting (or shocked)	:-?	pipe smoker
:-@	screaming	:-/I	no smoking
:,-(or :'-(	crying	:-) X	wearing a bow tie
~:-o	baby	{(:-)	wearing a toupee
]:-)>	devilish	:-{}	lipstick
):-)	impish	[:-)	stereo headphones
;->	lewd	d :-o	hats off
:-x	kiss	~:-(	has been flamed (or is on fire)
:-*	ready for a kiss (or just ate something sour)	~~:-(	has been flamed repeatedly
8-]	wow	)	Cheshire cat
:-J	tongue-in-cheek	(:-I	egghead
:-&	tongue-tied (or biting tongue)	3:-o	cow
:-p	no way! (or nyah nyah)	[: l]	robot
;-)	wink	M-)	see no evil

Smileys *(continued)*

Text	Meaning	Text	Meaning
'-)	one-eyed wink	:X)	hear no evil
:-7	wry statement (or tongue-in-cheek)	:-M	speak no evil
:-l :-l	déjà vu	*8((:	strange
?-(	sorry, I don't know what went wrong (or black eye)	O+	female
:-C	that's unbelievable! (or incredible!)	O->	male
B-D	serves you right	ll*(	handshake offered
:-B	drooling	ll*)	handshake accepted
:-*)	drunk	<{:-)}	message in a bottle
:-9	licking lips	(-: :-)	putting heads together
l-p	yuck!	[] or ()	hug given (name or initials can be included between the brackets)
:-b	sticking out tongue	((( )))	lots of hugs
-]:-)[-	impressed	((( ))):**	hugs and kisses
8-I or 8-l	in suspense	(::()::)	Band-Aid (or comfort)
l:-l	excessively rigid	@->—	a rose
:-]	obnoxious	@—>—	a long-stemmed rose
l-)	bored (or asleep)	@==	atomic bomb
l-I	asleep	<')))))-<	a fish
I^o	snoring	^	giggles

Alternate (Japanese) Smileys

Alternate smileys, which do not require users to tilt their heads sideways, were developed by Internet users in Japan and are becoming more common worldwide. Some versions of these emoticons leave out the ( ) brackets around the faces.

Alternate Smileys

Text	Meaning
(^_^)	male smiley
(^.^)	female smiley
(^L^) or (^(^)	happy
(-_-)	secret smile
(^o^)	laughing out loud
(^_^;)	laughing to cover nervousness
(^_^)/	waving hello
(;_;)/	waving good-bye

Alternate Smileys *(continued)*

Text	Meaning
(^_~) or (^_-)	winking
(*^o^*) or (*^.^*)	exciting
\(^_^)/	joyful
(;_;) or (~~>.<~~)	crying
(>.<) or (>_<)	angry
(v_v)	expressionless
(^o^;>	excuse me?
(*^_^*)	blushing (or shy)
(^_^;;;)	embarrassed (or in a cold sweat)
(?_?)	confused (or wondering)
(!_!) or (o_o)	shocked
(*_*)	frightened (or in love)
(=_=)~	sleepy
(u_u)	sleeping
(@_@)	stunned
'\=o-o=/'	wearing glasses
m(_)m	humble bow of thanks or apology

Acronyms and Shorthand

The first emotional indicators in newsgroups and e-mail were acronyms designed to give readers clues to the attitude and intent of the sender. Acronyms also quickly developed as keyboarding shortcuts. Use of acronyms is particularly prevalent in instant messaging, primarily to maintain the pace of real-time conversation.

Acronyms

Text	Meaning	Text	Meaning
AAMOF	as a matter of fact	JW	just wondering
AAR	at any rate	K	okay
ADN	any day now	KWIM	know what I mean?
AFAIK	as far as I know	L (or <L>)	laughing
AFK	away from keyboard	L8R	later
AFKBRB	away from keyboard, be right back	LJBF	let's just be friends
ASAP	as soon as possible	LOL	laughing out loud
A/S/L	age/sex/location	LTNS	long time no see
B2W	back to work	MHBFY	my heart bleeds for you
B4N (or BFN)	bye for now	MHOTY	my hat's off to you

Acronyms (*continued*)

Text	Meaning	Text	Meaning
BAK	back at keyboard	MOTAS	member of the appropriate sex
BBL	be back later	MOTD	message of the day
BBS	be back soon	MYOB	mind your own business
BCNU	be seeing you	NBD	no big deal
BF (or B/F)	boyfriend	NBIF	no basis in fact
BMN	but maybe not	NOYB	none of your business
BRB	be right back	NP	no problem
BTDT	been there, done that	NRN	no response necessary (or no reply necessary)
BTDTBTT	been there, done that, bought the tape	OIC	oh, I see
BTDTGTTS	been there, done that, got the t-shirt	OM	oh my (or old man, as in husband)
BTDTGTTSAWIO	been there, done that, got the t-shirt, and wore it out	OOI	out of interest
BTW	by the way	OOTB	out of the box
BYKT	but you knew that	OTL	out to lunch
CIO	cut it out	OTOH	on the other hand
CMIIW	correct me if I'm wrong	OTTH	on the third hand
CU (or CYA)	see you	PAW	parents are watching
CUL (or CUL8R)	see you later	PC	politically correct
DIY	do it yourself	PDA	public display of affection
DYJHIW	don't you just hate it when	PEST	please excuse slow typing
EAK	eating at keyboard	PI (or PIC)	politically incorrect
EOL	end of lecture	PKB (or P/K/B)	pot, kettle, black (or pot calling the kettle black)
EOM	end of message	PMBI	pardon my butting in
F2F (or FTF)	face to face	PMFJI	pardon me for jumping in
FAPP	for all practical purposes	POS	parent over shoulder (or parents over shoulder)

Acronyms *(continued)*

Text	Meaning	Text	Meaning
FOFL (or FOTFL)	falling on the floor laughing	POS	parent over shoulder (or parents over shoulder)
FTR	for the record	POV	point of view
FWIW	for what it's worth	PPL	people
FYA	for your amusement	PTB	powers that be
FYEO	for your eyes only	R (or r)	are
FYI	for your information	REHI	re-hello (following a short time away) (or hi again)
g (or <g>)	grin	RFC	request for comment
G (or <G>)	big grin	RL	real life
G2G (or GTG)	got to go	ROTFL	rolling on the floor laughing
GAL	get a life	ROTFLOL	rolling on the floor laughing out loud
GD&H	grinning, ducking, and hiding	RSN	real soon now
GD&R	grinning, ducking, and running	S (or <S>)	smile
GD&RVVF	grinning, ducking, and running, very, very fast	SCNR	sorry, could not resist
GF (or G/F)	girlfriend	SITD	still in the dark
GG	gotta go (or good game)	SOP	standard operating procedure
GIWIST	gee, I wish I said that	SPMD	some people may differ
GMTA	great minds think alike	SUP	what's up?
GoAT	go away, troll	TBE	to be expected
HAK	hugs and kisses	THX (or TX)	thanks
HAGD	have a great day	TIA	thanks in advance
HAND	have a nice day	TANJ	there ain't no justice
HEH	a courtesy laugh	TIC	tongue-in-cheek
HHOS	ha-ha, only serious	TPHB	the pointy-haired boss
HTH	hope this helps (or hope that helps)	TPTB	the powers that be
IAE	in any event	TTBOMK	to the best of my knowledge

Acronyms *(continued)*

Text	Meaning	Text	Meaning
HW	homework (or hardware)	TTFN	ta-ta for now
IANAL	I am not a lawyer	TTYL	talk to you later
IC	I see	TVM	thanks very much
ICBW	I could be wrong (or it could be worse)	TVMIA	thanks very much in advance
IDTS	I don't think so	TYVMIA	thank you very much in advance
IINM	if I'm not mistaken	U	you
IIRC	if I recall correctly	UW	you're welcome
IIUC	if I understand correctly	VBG (or <VBG>)	very big grin
IMCO	in my considered opinion	WB	welcome back
IME	in my experience	WCD	what's cookin' doc?
IMHO	in my humble opinion	WHBT	we have been trolled
IMNSHO	in my not-so-humble opinion	WOA	work of art
IMO	in my opinion	WRT	with regard to (or with respect to)
IOW	in other words	WTG	way to go
IRL	in real life	WTH	what the heck?
ISTM	it seems to me	Y (or <Y>)	yawning
ISWYM	I see what you mean	YHBT	you have been told (or you have been trolled)
ITRW	in the real world	YHBW	you have been warned
J (or <J>)	joking	YHGMTPOTG	you have greatly misinterpreted the purpose of this group
JC	just chillin'	YHM	you have mail
JIC	just in case	YMMV	your mileage may vary
JK (or J/K)	just kidding (or that was a joke)	YOYO	you're on your own
JTYWTK	just thought you wanted to know	YWSYLS	you win some, you lose some

Appendix B
Internet Domains

Top-Level Domains: Organizational

Domain	Type of Organization
.aero	Air-transport industry
.biz	Businesses
.com	Commercial
.coop	Cooperatives
.edu	Educational
.gov	Nonmilitary agency, United States federal government
.info	Unrestricted use
.int	International organization
.mil	United States military
.museum	Museums
.name	Individuals
.net	Network provider
.org	Nonprofit organization
.pro	Professional workers

Top-Level Domains: Geographic

Domain	Country/Region	Domain	Country/Region
.ac	Ascension Island	.lb	Lebanon
.ad	Andorra	.lc	St. Lucia
.ae	United Arab Emirates	.li	Liechtenstein
.af	Afghanistan	.lk	Sri Lanka
.ag	Antigua and Barbuda	.lr	Liberia
.ai	Anguilla	.ls	Lesotho
.al	Albania	.lt	Lithuania
.am	Armenia	.lu	Luxembourg
.an	Netherlands Antilles	.lv	Latvia
.ao	Angola	.ly	Libya
.aq	Antarctica	.ma	Morocco
.ar	Argentina	.mc	Monaco
.as	American Samoa	.md	Moldova
.at	Austria	.mg	Madagascar
.au	Australia	.mh	Marshall Islands
.aw	Aruba	.mk	Macedonia, Former Yugoslav Republic of
.az	Azerbaijan	.ml	Mali
.ba	Bosnia and Herzegovina	.ml	Mali

Top-Level Domains: Geographic *(continued)*

Domain	Country/Region	Domain	Country/Region
.bb	Barbados	.mm	Myanmar
.bd	Bangladesh	.mn	Mongolia
.be	Belgium	.mo	Macau SAR
.bf	Burkina Faso	.mp	Northern Mariana Islands
.bg	Bulgaria	.mq	Martinique
.bh	Bahrain	.mr	Mauritania
.bi	Burundi	.ms	Montserrat
.bj	Benin	.mt	Malta
.bm	Bermuda	.mu	Mauritius
.bn	Brunei	.mv	Maldives
.bo	Bolivia	.mw	Malawi
.br	Brazil	.mx	Mexico
.bs	Bahamas, The	.my	Malaysia
.bt	Bhutan	.mz	Mozambique
.bv	Bouvet Island	.na	Namibia
.bw	Botswana	.nc	New Caledonia
.by	Belarus	.ne	Niger
.bz	Belize	.nf	Norfolk Island
.ca	Canada	.ng	Nigeria
.cc	Cocos (Keeling) Islands	.ni	Nicaragua
.cd	Congo (DRC)	.nl	Netherlands, The
.cf	Central African Republic	.no	Norway
.cg	Congo	.np	Nepal
.ch	Switzerland	.nr	Nauru
.ci	Côte d'Ivoire	.nu	Niue
.ck	Cook Islands	.nz	New Zealand
.cl	Chile	.om	Oman
.cm	Cameroon	.pa	Panama
.cn	China	.pe	Peru
.co	Colombia	.pf	French Polynesia
.cr	Costa Rica	.pg	Papua New Guinea
.cu	Cuba	.ph	Philippines
.cv	Cape Verde	.pk	Pakistan
.cx	Christmas Island	.pl	Poland
.cy	Cyprus	.pm	St. Pierre and Miquelon
.cz	Czech Republic	.pn	Pitcairn Islands
.de	Germany	.pr	Puerto Rico
.dj	Djibouti	.ps	Palestinian Authority
.dk	Denmark	.pt	Portugal
.dm	Dominica	.pw	Palau

Top-Level Domains: Geographic *(continued)*

Domain	Country/Region	Domain	Country/Region
.do	Dominican Republic	.py	Paraguay
.dz	Algeria	.qa	Qatar
.ec	Ecuador	.re	Reunion
.ee	Estonia	.ro	Romania
.eg	Egypt	.ru	Russia
.er	Eritrea	.rw	Rwanda
.es	Spain	.sa	Saudi Arabia
.et	Ethiopia	.sb	Solomon Islands
.fi	Finland	.sc	Seychelles
.fj	Fiji Islands	.sd	Sudan
.fk	Falkland Islands (Islas Malvinas)	.se	Sweden
.fm	Micronesia	.sg	Singapore
.fo	Faroe Islands	.sh	St. Helena
.fr	France	.si	Slovenia
.ga	Gabon	.sj	Svalbard and Jan Mayen
.gd	Grenada	.sk	Slovakia
.ge	Georgia	.sl	Sierra Leone
.gf	French Guiana	.sm	San Marino
.gg	Guernsey	.sn	Senegal
.gh	Ghana	.so	Somalia
.gi	Gibraltar	.sr	Suriname
.gl	Greenland	.st	São Tomé and Príncipe
.gm	Gambia, The	.sv	El Salvador
.gn	Guinea	.sy	Syria
.gp	Guadeloupe	.sz	Swaziland
.gq	Equatorial Guinea	.tc	Turks and Caicos Islands
.gr	Greece	.td	Chad
.gs	South Georgia and the South Sandwich Islands	.tf	French Southern and Antarctic Lands
.gt	Guatemala	.tg	Togo
.gu	Guam	.th	Thailand
.gw	Guinea-Bissau	.tj	Tajikistan
.gy	Guyana	.tk	Tokelau
.hk	Hong Kong SAR	.tm	Turkmenistan
.hm	Heard Island and McDonald Islands	.tm	Turkmenistan
.hn	Honduras	.tn	Tunisia
.hr	Croatia	.to	Tonga
.ht	Haiti	.tp	East Timor

Top-Level Domains: Geographic *(continued)*

Domain	Country/Region	Domain	Country/Region
.hu	Hungary	.tr	Turkey
.id	Indonesia	.tt	Trinidad and Tobago
.ie	Ireland	.tv	Tuvalu
.il	Israel	.tw	Taiwan
.im	Man, Isle of	.tz	Tanzania
.in	India	.ua	Ukraine
.io	British Indian Ocean Territory	.ug	Uganda
.iq	Iraq	.uk	United Kingdom
.ir	Iran	.um	U.S. Minor Outlying Islands
.is	Iceland	.us	United States
.it	Italy	.uy	Uruguay
.je	Jersey	.uz	Uzbekistan
.jm	Jamaica	.va	Vatican City
.jo	Jordan	.vc	St. Vincent and the Grenadines
.jp	Japan	.ve	Venezuela
.ke	Kenya	.vg	Virgin Islands, British
.kg	Kyrgzstan	.vi	Virgin Islands
.kh	Cambodia	.vn	Vietnam
.ki	Kiribati	.vu	Vanuatu
.km	Comoros	.wf	Wallis and Futuna
.kn	St. Kitts and Nevis	.ws	Samoa
.kp	North Korea	.ye	Yemen
.kr	Korea	.yt	Mayotte
.kw	Kuwait	.yu	Yugoslavia
.ky	Cayman Islands	.za	South Africa
.kz	Kazakhstan	.zm	Zambia
.la	Laos	.zw	Zimbabwe

Appendix C
Common File Extensions

Common File Extensions

File Extension	Type of File
.0	File containing information on hard disk compressed with DoubleSpace.
.123	Spreadsheet file in Lotus 123.
.4th	Source file in Forth.
.a	Source file in Macintosh Assembly.
.ad	Screensaver file in After Dark.
.ada	Source file in Ada.
.ai	Vector graphic file in Adobe Illustrator.
.aif	*See* .aiff.
.aifc	*See* .aiff.
.aiff	Audio file in the Apple Audio Interchange Format originally used on Apple and Silicon Graphics (SGI) computers.
.ani	1. Animated cursor file in Microsoft Windows 9x and Windows NT. 2. Animation file.
.aol	File related to America Online.
.aps	Source file in Microsoft Visual C++.
.arc	Archive file compressed with ARC.
.arj	Archive file compressed with ARJ.
.asc	1. ASCII text file. 2. File encrypted with PGP (Pretty Good Privacy).
.asf	File in Microsoft Advanced Streaming Format.
.asm	Source file in Assembler.
.asp	File in Active Server Page format, generally found on the World Wide Web.
.atm	File in Adobe Type Manager.
.au	Sound file, generally on UNIX systems or the World Wide Web.
.avi	Audio visual interleaved data file in the Microsoft RIFF format.
.bac	*See* .bak.
.bak	Backup file.
.bas	Source file in Basic.
.bat	Batch program file.
.bfc	Briefcase file in Microsoft Windows 9x.
.bin	1. Archive file compressed with MacBinary. 2. Binary file.
.bk	*See* .bak.
.bmk	Bookmarked file.
.bmp	Raster graphics file stored in bitmap format.

Common File Extensions *continued*

File Extension	Type of File
.box	Mailbox file in Lotus Notes.
.c	Source file in C.
.c++	Source file in C++.
.cab	Microsoft cabinet file—multiple files compressed into one and extractable with the extract.exe utility.
.cas	Comma-delimited ASCII text file.
.cb	Clean boot file in Microsoft Windows.
.cbl	Source file in Cobol.
.cca	E-mail message in Lotus cc:mail.
.cda	CD audio track.
.cdf	1. File in Microsoft Channel Definition Format. 2. File in Common Data Format.
.cdi	File in Phillips Compact Disk Interactive format.
.cdr	Vector graphics file in CorelDraw.
.cgi	File containing Common Gateway Interface scripts, generally for use on the World Wide Web.
.cgm	Vector graphics file in Computer Graphics Metafile format.
.chk	Portions of unidentifiable files saved in Windows by the Disk Defragmentor or ScanDisk utilities.
.chm	File containing compiled HTML.
.cil	Microsoft Clip Gallery download package.
.class	Class file in Java.
.clp	Temporary file created by Microsoft Windows Clipboard utility.
.cmd	Command file in Windows NT, OS/2, MS-DOS, and CP/M.
.cmf	File in Corel Metafile.
.cob	Source file in Cobol.
.com	Command file or program.
.cpl	Control Panel file in Microsoft Windows 9x.
.cpp	Source file in C++.
.crt	Certificate file.
.css	Cascading Style Sheet file, generally used in conjunction with Web sites.
.csv	Comma-delimited text file.
.ct	Graphics file in Paint Shop Pro.
.cur	Cursor file in Windows.
.cxx	Source file in C++.
.dat	Data file.
.dbf	Database in dBASE and FoxPro.
.dcr	Multimedia file in Macromedia Shockwave.

Common File Extensions *continued*

File Extension	Type of File
.dib	Graphics file in Device Independent Bitmap format.
.dif	File in Data Interchange Format.
.dll	Dynamic-link library file.
.doc	**1.** Document file in Microsoft Word.
	2. In the past, document file in Adobe FrameMaker or WordStar.
	3. Document file formatted for a word processor.
.dos	MS-DOS–related files in Microsoft Windows 9x.
.dot	Document template in Microsoft Word.
.drv	Device driver.
.dtd	Document Type Definition file in SGML or XML.
.dtp	Document file in Microsoft Publisher or PublishIt!
.dv	Video file.
.dvi	Document file in TEX Device Independent File format.
.emf	File in Enhanced Windows Metafile format.
.eml	Mail message in Microsoft Outlook Express.
.eps	Encapsulated PostScript file.
.exe	Executable program or file.
.F	Source file in Fortran.
.F77	Source file in Fortran 77.
.F90	Source file in Fortran 90.
.fax	Fax file in many Fax programs.
.fdf	File in Adobe Acrobat Forms.
.fla	Movie file in Macromedia Flash.
.fli	Animation file in AutoDesk FLIC file.
.flf	Device driver in OS/2.
.fm	Document file in Adobe FrameMaker.
.fon	System font file in Windows.
.for	Source file in Fortran.
.fp	File in FileMaker Pro.
.fpt	*See* .fp.
.frm	Document file in Adobe FrameMaker.
.gid	Index file in Windows 9x.
.gif	Raster image file in GIF format.
.giff	*See* .gif.
.gtar	UNIX archive file compressed in GNU tar utility.
.gz	UNIX archive file compressed by gzip.
.gzip	*See* .gz.
.h	Header file.
.hdf	File in Hierarchical Data Format.

Common File Extensions *continued*

File Extension	Type of File
.hex	File encoded with Macintosh BinHex utility.
.hlp	Help file in Microsoft Windows.
.hqx	File encoded with BinHex utility.
.htm	*See* .html.
.html	HTML file, most commonly used as a Web page.
.ico	Icon file in Microsoft Windows 9x.
.iff	1. Image or sound file in IFF format.
	2. Data file on Amiga systems.
.image	Image file in Macintosh Disk Image format.
.inf	Device information file, which contains scripts used to control hardware operations.
.ini	In MS-DOS and Windows 3.x, an initialization file, which contains user preferences and startup information about an application program.
.ins	File containing InstallShield install script.
.isu	File containing InstallShield uninstall script.
.jas	Image file in JAS format.
.jav	*See* .java.
.java	Source file in Java.
.jff	*See* .jpg.
.jfif	*See* .jpg.
.jpe	*See* .jpg.
.jpeg	*See* .jpg.
.jpg	Graphic image file encoded in the JPEG File Interchange Format.
.js	Source file in JavaScript.
.l	Source file in LISP.
.latex	Text file in LaTeX.
.lha	Archive file compressed with LZH.
.lib	Library file in many programming languages.
.lnk	Shortcut file in Windows 9x and Windows NT 4.
.log	Log file.
.lsp	Source file in LISP.
.lzh	*See* .lha.
.mac	Image file in MacPaint.
.mak	Project file in Microsoft Visual Basic or Microsoft Visual C++.
.man	Manual page in UNIX.
.mbox	Mailbox file in BSD UNIX.
.mbx	1. Address file in Microsoft Outlook.
	2. Mailbox file in Eudora.
.mcw	Document file in Microsoft Word for the Macintosh.

Common File Extensions *continued*

File Extension	Type of File
.mdb	Database in Microsoft Access.
.mic	Image file in Microsoft Image Composer.
.mid	Music file in MIDI format.
.midi	*See* .mid.
.mime	File encoded in MIME format.
.moov	Video file in Apple QuickTime.
.mov	*See* .moov.
.movie	*See* .moov.
.mp2	Audio file compressed and encoded according to the MPEG Audio Layer-2 standard.
.mp3	Audio file compressed and encoded according to the MPEG Audio Layer-3 standard.
.mpe	*See* .mpg.
.mpeg	*See* .mpg.
.mpg	Compressed video and audio file in MPEG format.
.mpp	1. Graphics file in CAD format. 2. File in Microsoft Project.
.msg	E-mail message in Microsoft Outlook.
.ncb	File in Microsoft Developer Studio.
.ncf	Command file in Novell NetWare.
.ncf	Temporary file created by Microsoft Windows Clipboard utility.
.net	Network configuration file.
.newsrc	Setup file for UNIX-based newsreaders.
.nlb	Data file in Oracle 7.
.nlm	Module file in Novell NetWare.
.nsf	Database in Lotus Notes.
.nws	News message file in Microsoft Outlook Express.
.obd	File in Microsoft Office Binder.
.ocx	Microsoft OLE control.
.ole	Microsoft OLE object.
.opt	*See* .ncb.
.p	Source file in Pascal.
.p65	Document file in PageMaker 6.5.
.pab	Address book file in Microsoft Outlook.
.pcd	Image file in Kodak Photo-CD.
.pcl	File in Hewlett-Packard Printer Control Language.
.pcx	Bitmapped image file in PC Paintbrush.
.pdf	Document file encoded in Adobe Portable Document Format.
.pgp	File encrypted in PGP (Pretty Good Privacy).

Common File Extensions *continued*

File Extension	Type of File
.pic	1. Image file in PC Paint format.
	2. *See* .pict.
.pict	Image file in the Macintosh PICT.
.pl	1. Source file in Perl.
	2. Source file in Prolog.
.png	Bitmap image file in PNG format.
.pps	1. Image file in Paint Shop Pro.
	2. Slide show file in Microsoft PowerPoint.
.ppt	Presentation file in Microsoft PowerPoint.
.prc	Text or program file for 3Com PalmPilot.
.prg	File in Microsoft FoxPro, Ashton-Tate dBase, or CA Clipper.
.ps	PostScript printer file.
.psd	Image file in Adobe PhotoShop.
.pst	Personal File Folder file in Microsoft Outlook.
.pub	Document file in Ventura Publisher, Adobe PageMaker, or Microsoft Publisher.
.pwd	Document file in Microsoft Pocket Word for handheld and palm-size computers.
.pwl	Password file in Microsoft Windows 9x.
.pxl	Spreadsheet file in Microsoft Pocket Excel for handheld and palm-size computers.
.qic	Backup file in Microsoft Backup.
.qif	*See* .qti.
.qt	*See* .qtm.
.qti	Image file in Apple QuickTime.
.qtif	*See* .qti.
.qtm	Movie file in Apple QuickTime.
.qts	*See* .qti.
.qtx	*See* .qti.
.qxd	Document file in QuarkXPress.
.ra	Sound file in RealAudio.
.ram	Metafile in RealAudio.
.ras	Raster image bitmap on Sun systems.
.rast	*See* .ras.
.raw	Bitmap file in RAW format.
.rdf	Resource Description Framework file in XML.
.rgb	*See* .raw.
.rif	Bitmap file in RIFF format.
.riff	*See* .rif.

Common File Extensions *continued*

File Extension	Type of File
.rle	Bitmap file in RLE compression scheme.
.rm	Video file in RealAudio.
.rtf	Document file in Rich Text Format.
.s	1. Source file in Assembler. 2. Source file in Scheme.
.sam	Document file in Lotus Ami Professional.
.sav	1. Saved file in many games. 2. Saved backup file.
.scc	File in Microsoft SourceSafe.
.scd	File in Microsoft Schedule+.
.scr	Screensaver file in Microsoft Windows.
.sea	Self-extracting Macintosh archive file compressed with StuffIt.
.set	File set in Microsoft Backup.
.sgm	File in SGML.
.sgml	*See* .sgm.
.shtml	1. File in HTML format that has SSI (server side includes). 2. Secure file in HTML.
.sig	Signature file for e-mail or Internet newsgroup use.
.sit	Macintosh archive file compressed with StuffIt.
.sm	Source file in Smalltalk.
.snd	1. Interchangeable sound file format used on Sun, NeXT, and Silicon Graphics computers, consisting of raw audio data preceded by a text identifier. 2. Sound resource file on the Macintosh.
.spl	File in Macromedia Shockwave Flash.
.sql	Query or report file in SQL.
.stm	*See* .shtml.
.sun	Raster graphics file in Sun systems.
.swa	Audio file in Macromedia Shockwave.
.swf	File in Macromedia Shockwave Flash.
.swp	Swap file in Microsoft Windows.
.sys	System configuration file.
.tar	Uncompressed UNIX archive in tar format.
.taz	UNIX archive file in Gzip or tar format.
.tcl	Source file in TCL.
.tga	Bitmap file in Targa format.
.tif	Bitmap images in TIFF format.
.tiff	*See* .tif.
.tmp	Temporary file in Windows.

Common File Extensions *continued*

File Extension	Type of File
.tsv	Tab separated values file.
.ttf	TrueType font file.
.txt	ASCII text file.
.udf	Database file in Microsoft Windows NT.
.uri	File containing list of URIs.
.url	Shortcut file on the Internet for a URL.
.uu	*See* .uud.
.uud	Binary file that has been translated into ASCII format using uuencode.
.uue	File that has been decoded from ASCII format back into binary format using uudecode.
.vbx	Custom control in Microsoft Visual Basic.
.vda	*See* .tga.
.vp	Document file in Ventura Publisher.
.vrm	**1.** *See* .vrml. **2.** Source file in Visual ReXX.
.vrml	A 3-D graphics file in VRML.
.vst	Bitmap image file in Targa.
.vxd	Virtual device driver in Microsoft Windows.
.wab	E-mail file in Microsoft Outlook Express.
.wav	Sound file stored in waveform (WAV) audio format.
.wmf	Vector image file encoded as a Microsoft Windows Metafile.
.wp	Document file in Corel WordPerfect.
.wp6	Document file in Corel WordPerfect 6.x.
.wpd	*See* .wp.
.wpg	Graphic file in Corel WordPerfect.
.wps	Document file in Microsoft Works.
.wri	Document file in Microsoft Write.
.xls	Spreadsheet file in Microsoft Excel.
.z	UNIX file archive compressed with gzip.
.Z	UNIX file archive compressed with compress utility.
.zip	Archive file compressed in ZIP format with PKZIP or WinZip.
.zoo	Archive file compressed with zoo.

Get a **Free**
e-mail newsletter, updates, special offers, links to related books, and more when you
register on line!

Register your Microsoft Press® title on our Web site and you'll get a FREE subscription to our e-mail newsletter, *Microsoft Press Book Connections*. You'll find out about newly released and upcoming books and learning tools, online events, software downloads, special offers and coupons for Microsoft Press customers, and information about major Microsoft® product releases. You can also read useful additional information about all the titles we publish, such as detailed book descriptions, tables of contents and indexes, sample chapters, links to related books and book series, author biographies, and reviews by other customers.

Registration is easy. Just visit this Web page and fill in your information:
http://www.microsoft.com/mspress/register

Microsoft